THE AUTOBIOGRAPHY OF AMERICAN BUSINESS

The Autobiography of American Business

Edited by

JOHN BROOKS

DOUBLEDAY & COMPANY, INC.
GARDEN CITY, NEW YORK
1974

Grateful acknowledgment is made for permission to reprint the following material:

Bernard M. Baruch: Excerpts from *Baruch: My Own Story*. Copyright © 1957 by Bernard M. Baruch. Reprinted by permission of Holt, Rinehart and Winston, Inc.

Bert Cantor: Chapters 2 and 15 from *The Bernie Cornfeld Story*. Copyright © 1970 by Bert Cantor. Published by arrangement with Lyle Stuart, Inc.

Andrew Carnegie: "The Homestead Strike" and "Problems of Labor," from *The Autobiography of Andrew Carnegie*. Copyright renewed 1948 by Margaret Carnegie Miller. Reprinted by permission of the publisher, Houghton Mifflin Company.

Peter Cohen: Excerpts from *The Gospel According to the Harvard Business School*. Copyright © 1973 by Peter Cohen. Reprinted by permission of Doubleday & Company, Inc.

Jerry Della Femina: Excerpts from *From Those Wonderful Folks Who Gave You Pearl Harbor*. Copyright © 1970 by Jerry Della Femina and Charles Sopkin. Reprinted by permission of Simon and Schuster, Inc.

John H. Dessauer: "The Incredible 914" and "The Impossible Dream Comes True," from *My Years with Xerox*. Copyright © 1971 by John H. Dessauer. Reprinted by permission of Doubleday & Company, Inc.

F. N. Doubleday: Excerpts from *Memoirs of a Publisher*. Copyright © 1972 by Nelson Doubleday. Reprinted by permission of Doubleday & Company, Inc.

Robert T. Elson: Pages 274–303 from *Time Inc.: The Intimate History of a Publishing Enterprise, 1923–1941*. Copyright © 1968 by Time Inc. Reprinted by permission of Time Inc. and Atheneum Publishers.

Henry Ford: "What I Learned About Business" and "The Terror of the Machine," from *My Life and Work* by Henry Ford, in collaboration with Samuel Crowther. Copyright 1922 by Doubleday & Company, Inc. Reprinted by permission of the Seabury Memorial Home.

Clayton W. Fountain: "Boardwalk Ballet," from *Union Guy*. Copyright 1949 by Clayton W. Fountain. Reprinted by permission of The Viking Press, Inc.

Gerard B. Lambert: Excerpts from *All Out of Step*. Copyright © 1956 by Gerard B. Lambert. Reprinted by permission of Doubleday & Company, Inc.

David E. Lilienthal: Abridged from *The Journals of David E. Lilienthal, Vol. III: Venturesome Years, 1950–1955*. Copyright © 1966 by David E. Lilienthal. Reprinted by permission of Harper & Row, Publishers, Inc.

J. C. Penney: "The Experiment That Seemed to Go Wrong," from *The Man with a Thousand Partners: An Autobiography,* as told to Robert W. Bruère. Copyright 1931 by Robert W. Bruère. Reprinted by permission of Harper & Row, Publishers, Inc.

Contents

Introduction

A COMPILATION OF AMERICAN BUSINESS autobiographies should begin with an explanation of what the term "autobiography" is taken to mean. The objective of the compiler is simple and straightforward: to get a subjective view of the American business experience, in its varied aspects, by collecting the most interesting and revealing available accounts of it by participants, mighty or lowly, in their own words. (Or more or less their own words; as we will see, in many cases the words are filtered through a ghost.)

Accordingly, ordinary business histories, whether commissioned by corporations or not, whether of particular companies or of eras and episodes, have been excluded at the outset on grounds that they are not autobiography but biography or history. (The single exception is Time Inc.'s company history, which seems to me to be corporate autobiography because it was composed by employees who had themselves taken part in the events being described.) Unsigned corporate releases of all sorts, although they technically come within the canon as corporate autobiography, have been arbitrarily excluded, for a variety of reasons. Company annual reports to stockholders, while they occasionally provide insight and often provide rich examples of unintentional humor, have been excluded because their content is too transient and their manner too impersonal. Proxy statements and prospectuses, revealing as they may sometimes be to the sophisticated reader, have been excluded as too technical and legalistic. Public relations department releases about business activities have been excluded on grounds that they are almost always the products of too many hands too inhibited by special interests to be very revealing. Public speeches by business executives, even those that include autobiographical touches, have been excluded, first, because they are hardly ever primarily the work of the speaker, who in many cases has never seen them until a couple of hours before he delivers them, and second, because they are generally dull—kindly, reassuring soporifics or comforting polemics against safe enemies, to go with cigars and brandy.

What remains, then, are the autobiographies, usually published in book form, of businessmen and businesswomen.

The strength of autobiography is self-revelation; its weakness is self-servingness. Both are found in business autobiography, perhaps the latter in greater abundance. Traditionally, the successful American businessman or woman in the fullness of years and fortunes concludes that he or she must leave the world a monument. Perhaps it should be an actual monument of stone or bronze; perhaps one of money (a foundation). Or perhaps, an autobiography. If the last, the autobiographer usually finds himself—however experienced and learned in the practice of business—without literary skill or, indeed, literary interest and ambition, and in the lifelong habit of dictating. Therefore he engages a writer to set down his thoughts in order and then revises the written text as he wishes. Let us hope for both his sake and the reader's that the resulting book has enough merit so that he need not pay a publisher to publish it ("vanity publishing"); if he is eminent enough in business and has been enough in the public eye, he need not, regardless of the book's merit. In either case, his motive for publishing differs from that of the ordinary writer—or, indeed, from that of his collaborator. Like a great literary artist, he writes not for monetary gain but for immortality. Unfortunately, the analogy is frail: as the literary artist writes to express himself and to discover universal truth, the businessman-autobiographer does so to commemorate and vindicate himself and his works.

Richard M. Huber, in his brilliant book *The American Idea of Success* (McGraw-Hill, 1971), has postulated that the job of American philosophers has always been to reconcile evangelical Christianity

with the goals of business. In nineteenth-century business autobiography, the businessman-autobiographer took over the task and
became a do-it-yourself philosopher, assiduously reconciling *his* goals
with those of evangelical Christianity. Thus Andrew Carnegie, the
first author in this gallery, who may have cheated in business and at
golf, nevertheless became the father of modern philanthropy. Unfortunately, the accepted prose style composed by (or for) nineteenth-
century businessmen ran to the pompous and turgid, and, in addition,
the enterprise of moral self-justification is one that by its nature leads
to mealy-mouthed writing. Therefore only a few representative
samples of that genre are included.

Huber's argument goes on to say that, as the development of mass-
production facilities changed the primary impetus of business from
that of building to that of selling, the American idea of success
changed in response. The businessman tended to abandon what Huber
calls the "character ethic" (elsewhere called the "Protestant ethic")
and to adopt a "personality ethic" (elsewhere called the "social
ethic"). Businessmen, that is, stopped reporting to God and began
reporting to their peers. (Henry Ford, who invented mass production, balanced on the knife edge: personally committed to the character ethic, he created the conditions for the personality ethic.) The
result, in spite of the obvious and much-discussed drawbacks of the
salesman personality, was a more relaxed, open, and forthright attitude of businessmen toward their lives and work and a good deal
more candor and humor in their autobiographies. This is one reason
that all but eight of the chapters in this book are principally concerned with events after World War II, the real beginning of the
modern era in American business as in American life.

A second reason is that the modern era has probably been the most
varied and interesting of any in the history of American business. In
one aspect a time of what William H. Whyte memorably called "the
organization man," in another aspect it has, paradoxically, been a
time of individualism rampant. The organizational housekeeping
necessary to manage huge corporations has led to the development of
fixed, stale molds—and to the necessity for bold, free-thinking men to
break them. The need to sell goods to the newly affluent many has

led to the rise of an advertising business that sometimes brings the "personality ethic" to a kind of farcical apotheosis. The emergence of the first mass stock market in the world's history has led rapidly to the appearance of new forms of investor exploitation and to the startling discovery that long-established financial institutions can be exploited almost as easily as innocent first-time investors. Meanwhile, companies like Xerox have shown that the character-ethic tradition of succeeding by simply working hard and making something new and useful is not dead. All of these trends, and others, are reflected in the selections that follow.

The ghost writer is so nearly ubiquitous in business autobiography (*hic et ubique,* as the disconcerted Hamlet exclaimed about his father's ghost), and his role in it so pervasive that a few words must be said on the subject. Of the nineteen pieces included in this compilation, one is an unabashedly fake autobiography, one is an outright collaboration among employees of a company to describe the company, and six others are apparently the sole work of the authors who signed them (in three cases, the writer's chief subject is a person or institution other than himself). The remaining eleven appear to be, in a literary sense, chiefly the work of someone other than the autobiographer—to round up the euphemistic descriptions of the situation, written "with" an "arranger," "edited by," "assisted by," with the "help of," "in collaboration with," or, occasionally, "as told to" a more or less professional writer. As a classic text on the position of the ghost vis-à-vis the tycoon, we have the account of Frank Nelson Doubleday, founder of Doubleday & Company, of his adventures writing the "autobiography" of John D. Rockefeller. (The account is contained in Doubleday's *Memoirs of a Publisher,* written in 1926 for the entertainment of his immediate family but published by his heirs in 1972.) The episode began with Doubleday wangling an invitation to play golf with the famous old man, and then—but let Doubleday tell the story himself:

* * *

A COUSIN OF MINE, Julia Doubleday, married one of Mr. Rockefeller's most important secretaries, Starr Murphy. I conceived the idea that Mr. Rockefeller's autobiography would be very interesting, but he was a shy bird, never appeared in the newspapers if he could avoid it, and covered himself with a fog of obscurity which few people were able to penetrate. However, I thought that I would take a chance and talk the matter over with Starr Murphy, who had as much influence with him, I think, as did anyone in his employ.

Much to my surprise, Mr. Murphy did not seem to think the scheme impossible—another example of an experience I have had a hundred times: that plans called impossible, when they are once properly approached, often prove to be not impossible or even very difficult.

To make a fairly long story fairly short, I found that Mr. Rockefeller was playing golf at the Bon Air, in Augusta. Mr. Murphy would not give me a letter of introduction, but he said that he would write to Mr. Rockefeller, and if Mr. Rockefeller was interested to meet me, he would hunt me up. So it fell out one day that the great oil king took notice of the insignificant publisher and invited me to play golf with him.

Rockefeller's golf was the exact reverse of Mr. Carnegie's golf. Carnegie could not stand being beaten and would take the utmost liberties with the score. Rockefeller was strictness itself in counting every stroke. I remember that one tee at Augusta faced a little swamp. If Rockefeller had the misfortune to drive into this morass, he would stop and put on a pair of rubbers, go into the mud, and hammer at his ball, accounting for every stroke. He would keep his score with the utmost care and mark his improvements day by day. Considering everything, he played a remarkable game, and always in strict conformity to the rules.

I could not help but notice that he kept his eye on me when I was not looking; I presume he was sizing me up. I said nothing about his memoirs, hoping against hope that he would introduce the subject himself. One day after eighteen holes he asked me to sit with him a few minutes on the piazza of the hotel. He said:

"I am inclined to ask you to do me a favor, but I fear it might be too much of a task."

I asked him what it was, and tried to indicate that it would be a pleasure to me.

He said: "I would like to tell you the complete story of my life, which I have never told to anybody as yet, not even my own son. In this way I would bring back into my memory things that might escape me, and which are of importance—some of them of public importance. But I would only be willing to ask you to listen with the distinct agreement that if you are bored you will tell me frankly and we will end the sessions."

I told him that I would take a chance on being bored, and if the worst came to the worst, I would stop him in his narrative.

So for two or three weeks every day we sat on the piazza and he told me of all the things that had happened to him since he was a small boy. It was really a tale of thrilling interest, told with a dramatic fervor which kept my attention from the start. Some of these things, of course, were never printed. At that time I think he had no idea of ever printing any of the material; he simply wanted to make a record of it. I feared that the revelations were so intimate that I would never even have the cheek to ask him to give them expression in ink and paper.

One particular story, which will never be printed, he related so cleverly that it gave me a real thrill. He was telling me of the panic of 1907 or 1908 when Mr. Morgan assumed the generalship of the financial world which Wall Street was supposed to give in a panic situation. I think Mr. Rockefeller never greatly admired Mr. Morgan, for the reason, so far as I can see, that Mr. Morgan tried to dominate him and get him to do things which Mr. Rockefeller did not care to do.

I have forgotten just how the subject came up, but Mr. H. H. Rogers, when the panic storm burst, found himself in a bad position with the Virginia Railway, which he owned by himself, I believe, with obligations for a large sum of money when money could not be bought for love nor money. Mr. Rogers finally turned to his old partner, Mr. Rockefeller, and went to his house one afternoon, feeling that he had come to the end of his tether, and unless money could be raised instantly, all his plans and prospects would go up in the air.

Mr. Rockefeller said that, as Mr. Rogers came into the room, he saw that he was trembling with the greatest excitement. He tried to calm him and to be reassuring. Mr. Rogers burst out finally and said that he was ruined—that unless he could have a very large sum immediately, he was beyond help financially.

Mr. Rockefeller moved forward and put his hand on Mr. Rogers's knee and said: "Before you leave this room, you will be in entire mental comfort."

Mr. Rogers was so affected that he almost collapsed. Suddenly he woke up again to his position and said: "What are you going to charge me for it?"

Mr. Rockefeller replied: "This is a matter of friendship, not of money. You will pay not a penny of interest or commission." Then he went to his safe, which he had in his library, and produced securities sufficient to answer Mr. Rogers's requirements and the day was saved.

But to get back to the Rockefeller autobiography. This tale of Mr. Rockefeller's life lasted, I think, for at least two weeks, and when I went home I had the story pretty clearly in my brain, but not a note of any kind. Greatly to my delight, Mr. John D. Rockefeller, Jr., sought me out and said that his father had told him that he had narrated his life story to me. His son was anxious to have me write it out as well as I could remember it and give it to him, as he said it came nearer to a record than anything else that the family had; and as his father was the most abused man in the United States at that time, he and his sisters were eager to have any record which would be of value to them.

I explained that I had made no notes, and I did not know if I could reproduce the conversation with any success, but I would try. I sat down for three or four days and cudgeled my brains to write out this story. I think it amounted to about forty thousand words, and when I finished I gave the record to John D., Jr., for what it was worth. He was very grateful, and asked me if I would go over the material with his father, and correct and amplify the story as I had set it down. This I agreed to do, and I had long sessions with Mr. Rockefeller, reading and rereading the whole story over and over again, chapter by chapter. I never met a man who was so particular to get things right in detail; sometimes he would make me read certain passages four or five times, and when I showed that I was rather tired of it, he would say, "We will get this right, then we need never think of it again."

When we got the manuscript done, I asked Mr. John D., Jr., if we could publish it in *The World's Work*. He gave me his cordial permission, after consulting with the old man. When we talked about printing it in the magazine, Mr. Rockefeller asked: "How much do you think these articles are worth to you?" and I said, "As I have done an awful lot of work on them, I think perhaps five hundred dollars apiece would be a fair price." He said that if that was satisfactory to me it would be to him, and he actually took the money, five hundred dollars for each article. I tried to get it away from him to give to a blind friend who needed about this sum, but although he gave me some money for my friend, he still retained the major part of it.

I have never been able to understand why this book, which we published under the title, *Random Reminiscences of Men and Events*, by John D. Rockefeller, did not sell. There are two chapters, "The Difficult Art of Making" and "The Difficult Art of Giving," which I think are classics; and coming from the richest man in the world, as he probably was then, they assume an importance which for some reason has never been appreciated.

The success of the articles in the magazine was most complete. They raised the circulation and caused everybody to say that we had sold out to the Standard Oil Company. One incident disabused the public of that idea. While the articles were being published, the Standard Oil Company fell into disrepute, having been proved to have bought the influence of Senator [Joseph B.] Foraker. Mr. Page thought that it was our duty to comment on this subject most severely, condemning the Standard Oil root and branch. I agreed with him, but I told him that I thought we ought to tell Mr. Rockefeller, which I did. Much to my surprise, Mr. Rockefeller said: "If you did not express your opinion honestly, I should think that you were dishonest yourself"; so, while Mr. Rockefeller was still contributing to *The World's Work*, we attacked the Standard Oil Company in the editorial section as only Mr. Page's trenchant pen could do.

Later on Mr. Rockefeller was brought into court to testify about the Standard Oil Company as a trust, and he put in as his evidence the complete contents of this book, and said that he was willing to swear by that and make it his statement of the case.

The book is forgotten, and the whole incident fades away, but to me it was a dramatic experience.

*   *   *

ALAS, *Random Reminiscences of Men and Events*—published by Doubleday, Page in 1909, with, incidentally, no acknowledgment of any kind of Mr. Doubleday's role in its creation—is less interesting than its ghost writer would have us believe. It is a mélange of such elements as the inevitable rags-to-riches story of the "autobiographer's" first job (bookkeeper's assistant at $50 for the first three months), boring reminiscences of and courtesy tributes to his business associates, descriptions of road building at his Pocantico Hills estate, a self-congratulatory account of Standard Oil Company's early risks and subsequent rewards, and platitudinous advice to aspiring businessmen. It does contain some lovely unintentional irony with regard to the beginnings of multinational business, in Rockefeller's statement that "One of our greatest helpers has been the State Department in Washington, [which has helped us] to push our way into new markets to the utmost corners of the world." Nevertheless, the book is probably rightly forgotten; the craftsman's account of his task is more memorable than the product itself.

We should note at once that the Doubleday-Rockefeller relationship differed from the usual ghost writer-tycoon relationship in a few important respects (apart from the fact, appalling to other writers, that the book seems to have been written in "three or four days"). For one thing, the ghost in this case was not a writer but a publisher; far from being paid for his role in the transaction, Doubleday paid Rockefeller (and he entertains us by relating that Rockefeller not only accepted the money but turned down Doubleday's suggestion that he donate the fee to charity). Secondly, the ghost writer approached the subject, rather than vice versa; and thirdly, at the time of the interviews the ghost writer did not even know that he was going to write a book and took no notes. Beyond those aspects, the case is all too typical. We find the nominal autobiographer excessively worried about being boring and consequently *being* boring. We find—as we might have suspected after reading the autobiography—that certain things the tycoon actually said during the interviews have been excised from the manuscript. (Doubleday gives us an example of an anecdote that was cut apparently because Rockefeller, on reading the manuscript, decided it was too self-serving.) We find the ghost writer subsequently a bit uneasy about his role and eager to justify himself by convincing us of his subject's high-mindedness. "The success of the articles [when the book was serialized in *The World's Work* magazine] was most complete," Doubleday tells us and adds ironically, "They raised the circulation and caused everybody to say that we had sold out to the Standard Oil Company." The magazine then felt obliged to retrieve its reputation by attacking Standard Oil on its editorial page.

The point is that ghosts tend to feel uneasy about their ghostliness and that their uneasiness damages their craftsmanship. Of course, there is really no reason for a ghost to be defensive if he is a good ghost. If he conceives his role as simply that of a sort of stenographer with special skills, filling a need created by the autobiographer's lack of time and literary ability, the role is an honorable and a useful one. However, human nature and the literary temperament being what they are, the ghost writer too often does feel a little tainted, and his most common reaction is to justify his enterprise to himself by becoming more Catholic than the Pope, making his subject appear far more spotless and sinless—and inhuman—than the subject himself would have wished to do or been able to do if he had written the book with his own hand. Ghost-writing is the curse of business autobiography, and if these words serve to persuade one future tycoon-autobiographer that he should bite the bullet and write his own book—or even talk it into a recording machine and then turn the tapes over to an editor—they will have served a good purpose.

In spite of its element of spookiness, American business autobiography contains many fresh perspectives and insights and—as I hope the following selections show—adds a new and rewarding dimension to the history of American business.

THE AUTOBIOGRAPHY OF AMERICAN BUSINESS

1. *Founding Father*

ANDREW CARNEGIE (1835–1919) was the most interesting of the great nineteenth-century American industrialists because the most complex, and at the same time he was the most representative of the industrial spirit of his age, combining as he did an astonishing drive for power with strong tendencies toward self-righteousness and moralizing in general. Born in Dunfermline, Scotland, into a family of radical populists, he came with his parents to the Pittsburgh area in 1848 and rose by rapid, apparently effortless steps to become one of the richest men in America and head of the giant Carnegie Steel Corporation. Through it all, he seemed to feel the need to keep his inherited radical credentials, and took to journeying every year to Britain where he regularly made vociferously radical pronouncements against all forms of special privilege. His rhetoric was much more measured when he was in and around Pittsburgh, but he did succeed in projecting himself as a friend of the working man and an apostle of "sweetness and light" in American labor-management relations. After selling out his steel interests to the newly formed United States Steel Corporation in 1901, he lived in retirement—mostly at his castle in Scotland—seeking to implement his theory that it is "a sin to die rich" by making such lavish and widespread benefactions as would win for him the title of "father of modern philanthropy" and pursuing such other avocations (nagging American Presidents with constant letters of advice, establishing a fund to promote heroism, and so on) as would establish him before his death as the very model of a modern dotty old multimillionaire. He died in 1919—not poor, to be sure, but having given away some $350 million.

As an autobiographer, Carnegie had the qualification, all but unique among American industrialists, of being a competent and experienced writer with his own hand. All his life he nourished an almost naïvely respectful attitude toward writers and writing, and he took his own literary ventures seriously. As a young man, when his net worth was still a mere $400,000, he considered quitting business to become editor of a highbrow newspaper or magazine that he would found in London. He never carried out this ambition, but throughout his career he regularly explained himself in essays composed without the help of ghosts, one of which—"The Gospel of Wealth" (1889), in which he sets forth his idea that rich men are "trustees" of their wealth with a fiduciary responsibility to use it for the public good—stands as a classic expression of the social rationalization of laissez-faire capitalism in his time. True, his *Autobiography*, jotted down in old age and published the year after his death, was put together with the help of what Carnegie called his "arranger," John C. Van Dyke. Nevertheless, it conveys his characteristic tone of self-satisfaction, piety, and arch humor as well as do any of his writings.

The 1892 strike at Carnegie's Homestead, Pennsylvania, steel works, which is discussed in the following passage, was the most serious setback in Carnegie's whole career and was, indeed, one of the bitterest industrial conflicts in American history, resulting in several deaths and many injuries, the near assassination of Carnegie's partner Henry Clay Frick, and eventually the crushing of the workers by the state National Guard. From whatever motives, the apostle of "sweetness and light" sat the whole thing out in Scotland, sending Frick periodic messages of encouragement. As Carnegie writes here, "No pangs remain of any wound received in my business career save that of Homestead." Still, even in dealing with it a quarter of a century later he cannot bring himself to describe what actually happened; rather, he gives a sort of lawyer's brief in his own defense without even summarizing the agreed-upon facts, far less stating the case against him.

In his general statements on management-labor relations he projects his characteristic attitudes: that workers without jobs are a class apart and an inferior one ("Only the inferior class as a rule is idle") and that they respond best to rough treatment, so long as it is forthright and fair ("That man Kelly was my stanch friend and admirer ever afterward"); but that in dealings with them there must be no back talk ("None of that, Billy!"). The trusteeship of wealth, after all, had, in his view, been conferred upon him by God.

As I have said, Carnegie was exaggeratedly worshipful of writers. It is amusing to see how one of the most famous of his time treated him. Mark Twain, whom Carnegie had sought out and who liked to call him "Saint Andrew," wrote him on his retirement a letter he was proud enough of to include in his *Autobiography:*

Dear Sir and Friend:
You seem to be prosperous these days. Could you lend an admirer a dollar and a half to buy a hymn-book with? God will bless you if you do; I feel it, I know it. So will I. If there should be other applications this one not to count.

Yours, Mark

P.S. Don't send the hymn-book, send the money. I want to make the selection myself.

M.

THE HOMESTEAD STRIKE

WHILE UPON THE SUBJECT of our manufacturing interests, I may record that on July 1, 1892, during my absence in the Highlands of Scotland, there occurred the one really serious quarrel with our work-

From *The Autobiography of Andrew Carnegie,* ed. by John C. Van Dyke (Houghton Mifflin, 1920), pp. 228–54.

men in our whole history. For twenty-six years I had been actively in charge of the relations between ourselves and our men, and it was the pride of my life to think how delightfully satisfactory these had been and were. I hope I fully deserved what my chief partner, Mr. Phipps, said in his letter to the "New York Herald," January 30, 1904, in reply to one who had declared I had remained abroad during the Homestead strike, instead of flying back to support my partners. It was to the effect that "I was always disposed to yield to the demands of the men, however unreasonable"; hence one or two of my partners did not wish me to return.[1] Taking no account of the reward that comes from feeling that you and your employees are friends and judging only from economical results, I believe that higher wages to men who respect their employers and are happy and contented are a good investment, yielding, indeed, big dividends.

The manufacture of steel was revolutionized by the Bessemer open-hearth and basic inventions. The machinery hitherto employed had become obsolete, and our firm, recognizing this, spent several millions at Homestead reconstructing and enlarging the works. The new machinery made about sixty per cent more steel than the old. Two hundred and eighteen tonnage men (that is, men who were paid by the ton of steel produced) were working under a three years' contract, part of the last year being with the new machinery. Thus their earnings had increased almost sixty per cent before the end of the contract.

The firm offered to divide this sixty per cent with them in the new scale to be made thereafter. That is to say, the earnings of the men

[1] The full statement of Mr. Phipps is as follows:

Question: "It was stated that Mr. Carnegie acted in a cowardly manner in not returning to America from Scotland and being present when the strike was in progress at Homestead."

Answer: "When Mr. Carnegie heard of the trouble at Homestead he immediately wired that he would take the first ship for America, but his partners begged him not to appear, as they were of the opinion that the welfare of the Company required that he should not be in this country at the time. They knew of his extreme disposition to always grant the demands of labor, however unreasonable.

"I have never known of any one interested in the business to make any complaint about Mr. Carnegie's absence at that time, but all the partners rejoiced that they were permitted to manage the affair in their own way." (Henry Phipps in the *New York Herald,* January 30, 1904.)

would have been thirty per cent greater than under the old scale and the other thirty per cent would have gone to the firm to recompense it for its outlay. The work of the men would not have been much harder than it had been hitherto, as the improved machinery did the work. This was not only fair and liberal, it was generous, and under ordinary circumstances would have been accepted by the men with thanks. But the firm was then engaged in making armor for the United States Government, which we had declined twice to manufacture and which was urgently needed. It had also the contract to furnish material for the Chicago Exhibition. Some of the leaders of the men, knowing these conditions, insisted upon demanding the whole sixty per cent, thinking the firm would be compelled to give it. The firm could not agree, nor should it have agreed to such an attempt as this to take it by the throat and say, "Stand and deliver." It very rightly declined. Had I been at home nothing would have induced me to yield to this unfair attempt to extort.

Up to this point all had been right enough. The policy I had pursued in cases of difference with our men was that of patiently waiting, reasoning with them, and showing them that their demands were unfair; but never attempting to employ new men in their places—never. The superintendent of Homestead, however, was assured by the three thousand men who were not concerned in the dispute that they could run the works, and were anxious to rid themselves of the two hundred and eighteen men who had banded themselves into a union and into which they had hitherto refused to admit those in other departments—only the "heaters" and "rollers" of steel being eligible.

My partners were misled by this superintendent, who was himself misled. He had not had great experience in such affairs, having recently been promoted from a subordinate position. The unjust demands of the few union men, and the opinion of the three thousand non-union men that they were unjust, very naturally led him into thinking there would be no trouble and that the workmen would do as they had promised. There were many men among the three thousand who could take, and wished to take, the places of the two hundred and eighteen—at least so it was reported to me.

It is easy to look back and say that the vital step of opening the works should never have been taken. All the firm had to do was to say to the men: "There is a labor dispute here and you must settle it between yourselves. The firm has made you a most liberal offer. The works will run when the dispute is adjusted, and not till then. Meanwhile your places remain open to you." Or, it might have been well if the superintendent had said to the three thousand men, "All right, if you will come and run the works without protection," thus throwing upon them the responsibility of protecting themselves—three thousand men as against two hundred and eighteen. Instead of this it was thought advisable (as an additional precaution by the state officials, I understand) to have the sheriff with guards to protect the thousands against the hundreds. The leaders of the latter were violent and aggressive men; they had guns and pistols, and, as was soon proved, were able to intimidate the thousands.

I quote what I once laid down in writing as our rule: "My idea is that the Company should be known as determined to let the men at any works stop work; that it will confer freely with them and wait patiently until they decide to return to work, never thinking of trying new men—never." The best men as men, and the best workmen, are not walking the streets looking for work. Only the inferior class as a rule is idle. The kind of men we desired are rarely allowed to lose their jobs, even in dull times. It is impossible to get new men to run successfully the complicated machinery of a modern steel plant. The attempt to put in new men converted the thousands of old men who desired to work, into lukewarm supporters of our policy, for workmen can always be relied upon to resent the employment of new men. Who can blame them?

If I had been at home, however, I might have been persuaded to open the works, as the superintendent desired, to test whether our old men would go to work as they had promised. But it should be noted that the works were not opened at first by my partners for new men. On the contrary, it was, as I was informed upon my return, at the wish of the thousands of our old men that they were opened. This is a vital point. My partners were in no way blamable for making the trial so recommended by the superintendent. Our rule never to employ new men, but to wait for the old to return, had not been violated so far. In regard to the second opening of the works, after the strikers had shot the sheriff's officers, it is also easy to look back and say, "How much better had the works been closed until the old men voted to return"; but the Governor of Pennsylvania, with eight thousand troops, had meanwhile taken charge of the situation.

I was traveling in the Highlands of Scotland when the trouble arose, and did not hear of it until two days after. Nothing I have ever had to meet in all my life, before or since, wounded me so deeply. No pangs remain of any wound received in my business career save that of Homestead. It was so unnecessary. The men were outrageously wrong. The strikers, with the new machinery, would have made from four to nine dollars a day under the new scale—thirty per cent more than they were making with the old machinery. While in Scotland I received the following cable from the officers of the union of our workmen:

"Kind master, tell us what you wish us to do and we shall do it for you."

This was most touching, but, alas, too late. The mischief was done, the works were in the hands of the Governor; it was too late.

I received, while abroad, numerous kind messages from friends conversant with the circumstances, who imagined my unhappiness. The following from Mr. Gladstone was greatly appreciated:

MY DEAR MR. CARNEGIE,

My wife has long ago offered her thanks, with my own, for your most kind congratulations. But I do not forget that you have been suffering yourself from anxieties, and have been exposed to imputations in connection with your gallant efforts to direct rich men into a course of action more enlightened than that which they usually follow. I wish I could relieve you from these imputations of journalists, too often rash, conceited or censorious, rancorous, ill-natured. I wish to do the little, the very little, that is in my power, which is simply to say how sure I am that no one who knows you will be prompted by the unfortunate occurrences across the water (of which manifestly we cannot know the exact merits) to qualify in the slightest degree either his confidence in your generous views or his admiration of the good and great work you have already done.

Wealth is at present like a monster threatening to swallow up the moral life of man; you by precept and by example have been teaching him to disgorge. I for one thank you.

Believe me

Very faithfully yours

(Signed) W. E. GLADSTONE

I insert this as giving proof, if proof were needed, of Mr. Gladstone's large, sympathetic nature, alive and sensitive to everything transpiring of a nature to arouse sympathy—Neapolitans, Greeks, and Bulgarians one day, or a stricken friend the next.

The general public, of course, did not know that I was in Scotland and knew nothing of the initial trouble at Homestead. Workmen had been killed at the Carnegie Works, of which I was the controlling owner. That was sufficient to make my name a by-word for years. But at last some satisfaction came. Senator Hanna was president of the National Civic Federation, a body composed of capitalists and workmen which exerted a benign influence over both employers and employed, and the Honorable Oscar Straus, who was then vice-president, invited me to dine at his house and meet the officials of the Federation. Before the date appointed Mark Hanna, its president, my lifelong friend and former agent at Cleveland, had suddenly passed away. I attended the dinner. At its close Mr. Straus arose and said that the question of a successor to Mr. Hanna had been considered, and he had to report that every labor organization heard from had favored me for the position. There were present several of the labor leaders who, one after another, arose and corroborated Mr. Straus.

I do not remember so complete a surprise and, I shall confess, one so grateful to me. That I deserved well from labor I felt. I knew myself to be warmly sympathetic with the working-man, and also that I had the regard of our own workmen; but throughout the country it was naturally the reverse, owing to the Homestead riot. The Carnegie Works meant to the public Mr. Carnegie's war upon labor's just earnings.

I arose to explain to the officials at the Straus dinner that I could not possibly accept the great honor, because I had to escape the heat of summer and the head of the Federation must be on hand at all seasons ready to grapple with an outbreak, should one occur. My embarrassment was great, but I managed to let all understand that this was felt to be the most welcome tribute I could have received—a balm to the hurt mind. I closed by saying that if elected to my lamented friend's place upon the Executive Committee I should esteem it an honor to serve. To this position I was elected by unanimous vote. I was thus relieved from the feeling that I was considered responsible by labor generally, for the Homestead riot and the killing of workmen.

I owe this vindication to Mr. Oscar Straus, who had read my articles and speeches of early days upon labor questions, and who had quoted these frequently to workmen. The two labor leaders of the Amalgamated Union, White and Schaeffer from Pittsburgh, who were at this dinner, were also able and anxious to enlighten their fellow-workmen members of the Board as to my record with labor, and did not fail to do so.

A mass meeting of the workmen and their wives was afterwards held in the Library Hall at Pittsburgh to greet me, and I addressed them from both my head and my heart. The one sentence I remember, and always shall, was to the effect that capital, labor, and employer were a three-legged stool, none before or after the others, all equally indispensable. Then came the cordial hand-shaking and all was well. Having thus rejoined hands and hearts with our employees and their wives, I felt that a great weight had been effectually lifted, but I had had a terrible experience although thousands of miles from the scene.

An incident flowing from the Homestead trouble is told by my friend, Professor John C. Van Dyke, of Rutgers College.

In the spring of 1900, I went up from Guaymas, on the Gulf of California, to the ranch of a friend at La Noria Verde, thinking to have a week's shooting in the mountains of Sonora. The ranch was far enough removed from civilization, and I had expected meeting there only a few Mexicans and many Yaqui Indians, but much to my surprise I found an English-speaking man, who proved to be an American. I did not have long to wait in order to find out what brought him there, for he was very lonesome and disposed to talk. His name was McLuckie, and up to 1892 he had been a skilled mechanic in the employ of the Carnegie Steel Works at Homestead. He was what was called a "top hand," received large wages, was married, and at that time had a home and considerable property. In addition, he had been honored by his fellow-townsmen and had been made burgomaster of Homestead.

When the strike of 1892 came McLuckie naturally sided with the strikers, and in his capacity as burgomaster gave the order to arrest the Pinkerton detectives who had come to Homestead by steamer to protect the works and preserve order. He believed he was fully justified in doing this. As he explained it to me, the detectives were an armed force invading his bailiwick, and he had a right to arrest and disarm them. The order led to bloodshed, and the conflict was begun in real earnest.

The story of the strike is, of course, well known to all. The strikers finally defeated. As for McLuckie, he was indicted for murder, riot, treason, and I know not what other offenses. He was compelled to flee from the State, was wounded, starved, pursued by the officers of the law, and obliged to go into hiding until the storm blew over. Then he found that he was blacklisted by all the steel men in the United States and could not get employment anywhere. His money was gone, and, as a final blow, his wife died and his home was broken up. After many vicissitudes he resolved to go to Mexico, and at the time I met him he was trying to get employment in the mines about fifteen miles from La Noria Verde. But he was too good a mechanic for the Mexicans, who required in mining the cheapest kind of unskilled peon labor. He could get nothing to do and had no money. He was literally down to his last copper. Naturally, as he told the story of his misfortunes, I felt very sorry for him, especially as he was a most intelligent person and did no unnecessary whining about his troubles.

I do not think I told him at the time that I knew Mr. Carnegie and had been with him at Cluny in Scotland shortly after the Homestead strike, nor that I knew from Mr. Carnegie the other side of the story. But McLuckie was rather careful not to blame Mr. Carnegie, saying to me several times that if "Andy" had been there the trouble would never have arisen. He seemed to think "the boys" could get on very well with "Andy" but not so well with some of his partners.

I was at the ranch for a week and saw a good deal of Mc-Luckie in the evenings. When I left there, I went directly to Tucson, Arizona, and from there I had occasion to write to Mr. Carnegie, and in the letter I told him about meeting with Mc-Luckie. I added that I felt very sorry for the man and thought he had been treated rather badly. Mr. Carnegie answered at once, and on the margin of the letter wrote in lead pencil: "Give McLuckie all the money he wants, but don't mention my name." I wrote to McLuckie immediately, offering him what money he needed, mentioning no sum, but giving him to understand that it would be sufficient to put him on his feet again. He declined it. He said he would fight it out and make his own way, which was the right-enough American spirit. I could not help but admire it in him.

As I remember now, I spoke about him later to a friend, Mr. J. A. Naugle, the general manager of the Sonora Railway. At any rate, McLuckie got a job with the railway at driving wells, and made a great success of it. A year later, or perhaps it was in the autumn of the same year, I again met him at Guaymas, where he was superintending some repairs on his machinery at the railway shops. He was much changed for the better, seemed happy, and to add to his contentment, had taken unto himself a Mexican wife. And now that his sky was cleared, I was anxious to tell him the truth about my offer that he might not think unjustly of those who had been compelled to fight him. So before I left him, I said,

"McLuckie, I want you to know now that the money I offered you was not mine. That was Andrew Carnegie's money. It was his offer, made through me."

McLuckie was fairly stunned, and all he could say was:

"Well, that was damned white of Andy, wasn't it?"

I would rather risk that verdict of McLuckie's as a passport to Paradise than all the theological dogmas invented by man. I knew

McLuckie well as a good fellow. It was said his property in Homestead was worth thirty thousand dollars. He was under arrest for the shooting of the police officers because he was the burgomaster, and also the chairman of the Men's Committee of Homestead. He had to fly, leaving all behind him.

After this story got into print, the following skit appeared in the newspapers because I had declared I'd rather have McLuckie's few words on my tombstone than any other inscription, for it indicated I had been kind to one of our workmen:

"JUST BY THE WAY"

Sandy on Andy

Oh! hae ye heared what Andy's spiered to hae upo' his tomb,
When a' his gowd is gie'n awa an' Death has sealed his doom!
Nae Scriptur' line wi' tribute fine that dealers aye keep handy,
But juist this irreleegious screed—"That's damned white of
    Andy!"

The gude Scot laughs at epitaphs that are but meant to flatter,
But never ane was sae profane, an' that's nae laughin' matter.
Yet, gin he gies his siller all awa, mon, he's a dandy,
An' we'll admit his right to it, for "That's damned white of Andy!"

There's not to be a "big, big D," an' then a dash thereafter,
For Andy would na spoil the word by trying to make it safter;
He's not the lad to juggle terms, or soothing speech to bandy.
A blunt, straightforward mon is he—an' "That's damned white of
    Andy!"

Sae when he's deid, we'll gie good heed, an' write it as he askit;
We'll carve it on his headstone an' we'll stamp it on his casket:
"Wha dees rich, dees disgraced," says he, an' sure's my name is
    Sandy,
'T wull be nae rich man that he'll dee—an' "That's damned white
    of Andy!"[2]

---

[2] Mr. Carnegie was very fond of this story because, being human, he was fond of applause and, being a Robert Burns radical, he preferred the applause of Labor to that of Rank. That one of his men thought he had acted "white" pleased him beyond measure. He stopped short with that tribute and never

PROBLEMS OF LABOR

I SHOULD LIKE to record here some of the labor disputes I have had to deal with, as these may point a moral to both capital and labor.

The workers at the blast furnaces in our steel-rail works once sent in a "round-robin" stating that unless the firm gave them an advance of wages by Monday afternoon at four o'clock they would leave the furnaces. Now, the scale upon which these men had agreed to work did not lapse until the end of the year, several months off. I felt if men would break an agreement there was no use in making a second agreement with them, but nevertheless I took the night train from New York and was at the works early in the morning.

I asked the superintendent to call together the three committees which governed the works—not only the blast-furnace committee that was alone involved, but the mill and the converting works committees as well. They appeared and, of course, were received by me with great courtesy, not because it was good policy to be courteous, but because I have always enjoyed meeting our men. I am bound to say that the more I know of working-men the higher I rate their virtues. But it is with them as Barrie says with women: "Dootless the Lord made a' things weel, but he left some michty queer kinks in

asked, never knew, why or how the story happened to be told. Perhaps this is the time and place to tell the story of the story.

Sometime in 1901 over a dinner table in New York, I heard a statement regarding Mr. Carnegie that he never gave anything without the requirement that his name be attached to the gift. The remark came from a prominent man who should have known he was talking nonsense. It rather angered me. I denied the statement, saying that I, personally, had given away money for Mr. Carnegie that only he and I knew about, and that he had given many thousands in this way through others. By way of illustration I told the story about McLuckie. A Pittsburgh man at the table carried the story back to Pittsburgh, told it there, and it finally got into the newspapers. Of course the argument of the story, namely, that Mr. Carnegie sometimes gave without publicity, was lost sight of and only the refrain, "It was damned white of Andy," remained. Mr. Carnegie never knew that there was an argument. He liked the refrain. Some years afterward at Skibo (1906), when he was writing this Autobiography, he asked me if I would not write out the story for him. I did so. I am now glad of the chance to write an explanatory note about it. . . . *John C. Van Dyke.*

women." They have their prejudices and "red rags," which have to be respected, for the main root of trouble is ignorance, not hostility. The committee sat in a semicircle before me, all with their hats off, of course, as mine was also; and really there was the appearance of a model assembly.

Addressing the chairman of the mill committee, I said:

"Mr. Mackay" (he was an old gentleman and wore spectacles), "have we an agreement with you covering the remainder of the year?"

Taking the spectacles off slowly, and holding them in his hand, he said:

"Yes, sir, you have, Mr. Carnegie, and you haven't got enough money to make us break it either."

"There spoke the true American workman," I said. "I am proud of you."

"Mr. Johnson" (who was chairman of the rail converters' committee), "have we a similar agreement with you?"

Mr. Johnson was a small, spare man; he spoke very deliberately:

"Mr. Carnegie, when an agreement is presented to me to sign, I read it carefully, and if it don't suit me, I don't sign it, and if it does suit me, I do sign it, and when I sign it I keep it."

"There again speaks the self-respecting American workman," I said.

Turning now to the chairman of the blast-furnaces committee, an Irishman named Kelly, I addressed the same question to him:

"Mr. Kelly, have we an agreement with you covering the remainder of this year?"

Mr. Kelly answered that he couldn't say exactly. There was a paper sent round and he signed it, but didn't read it over carefully, and didn't understand just what was in it. At this moment our superintendent, Captain Jones, excellent manager, but impulsive, exclaimed abruptly:

"Now, Mr. Kelly, you know I read that over twice and discussed it with you!"

"Order, order, Captain! Mr. Kelly is entitled to give his explanation. I sign many a paper that I do not read—documents our lawyers and partners present to me to sign. Mr. Kelly states that he signed this document under such circumstances and his statement must be received. But, Mr. Kelly, I have always found that the best way is to carry out the provisions of the agreement one signs carelessly and resolve to be more careful next time. Would it not be better for you to continue four months longer under this agreement, and then, when you sign the next one, see that you understand it?"

There was no answer to this, and I arose and said:

"Gentlemen of the Blast-Furnace Committee, you have threatened our firm that you will break your agreement and that you will leave these blast furnaces (which means disaster) unless you get a favorable answer to your threat by four o'clock to-day. It is not yet three, but your answer is ready. You may leave the blast furnaces. The grass will grow around them before we yield to your threat. The worst day that labor has ever seen in this world is that day in which it dishonors itself by breaking its agreement. You have your answer."

The committee filed out slowly and there was silence among the partners. A stranger who was coming in on business met the committee in the passage and he reported:

"As I came in, a man wearing spectacles pushed up alongside of an Irishman he called Kelly, and he said: 'You fellows might just as well understand it now as later. There's to be no d——d monkeying round these works.'"

That meant business. Later we heard from one of our clerks what took place at the furnaces. Kelly and his committee marched down to them. Of course, the men were waiting and watching for the committee and a crowd had gathered. When the furnaces were reached, Kelly called out to them:

"Get to work, you spalpeens, what are you doing here? Begorra, the little boss just hit from the shoulder. He won't fight, but he says he has sat down, and begorra, we all know he'll be a skeleton afore he rises. Get to work, ye spalpeens."

The Irish and Scotch-Irish are queer, but the easiest and best fellows to get on with, if you only know how. That man Kelly was my stanch friend and admirer ever afterward, and he was before that one of our most violent men. My experience is that you can always rely upon the great body of working-men to do what is right, provided they have not taken up a position and promised their leaders to stand by them. But their loyalty to their leaders even when mistaken, is something to make us proud of them. Anything can be done with men who have this feeling of loyalty within them. They only need to be treated fairly.

The way a strike was once broken at our steel-rail mills is interesting. Here again, I am sorry to say, one hundred and thirty-four men in one department had bound themselves under secret oath to demand increased wages at the end of the year, several months away. The new year proved very unfavorable for business, and other iron and steel manufacturers throughout the country had effected reductions in wages. Nevertheless, these men, having secretly sworn months previously that they would not work unless they got increased wages, thought themselves bound to insist upon their demands. We could not advance wages when our competitors were reducing them, and the works were stopped in consequence. Every department of the works was brought to a stand by these strikers. The blast furnaces were abandoned a day or two before the time agreed upon, and we were greatly troubled in consequence.

I went to Pittsburgh and was surprised to find the furnaces had been banked, contrary to agreement. I was to meet the men in the morning upon arrival at Pittsburgh, but a message was sent to me from the works stating that the men had "left the furnaces and would meet me to-morrow." Here was a nice reception! My reply was:

"No they won't. Tell them I shall not be here to-morrow. Anybody can stop work; the trick is to start it again. Some fine day these men will want the works started and will be looking around for somebody who can start them, and I will tell them then just what I do now: that the works will never start except upon a sliding scale based upon the prices we get for our products. That scale will last three years and it will not be submitted by the men. They have submitted many scales to us. It is our turn now, and we are going to submit a scale to them.

"Now," I said to my partners, "I am going back to New York in the afternoon. Nothing more is to be done."

A short time after my message was received by the men they asked if they could come in and see me that afternoon before I left.

I answered: "Certainly!"

They came in and I said to them:

"Gentlemen, your chairman here, Mr. Bennett, assured you that I would make my appearance and settle with you in some way or other, as I always have settled. That is true. And he told you that I would not fight, which is also true. He is a true prophet. But he told you something else in which he was slightly mistaken. He said I *could* not fight. Gentlemen," looking Mr. Bennett straight in the eye and closing and raising my fist, "he forgot that I was Scotch. But I will tell you something; I will never fight you. I know better than to fight labor. I will not fight, but I can beat any committee that was ever made at sitting down, and I have sat down. These works will never start until the men vote by a two-thirds majority to start them, and then, as I told you this morning, they will start on our sliding scale. I have nothing more to say."

They retired. It was about two weeks afterwards that one of the house servants came to my library in New York with a card, and I found upon it the names of two of our workmen, and also the name of a reverend gentleman. The men said they were from the works at Pittsburgh and would like to see me.

"Ask if either of these gentlemen belongs to the blast-furnace workers who banked the furnaces contrary to agreement."

The man returned and said "No." I replied: "In that case go down and tell them that I shall be pleased to have them come up."

Of course they were received with genuine warmth and cordiality and we sat and talked about New York, for some time, this being their first visit.

"Mr. Carnegie, we really came to talk about the trouble at the works," the minister said at last.

"Oh, indeed!" I answered. "Have the men voted?"

"No," he said.

My rejoinder was:

"You will have to excuse me from entering upon that subject; I said I never would discuss it until they voted by a two-thirds majority to start the mills. Gentlemen, you have never seen New York. Let me take you out and show you Fifth Avenue and the Park, and we shall come back here to lunch at half-past one."

This we did, talking about everything except the one thing that they wished to talk about. We had a good time, and I know they enjoyed their lunch. There is one great difference between the American working-man and the foreigner. The American is a man; he sits down at lunch with people as if he were (as he generally is) a gentleman born. It is splendid.

They returned to Pittsburgh, not another word having been said about the works. But the men soon voted (there were very few votes against starting) and I went again to Pittsburgh. I laid before the committee the scale under which they were to work. It was a sliding scale based on the price of the product. Such a scale really makes capital and labor partners, sharing prosperous and disastrous times together. Of course it has a minimum, so that the men are always sure of living wages. As the men had seen these scales, it was unnecessary to go over them. The chairman said:

"Mr. Carnegie, we will agree to everything. And now," he said hesitatingly, "we have one favor to ask of you, and we hope you will not refuse it."

"Well, gentlemen, if it be reasonable I shall surely grant it."

"Well, it is this: That you permit the officers of the union to sign these papers for the men."

"Why, certainly, gentlemen! With the greatest pleasure! And then I have a small favor to ask of you, which I hope you will not refuse, as I have granted yours. Just to please me, after the officers have signed, let every workman sign also for himself. You see, Mr. Bennett, this scale lasts for three years, and some man, or body of men, might dispute whether your president of the union had authority to bind them for so long, but if we have his signature also, there cannot be any misunderstanding."

There was a pause; then one man at his side whispered to Mr. Bennett (but I heard him perfectly):

"By golly, the jig's up!"

So it was, but it was not by direct attack, but by a flank movement. Had I not allowed the union officers to sign, they would have had a grievance and an excuse for war. As it was, having allowed them to do so, how could they refuse so simple a request as mine, that each free and independent American citizen should also sign for himself? My recollection is that as a matter of fact the officers of the union never signed, but they may have done so. Why should they, if every man's signature was required? Besides this, the workmen, knowing that the union could do nothing for them when the scale was adopted, neglected to pay dues and the union was deserted. We never heard of it again. [That was in 1889, now twenty-seven years ago. The scale has never been changed. The men would not change it if they could; it works for their benefit, as I told them it would.]

Of all my services rendered to labor the introduction of the sliding scale is chief. It is the solution of the capital and labor problem, because it really makes them partners—alike in prosperity and adversity. There was a yearly scale in operation in the Pittsburgh district in the early years, but it is not a good plan because men and employers at once begin preparing for a struggle which is almost certain to come. It is far better for both employers and employed to set no date for an agreed-upon scale to end. It should be subject to six months' or a year's notice on either side, and in that way might and probably would run on for years.

To show upon what trifles a contest between capital and labor may turn, let me tell of two instances which were amicably settled by mere incidents of seemingly little consequence. Once when I went out to meet a men's committee, which had in our opinion made unfair demands, I was informed that they were influenced by a man who secretly owned a drinking saloon, although working in the mills. He was a great bully. The sober, quiet workmen were afraid of him, and the drinking men were his debtors. He was the real instigator of the movement.

We met in the usual friendly fashion. I was glad to see the men, many of whom I had long known and could call by name. When we sat down at the table the leader's seat was at one end and mine at the other. We therefore faced each other. After I had laid our proposition before the meeting, I saw the leader pick up his hat from the floor and slowly put it on his head, intimating that he was about to depart. Here was my chance.

"Sir, you are in the presence of gentlemen! Please be so good as to take your hat off or leave the room!"

My eyes were kept full upon him. There was a silence that could be felt. The great bully hesitated, but I knew whatever he did, he was beaten. If he left it was because he had treated the meeting discourteously by keeping his hat on, he was no gentleman; if he remained and took off his hat, he had been crushed by the rebuke. I didn't care which course he took. He had only two and either of them was fatal. He had delivered himself into my hands. He very slowly took off the hat and put it on the floor. Not a word did he speak thereafter in that conference. I was told afterward that he had to leave the place. The men rejoiced in the episode and a settlement was harmoniously effected.

When the three years' scale was proposed to the men, a committee of sixteen was chosen by them to confer with us. Little progress was made at first, and I announced my engagements compelled me to return the next day to New York. Inquiry was made as to whether we would meet a committee of thirty-two, as the men wished others added to the committee—a sure sign of division in their ranks. Of course we agreed. The committee came from the works to meet me at the office in Pittsburgh. The proceedings were opened by one of our best men, Billy Edwards (I remember him well; he rose to high position afterwards), who thought that the total offered was fair, but that the scale was not equitable. Some departments were all right, others were not fairly dealt with. Most of the men were naturally of this opinion, but when they came to indicate the underpaid, there was a difference, as was to be expected. No two men in the different departments could agree. Billy began:

"Mr. Carnegie, we agree that the total sum per ton to be paid is fair, but we think it is not properly distributed among us. Now, Mr. Carnegie, you take my job—"

"Order, order!" I cried. "None of that, Billy. Mr. Carnegie 'takes no man's job.' Taking another's job is an unpardonable offense among high-classed workmen."

There was loud laughter, followed by applause, and then more laughter. I laughed with them. We had scored on Billy. Of course the dispute was soon settled. It is not solely, often it is not chiefly, a matter of dollars with workmen. Appreciation, kind treatment, a fair deal—these are often the potent forces with the American workmen.

Employers can do so many desirable things for their men at little cost. At one meeting when I asked what we could do for them, I remember this same Billy Edwards rose and said that most of the men had to run in debt to the storekeepers because they were paid monthly. Well I remember his words:

"I have a good woman for wife who manages well. We go into Pittsburgh every fourth Saturday afternoon and buy our supplies wholesale for the next month and save one third. Not many of your men can do this. Shopkeepers here charge so much. And another thing, they charge very high for coal. If you paid your men every two weeks, instead of monthly, it would be as good for the careful men as a raise in wages of ten per cent or more."

"Mr. Edwards, that shall be done," I replied.

It involved increased labor and a few more clerks, but that was a small matter. The remark about high prices charged set me to thinking why the men could not open a coöperative store. This was also arranged—the firm agreeing to pay the rent of the building, but insisting that the men themselves take the stock and manage it. Out of that came the Braddock's Coöperative Society, a valuable institution for many reasons, not the least of them that it taught the men that business had its difficulties.

The coal trouble was cured effectively by our agreeing that the company sell all its men coal at the net cost price to us (about half of what had been charged by coal dealers, so I was told) and arranging to deliver it at the men's houses—the buyer paying only actual cost of cartage.

There was another matter. We found that the men's savings caused them anxiety, for little faith have the prudent, saving men in banks and, unfortunately, our Government at that time did not follow the British in having post-office deposit banks. We offered to take the actual savings of each workman, up to two thousand dollars, and pay six per cent interest upon them, to encourage thrift. Their money was kept separate from the business, in a trust fund, and lent to such as wished to build homes for themselves. I consider this one of the best things that can be done for the saving workman.

It was such concessions as these that proved the most profitable investments ever made by the company, even from an economical standpoint. It pays to go beyond the letter of the bond with your men. Two of my partners, as Mr. Phipps has put it, "knew my extreme disposition to always grant the demands of labor, however unreasonable," but looking back upon my failing in this respect, I wish it had been greater—much greater. No expenditure returned such dividends as the friendship of our workmen.

We soon had a body of workmen, I truly believe, wholly unequaled —the best workmen and the best men ever drawn together. Quarrels and strikes became things of the past. Had the Homestead men been our own old men, instead of men we had to pick up, it is scarcely possible that the trouble there in 1892 could have arisen. The scale at the steel-rail mills, introduced in 1889, has been running up to the present time (1914), and I think there never has been a labor grievance at the works since. The men, as I have already stated, dissolved their old union because there was no use paying dues to a union when the men themselves had a three years' contract. Although their labor union is dissolved another and a better one has taken its place—a cordial union between the employers and their men, the best union of all for both parties.

It is for the interest of the employer that his men shall make good earnings and have steady work. The sliding scale enables the company to meet the market; and sometimes to take orders and keep the works running, which is the main thing for the working-men. High wages are well enough, but they are not to be compared with steady employment. The Edgar Thomson Mills are, in my opinion, the ideal works in respect to the relations of capital and labor. I am told the men in our day, and even to this day (1914) prefer two to three turns, but three turns are sure to come. Labor's hours are to be shortened as we progress. Eight hours will be the rule—eight for work, eight for sleep, and eight for rest and recreation.

There have been many incidents in my business life proving that labor troubles are not solely founded upon wages. I believe the best preventive of quarrels to be recognition of, and sincere interest in, the men, satisfying them that you really care for them and that you rejoice in their success. This I can sincerely say—that I always enjoyed my conferences with our workmen, which were not always in regard to wages, and that the better I knew the men the more I liked them. They have usually two virtues to the employer's one, and they are certainly more generous to each other.

Labor is usually helpless against capital. The employer, perhaps, decides to shut up the shops; he ceases to make profits for a short time. There is no change in his habits, food, clothing, pleasures—no agonizing fear of want. Contrast this with his workman whose lessening means of subsistence torment him. He has few comforts, scarcely the necessities for his wife and children in health, and for the sick little ones no proper treatment. It is not capital we need to guard, but helpless labor. If I returned to business to-morrow, fear of labor troubles would not enter my mind, but tenderness for poor and sometimes misguided though well-meaning laborers would fill my heart and soften it; and thereby soften theirs.

Upon my return to Pittsburgh in 1892, after the Homestead trouble, I went to the works and met many of the old men who had not been concerned in the riot. They expressed the opinion that if I had been at home the strike would never have happened. I told them that the company had offered generous terms and beyond its offer I should not have gone; that before their cable reached me in Scotland, the Governor of the State had appeared on the scene with troops and wished the law vindicated; that the question had then passed out of my partners' hands. I added:

"You were badly advised. My partners' offer should have been accepted. It was very generous. I don't know that I would have offered so much."

To this one of the rollers said to me:

"Oh, Mr. Carnegie, it wasn't a question of dollars. The boys would have let you kick 'em, but they wouldn't let that other man stroke their hair."

So much does sentiment count for in the practical affairs of life, even with the laboring classes. This is not generally believed by those who do not know them, but I am certain that disputes about wages do not account for one half the disagreements between capital and labor. There is lack of due appreciation and of kind treatment of employees upon the part of the employers.

Suits had been entered against many of the strikers, but upon my return these were promptly dismissed. All the old men who remained, and had not been guilty of violence, were taken back. I had cabled from Scotland urging that Mr. Schwab be sent back to Homestead. He had been only recently promoted to the Edgar Thomson Works.

He went back, and "Charlie," as he was affectionately called, soon restored order, peace, and harmony. Had he remained at the Homestead Works, in all probability no serious trouble would have arisen. "Charlie" liked his workmen and they liked him; but there still remained at Homestead an unsatisfactory element in the men who had previously been discarded from our various works for good reasons and had found employment at the new works before we purchased them.

2. A Classic Fake

DANIEL DREW (1797–1879) is recognized as the embodiment of predatory sneakiness, sanctimony, and parsimony in the jungle of nineteenth-century Wall Street. Originally a cattle drover from up the Hudson River, he came to Wall Street in 1844, forced his way into a directorship of the Erie Railroad (one of the nation's largest commercial enterprises in those days) in 1857, systematically looted it over the subsequent years, defeated Commodore Cornelius Vanderbilt by foul means in the celebrated "Erie War" of 1866–68, was later betrayed by his former allies Jay Gould and Jim Fisk, and went bankrupt in 1876, three years before his death. In his heyday, he endowed Drew Theological Seminary (now part of Drew University) with $250,000—or rather, he announced his intention to so endow it and paid annual interest on the sum as earnest of his intention. Alas for the seminary, his bankruptcy intervened before the cash was forthcoming. *The Book of Daniel Drew*, published in 1910 and allegedly based on a Drew diary that surfaced in New York in 1905, has done more than any other book to shape the legend of Daniel Drew. It has been solemnly quoted and cited by one social and financial historian after another, over the years; its story (included here) about the origin of "stock watering" is accepted as gospel by social historians; and—far more than *Chapters of Erie,* a sober account by Charles Francis Adams and Henry Adams—it has supplied matter for later accounts of the Erie War: Drew's cool scheming, Fisk's droll appeal to the principle of press freedom in connection with the improper printing of Erie stock certificates, Vanderbilt's eventual pronouncement that the encounter with Drew "taught me it never pays to kick a skunk."

But is it authentic? Hardly likely. I put the question recently to Kenneth E. Rowe, librarian of Drew University, in Madison, New Jersey, and received the following deadpan reply: "Since [Bouck] White was only five years old when Daniel Drew died, there is little chance that he could have gathered information directly from Drew himself. The Drew diary which he cites in his preface . . . has not survived to my knowledge . . . White . . . seldom uses what I would call primary materials . . . Instead, he 'quotes' liberally from Drew's enemies." What we have, then, is a concocted "autobiography," complete with an earnest attempt to simulate the supposed autobiographer's style, that differs from Clifford Irving's celebrated one of Howard Hughes chiefly in the fact that it avoids criminal fraudulence because its inauthenticity is unconcealed, indeed cheerfully self-evident. Yet it has become a semistandard historical source.

Who was Bouck White? According to his obituary in the New York *Times* (January 9, 1951), he was a graduate of Harvard and Union Theological Seminary and a "philosopher, pottery maker, and former Socialist." Besides *The Book of Daniel Drew,* he wrote two books about the life of Jesus. Like Clifford Irving, he did a term in jail, though not for literary fraud; White's imprisonment in 1917 resulted from his burning of an American flag (along with the flags of nine other nations) as a "symbol of internationalism." He was expelled from the Socialist party in 1919. In 1927, in Paris, he perfected a process for making pottery without fire. He spent his last years at a castlelike retreat in the Helderberg Mountains near Albany, making pottery and dispensing philosophy. An example, then, of one of the familiar glories of American life, the idealist-nut, who, if he happens to have genius, is a John Brown or a Henry Ford.

The following excerpts from *The Book of Daniel Drew* are included here not for documentation, God forbid, but for their intrinsic interest and as an object lesson on the nature of American business-financial autobiography and the creation of American business-financial "history."

FORMERLY drovers into New York City had to take their droves to the old "Bull's Head," which was on the Bowery Lane, not far from where the Bowery Theatre stands. There the butchers from the stalls down on Fulton Street would meet the drovers coming into town and buy their stock.

But there was a butcher by the name of Astor—Henry Astor, his name was—who got into the habit, whenever a drover would be reported as coming into town, of leaving his brother butchers tippling at the Bowery "Bull's Head," skip out through the back door of the tavern, mount his horse, ride up the Bowery Road, and meet the drove before it got down to where the other butchers were waiting. Astor would stop the drove and pick out the prime beeves before any one else had a chance at them. By and by the other butchers got on to his trick and also began to ride up to the Bowery to meet the herds. In this way a new "Bull's Head" was established, way out on the Boston Road, where Twenty-sixth Street now is. (The "Boston Road" is now Third Avenue.) By my time this new "Bull's Head" had got to be the cattle market, the drovers' headquarters for the city.

Henry Astor—I got to know him well—was one of the most thriving butchers in the city. He was a German. He had come over in the Revolutionary War as a sutler following the Hessian Troops. His brother, John Jacob Astor, came over a little later; and Henry started him in business as a peddler of knickknacks among the trading sloops that were tied up at the wharves. It was in this way, I guess, that John Jacob got in with the fur traders, and later made a peck of money; so that his son gave the Astor Library there, a little below where my "Bull's Head" tavern was located. But this is getting ahead of my story.

From *The Book of Daniel Drew*, by Bouck White (Doran, 1910).

As I was driving my herd down through the Harlem valley one day, I got to thinking how anxious Henry Astor always was to get fat cattle. (I worked the scheme on any number of the New York butchers as time went on, so it will be understood that I'm now taking Astor merely as a type, because he is one of the best-known butchers of that time and because I got to know him perhaps better than I did the others.) As I was riding along, suddenly I hit upon the idea. And with me, to think of doing a thing means to begin to do it.

We came on along the Bronx River by old man Williams's bridge and across Gun Hill Road, which was deep and heavy—almost as heavy, I reckoned, as the time when the cannons sunk on that hill up to the hubs and General George Washington had to leave them to the British. Then crossing the Harlem on the King's Bridge, I brought the drove over to Harlem Village on the easterly side of the Island, about where Third Avenue now crosses 125th Street. There I put up for the night, since there was a good inn with several pasture lots alongside, in that village. I told my cattle boys to turn in early and get a good sleep, for we would be in New York City on the morrow.

That night, when all the rest were asleep—the cattle boys used to sleep in the barn on the hayloft—I went out to the drove in the pasture alongside the tavern, and emptied sacks of salt on the ground, scattering it so every critter could get some. Then I saw that all the bars were tight. I didn't want any of them to get out and drink. I'll explain why when I get along a little further. . . .

After the cattle had been well salted and the bars all safe and tight, I turned in and went asleep. Next morning I got up good and early. Didn't need any one to wake me. The cattle were lowing long before the sun was up, as though they wanted something or other almighty bad. By the time I got downstairs a couple of cattle boys were up and getting ready to let down the bars, to lead them out to water.

"Hey, there, what are you louts doing?" I called out. "Put up those bars right away and bring back that critter you've let out."

"But, boss," said one of them, "they're choked for water."

"What if they are?" said I. "Would you poison these critters by giving them water they aren't used to? These cattle are fresh from the country. This here is an island surrounded by the salt sea. The water here isn't what it is up country. We must get them used to this new region first. I guess I know my business. Not one of these critters gets a smitch of water until I give the word. D'ye hear? Go now; get a bite of feed, and we'll start for the city."

Thus I kept the drove from water; and as soon as breakfast was over, started them along the turnpike. At the same time I sent word ahead by a rider to Henry Astor, telling him that I was coming with some prime cattle and for him to meet me at the "Bull's Head" about noon. We trudged along, going slow; it was hot as mustard, and I didn't want to sweat any meat off my critters.

Below Yorkville—that's the village that used to be over on the Boston Road, about where Eighty-sixth Street now crosses it—was a little stream called the Saw-Kill, with a bridge crossing it. It was called "Kissing Bridge," because couples walking out that way used to kiss whenever they came to the bridge. It was a recognized custom. The bridge itself was below Yorkville, not far from where Seventy-seventh Street now cuts through. It was a low stone bridge, and hardly to be told from the road itself. But I guess young sparks and their sweethearts never failed to know when they were crossing it. Well, by the time the cattle got to that stream, on the drive down from Harlem Village, they were all-fired thirsty. The cattle boys, too, were glad to see the water. (We used to call these boys "ankle beaters," because they had orders when they were beating the cattle not to strike any higher than the ankle, for fear of bruising the flesh and making it unsound for market.) The boys had been feeling for the poor, suffering critters, and now were laying out to give them a good, long drink. But I had other fish to fry. I rode back to where they were. In taking a drove along the turnpike I used to ride ahead to pick out the road, leaving the boys to follow behind with the cattle. I said to them: "Boys, line up along the road there by the bridge, or those critters will get off away from you."

"Oh, they'll be all right," piped up one of the lads. "They smell the water already, and will make for it without any help from us."

"Make for nothing!" said I. I knew how to put command in my tone, when it was herd-boys I was dealing with. "I don't want one of those critters to get to that there brook. Didn't you hear me tell you this morning about the poison that's in this salt air and this island water, to critters that have been raised in fresh water-regions? Not a drop do they get, and pelt them with dirt clods if you've got to. Get them over the bridge dry-shod."

They minded me. They had to. They had seen me plaster mud all over a steer when he didn't go to suit me, and they knew I could do it to them, too, if they didn't mind. I got the drove over the bridge high and dry. Pretty soon we were at the "Bull's Head." I told the boys to take the cattle into the pasture pen that was back of the tavern, where the well was. Then I went around in front to the tap-room, as soon as I had put my horse out, to look for Astor. He wasn't come yet, so I went in to dinner. Then I waited for him on the stoop in front of the tavern, alongside the Boston Road. Pretty soon I saw him come up the turnpike, riding his horse. I got up and shook him by the hand.

"Got my message, I see," said I, as he was getting off his horse. "You know whom to come to when you want prime stock."

"Well," said he. "I don't know as I'm buying much to-day. Market's mighty poor. But thought I would ride up for friendship's sake, and take a look at your critters." (Being a German, he spoke crooked English. It was curious to hear him. I wish I could set it down here the way he spoke it.)

I was in hopes he'd go into the tap-room and take something. Because when you're bargaining with a man it's always easier if he's got something inside. For then he takes a rosy view of things and doesn't stop to haggle over pennies. Get ale inside of a man, it makes him speak as he thinks. But Astor wouldn't take anything. He only asked the landlord for a drink of water. Then I saw that I had an uphill job on my hands. I was glad that he hadn't come in a gig and brought his wife along, because then I'd have had two of them against me; and Hen Astor's wife, Dorothy, was a money-maker, just like himself. She used to help him in the slaughter-house, doing up butcher's small meats—that is, the tongue, liver, kidneys and such-like; she helped make him the rich man that he got to be after a while. I knew that with Hen Astor by himself I was going to have my hands full. But I went to it with a will. I asked him to wait for me a minute while I stepped out to see if my horse was being fed.

With this as an excuse, I skipped around to where my cattle boys were. I said: "My lads, I guess those critters are used to the climate by this time, and can now drink in safety. Buckle to and give them all the water they can drink."

You should have seen them get to work. Cattle boys get real fond of their critters. A drover likes his critters because they mean money to him. "Ankle-beaters" often get to like them out of real affection. And you should have seen the cattle go at it, too. You'd have thought they'd not had a drink for an age. The salt had done its work. A quart of salt to every pair of cattle is a fair allowance; in the present case I had allowed them a little more than that. So that now they sucked the water in like sponges. Do the best they could, the boys couldn't keep the trough full. The steers fairly fought with each other for a drink. So I told off a couple of the boys to take part of the herd over to another pasture across the road, where there was a big pump, and start that going too. Then, when I saw that the thing was nicely under way, I went back to the tavern, where Astor was waiting for me.

"It beats all how these hostlers need looking after," said I. "If I hadn't gone out there to the barn they'd have starved that mare of mine. A thimbleful of oats no bigger than that, as true as you live, that's what they were giving my mare. And she as big as two ordinary horses. But how are you, anyhow?" And I seated myself beside him on the stoop. I took a fresh chew of tobacco, and offered him some. I thought it a good plan to sit and visit for a spell. It gets your customer into a neighbourly frame of mind; and then, too, in this present case it would give my boys time for the watering.

"I'm not so very chirpy," he grumbled. "How are you?"

"Fine as a fiddle," said I; "and what's ailing you?"

"All kinds of troubles," he went on. "The life of a cattle butcher, Dan, isn't what it used to be. There are so many in the business nowadays. And housewives come to my stall there in the Fulton Market and buy my best meats—top slices, no second cuts for them—and then, when I or Dorothy go to see them, they won't pay their bills. And the stall is getting so crowded, the hucksters and salad women have been signing a paper against me, because, they say, I've built my stall across the whole end of the market, and have crowded them out under the eaves, where they're exposed to the sun and weather. I'm a licensed victualler—I guess I've got some rights there. And then, too, the city fathers these days are getting so pernickety. You remember the market used to be on Maiden Lane—it was built over a running stream that was used as a city sewer. Very handy for us, because we could drop the swill and such-like right through a hole in the floor. But the City Board didn't do anything else but talk everlastingly about 'nauseous and pestilential vapours,' and kept it up till we moved the market up onto Fulton Street. And now they're getting more pernickety still. Why, Dan, since the small-pox came they are getting so they won't allow our hogs to run in the streets any longer."

"Heinrich Astor!" said I (he liked to be called by his German name); "what won't they be ordering next? Pigs in the street are the best scavengers a city can have. You mark what I tell you, Hen; if they shut the pigs up, the gutters will get so full of slops and stuff, there won't be any living inside the city limits. Why, it would take a herd of swine to clean up what your slaughter-houses alone dump into the street."

"There you are again," he broke in. He was getting riled up. "That fussy old board of city fathers have gone and passed another ordinance, that butchers mustn't empty any more refuse in the street gutters. So now we have to cart the blood and slops way over to the river. I'd like to know how dogs, to say nothing of the hogs, are going to get a living inside the city limits, if this sort of thing keeps on. And without dogs, where would we be, at night? Why, just the other day a farm below me on the Bowery Road lost no end of chickens by the foxes."

"That loss of poultry will make more call for cow meat," said I; "and, Hen, between you and me, I've brought you some of the fittest beeves this trip that ever set foot on Manhattan Island. We'll step out and take a look, if you say so." I knew by this time that the boys would be through with the watering. So we went out.

Sure enough, when we got out into the pasture, you couldn't see a sign of a water-pail. And there, as plump and fat-looking as a man ever saw, stood the critters. I noticed out of the tail of my eye that Astor got interested all to once.

"There are two or three good-sized ones in the bunch," he remarked. "I suppose you want to sell the drove at a lump sum. I wasn't calculating on buying any stock to-day. But seeing it's you, I might be able to make an offer for the drove as a whole—say, at so much a critter."

"No," said I, "they go by the pound, this trip. Prime cattle such as these take a sight of time and fodder to fatten. I've had to get this herd together one at a time, the very best from a hundred farms. But it's worth the pains," I added, "when a fellow can bring to market a drove like this." He punched his thumb into two or three of the critters, and found them firm and solid.

"Tolerable good," said he, "tolerable good. But I'm afeared most of them will be tough. I suppose, though, I could use them up for soup meat. Tell you what I'll do. I'll give you two and a quarter a pound just as they stand, and for one or all."

I said that the figure I had set for this drove was four cents. He gave a snort and started towards the tavern as though disgusted. I didn't make any move to call him back; I knew that when a butcher finds what he thinks to be a drove of fat cattle, he isn't going to give up at the first crack. He likes the thought of a nice, fat carcass hanging from the hooks at his stall in the market. So, pretty soon, back he came.

"Donner and Himmel!" he exclaimed, and he was red in the face. "You drovers take us townspeople for suckers. I'll give you two and a half, and not a speck more. You can take it or leave it. Anyhow, I'm expecting another drover in from Long Island next week, and only came up to-day to just kind of look around."

I met him by coming down half a cent. I hadn't thought for a minute that I could get the four-cent price I had named. I had mentioned that figure in order to have something to back away from, when we got down to business. You must ask much to get a little.

He snorted off once more; but he didn't get so far this time. "Two and three quarters," said he, coming back. "And there isn't a cent in it for me at that figure, so help me Gott!"

I told him the very best I could do was three and a quarter, and only made it that figure because he was willing to take the whole drove. "It's the beneathenest price I ever saw offered for choice stock such as these," said I. "It costs money, Hen, to pump corn into a heifer until her loins stand out like the hams on a hog."

He backed away. We dickered a spell longer. Finally we hit on a flat three-cent price. The cattle were driven on the scales. (They weighed up fine, as you can believe.) He paid over the money, and took them off down to his slaughter-pen, not far from the Bowery. I was happy, and he went off happy, too. Because a butcher likes to get heavy critters. To be sure they cost him more, but fat beef in a butcher's stall goes like hot cakes, where stringy joints wouldn't sell at all. So it was what I call a good bargain, seeing that both of us were pleased.

It can be seen now what a lucky thought it was for me—that salting device. The salt cost but a few pennies a bag, and by means of it nigh onto fifty pounds had been added to the selling weight of every critter in the drove—a full-grown critter will drink that weight of water if you get her good and thirsty. Thus I took in as my profits on this trip as fine a penny as a man could ask.

I FELT SO RICH from my stock-watering deal that I stayed at the "Bull's Head" tavern a spell. And, a day or two after the business with Astor, I started down to the city to see about getting a new saddle. My old one was so worn that the stuffing was coming out; for, although I had been making money for some years back, I hadn't felt like spending any more of it than I could help. My idea in those days was: Better a hen to-morrow than an egg to-day. Small savings, if you keep them up long enough, mean big savings by and by. If a fellow is going to be rich, he must get money working for him early in life. A swarm of bees in May is worth a load of hay; but a swarm in July isn't worth a fly.

Now, however, I felt rich enough to afford a new saddle. So I mounted my mare and started down to New York. . . .

Reaching Wall Street, I hitched my mare to a lamp-post and started out to the saddler's. There were a number of good hotels down in New York at this time, with horse sheds attached, such as the Franklin House, over on the Broadway, corner of Dey Street, and the Park Place Hotel, corner of Park Place. But the hostlers in those city hotels charged a fee even for tying your horse under the shed. It has always been my motto: Never feel rich, even though you have money in every bank in town. There are some young men so spendthrifty, they eat

the calf while yet inside the cow. But not I. In those days a lamp-
post was just as safe a place for a quiet mare as a hotel shed; and was
good enough for me.

I soon found that my dodging of Astor's place on the Bowery had
been in vain. Because, as I was walking down towards "Dirty Lane"
—that's the name that used to be given to South William Street—I
happened to look back and spied him a-hurrying after to catch up
with me. He must have seen me cut across lots to dodge going by his
house; or maybe he had come over from his stall at the Fulton Market
onto Wall Street, and had chanced to spy me. At any rate, there he
was, a-following after. I didn't want to meet him just then and there;
I could see that he was in a temper. So I turned the corner into William Street, and stepped into a tavern that was not far down the street.
I guess I wasn't quick enough; for a minute or two later Astor came
in the front door also.

"Hey, you," said he, busting in through the door and puffing hard;
"you damned Dan Drew! You think you can sell me pump water at
three cents a pound, do you? I want to speak just one word with you,
you damned ——"

But I didn't wait. It never pays to argue with a man when he's excited, and Hen now was very red in the face; I saw at a glance, that
he was in no state of mind to talk a matter over calmly. So I hurried
on through the tavern and out by the back door. There I cut over onto
the other street through a lane before he could see which way I went,
and so lost him.

I decided, after thinking the matter over, that I wouldn't stay in
the city to get a saddle this trip, after all. So I went back to my mare,
unhitched her, and was soon back to the "Bull's Head," safe and
sound. Then I rode away to Putnam County for another drove of
cattle.

The saying, "selling watered stock," has now got to be well-known
in the financial world. So I've wrote down in this paper about the
affair of salting my critters. Some time later I became an operator
in the New York Stock Exchange; I hung out my shingle on Broad
Street. And the scheme was even more profitable with railroad stocks.
If a fellow can make money selling a critter just after she has drunk

up fifty pounds of water, what can't he make by issuing a lot of new shares of a railroad or steamboat company, and then selling this just as though it was the original shares? But for this drover time in my life, these smaller profits seemed mighty big.

For I didn't let the salting scheme rest with only the one trial. After I got back to Putnam County I lost no time in getting another drove together and hurrying it back to the city. Astor didn't care to buy of me this second trip. Not that he kept mad for any length of time. He was the kind of a fellow to cool off after a few weeks. On this, my next trip to the city, I found him as civil as I could wish. But he wouldn't buy my cattle—made a number of excuses. He showed his friendly spirit, however, by introducing me to one of his fellow butchers in the Fulton Market; so that on the present trip I dealt with this other butcher. In fact, I found that the stock-watering plan, while a money-maker, had certain drawbacks. Because from now on it compelled me to deal with a different butcher 'most every trip. But that wasn't so bad as it might seem. For there were lots of butchers in the city; and in most cases I found that the butcher I'd dealt with the last time was willing to introduce me to one of his competitors, as a drover that handled choice stock. I took in profits with a big spoon . . .

THE ERIE WAR was now about to open. It was the biggest fight I was ever in. So I was glad I had got an able helper like Jim Fisk; for I was going to need partners now as never before.

It was a fight, as anybody might know, between Vanderbilt and me. Pretty much all our lives we have been fighting each other. When he had a good thing, it always kind of seemed as though I wanted it, too; and when I had a good thing, he never slept easy till he had a finger in it. That had been the case with steamboats, and it was now to be the case, also, with the Erie Railroad.

Vanderbilt's make-up and mine were different. I suppose that accounts for our everlastingly crossing horns. His way was to break down opposition, by rushing straight through it; my way was to go around it. He was the dog, I the cat. A cat believes in going soft-footed—in keeping its claws hid till the time comes to show them. A dog goes with a big bow-wow; my plan has always been to go at a thing quieter. A cat won't spring at a dog from in front—'tisn't good tactics.

She gets around on the flank, claws the dog from behind, and so does a lot of damage without being in any danger herself.

The Commodore was a lordly fellow. He used to drive a team of horses, and would go riding up Fifth Avenue as though he owned both sides of it. His house was down on Washington Square among the silk-stockings. In winter he would wear a fur-lined coat and a stove-pipe hat; was very proud of his person. As for me, I was never a hand for vainglory. Top-boots, such as I used to wear in drover days, have always been good enough for me. And I never could see the use of paying expensive prices to a tailor when you can get a suit ready-made for less than half the sum. As for cutting a wide swath, I never did take to it. My turn-out of one horse and a doctor's gig was good enough for me. When the Broadway stages started in, they were cheaper yet; so I used them.

Some of my friends used to scold me because I didn't dress up. They'd say: "Uncle Dan, why on earth do you walk around with such an old stick as that for a cane?" But I told them I wasn't proud. That stick had once been the handle of an almighty good umbrella. And now that the umbrella part was of no use any more, I felt it would be a shame to throw away the stick; because the stick was in just as good a condition as when I had bought the umbrella years before.

Another difference between the Commodore and me was that he was by make-up a Bullish fellow, whereas most of my life I have been on the Bear side of the market. It used to be one of his mottoes: "Never sell short." Even in the darkest hours of the Civil War, he had lots of faith in the future of the country. He seemed to think that in America 'most any kind of stock would go up and be valuable if he only waited long enough. "I bide my time," he used to say to me, when I would tell him he'd better sell such and such a stock and get it off his hands. "Get it off my hands?" he'd exclaim. "Not by a jugful! I bought that stock as an investment; it's going to reach par some day, and don't you forget it."

Yes, he was a natural-born hoper. I have always been more con-servative have never allowed myself to paint the future in too bright colours. The Commodore made most of his money by stocks going up. I made most of mine by stocks going down. I wish now I'd been a Bull instead of a Bear. Because a Bull makes money when everybody's happy, that is, when stocks are on the upward move; so that people are willing to see him get rich. But a Bear makes his money when other people are unhappy. Because, in order for him to make, others have got to lose; for him to get rich means that there is a line of bankrupts in his train; and people cuss him so for taking money away from them, that his fortune doesn't give him so very much satisfaction.

Vanderbilt's faith in the future of our country sometimes led him into reckless expenditures. During the Civil War he was willing to have that conflict come to an end, even though it was making good business for us operators in Wall Street; because he figured that, with the country prosperous once more, he would be prosperous also. He even gave a million-dollar boat outright to the Government, for use as a gun-boat, to help hurry the War to an end. He seemed to think the country's interests and his own were one and the same—a position which leads a fellow into all kinds of extravagance. It's all right to love your country; but a fellow ought to love himself, too. I loaned some of my Stonington Line boats to the Government during the War; but I charged rent. In the year '62 alone, Abe Lincoln paid me $350,-000 for the use of the boats. So I was really sorry when the Civil War was over. For then an era of prosperity set in; and prosperity isn't good for a Bear operator.

The Commodore gave a million dollars to Vanderbilt University—right out of hand. He didn't seem to have any fear of losing his fortune and dying poor. I have believed in giving sort of cautious-like. I gave a quarter-million as an endowment to found Drew Theological Seminary. But I kept the principal in my own hands—only paid over the interest each year—that is, I paid the interest as long as I was able. I have always believed that a man should be handier with a rake than with a fork.

Well, the Erie fight was between Vanderbilt and me. I had been the ruling spirit in Erie now for ten years, and had made so much money out of that road that other people got jealous. Part of those ten years was Civil War time. Stocks were bobbing up and down like a boy's kite. I was on the inside and could take advantage of these jumps.

The Civil War was over; Vanderbilt now vowed that he would get control of the Erie Road and put me and my crowd out of business for good and all. He said we were nothing but a nest of gamblers, that we were unsettling the entire market by our speckilations, and that he wouldn't feel safe for his other properties until the Erie Railroad had also been placed in what he called safe hands. So he set out to buy a controlling interest in the stock.

I guess what made him so mad was a "Convertible Bond" scheme that I worked about this time. The Erie Road wanted three million dollars to make some improvements. I loaned her the money, and took as security for the loan three million dollars of bonds which were convertible into stock; and also twenty-eight thousand shares of unissued stock which the road just then had on hand. This provided me in all with fifty-eight thousand shares of stock. Thus fortified—and when the Street didn't know that I held these shares—I went onto the Exchange and sold Erie heavily short. Erie was then at 95, and promised to go still higher. People reckoned that I was a reckless plunger. The weeks ran along. Pretty soon it came time for me to deliver. The price held strong at 95. My enemies began to snicker. They said I was cornered. But I took the twenty-eight thousand shares I had kept up my sleeve, and dumped them into the market all to once. It was probably the biggest surprise Wall Street up to that time had known. Prices were knocked into a cocked hat. Erie gave one plunge—fell to 47. Which means, I made the other fellows pay me $95 a share for stock which was costing me now only $47. So I cleaned up $48 on every share dealt in. It was the finest scoop I had ever made. It is true, those 58,000 shares had been intrusted to me only to hold as security until the road should pay back my loan. But in a business deal, you can't stop for every little technicality.

Vanderbilt said that sort of thing had to stop. And he was going to be the one to stop it. So he started in. He didn't try to conceal his moves. He let everybody know. He went out in the open market and made his bids. He said that the Erie Road, in spite of all the dirty water—as he called it—in its stock, could be made once more into a dividend-earning property; and that it would be worth money to him and to the public generally to make it into a good road once more. At least he was willing to put his fortune into the attempt. So he gave his brokers unlimited orders. "Buy Erie," was what he told them. "Buy it at the lowest figure you can; but buy it!" And he swore an awful oath that the moment he got control of the road, there would be such a cleaning out of the Erie stable as it hadn't known for years.

One of his first moves was to get in with a Boston set that owned a large block of the stock—the "Boston, Hartford and Erie" crowd. Almost before I knew it, he had worked up this combination among the directors, so that I was likely to be defeated for reëlection to the Erie Board. I went to the Commodore to soften him down. I said I'd try to do better from now on, if he'd let me stay in the Board. Besides, he needed me, even though maybe I wasn't just the kind of an Erie manager that he'd like to have. He thought I was a selfish director; but there was a set of men now getting in who were really and wilfully thievish.

"You think I'm a director who is working only for my own pocket," said I. "Well, I'll promise from now on to work for the interests of the road. But there is a set of bad men now getting in, who are unregenerate. Commodore, you can't fight them alone. What you need is a partner who is on the inside, and who can, therefore, fight those fellows for you better than you can do it yourself."

"Yes," said he, "but where in time could I find such a man?"

"I'm the one," and I spoke up good and prompt.

He laughed a great big laugh. (Vanderbilt had a hearty way of laughing, as though he wasn't afraid of anything or anybody. He used to poke fun at me—on the occasions when he and I were on good terms—because I didn't laugh a good loud laugh like he did. "Why in thunder, Dan, don't you laugh when you set out to do it," he used to say, "and quit that hen cackle of yours, which is no nearer a real laugh than one of my old Staten Island periaugers would be to a modern paddle-wheel boat?") He gave one of those laughs of his now.

"That would be a bully good idea!" he said. "You are just the fellow to take in as confidential friend and partner. Drew, you're as crooked as a worm fence. You'd betray me inside of twenty-four hours."

"I wouldn't betray you at all," said I. "I guess I haven't forgotten the time when we used to be friends together in the old steamboat days. Why, back there in that *Waterwitch* affair ——"

"Yes, yes," said he. "I remember old steamboat days. We have known each other quite a while, haven't we? I don't know but what

I might give you one more trial." He thought for a spell. "Do you really think, Dan, if I took you back, that you could play fair?"

"I don't believe anything about it," said I. "I know I could. And I'm in a position to do you a whole lot of help."

"I declare, I believe I'll try it," said he. "But wait. I gave my promise to put you out. The Boston crowd wants to get rid of you. And I told them that at this next annual meeting I'd see to it that you were not reëlected."

"Yes," said I; "but you can tell them you have changed your mind."

"That isn't the way I do things," said he. "A promise is a promise."

"Well, if that is the way you feel," I answered, "why not work it this way? We'll go ahead and hold the election. I will be left out. We'll put a dummy in the place instead of me. Thus you'll be keeping your promise with the Boston crowd. Then, after the election is over, the dummy can resign and I will be appointed in his place."

"That's certainly a fruitful noddle you've got there, Uncle," said the Commodore. "I don't just take to that way of getting out of the difficulty. But maybe it's as good as any. We'll call it settled."

The election was held. My name didn't appear in the list of those reëlected to the Board. It looked as though I was out of Erie for good and all. But the next day the dummy resigned—said that on further thought he was not able to take it and would have to be relieved. We relieved him. I stepped into his shoes. I was back into my old place.

Now, I was ready for work. I started in. There was no time to be lost. Vanderbilt would soon have complete control of Erie unless I blocked him. Already I had Fisk with me as a partner. I needed another man. This other man I found in Jay Gould.

Jay had been worming his way inside of Erie for some time back. He had given up writing histories—had also sold his tannery business out in Pennsylvania. He had come to New York with a patent rat-trap to sell. Then he got into the Street. First along he dealt in small railroads. But when he saw what a bag of money I was making out of Erie he began to invest in its stock. He got in with some of the stockholders, and by now had become a director himself and one of the powers in the road. I took him now as a partner. He was at the head of a clique in the Board of Directors that I needed in my fight against

Vanderbilt. So he and Jim Fisk and I now stood together like three blood-brothers against the Commodore, our common foe.

Gould was just the criss-cross of Fisk. He was an undersized chap, and quiet as a mouse. I never liked his face. It was dark, and covered all over with whiskers so you could hardly see him. As to Fisk, you couldn't help but like him. Jimmy did me one or two dirty deals before he died. However, I could take it from him, he was that big and warm-hearted in it all. But Jay was so almighty silent. And he wasn't a healthy man, either. He was as lean as a parson's barn. Never seemed to me that he ate enough. Jimmy used to put his purse into his belly. Jay put his belly into his purse. So that, though he himself was thin, his purse was fat as a porker. Jimmy used to say:

"The difference between Jay and me is, I have more trouble to get my dinner than to digest it, and Jay has more trouble to digest it than to get it."

As I said, I couldn't help but like Fisk, no matter how wicked a man he was; and he was wicked. He was very carnal. The way he used to carry on with women was something scandalous. He used to bring them right down to the office. Didn't make any bones about it. He would drive down in a barouche with a darkey coachman and four horses, and have two or three ladies of pleasure in the carriage with him. Sometimes we would be in the middle of a hard day's work. A carriage would drive up; a couple of ballet dancers would get out, bounce into the office where we were, trip up to Fisk and say, "Hello, we've come to spend the day."

I'd look up as much as to say: "You're going to put them out, aren't you?"

But he would answer my look and say: "Uncle, I've got a previous engagement with my Sweet-lips here, and this railroad matter will have to wait over until to-morrow. And this other female charmer here—Mr. Drew, allow me to make you acquainted with the prima donna of "Mazeppa" and "The French Spy." Then he would send out for a restaurant man, have victuals brought in, and would serve up a banquet to his ballet dancers right in his private office. He wouldn't care what the expense was; and he didn't mind whether he had known the girls before or not. Sometimes they would bring in another girl, one he had never met, and say:

"We've brought Annie along. You must meet her. They all say she's the sassiest queen in town."

"That's fine," he would answer; "and she's a lu-lu, too; she shall enjoy the carousal with us. The more the merrier. The world can never have too many girls of the kind that are toyful and cuddlesome."

I used to scold Jimmy for these wenching bouts of his; but my scoldings didn't count for much.

"That's all right, Uncle," he'd answer. "You're old and dried up. There's no fire in your veins. But for a gay young buck like me, a little spice in the midst of a hard day's work is needed. I never was one of your Josephs—woman-proof."

So I didn't have much peace of soul with either of these partners of mine. Gould, quiet as a clam; and Fisk, the devil's own. But both of them were handy in a stock-market dicker; and that was what I needed just now. The Erie war was rapidly coming on. I had to have partners that could help.

WHEN you set out to ride a colt, see that your saddle is girt good and tight. That's what I did now. I didn't want to tackle the Commodore before I had first made good and ready. This is the way I set about it:

At one of the meetings of the Erie Board of Directors I got the matter of steel rails to take the place of the old and unsafe iron rails acted upon by the Board. Our road, further, was being hurt because it had a six-foot track, whilst the other railroads were being built with only a narrow, that is, the present standard-gauge, track. Their cars couldn't go on our road, nor ours on their road. It had been proposed that the Erie lay a third rail inside the other two rails, in order that narrow-gauge rolling stock could run on the track in the same train, if need be, with our own broad-gauge cars. This, and the steel rails to replace the iron ones, were two such needed improvements that I now made them an excuse for getting the road to issue some new shares of stock. By means of my control of the Executive Committee, I got them to vote to issue ten million dollars of convertible bonds, the proceeds of which—so they supposed—were to go into these improvements.

The advantage of convertible bonds was this: There was a provision in the charter forbidding the Erie Road to issue new stock except at par—which wouldn't have suited my purpose. Bonds would have been equally useless, seeing they are of no value in stock-exchange dickers. Bonds convertible into stock, however, were just the thing. Because it was only another name for an issue of stock at the market rate.

So now I had one hundred thousand shares of stock at my disposal, whenever I should care to turn the trick. Of course, legally speaking, these shares were not just at my disposal, either; because they were meant as a means of raising money to be put into the improvements and repairs that the road then needed. But all's fair in love and war. And in this particular case I felt that I was more in need of this nine or ten million than the Erie Road was. The road was under my management, because I controlled the Executive Committee, and, therefore, the finances. I felt that I was entitled to a few pickings, as it were. It's an ill cook that can't lick his own fingers. So, instead of using the money to buy steel rails, I had the old iron rails turned, in order to bring the unworn outside edge onto the inside now. Of course, this wasn't altogether as safe as new steel rails would have been. But I needed in my stock-market operations the money which this new bond issue was raising. And inasmuch as I had put in a good deal of valuable time as treasurer of the Erie Railroad, I felt I had a right now to sluice off some of her revenues into my own pocket. When you own a cow, you own her milk also. As to legal objections, by getting one of the judges on my side—as will be seen later—we got the law courts so jummixed up that they didn't know where they stood; and so the law couldn't touch me.

Whilst in the midst of these busy preparations, I had to cease operations for a couple of days and go out to the formal opening of my theological seminary at Madison, N. J. It was an occasion of great spiritual refreshment, and I'll write about it later. Just now I must finish telling about this Erie Railroad affair.

Supplied with ammunition in the shape of this fine, big issue of stock, I was now prepared for war. And I wasn't a moment too soon, either. Vanderbilt was already at work. He was out in the open market buying Erie with the boldness of a lion. I guess he was figuring that I was on his side, or he might never have been so bold and confident. Anyhow, he was going ahead as though there was nothing now that could stop him. I didn't say anything. I thought I'd let him go ahead, and sort of take him by surprise when the time came.

Vanderbilt wanted to buy Erie shares. All right. I was willing he should buy all he wanted. In fact, I thought I would help him in the matter. So I went onto the market, and sold Erie short in enormous quantities.

My friends thought I was going it wild. "What in the world, Uncle, are you up to?" they said to me. "Don't you remember those luckless Bears that went short of Harlem and got their feet caught in the trap? That's just what you're doing now. The Commodore is going to corner you tight as a fly in a tar-barrel." But I only smiled.

The Commodore now learned that I was against him, and got very much het up. His crowd taunted me.

"You're already beginning to count your profits?" said I to them. "Don't boil the pap till the child is born, that's all." And I went on selling the stock short.

Vanderbilt now made a move which he hadn't tried before. He went to the law courts and got out an injunction forbidding me and my crowd to issue any more shares of Erie stock. This last was a proceeding I was not willing to stand for. As chief director of Erie, I had a right to operate her as I saw fit. But here was Vanderbilt going to the law courts and putting a higher power over Erie's affairs than I was. He was tying my hands. So I went into the law-court business, too. I called a council of Gould and Fisk. We decided, since Vanderbilt had got a judge of the Supreme Court on his side to issue injunctions for him, that we'd get a judge too. So we went out to Binghamton, and got a judge there. Vanderbilt's judge had enjoined us from issuing any more Erie stock. This new judge of ours now got out an injunction commanding us to issue more stock. He wasn't a New York City judge. But he had as much power, so far as his legal standing was concerned. Because these Circuit Court judges work side by side. Any one judge has power extending over the entire state. Ordinarily they are supposed to stand by each other; but this was just after the Civil War, when things were topsy-turvy. Johnson was being impeached. The legal machinery of the country was that unsettled, we could do with it 'most anything we wanted.

When Vanderbilt had got out his injunction, restraining us from manufacturing any new certificates of Erie stock, he thought that he had all the leaks corked up at last good and tight. He supposed, therefore, that in issuing orders to his brokers to take all the Erie that was offered, he wasn't in any possible danger. I went onto the Exchange as though nothing had happened, and proceeded to sell more Erie. I sold all that I could—didn't set any limits—agreed to deliver all the stock I could find buyers for. Of course, in the Commodore I found a ready buyer.

People now thought me plumb crazy. "Uncle Daniel has gone clean off his head," said they. "It's got to be second nature with him to sell stock short. He goes onto the Bear side by force of habit. In this deal he hasn't any more chance than a grasshopper in January. The Commodore has got him this time. He's fixed it so that Drew and his crowd can't manufacture any new stock, and he has roped in all the floating supply that is still on the market. And yet here is Uncle Daniel still offering to deliver the stock in unlimited amounts. Where's he going to get it when these contracts mature? Drew is daft. He's going it blind, and will run his head against a post." Thus they talked. I let them. I was still able to find my way around in a Wall Street transaction—as they soon found out.

By and by the time drew near when these short contracts of mine would mature. (I say "mine." Of course, Fisk and Gould were with me. But I was the leader of the party, so I speak of it in my own name.) Jimmy came to me and said: "Guess it's about time to play our ace of trumps, don't you think so? We'll make Rome howl." I said I guessed he was right. So we called in Jay. We held a council of war. We decided that the time had come to set off the gunpowder.

Accordingly, we went to a printing-house and got them to print a hundred thousand shares of Erie. (It was those convertible bonds now being turned into stock.) Of course, the printer could turn out only the blank forms; but since we were the officers of the road, or controlled the officers, such as the Secretary and such-like, we could get any amount of printed blanks signed in legal manner and made thus into good financial paper.

It was a helpful sight to see that printing press work so smooth and fast. For we had only a few days more in which to make our deliveries. All the Street thought we were cornered. In fact, Vanderbilt himself was beginning to tell around that he was going now to clean up the Erie stable inside and out—wasn't going to leave so much as a grease spot of us behind. It was an exciting time. The Street knew that big things were about to happen. For this was a battle of the giants. Vanderbilt and I were the two biggest men in Wall Street. When the two big roosters on the dung-pile cross spurs, there's going to be some feathers flying.

Gould and Fisk stood with me watching the printing press as she turned out for us the bright, new stock certificates. Each one of those sheets of paper was of enormous value to us. Not just because of the amount of money it would bring in dollars. But this was a war, and each of these crisp certificates was a cannon ball, so to speak. If we could pound the Commodore hard enough that he wouldn't have time to recover between the blows but would be forced to knuckle under, then we'd have him at our mercy, and all of his property also. Besides, with him busted up, there would be a great smash in values, and we on the Bear side of the market would then profit all along the line. It's far more important in a business war to break down the man himself, than to break down any particular piece of his property. Because when the man goes under, all of his fortune is at your disposal. So these bright new sheets of paper looked very beautiful to us. They were just so many additions to our ammunition supply. I could almost have hugged that printing press, she was that friendly to us. Jimmy, of course, had to have his joke.

"That injunction of the Commodore's," said he, "was aimed against the freedom of the press. As freeborn Americans we couldn't stand for that. Give us enough rag paper and we'll hammer the everlasting tar out of that mariner from Staten Island."

"Oh, come now," said Jay; "let's don't get rambunctious. We're not out of the woods yet. Our contracts to deliver the stock are rapidly maturing. We have engaged to hand over to the Commodore such enormous blocks of it that I can't sleep nights, thinking of it. And something may happen yet to get in our way."

"Happen!" said Jimmy, and he was as calm as a cat with kittens; "I'd like to see anything happen! If this printing press don't break down, we'll give the old hog all the Erie he wants."

I scolded him. But in my heart I was glad to have a partner who was so cock-sure. For we were in a ticklish place. If any hitch should come, we would certainly find ourselves in the tightest corner a man was ever in, and got out alive. Jimmy's spirit kept us in heart. Fortunately, the printing press didn't break down. It kept on with its klickety-klack, smooth as clock-work. As fast as the blank certificates were turned out and the printer's ink had dried, Fisk took them and made them valid by putting in the proper signatures. "The Devil has got hold of me," he remarked; "I might as well keep on signing." Soon the entire issue was finished, and tied up in a neat bundle at the Company's office. The stock was now good financial paper.

But there was still a danger. And because the amounts at stake were so high, we determined to take no chances. The Commodore might hear that our printing press had been once more at work, and get his judge to enforce his injunction, by attaching this new bunch of Erie shares. In which case we wouldn't have time to print any more; for our deliveries were maturing the very next day. The Commodore's judge was in New York City, right at the seat of war. Whereas our judge was way out in Binghamton; so that the Commodore could act more quickly than we; and this was a time when minutes would count.

So we took measures. The new stock was over in the Erie office on West Street. We tied up the books of newly printed certificates in a neat paper bundle. Then we called the office boy and told him to take that bundle over to the Transfer Office on Pine Street. He started out with it. When he was just outside the door, something happened. He returned empty-handed, and white as a sheet. He said that a man—a big blonde individual, with a yellowish moustache and a large shirt front—had rushed upon him whilst he was in the hall, grabbed the bundle from him, and had whisked off with it before he could say "boo."

"Dear, dear!" said the Secretary (he was the one who had been enjoined from issuing this stock) "that's too bad!" But he told the boy not to mind; he had done his best, anyhow; it wasn't his fault; and sent him back to his desk. We all pretended to be het up over the matter; but we were pretty calm inside. Because we could have made a pretty close guess as to who had grabbed the bundle away from the boy. But, of course, if it had come to the taking of evidence in court, the Secretary could now clear his skirts; because the stock had been snatched out of his keeping. That same afternoon those shares turned up at the office of our broker. He parcelled fifty thousand of them out to his subagent in ten-thousand share lots. Now we were ready for operations.

The next morning the Stock Exchange opened calm and clear, as though it was a time of perfect peace. The president of the Board called out the shares of the various railroads in usual order: "Union Pacific!" "Wabash!" "New York Central!"—no response. He met with a dead silence. Then he called out "Erie!" Things broke loose at once. One of our brokers jumped out onto the floor and offered a block of one thousand shares of Erie; he followed this up with another thousand; that with another; until he had offered five thousand shares of Erie—wanted to sell them right then and there. Vanderbilt's brokers took the first two or three thousand-share blocks cheerfully. But it was noticed that they looked surprised. Then, almost before our first broker had got through, another sprang forward and offered blocks of Erie for sale—ten thousand in all. Our first broker followed up his previous offerings with five thousand more (that made up his ten thousand). Still another of our brokers came and helped push along the landslide. He yelled out: "A thousand shares of Erie for sale! A thousand more of Erie! A block of five thousand shares of Erie!" And so on until his ten thousand shares were offered.

By this time the Vanderbilt brokers were scared out of their wits. They got into communication with their master. "Hell has broke loose," they sent word to him. "Thirty thousand shares of Erie have come raining down on us in the last half-hour, with more coming out every minute. What shall we do?"

All the answer he gave was: "Support the market."

As he didn't seem at all flustered, his brokers got courage, went back and took our offerings. They succeeded in absorbing the whole fifty thousand shares without letting the market sag more than a point or two.

But now came the death stroke. These deliveries of stock were made right away. As soon as the Exchange saw that these certificates were crisp and new, with the printer's ink hardly dry on them, the secret was out. In defiance of Vanderbilt's injunction, we had set our printing press to work.

The landslide then broke loose. For if we had been able to cut the legal red tape with which Vanderbilt had tried to tie our hands—had found a way to start the printing press to work once more—why, it was good-night to the Commodore. Because there is no limit to the amount of blank shares a printing press can turn out. White paper is cheap—it is bought by the ream. Printer's ink is also dirt cheap. And if we could keep on working that kind of deal—make Vanderbilt pay us fifty or sixty dollars for little pieces of paper that hadn't cost us two cents, we would very soon have all of his cash ladled out of his pocket into ours.

It was, I guess, the darkest hour in Vanderbilt's life. He had staked his reputation and a good share of his fortune on this Erie fight; and now we had suddenly unmasked a battery that was pouring hot shot into his ranks thick and fast. No wonder his followers began to desert him. They fell off by twos and threes. There was a small-sized panic all through the Vanderbilt party. Until now they had looked upon their leader as able to take care of them. Some of them had begun to think that he was a sort of supernatural person, one that couldn't be touched by mortal hands. But now his career seemed to have come to an end. He was no longer the high and mighty one that he had been.

This was the moment we had been waiting for. In war it is good generalship to know when to strike. We now dumped the other fifty thousand shares onto the floor of the Exchange all to once. The price, which had been at 83, dropped like a dead heifer. It was as though the bottom had fallen out—nothing was left to support things. Down and down and down it went, clean to 71. Considering the number of shares involved, and the size of the transactions, it was the biggest stroke Wall Street had ever seen. The Commodore himself wasn't able to stand out any longer. The price rallied a little before the day was over, for it was seen that the Commodore wasn't as yet entirely swamped—he took all the stock that we offered, even the last fifty thousand, and paid over his good cash for it. But the market had made a fatal break. Nothing he or his friends could do would bring it back again. And the day closed with me and my crowd gloriously on top.

THIS was Tuesday, early in March. The next day, Wednesday, we met at our Erie Railroad office on West Street, to count our profits. It was a happy hour. Seven million dollars of Vanderbilt's had been scooped out of his pocket into ours. Four millions of it was in legal-tender notes, good crisp greenbacks. We hardly knew where to stow the money. We set to work tying it up in bundles. We were in high spirits. Jimmy couldn't get over laughing and talking about the "green goods." He said how the Commodore was all right for Staten Island, but he ought to have stayed down there along with the other farmers; because the streets of New York were not safe for people who didn't know the game. We were all in good heart.

3.   The Park-Bench Sage

FROM HIGH ROLLER to elder statesman with the greatest of ease—so have moved a handful of Americans, perhaps most eminently Joseph P. Kennedy and, before him, Bernard M. Baruch. Baruch (1870–1960) was born in Camden, South Carolina, the son of a successful physician of German-Jewish origin who had served in the Confederate Army in the Civil War and been captured at Gettysburg. The family moved to New York City in 1880, whereupon Bernard Baruch attended City College (and subsequently became its most famous graduate), then went into Wall Street where he accumulated a fortune before he was thirty. In World War I he served as chairman of the War Industries Board and in World War II and afterward as special adviser to James F. Byrnes, in various posts. In 1946 he became United States representative to the United Nations Atomic Energy Commission and helped formulate plans for international control of atomic energy. *Passim,* he served as unofficial park-bench adviser to practically everybody in high federal office. Just how his high-rolling activities prepared him for these elder-statesman activities is not clear, nor is the same thing clear as regards to others who have made the same transition. We do not elevate to high office or to positions of trust successful gamblers who operate only in card games; it seems illogical that we should so elevate those like Baruch who operate in card games *and* in Wall Street. Yet by most accounts, Baruch seems to have paid his dues as a wise man; perhaps, indeed, there is some wisdom-imparting quality in stock speculation, or perhaps it was just luck.

Included here are Baruch's vivid first-hand account of the great Northern Pacific panic of 1901, in which the Hill-Morgan and the Harriman-Kuhn, Loeb forces fought to a virtual standoff while the stocks of most other companies crashed (and in which, as he blandly relates, Baruch made a huge profit based on insider information); a short, flavorful account of Baruch's participation in gambling of the traditional sort; and his "investment philosophy," in which he seems to advance gambling or its equivalent not as a risky entertainment or a way of getting rich but as a high moral cause.

In the introduction to his autobiography Baruch acknowledges the "help" of no fewer than three persons: Harold Epstein, Samuel Lubell, and Herbert Bayard Swope.

RATHER OFTEN I am asked why it is that we do not have any present-day equivalents to the financial giants who dominated Wall Street at the turn of the century. Is it that Americans have really become a new and softer breed?

Part of the answer, of course, is that today's stock market is drastically different from what it was in the days of Morgan, Rockefeller, Edward H. Harriman, and others. Government regulation has made illegal many of the practices engaged in even as late as 1929. The kind of trading that I did for Thomas Ryan in his tobacco war with James Duke would not be possible today; nor what I had done with Amalgamated Copper.

And, of course, the level of present-day taxes means that no matter how huge one's profits may be, a considerable part of them goes to the government.

From *Baruch: My Own Story,* by Bernard M. Baruch (Holt, 1957), pp. 133–49, 180–82, 247–49.

Still, I believe, the main reason why Wall Street has lost that quality of dramatic personal adventure which was so marked in my youth will be found in the astonishing extension of the range and area of economic interests covered by the market's activities.

This change, in turn, reflects the equally astonishing transformation of America from a frontier-pushing people, concerned mainly with subduing a continent, to the prime stabilizing force for the whole of western civilization.

One might label this change as a shift from an era of almost unrestrained individualism to one of global responsibility. The meaning of this shift is something I would like to come back to later in this narrative, because it covers so much of our national history and remains one of the keys of understanding which may help us unlock the future.

My own career seems almost to have been a span between these two eras, not because I foresaw what was coming but primarily because I was thrust into the picture in such a way that I could hardly help but contribute to this transition. I came into the world of business and finance just in time to see the titans of finance at the zenith of their power. From the atmosphere generated by their example—and struggle—I was thrust abruptly into all the problems of global responsibility by my appointment as chairman of the War Industries Board in World War One.

After that war was over, when others sought a return to "normalcy," I continued to grapple with these problems in successive posts, from being an adviser to Woodrow Wilson at the Paris Peace Conference to representing the United States on the United Nations Commission on Atomic Energy.

For forty-odd years, in fact, I have found myself in the position of trying to reconcile what I learned about business in my earlier years with the newer national and global needs that a shrinking world has forced on us.

The extent to which the Wall Street of fifty years ago was subject to the influence, if not domination, of a few individuals may be difficult to realize, since it differs so markedly from today. The glamour figures of those days were largely financiers, with the newspapers and Sunday supplements generating much mystery and intrigue over what "they" were doing—the "they" being the Morgans and Harrimans, the Ryans, Rockefellers, and other financial "big shots."

As an amusing example of how the market could seem to be dominated by some bold figure, I recall a story about Dan Reid, who was a director of U. S. Steel but who still liked to play the role of the great big bear from time to time.

During one heavy stock decline, Reid raided stock after stock until he seemed to be in full control of the whole market. Actually his "raids" were made possible by an unsound market condition which gave a man with abounding courage an advantage that could be only temporary. None knew this better than Reid. Just the same, even the most powerful bankers were afraid of what Reid might do.

Reid happened to be quite fond of Henry P. Davison, then rightfully the most important junior partner of J. P. Morgan's. One day Reid telephoned Davison and asked:

"Harry, do *you* know what I am going to do?"

"No," said Mr. Davison.

"Do you *want* to know what I am going to do?"

"Yes," said Davison eagerly.

"You *really* want to know?"

"Yes," said Davison, ready to expect anything.

"Well," replied Reid, "I'm not going to do a damn thing."

Almost at once the market righted itself. Today, of course, no one man could run the market ragged for even a few days or stabilize it by a telephone call.

Perhaps an even more revealing illustration of the compact intimacy of the old stock market could be seen in the old Waldorf-Astoria, then located where the Empire State Building now stands. In those days, after the closing gong had sounded on the Exchange, most of the traders would gather at the Waldorf. To belong to the "Waldorf crowd" meant that a man had arrived. I had won admittance to this circle on the strength of the reputation I made in the purchase of the Liggett & Myers Tobacco Company.

On an afternoon or two at the Waldorf one might brush elbows with Richard Harding Davis, Mark Twain, Lillian Russell, Gentleman Jim Corbett, Admiral Dewey, Mark Hanna, Chauncey Depew, Diamond Jim Brady, Edwin Hawley, and countless presidents of banks and railroads. Judge Elbert Gary, the head of U. S. Steel, lived there, as did Charley Schwab and James Keene. It was at a private dinner party in the Waldorf that I saw John W. Gates place a $1,000,000 bet in a game of baccarat.

The fact that nearly everyone of importance in Wall Street could be found at the Waldorf made it a highly revealing laboratory for the study of human nature. Once . . . I used this fact to conduct an experiment in human psychology, by which a company was financed through the mere showing of a certified check. The various "rooms" of the Waldorf-Astoria—the Empire Room or Peacock Alley, the billiard room, or the Men's Café with its famous four-sided mahogany bar—were really like so many exhibition galleries in which every human trait was on display.

Sitting in these rooms, it was always an intriguing exercise to try to detect the doers from the braggarts, the genuine human article from the spurious. Nor will I ever forget how panic struck the Waldorf one night and transformed it from the preening ground of all that was fashionable to a lair of frightened animals.

It was the first time that I had witnessed a panic, and it lasted for only one night. Other panics I later experienced, such as those of 1907 and 1929, had far more devastating effects on the economy. Still, this particular panic of May 8, 1901, seemed all the more revealing, perhaps because it came and went so swiftly or because through chance I was able to watch it as if I were a spectator and not one of its hapless victims.

2

As with most financial panics the stage had been set in advance by extravagant hopes and talk of a "New Era." Varied factors contributed to this surge of optimism. Our victory over Spain had stirred fantastic dreams of imperialism and dazzling predictions of new foreign markets. The public was in the stock market as never before.

It was at this time, I believe, that women came into the market for the first time in any numbers. Over their teacups in the Waldorf's glass-enclosed Palm Room they talked knowingly of what U. S. Steel or Union Pacific or Amalgamated Copper was bound to do. Bellboys, waiters, barbers—everyone—had a "tip" to pass on. Since the market was rising, every bullish tip came true and every tipster seemed a prophet.

Several times it seemed that the market had run its course and that a healthy reaction was on the way. Then a new stock would be brought forward and there would be another balloon ascension. On the last day of April, 1901, the market had the biggest day in its history to that time—3,270,884 shares were traded. This represented an average of a million dollars a minute changing hands during the five hours the Exchange was open. The commissions to brokerage houses alone aggregated $800,000.

On May 3 the market broke from seven to ten points. Many persons, including myself, thought this was a sign that the long-anticipated decline had come. But then on Monday, May 6, a strange new factor entered the market—a spectacular rise in Northern Pacific.

In my entire career on the Stock Exchange, I do not recall another opening similar to this one. The first sale of Northern Pacific was at 114, or four points above its Saturday closing. On the second sale it jumped to 117. Thereafter the day was marked by spasmodic up-rushes as Eddie Norton, the floor member of Street & Norton, bought every share in sight at the market.

No one seemed able to fathom the cause of this rise. Directors of the Northern Pacific could not explain it. Bankers could not explain it. Eddie Norton, who was doing the buying, was not talking.

By a rare piece of good fortune I was one of the few persons in the world who knew, on that fateful Monday morning, the central fact behind the Northern Pacific's puzzling performance—that it represented not some mere market manipulation but a mighty battle for control of the road between E. H. Harriman and James Hill, represented by their respective bankers, Kuhn, Loeb & Company and J. P. Morgan.

Before disclosing the curiously informal manner in which I learned this information, let me sketch what was at issue between the contending giants.

The rise of Edward H. Harriman, who had come to Wall Street as an office boy, had long been a thorn in Mr. Morgan's side. Early in Harriman's climb he had met and bested Morgan not once but two or three times. A violent personal enmity grew up, which Mr. Morgan did not temper by his habit of referring to Harriman as "that two-dollar broker."

In the late nineties the Union Pacific seemed one of the most hopeless roads in the country. After Morgan refused to reorganize it, Harriman bought control, rehabilitated, and extended the road. He not only made it pay handsomely but he turned it into a worthy rival of the Great Northern and the Northern Pacific, which were under Hill-Morgan control.

Then Harriman bought the Southern Pacific, moving, as always, so quickly and silently that his object was accomplished before his adversaries knew what was in the wind. Thus did "that two-dollar broker" become one of the foremost railroad men of the world.

Incidentally, our firm did a large business for Mr. Harriman which was handled first by Arthur Housman and then by Clarence Housman. In 1906 Harriman had the Housmans place heavy bets on Charles Evans Hughes in his race for Governor of New York against William Randolph Hearst. After several hundred thousand dollars had been wagered, the Housmans stopped. Hearing of this, Harriman called them up.

"Didn't I tell you to bet?" he demanded. "Now go on."

Clarence Housman told me that when he was admitted into Harriman's office to report how much had been bet, he saw "Fingy" Conners, the Democratic boss of Buffalo. Conners may have been there to talk about contracts for handling Buffalo's wharf freight, but we were more cynical in explaining his presence there.

Harriman's purchase of the Southern Pacific was also handled largely through A. A. Housman & Company. Edwin C. Hawley conducted most of the operation. However, I had no part in the transaction and at the time did not know Mr. Harriman.

I do remember one day seeing on the floor of the Exchange a slightly bow-legged, nervous little man, with large round spectacles. Turning to one trader, I asked, "Who is that little fellow buying all that U.P. preferred?"

I was told he was Edward Harriman. I have no idea why he happened to be on the floor of the Exchange that day. I never saw him there again.

With Harriman controlling Union Pacific and Southern Pacific, the Hill-Morgan interests needed an entrance into Chicago. So they bought the Burlington, on which Harriman also had his eye. Harriman asked for a third interest in the purchase. Morgan refused. Harriman's response was one of the most audacious strokes in Wall Street's history—a secret move to purchase in the open market a majority of the $155,000,000 common and preferred stock of the Northern Pacific Railroad.

Early in April, after refusing Harriman an interest in the Burlington, Morgan sailed for Europe. Harriman and Jacob H. Schiff, the senior partner of Kuhn, Loeb & Company, began purchasing the stock of the Northern Pacific.

Under the spur of this buying, N.P. rose about twenty-five points. But with the whole market surging forward, little was thought of it. Ironically, the general view was that N.P. was being bought by the public in anticipation of the strong position it would attain because of the Burlington deal. Even some Morgan and Northern Pacific insiders, tempted by the high prices, sold their Northern Pacific stock.

Late in April, James Hill, the veteran president of the Great Northern, in far-off Seattle, smelled a mouse. Ordering a special train and a clear track, Mr. Hill broke the existing record on a run to New York. He arrived on a Friday, May 3, and put up, as was his custom, at the Netherlands Hotel. That night Mr. Schiff informed him that Harriman controlled the Northern Pacific.

The shaggy-haired Westerner refused to believe it. Mr. Schiff, always the suavest of men, assured him that it was true.

Schiff, though, it turned out, was not entirely right. Harriman held a clear majority of the preferred stock and a clear majority of the aggregate capital stock, common and preferred, but not a majority of common alone. On the next day, a Saturday, Harriman telephoned Kuhn, Loeb to buy 40,000 shares of N.P. common, which would have given him a majority. The partner who took the message waited to consult Mr. Schiff, who was at a synagogue. Schiff said not to make the purchase that day.

By Monday it was too late. After his talk with Schiff, Hill had sought out Robert Bacon of J. P. Morgan & Company. A cable was sent to Morgan in Europe. On Sunday, May 5, Mr. Morgan replied, authorizing the purchase of 150,000 shares of Northern Pacific common at the market. What Schiff had overlooked was that the Northern Pacific directors had the power to retire the preferred stock and thus, through control of the common stock, still could retain control of the railroad.

It was at this point that I got my line on what was going on. This is how it happened.

3

As an office boy at Kohn's I had acquired the habit of getting downtown an hour or two before the Exchange opened to see whether the London quotations offered opportunities for making an arbitrage profit. On Mondays in particular I did that to take advantage of possible developments over the week end.

On the Monday morning that was the beginning of the puzzling day in Northern Pacific, I was standing at the arbitrage desk where London cables were sent and received. Beside me stood Talbot Taylor, one of the better brokers and the son-in-law of James Keene, who was the man the Morgans usually turned to for difficult market operations.

I drew Taylor's attention to the fact that Northern Pacific could be bought in London several points below the New York price.

Taylor's brown eyes regarded me intently. His face was expressionless.

"Bernie," he said, tapping his lips with the butt end of his pencil, "are you doing anything in Northern Pacific?"

"Yes," I replied, "and I'll tell you how to make some money out of it. Buy in London, sell here, and take an arbitrage profit."

Taylor went on tapping his lips, then his forehead, with the pencil. At length he said, "I would not arbitrage if I were you."

I did not ask why. If Taylor wanted me to know he would tell me. I offered to let him have some of my previous London purchases if they would help him any.

"All right," he agreed, "you can buy N.P. in London, but if I need the stock I want you to sell it to me at a price and a profit that I will fix."

To this I agreed. Taylor stood there for an instant. Then, taking my arm, he led me out of earshot of anyone else.

"Bernie," he said in almost a whisper, "I know you will do nothing to interfere with the execution of the order. There is a terrific contest for control and Mr. Keene is acting for J. P. Morgan.

"Be careful," concluded Taylor, "and don't be short of this stock. What I buy must be delivered now. Stock bought in London will not do."

With this priceless information, Eddie Norton's buying later that day was no mystery to me, of course. I could have told others what was going on and, if I had, much of what later happened may never have taken place. But that would have meant breaking Taylor's confidence. Once the word got around, Taylor would have found it more difficult to execute the purchase orders that had been given his firm.

Brokers often have told me in confidence of their orders, knowing that I would keep their secret and not upset their operations. Usually I tried to avoid such confidences since they could prove embarrassing. Several times I have been forced to abandon actions I had already decided upon so it would not appear as if I were using confidential information against the people who had given it to me. Still, this was one occasion when a fellow broker's confidence did mean a great deal.

As I walked away from the arbitrage desk I pondered what Keene's son-in-law had told me. With Morgan and Harriman eager to acquire every possible share, the available supply of Northern Pacific stock was likely to be "cornered" rather quickly. Traders who had sold the stock short, anticipating its decline, would be unable to cover themselves. They would be forced to bid fantastic prices for Northern Pacific. To cover these losses they would have to dump other securities. A corner in Northern Pacific, in other words, would produce a general collapse in the market.

And so I decided to go short in several other leading stocks in the market, to profit when these securities were dumped. I resolved not to do any trading at all in Northern Pacific. As it turned out, being on the sidelines proved the best place from which to observe the wildest situation the Stock Exchange had ever known.

On the following day, Tuesday, May 7, it was clear that the stock had been cornered. There was virtually no Northern Pacific stock that anyone wanted to sell. During the trading it touched 149 and closed at 143. But the really wild scramble came after the three o'clock gong.

Under the Stock Exchange's rules of that day, all stock bought or sold had to be delivered by the next day. If someone sold a stock short, the practice was to borrow the stock certificate from some broker, if necessary, paying a premium for its use. If a trader couldn't borrow the stock certificates he needed, the man to whom the stock had been sold could go into the market and pay any price for it. The trader who had been caught short would have to make good this price.

But in the case of Northern Pacific there simply weren't enough stock certificates to cover the needs of all the traders who had sold short. When the closing gong sounded the frantic traders surged around the Northern Pacific trading post bidding premium rates for any stock that might be available.

I have used the files of the New York *Herald* to stimulate my recollection of the scenes that took place. The picture this newspaper gives of the wild scramble on that day is not overdrawn if my memory is any criterion.

When one broker walked into the crowd, other traders, thinking he might have some Northern Pacific stock, charged him, banging him against the railing.

"Let me go, will you?" he roared. "I haven't a share of the d———d stock. Do you think I carry it in my clothes?"

Then, through the desperate crowd strode Al Stern, of Herzfeld & Stern, a young and vigorous broker. He had come as an emissary of Kuhn, Loeb & Company, which was handling Harriman's purchases of Northern Pacific. Stern blithely inquired: "Who wants to borrow Northern Pacific? I have a block to lend."

The first response was a deafening shout. There was an infinitesimal pause and then the desperate brokers rushed at Stern. Struggling to get near enough to him to shout their bids, they kicked over stock tickers. Strong brokers thrust aside the weak ones. Hands were waving and trembling in the air.

Almost doubled over on a chair, his face close to a pad, Stern began to note his transactions. He would mumble to one man, "All right, you get it," and then complain to another, "For heaven's sake, don't stick your finger in my eye."

One broker leaned over and snatched Stern's hat, with which he beat a tattoo on Stern's head to gain attention.

"Put back my hat!" shrieked Stern. "Don't make such a confounded excitement and maybe I can do better by you."

But the traders continued to push and fight and nearly climb over one another's backs to get to Stern. They were like thirst-crazed men battling for water, with the biggest, strongest, and loudest faring best.

Soon Stern had loaned the last of his stock. His face white, and his clothes disheveled, he managed to break away.

The next day, May 8, the corner in Northern Pacific was acknowledged and the panic spread. The shorts, knowing that they would have to acquire stock to cover themselves before the day's trading was over, bid wildly. The stock opened at 155, twelve points above the last quotation of the previous day. Soon it advanced to 180.

During the day Mr. Schiff made the public announcement that Harriman controlled the Northern Pacific. But the Hill-Morgan forces refused to strike their flag. They were banking on the judgment of their field marshal, James Keene, the greatest market operator of his time.

Keene never appeared on the floor during this or any other of his operations. He was not, indeed, a member of the Exchange. Throughout the Northern Pacific contest he remained inaccessible in the office of Talbot Taylor's firm. To send reports to Keene, Eddie Norton would pass the word to Harry Content, who in turn would wander around the room a bit and then come up to Taylor and give him the information for Mr. Keene.

On the Exchange floor fear had completely taken the place of reason. Stocks were being dumped wildly, dropping from ten to twenty points. There were rumors of corners in other stocks.

In a panic it is not easy to avoid being swept along with the mad tide. In this case, however, having made my plans in advance, I was able to step aside and keep my wits. When stocks were dumped I bought—my net profit that day was more than I made on any other one day before or after.

I also decided that there would be no corner in any other stock. I reasoned the railroad bankers had had just about enough and soon would be trying to bring the panic to an end. The whole situation, as I saw it, was in the hands of two titanic forces who would have to compromise sooner or later—I felt sooner.

Still, the scenes of that afternoon and evening, after the gong put an end to the trading, showed no surface indications of peace between the warring factions.

Pandemonium reigned in the loan crowd from three until four-thirty. When Al Stern appeared again, he was shoved against a pillar as the traders surged upon him to renew the loans of the day before. Stern climbed on a chair and cried to the traders to keep off and listen to what he had to say.

When the crowd finally quieted, Stern broke the crushing news—those who had borrowed his stock would have to turn it in as he could renew no loans.

This action, I might explain, was not taken to squeeze the shorts to make them pay to the last dollar of ability as Jay Gould did in his Chicago & Northwestern corner of 1872. The reason for the action was that the Harriman and Morgan forces were at the showdown point in their struggle for control of the Northern Pacific. Neither could tell how much of the stock each side would be able to vote until the actual stock certificates were in hand.

That night the public rooms and corridors of the Waldorf were jammed, but by a far different kind of crowd than had peopled this palace of leisure and gaiety only a few days before. The ladies were gone. Men neglected the amenity of formal clothes.

Have you ever noticed how animals behave on a sunny day when no danger threatens? They lick their coats, preen themselves, strut and sing, each trying to put on a better show than the other fellow. So with human beings. And like animals, when fear strikes their hearts, they forget their elegances and sometimes even the common courtesies.

One look inside the Waldorf that night was enough to bring home this truth of how little we differ from animals after all. From a palace the Waldorf had been transformed into the den of frightened men at bay. Men milled about from one throng to another, eager to catch the news of any change in the situation. Some men were too frightened to take a drink; others were so terrified they could only drink. It was, in short, a mob, swayed by all the unreasonable fears, impulses, and passions that play on mobs.

Only the stoutest could maintain outward signs of composure. I saw Arthur Housman in the company of John W. Gates of "Bet a Million" fame. The bluff, breezy Chicagoan kept up his old bravado. He denied all rumors connecting him with a short interest in Northern Pacific, saying that he had not lost a cent and that if he had, he wouldn't squeal.

The latter part of this statement was true, if the first part was not. As a matter of fact, all the millions Gates had made were in jeopardy. He and other big fellows were asking one question—would compromise be reached in the course of the night?

4

The next morning a tense, white-faced, almost silent band of men surrounded the Northern Pacific trading post. No word of compromise, no hope for truce had emanated from behind the guarded doors where sat the rival generals and their chiefs of operation.

A babble of voices drowned the echo of the gavel. Within an hour Northern Pacific was selling at $400 a share. Before noon, it was $700. Shortly after two o'clock 300 shares were sold for $300,000 cash—$1000 a share.

I happen to know that Eddie Norton personally sold that stock short. As he told me later, he was gambling that the price could not stay that high and that if it did, there would be general ruin in the market.

With Northern Pacific soaring, the rest of the list collapsed, losing up to 60 points as stocks were thrown over at any price. Call money loaned by banks to brokers opened at 40 per cent and touched 60. All sense of value and sanity was gone.

Eddie Norton stood with tears in his eyes at the thought of the imminent ruin of many of his friends. The wildest rumors sped to and fro. One report, which I later learned was cabled to London, was that Arthur Housman had dropped dead in our office. To contradict this he had to show himself on the floor of the Exchange.

Scenes in the brokerage offices were as heartrending as those on the floor. My friend Fred Edey, of H. B. Hollins & Company, rushed to the offices of J. P. Morgan to warn that there would be twenty failures by nightfall if loans were not forthcoming. From banker to banker Edey went, pleading and persuading. His efforts brought millions of dollars into the Exchange and helped parry disaster.

Two-fifteen was the deadline when the shorts had to put up the stock certificates to cover their sales of the previous day. A few minutes before, Al Stern, the Kuhn, Loeb emissary, came onto the floor. Mounting a chair and shouting to make himself heard, he announced that his firm would not enforce delivery of Northern Pacific purchased yesterday.

Stern was followed by Eddie Norton, who announced that his firm as well would not demand delivery of 80,000 shares due them.

The crisis was over. Northern Pacific sold off to 300. The general list steadied.

At five that evening the crowds at the Waldorf were relieved by a bulletin over the ticker that said Morgan and Kuhn, Loeb would provide stock for those short of it at 150. These were much more generous terms than most of the shorts had expected to get. The panic was ended.

No man was more relieved than the picturesque Gates, who no longer had been able to conceal the truth of his position. He held court that night in the Men's Café of the Waldorf, flanked by Max Pam, his attorney, and Arthur Housman, while people fought to get near him. He was chipper but it required a good deal of effort.

"What do you think of the flurry, Mr. Gates?" he was asked.

"Flurry?" he retorted. "If you call that a flurry, I never want to be in a cyclone."

"Are you broke?" someone asked impertinently.

"Just badly bent," retorted the game old warhorse. "You know, I feel like a dog I used to own out in Illinois. That dog got kicked around so much he walked sort of sideways. Finally he got accustomed to the kicks and did not mind them and walked straight. A while ago I was walking sideways. I was kicked all out of shape but along about sunset this evening I managed to right myself. Now I am able to walk as straight as the next fellow and look forty ways for Sunday."

A day or so later Mr. Gates sailed for Europe with the whole affair dismissed from his mind, or at least so far as anyone could judge from outward appearances.

When the smoke blew away there was some question as to who, after all, controlled the Northern Pacific. Harriman was a lion. He was ready to fight on. But Morgan and Hill had had enough. They were willing to compromise to avoid future hostilities. An agreement was reached whereby Harriman obtained representation on the boards of both the Burlington and the Northern Pacific, which was more than he had asked for in the first place.

HIGH ROLLING

[I RECALL] A DINNER PARTY at the Waldorf. It was given [in 1902] for "Hi" Barber, president of the Diamond Match Company.

After a cold buffet, the table was made ready for baccarat. John Drake, who had been a partner with Gates in backing Royal Flush for the Goodwood Cup, and Loyal Smith, a real estate operator, were co-bankers. We took our places and bought chips. White chips represented the smallest denomination. They were $1000 apiece.

Gates was playing the tableau opposite mine. After a few rounds of two-, three-, and five-thousand-dollar bets he began to call us pikers and to raise his stake. Harry Black and "Huddie" Hudson followed him up to $25,000; then Hudson refused to go any higher. I saw Gates was fixing to plunge, and placed a limit of $5000 on my bets. My precaution was emulated by at least two of the other guests, Hugh Wallace, later ambassador to France, and Willis McCormick.

This annoyed Loyal Smith, who was taking in the winnings and paying out the losses of the bank. "I can't bother with you pikers," he said. "You'll have to pay in and take out for yourselves."

Up went the betting—fifty, seventy-five thousand dollars on a play.

What is it that turns ordinary betting into a reckless gamble? Desperation on the part of a heavy loser is one factor. Again, I have seen a run of luck go to a fellow's head and make him think how much more he might win if the stakes were raised. But in this game there were no heavy losers or heavy winners. All through the evening the game ran strangely even for both the large and small bettors. It was lose and win, then win and lose, with no one getting far either way.

Perhaps it was the inconclusive nature of the play that bothered Gates. Anyhow he tossed out two yellow chips, worth $50,000 apiece. The bank accepted the bet. Other players raised their bets as well, but I stuck to my limit of not more than five $1000 chips.

It was the first time in my life I ever had seen $100,000 risked by one man on the turn of a card. For a moment I wondered if it was real money. When I saw the look on the faces of Drake and Smith, I knew it was.

Gates wasn't satisfied. He tossed four yellow chips onto the table. The bankers consulted each other and accepted the dare. No one attempted to duplicate that bet. At $200,000 a play, all of us were pikers now. Gates made several more such bets only to find that he stood even.

Then he picked up his chips, chinked them together for a moment, and with a dexterous movement of his stubby fingers laid out two equal stacks before him. He placed one stack on his own tableau and the second stack on the tableau I was playing. Each stack stood ten yellow chips high—$1,000,000 in all!

"Just a little light bet," Gates said, looking up expectantly into the faces of the bankers. If he breathed a bit heavily, as he sometimes did under the stress of excitement, or if there were an unnatural note in his voice, I could not detect it.

The rest of us looked at the bankers, too. Smith demurred. He said that was too much for him to risk.

"Come on," urged Drake, "let's give him a run for his money."

After some persuading Smith consented to accept the bet. Drake picked up the cards to deal. His face was pale but his hands were steady. Behind him stood Smith, white as a ghost, with perspiration trickling from his forehead.

I looked at my two cards. They showed a natural nine, which I exposed quickly. Gates, who was wagering on my cards as well as on his, had won the first bet of $500,000.

Then Gates turned his cards up on the other side of the table. They did not suit him. He drew to improve and lost. Gates and the bank were even.

Even Drake, one of the nerviest men I have known, was satisfied with this outcome. But Gates was not. When he bet, he bet to win.

The rest of the evening was anticlimactic, the bank having announced it would cover no more $500,000 bets. We played for quite a time, though, with the stakes high enough to suit me. Too high, in fact, so I just trailed along with my white chips, and never more than five of them on the line at a time.

Strangely, the balanced run of the cards continued. The large bettors broke about even. The heaviest loser was the one man who of all those present could least afford to lose. I myself quit $10,000 behind.

MY INVESTMENT PHILOSOPHY

I HAVE HEARD attributed to Sir Ernest Cassel, who was the private banker to King Edward VII, a remark that I wish I had thought of first.

"When as a young and unknown man I started to be successful I was referred to as a gambler," Sir Ernest said. "My operations increased in scope and volume. Then I was known as a speculator. The sphere of my activities continued to expand and presently I was known as a banker. Actually I had been doing the same thing all the time."

That observation is particularly worth pondering by those who may think that there is such a thing as a sure investment. The elder J. P. Morgan could gag at the word "gamble" when I used it. Still, the truth is there is no investment which doesn't involve some risk and is not something of a gamble.

We all have to take chances in life. And mankind would be vastly poorer today if it had not been for men who were willing to take risks against the longest odds. In setting out to discover a new route to India, Columbus was taking a chance that few men of his time were willing to hazard. Again, in our own age when Henry Ford started to make the first Model T, he was embarking on one of the most gigantic speculations of all time.

Even if it could be done—and it cannot—we would be foolish to try to stamp out this willingness in man to buck seemingly hopeless odds. What we can try to do perhaps is to come to a better understanding of how to reduce the element of risk in whatever we undertake. Or put another way—and this applies to governmental affairs as well as money making—our problem is how to remain properly venturesome and experimental without making fools of ourselves.

As I already have pointed out, the true speculator is one who observes the future and acts before it occurs. Like a surgeon he must be able to search through a mass of complex and contradictory details to the significant facts. Then, still like the surgeon, he must be able to operate coldly, clearly, and skillfully on the basis of the facts before him.

What makes this task of fact finding so difficult is that in the stock market the facts of any situation come to us through a curtain of human emotions. What drives the prices of stocks up or down is not impersonal economic forces or changing events but the human reactions to these happenings. The constant problem of the speculator or analyst is how to disentangle the cold, hard economic facts from the rather warm feelings of the people dealing with these facts.

Few things are more difficult to do. The main obstacle lies in disentangling ourselves from our own emotions.

4. *The Golden Rule*

THE CHAIN-STORE MAGNATE J. C. Penney (1875–1971) was a paradigm of the Fundamentalist American success seeker and his autobiography is an anthology of Fundamentalist American business thought. If a novelist had invented him, the resulting character would surely have been ridiculed by critics as too typecast, too broadly drawn for belief. Even his name was too good to be true: J. C. (Jesus Christ?) Penney—the meeting of religion and money. Born in Hamilton, Missouri, the son of a Primitive Baptist minister, Penney made money as a boy by raising pigs and watermelons, later ran a butcher shop that failed because he would not deal with hotels that served liquor, then worked for a time in a retail dry goods store in Kemmerer, Wyoming. In 1902 he was able to buy a one-third interest in the store, thereby launching his career. He called the chain that gradually developed from that beginning the "Golden Rule Stores." He never touched alcohol or tobacco and for many years forbade his employees to do so. He believed, as he says in the following excerpt, that anyone and everyone has in him the latent capacity to become "a human dynamo, capable of accomplishing anything to which he aspires"; he was against debt; he put emphasis in his organization on energy, integrity, and loyalty. He made it a principle to offer a new executive less than he had been paid in his previous job, as a test of loyalty and faith—and also, no doubt, as a measure of thrift. Late in his life, when his chain had grown to become the nation's fifth largest merchandising operation with 1,600 stores ("partners") nationwide and annual sales of over $4 billion, he proclaimed that "the company's success is due to the application of the Golden Rule to every individual, to the public, and to all of our activities."

"What a bore!" we may be tempted to exclaim. But like so many American primitives of commerce, past and present—and, indeed, like the American primitives of art—he was more complex and interesting than he appears at first, as the following passage suggests. In it he tells about the career of George H. Bushnell, whom Penney, in 1913, hired away (at a reduced salary) from a farm implement firm in Ogden, Utah. Bushnell went on eventually to become first vice president of Penney's chain, although his first assignment for it, that of setting up a warehouse in Salt Lake City, was a failure and his second, establishing a new and heroically detailed inventory-control system, apparently involved almost superhuman effort. Penney presents the story as an object lesson in loyalty and hard work and their rewards; the interesting point, though, is that in this "as-told-to" account he allows Bushnell to have his say, however briefly, in direct quotations. "That experience," Bushnell is quoted as saying about the inventory project, "ruined my disposition. Mr. Penney says it made me. I do not agree with him. It ruined my disposition and came near to breaking me."

So the reward of loyalty and hard work came to a man by his own account nearly broken and with a "ruined disposition." What a story, here left to implication, might have been told by the first vice president about working for the proprietor of the Golden Rule Stores!

AN EXPERIMENT THAT SEEMED TO GO WRONG

BY 1910 OUR CHAIN and our partnership-branching chains were in full swing. I knew how to run a store of our type, I knew how to get at the needs and the hearts of our kind of people. I knew how to select locations in towns where there was a commodity vacuum, where people were eager to welcome the kind of service we were prepared to offer. I had learned how to select men, men of the right type, men of character, energy, and enthusiasm. My wife was a great help in this; I have rarely met her equal in soundness of judgment with respect to our type of men. A glance at the list of stores opened after 1908 will show that my partners had struck their strides too. In 1908 we had four stores with gross sales of $218,432.35; in 1909, six stores with gross sales of $310,062.16; in 1910, fourteen stores with gross sales of $662,331.16. In 1911, the number of our stores jumped to twenty-two and our gross sales passed the million mark.

We were all small-town and country boys, many of us had made a fumbling start, but we worked hard and caught the fire of an idea. Any number of young men are groping about without any vision of where they are going. They are like a man in deep water who has not yet learned to swim. Some men lack stamina, or perhaps their judgment is undeveloped; but it does not necessarily follow that such a man is doomed to failure. In every man's life there lies latent energy only waiting for a spark which if it strikes will set the whole being afire, and he will become a human dynamo, capable of accomplishing anything to which he aspires. With us the partnership idea supplied that spark. We were inspired by the consciousness that we were a fellowship every member of which was dependent upon the energy, integrity, and loyalty of every other member for security and success.

From *The Man with a Thousand Partners,* an autobiography of J. C. Penney, as told to Robert W. Bruère (Harper, 1931), pp. 84–103.

Furthermore, we realized that the partnership idea, to be effective, must be carried over into our relations with our customers, that there could be no lasting prosperity for us unless the people of our communities were better off and happier for our being among them. We operated in small towns and villages, and as small-town men we understood our new neighbors as readily as they understood us. It wasn't as if we had been a bunch of raiders swooping down upon them out of nowhere like the patent medicine and gold brick gentlemen who used to flash through that pioneering country for a quick cleanup and then disappear into nowhere, leaving those simple, hard-working people with a headache and empty pockets.

We were among them to stay. We built upon their satisfaction and good will. If when they got their purchases home they were not fully satisfied, they knew they could always bring them back and receive their money, or a fair exchange, with courtesy and as a matter of course. Our stores were the simple kinds of places they felt at home in, we were their kind of people. They liked our cash and carry plan. They knew that they usually paid dearly for credit, which with many of them, the miners especially, meant a coupon system that kept them in a kind of bondage by depriving them of the full and free control of the money they earned when they earned it. We had no sure-fire efficiency system, but we had certain clear, time-tested policies out of which in the course of years a system emerged, though even today it is a highly flexible system always subject to modification to meet new conditions as they arise. The system grew out of experience; experience was never dictated by a foreordained system. My older associates in referring to the practices of those early days do not speak of a system but of "the original body of doctrine."

By 1910, when we had fourteen stores doing more than six hundred thousand dollars of business, I felt that our experience had made it clear that we were spending too much time and money at the wholesale end of the business. As the rate of growth increased, we were increasingly dependent upon the managers to find, select, and train new men. The ability to train men has always with us been a cardinal requirement; new stores cannot be opened without trained and tried out men to take charge of them. With growth, competition grew keener, the managers needed to keep their eyes close to their clerks and their customers. They were spending too much time in the wholesale markets.

Our stores were sufficiently alike so as to have a common and steady demand for certain lines of staple goods, such as overalls, notions, sweaters, shoes and even women's ready-to-wear, since in those days a great many household garments were less subject to style changes than they are now. It was our custom to go to the wholesale markets in groups, to St. Louis and New York especially, each manager being held finally responsible for buying the right goods for his store. We made these trips as a rule twice a year. But in the intervals one store would develop an unanticipated popular demand for one line of goods, another store for another, and just when the manager was needed most in the store, he might have to hurry off to the wholesale market. Even the regular buying trips were costly in money and in time, when it is remembered that we bought most of our goods in New York, four days distant from Kemmerer [Wyoming] or Salt Lake City by fast train.

Such considerations led me to the conviction that it would be of great advantage to all of us if we could establish a great storage warehouse in Salt Lake City, which was a convenient distributing point to all our stores. My idea was not only to warehouse goods so as to have them ready at hand when special calls for them developed, but also to employ a man with expert training and experience in our lines, who would do the bulk of the staple buying for all of us. This would leave us correspondingly free to keep close watch on our own stores, to perfect ourselves as retail merchants, to make the rounds of the stores and share our experience with the younger managers, to keep our eyes open for new locations and for the right men to take charge of them. I was on the point of discovering what is one of the greatest economic advantages of the chain store form of organization: The chain makes it possible for one highly trained man to serve as buyer or bookkeeper for twenty stores, and thus greatly to reduce the burden of overhead costs.

At that time the idea was new and outside of our experience. My partners did not take kindly to the suggestion. They liked to do their own individual buying. They felt that no one not directly in touch with the customers could buy as true to the demand as they could. We were all trained to the importance of rapid turnover. Our ability to sell goods of quality at lower prices than our competitors—to pack the customer's dollar full of value—depended upon volume and volume depended upon sure judgment as to what the people of our town wanted. A turnover of six and even ten times in the year was not unusual. My partners did not want to let this important part of their business get out of their hands. I was glad to find them so keen to drive straight ahead along the paths I had blazed and started them in.

But by 1910 I was a different person from the Me of Hamilton [Missouri] and Longmont [Colorado] and the first year or two in Kemmerer. I had learned that the vitality of a business depends upon the determination to find better ways of doing business through experiment. I had opened more stores than any of my associates, as was inevitable simply as a matter of time; I commanded more ready capital; I was not afraid to experiment. Indeed, I had come to feel that it was a part of my duty to search for and try out new ways of strengthening and developing the organization. Accordingly, after weighing all the arguments against it, I decided to go ahead with the warehouse, with my own capital and at my own sole risk. If it succeeded and my associates were convinced, we would incorporate it into the business and share its advantages.

I found a man who had made a conspicuous success as a buyer and who had a good reputation as an all-round dry goods merchant. I supplied the capital and he and I launched a wholesaling and warehouse company under his name. Because my associates were skeptical and I didn't want to entangle them against their free will, I tried to keep even my own connection with the experiment a secret. My expert began to buy; he bought certain lines in such quantities that there could be no danger of running out even though all the stores should turn to him for special orders at one time. The managers of the stores had been asked to cooperate by telling him what lines they particularly wanted, and he was to go to the wholesale markets more or less as their agent. But he and they didn't click. He didn't always follow their suggestions. They were accustomed to handle certain brands of underwear, for example, but when he felt he could get them better values in other brands he bought against their judgment. They went ahead and bought the brands they believed their customers perferred. He was unwise in forcing this issue. On the other hand, there was a certain prejudice among the managers against any man who had not taken the regular course, who had not been tried out and come up through the stores. Goods began to accumulate in the warehouse. The managers increasingly fought shy of my confidential wholesale associate. He failed to get either his goods or himself across to them. They were then, as they are today, the final judges of what they would undertake to sell, so long as they made good on their judgment. I could reason with them, but I had no desire to bring pressure upon them. That would have been contrary to the basic spirit of our partner-manager principle which I have always held inviolate. I was eager to lead, but I was never willing to dominate.

The result was that the buyer soon had some hundreds of thousands of dollars tied up in merchandise that he was unable to sell. The plan was not working; something had to be done. It was a rule with me never to be bullheaded about a theory that didn't work. The proof of a theory is in the carry-through. I never hesitated to break away from any scheme once it became clear that it was not effective. I had by that time employed a man to act as auditor for all the stores in which I had a financial interest. He proved the man for the hour. By herculean labor he managed to get rid of that dead stock, of the warehouse, and incidentally of my partner in that abortive wholesaling experiment.

When I moved my headquarters from Kemmerer to Salt Lake City I had in mind not only centralized buying, but also centralized bookkeeping, accounting, and finance, for the stores in which I had a financial interest to begin with, but ultimately for all the stores. None of us who had developed the business up to that time had any experience in modern accounting. I knew how to strike a trial balance, to make a statement, and to keep track of my bank accounts, but my bookkeeping knowledge was limited to the elements of single entry. I always knew where I was at, by and large, but I had no means of keeping current tab on the transactions of all my stores. There was no one point where I could put my hand on everything that I found it convenient to know. I wanted a system of accounting that would give me a consolidated picture of the business as a whole, as well as a current analysis that would show the strength and weakness of individual store managements.

Early in 1911, I met Mr. John I. H. Herbert, who came to Salt Lake as my bookkeeper and accountant. Mr. Herbert had had banking experience. Under difficult conditions he developed a system of accounting for me. He became the watchdog of my funds, as he later became the guardian of the funds of the company. In 1913, at the first meeting of our board of directors under our charter of incorporation, he was elected treasurer of the company, an office he has held ever since.

But the man whom I associate with that warehouse experiment in a way that still makes it seem worth all it cost is Mr. George H. Bushnell, who, when I first heard of him, was employed by a firm of farm implement dealers in Ogden, Utah. His work frequently took him to the neighboring town of Preston, where I had started my second store out of Kemmerer. He had the habit of working late into the night. Returning to his room at one or two o'clock in the morning, he would often see the manager of the Golden Rule Store in Preston still busy with one or two of his helpers. This aroused his curiosity. He dropped in upon the manager and commented upon the similarity of their addiction to late hours. The manager asked him what interest he owned in his business. He said he owned none, just worked on a salary. "From the hours you keep," said our manager-partner, "I thought you must have a share in it." This stirred his curiosity still further. He learned about our partnership plan. "Some day," said the manager, "I may have something to say to you." This led to the meeting between Mr. Bushnell and me.

We first met in the old Pocatello station of the Union Pacific Railroad. My train was leaving at two o'clock in the morning and I was not in the habit of spending money on a hotel for so small a part of the night. The thermometer was about forty below zero. There was no fire in the station. The oil lamp served for warmth as well as for light. We spent some hours there together just talking about things in general. We didn't get down to business that night. But after taking time to weigh my impressions, I wrote Mr. Bushnell a letter telling him that as I saw it there was not much work for him with us in Salt Lake City, but that if he should decide to come down there I would pay him eighty dollars a month and that he could probably get some night work on the side that would enable him to get along. He answered that he could not conscientiously consider a drop from one hundred and seventy-five dollars a month and expenses most of the time, to eighty dollars a month. It was always a conviction with me that if a man would not come to us for less than he was getting elsewhere he had no proper insight into the opportunities offered by our partnership plan. I never made promises, and I rarely raised my price once I had made an offer. But under the circumstances, which were out of the ordinary, I wrote Mr. Bushnell again, offered him ninety dollars and asked him when I might expect him to report.

"I took that second letter home," Mr. Bushnell recalls. "We owned our own home there in Ogden and most of our friends lived there. My wife and I discussed Mr. Penney's proposition pro and con. It looked sort of ridiculous, and yet there was a strong attraction in it, a strange attraction in the man behind it.

"Finally I went to a state senator who was a very good friend of mine. 'Here is an offer that puzzles me,' I told him. 'It looks like the kind of opportunity I have been waiting for, but I want to know something about this man J. C. Penney.'

"The senator said that he . . . knew *about* J. C. Penney. He thought that there was a wonderful career ahead of me if I could connect up with him and strongly advised me to go at any price.

"Finally I wrote Mr. Penney that I would try to sell my home, come down there and take my chances on the future, whatever it might be. When I didn't hear from him as soon as I expected, I went down to Salt Lake City to see him. He was not there. So I went back to Ogden and resigned my position anyway, after having been there nearly eight years. I just pulled up stakes and reported to Salt Lake City in the fall of 1911."

That act of faith is a thing I remember with gratitude. In retrospect it appears the more significant because in that midnight meeting at the station in Pocatello I made Mr. Bushnell no promises. When he pulled up stakes in Ogden and came to Salt Lake City, he was taking his chances without the usual prospect of the men who entered our stores as clerks. They knew that if they made good they would be put out as managers with a financial interest in their first store and with the further prospect of an interest in such other stores as might bud off from those first ones. With them the salary was a secondary consideration, it was simply what we often called a drawing account to cover their minimum living expenses. With Mr. Bushnell, as with Mr. Herbert before him, the salary was the only guaranteed income, and in his case it was less than half of what he had been earning, for we were not long on expense accounts, as he was to learn almost instantly after his arrival in my office.

"I went into the office," Mr. Bushnell continues, "a little room, thirty by thirty-five or so, with a cement floor, one flat top desk that had been loaned to Mr. Penney by a friend of his, and one of those old-fashioned standing desks designed to keep bookkeepers awake. 'There is your desk,' Mr. Herbert said; 'just get busy and do whatever is necessary.' He was passing on the only instructions Mr. Penney had given to him.

"Well, I began looking for a place to live, and just to show how tight and thrifty everything was at that time, after I had worked one day I decided to take a day off and find a place to live. I went out and found a two-room apartment for $25 a month. It was handy to the office, so I took it, sent word to my family and had them come down. When I got my first pay check I found that I had been docked for that day. I began to wonder where this thing was going to wind up; but I let it go, and I have since had more than my money's worth of fun out of those three dollars."

What we needed, Mr. Bushnell concluded, was system as an accountant understood system. He and Mr. Herbert have always contended that we had no system whatever when they joined up with me there in Salt Lake City. But that is overstretching the bow. We did have a system of a kind, though its outlines would naturally seem rather hazy to a full-fledged accountant. I probably complicated matters a bit by insisting that they should open a set of double entry books without taking an inventory of the stores. And they were outsiders, too; they hadn't come up through the regulation course of store training and the managers knew that our methods were so peculiar to ourselves that they were always skeptical of the ability of an outsider to understand them. Their own experience had convinced them of that.

"Few people can realize the difficulties that John Herbert and I had to meet up with," Mr. Bushnell insists. "We would go to the men in the stores—*They* were *Partners*. We would ask for definite information. We would suggest various things that would help us to keep the records clearly. The managers were very trying. They were partners! They were not bookkeepers or accountants. They did not care two raps about accounting. They were interested in selling merchandise and they didn't want any red tape to get between them and their customers! It was only by hammering away at them, working anywhere between eighteen and twenty hours a day, year in and year out without any break for a holiday, that we were finally able to get our system to where it was down to working order."

And during all this time Mr. Bushnell and Mr. Herbert saw little of me. I had other matters to attend to; I didn't know the answer to their problem; I shouldn't have brought them in there if I had known. Besides, I always placed upon men all the responsibility they could possibly carry. From my own experience . . . I was convinced that there is nothing like responsibility to make men. To this day, Mr. Bushnell thinks it odd that at such a crucial juncture they should have seen so little of me.

"Mr. Penney would come to the office when he was in the city," Mr. Bushnell recalls. "He would come in at eight o'clock in the morning, go to work at his mail, and at twelve he would put on his hat. 'Let's go to lunch,' he would say. We would rush across the street to a lunch counter and have a ham and egg sandwich and a cup of coffee or a glass of milk—Mr. Penney never drank coffee. Then we would rush back to the office, be gone barely ten minutes; and then the same hammering away. Along about seven o'clock we would decide to go home to supper, but at eight we were back at the job again and stayed there until midnight or later.

"We had absolutely no equipment," Mr. Bushnell says, as if he had expected to find all the tools of an accountant in an office where there had never been an accountant. "Mr. Penney would go to his mail and as he opened his letters he was very careful of the envelopes. He would turn them upside down on his desk, slit them, stack them up in a neat pile and then use the backs of those envelopes for memoranda. One of the first things that struck me when I got there—and there were already twenty-two stores doing a business of more than a million dollars—was that there were no inkwells or pencils or things of that kind, to say nothing of such a thing as a typewriter. As we absolutely needed them, we would go out and buy penny pencils and a single bottle of ink, a penholder and a nickel's worth of pens. John Herbert and I worked out a consolidated statement system for the payment of bills of all those twenty-two stores and the record will show that every one of those payments was made out in long hand."

But they "made it," to use my father's phrase, which I always carried in my mind as a measuring rod; they worked out a system fitted to our particular set-up. They hammered it out. I was so much impressed that I decided to send Mr. Bushnell into the warehouse to see what he could do about that. Mr. Sams wanted him to go to Eureka, the headquarters of his chain, to be his accountant. But he went to the warehouse and dug in. That was in 1912. He put in an accounting system and found that I was losing money. In 1914, we decided to wind up that experiment. Several hundred thousand dollars' worth of merchandise was tied up in the warehouse. Something had to be done with it. We never hold sales. If a manager buys more than he can sell at a fair profit, or buys the wrong kind of merchandise, he simply marks it down, changes the price tag without advertising and takes his loss. I decided to follow the same practice with that bulging warehouse and take my loss. A committee of managers was appointed and they came down and went through the building from cellar to roof. They went through all this merchandise and put a price on it. There were thousands of dollars' worth of sweaters alone. When they got through pricing it, they agreed to take whatever Mr. Bushnell would figure out as their quota. He shipped them what he saw fit and they took it. Before 1915 was many months old the whole stock was cleared out and the warehouse was closed.

The experiment seemed to have failed. I say seemed, because it was only that first attempt that failed, not the idea. The idea was sound and is today established in our merchandising practice. Before the warehouse was closed, we established connections with a firm in St. Paul who did a large volume of wholesaling for us on a commission basis. Later we opened another warehouse of our own in New York and later still another great modern warehouse in St. Louis.

The idea was sound and ultimately worked out. But I have always contended that one of the greatest values we derived from that experiment was the making of Mr. Bushnell into the man who became the comptroller of the company and later its first vice-president. He began by opening for every store a set of books through which their daily transactions could be recorded in the central office. We still keep such books. As we grew he added what he called a set of control books, a set of books for the operating accounts of the stores which gave us a double check on every transaction. Periodically—daily at first, and later every ten days—each manager sent in his reports to the comptroller's department. It was not long before this came to involve the current auditing of millions of transactions.

In 1916, when we had one hundred and twenty-seven stores, our credit requirements had reached formidable proportions. The bankers suggested the desirability of an audit by a firm of certified public accountants. Mr. Bushnell still remembers with a tingle of excitement that searching examination; his records were checked against a complete inventory of all of the stores. There was no other organization like ours in the country. Our system of accounting had been invented to meet our peculiar requirements. The public accountants had never seen anything like it. They went over the records of every single transaction, they took inventory of all the assets of the stores, and when they finished they gave Mr. Bushnell a clean sheet. Not a figure but stood exactly as he had entered it.

And I have always credited that record in considerable part to the warehouse. Mr. Bushnell does not agree with me. "That experience," he protests, "ruined my disposition. Mr. Penney says it made me. I do not agree with him. It ruined my disposition and came near to breaking me."

But we have never quarreled over that difference in judgment. I like to remember what he once said to a friend of mine who was discussing the episode with him. "You do not know me," he said to this friend, "and I do not know whether Mr. Penney has ever told you anything about me; but they say of me that I shoot pretty hard sometimes and say exactly what I think. That has been one of the fine things in my experience with Mr. Penney. I always feel I can go in and sit down and talk to him across the table, just as I am talking to you, and it has just been a happy experience to me through all these years."

Mr. Bushnell had proved himself. He had no time to look up new locations or to train new men. It was not possible for him to act as comptroller and a store manager at the same time. But we wanted to bring him into the partnership. Accordingly I sold him an interest first in my store in Kemmerer and then in other stores. Others of the founding partners followed my example, and in the course of time both Mr. Bushnell and Mr. Herbert acquired classified stock in various stores and became partners. This precedent was followed in the case of all other headquarters executives who met the test of ability and character fundamental to the partnership plan. Year after year, Mr. Bushnell grew in spiritual stature and in his mastery of the business. He has been friend as well as wise counselor to hundreds of men in our company, who often in affection refer to him as the "steel framework" of the organization. And to this day I contend that it was the warehouse that made him.

5.   A Merchant Prince

IN GERARD B. LAMBERT (1886–1967) we find the almost-perfect type of a once familiar and still important kind of American businessman, the merchant prince. Born to his nation's version of the purple —but, unlike traditional royalty, oriented toward commerce and profit—as a matter of course such a man is elegantly educated, and as a matter of training he believes that all things are possible to him. With his estates and yachts and habits of international travel, he lives in the high style, aiming for self-fulfillment through self-entertainment —unless he goes the other way and becomes exaggeratedly sober and responsible, as, for example, the Rockefeller heirs have tended to do. If, like Gerry Lambert, he goes into active business, by the nature of his background and circumstances he brings to it a casualness and a freedom that may be either creative or destructive.

Gerard Lambert came from a rich Virginia landowning family; his father, Jordan Wheat Lambert, had been the founder and sole owner of the Lambert Pharmacal Company (now part of Warner-Lambert Company) and the developer of Listerine, a product for whose trade name permission had been obtained from Joseph Lister himself. At Princeton (class of 1908), Gerry rode a chauffeured car, had a tax-free income of $30,000 a year, and belonged to Ivy, most exclusive of the undergraduate eating clubs that tended to dominate student social life at Princeton in those days. After doing postgraduate study first in architecture and then in law, almost like a Renaissance prince, he went on a decade-long spending spree, as a result of which he astonishingly managed to end up deeply in debt. In 1922, already in his thirties, he came to work at his father's company (by then actually *his* company), where he achieved distinction—very marked distinction, indeed, in commercial if not in esthetic terms—by conceiving the famous "halitosis" advertising campaign that vastly increased sales of Listerine. Meanwhile he founded an advertising agency, Lambert & Feasley. In 1928 and 1929, just ahead of the great stock market crash, he sold his company holdings for $25 million, and, as he wrote in his autobiography in 1956, "From that day to this I have never tried to make another dollar."

In the first and third of the following excerpts, he comments on his benefactions and extravagances and expresses some shrewd insights into the psychology of the American rich (along with some bitterness and more self-congratulation). In the second, he tells how during the Depression years, summoned out of retirement by a Morgan partner, he insouciantly (and without salary) accepted the presidency of the Gillette Safety Razor Company, insouciantly launched the company's "Blue Blade" and put it on a sounder financial footing, and then insouciantly resigned to go back to his yachts and estates. At the end of this account, he speculates that perhaps "subconsciously" his real motivation for becoming involved with Gillette at all was merely to give him something to do while he waited out a divorce.

Freed from commercial pressures, the merchant prince, provided he happens to have it in him, can sometimes bring to business a creativity that others, caught in the bureaucratic toils and the struggle for advancement, cannot. Gerard Lambert epitomizes the elegant amateur in American business.

GIVING

I HAVE KEPT NO RECORD of my total gifts to tax-free charitable and educational institutions, although I suppose it could be dug up. But I am not interested in the amount. I have given as I thought I should give. I do know it is a large amount. I remember that one year I gave to various institutions $600,000 of annuities that I had purchased to bring me an income. Twenty-one thousand of this annuity income goes each year to institutions in the town of Princeton (a fact known to very few people there).

There has been another form of disbursement.

I have loaned more than $1,000,000 to personal friends. None of these loans has been paid off except in two cases. The amounts were not large, but they were paid back in full with interest. Needless to say, except in those two instances, I have lost all of the other borrowers as friends. Sometimes these people have prospered and later have made substantial amounts for themselves, but they have not paid me back. In one case I loaned well over half a million dollars to a friend. At that time he was earning more than $100,000 a year in salary. It occurred to me that if I died my executors would enforce payment of this debt, which would ruin him. So one day I forgave him the debt, although he had not paid one penny back. The federal government considers such a forgiveness to be a gift and so, in addition to losing the original sum, I had to pay the government the gift tax for the opportunity of releasing my friend from his obligation. I was able to reduce the amount upon which the tax was calculated because I could show that in his life he would be unable to pay the whole sum. After conferences in Washington with officials it was agreed that a portion could be written off as a bad debt. Nevertheless, the gift tax

---

From *All Out of Step: A Personal Chronicle,* by Gerard B. Lambert (Doubleday, 1956), pp. 152–54, 185–95, 301–3.

was very large. As I write, my friend still has an income of more than $65,000 a year.

In reviewing my life, then, I find that a great deal of this money has gone to benefit others; and that is as it should be.

But what about the money spent on my own extravagances? Was it ostentation? The only amounts of any consequence have gone into two things, large houses and yachts. I have realized only lately that of the many houses I have built or remodeled I have ended by selling them all (except the small ones we are living in at the moment), and moving away. Why? Because I have a terrific creative urge. I create a house and move on to another. I am really like any creative artist, architect, or writer. I cannot imagine an artist making one painting and sitting there and looking at it for the rest of his life, nor a writer reading his one book over and over. So I have spent money on houses because I want to bring them into being. They have never been used for show or ostentation. One very large house, which was our most elaborate one and fully staffed with servants, we held onto for seven years, and we *never gave a dinner party!*

Referring to yachts, the other major category of expense, I find another interesting thing. Without exception I have owned only racing yachts, sailing yachts that I have raced myself. I have never *built* a yacht. They have all been bought secondhand and at relatively low prices, a fraction of their original cost. It has been an expensive sport, it is true, but I bought them to engage in a sport. I have never owned a power yacht, which might be considered, I suppose, a means for ostentation by some people. I have owned and sailed some small racing yachts. For instance, I had and raced one of the Internationals on Long Island Sound. But it did not satisfy me; it was the more powerful and more thrilling ones I wanted.

WHEN I RETURNED TO THIS COUNTRY [in 1931] from the Grand National I found several important messages waiting for me. Among them was word from George Whitney, a partner in J. P. Morgan and Company. George asked me to come down to see him. I went down and asked what was on his mind. He told me that the Gillette Safety Razor Company in Boston was in quite a mess and that the Boston crowd had asked the Morgan group to tell them of someone who might pull it out. Their answer was to recommend me. I told George I didn't know a damn thing about razor blades, but he insisted that I take the job. While he was talking I had been doing some pretty fast thinking, and I told him then and there that I would take the morning train for Boston.

The fast thinking involved a personal problem between me and Ray. For some months we had begun to realize that inevitably our marriage was nearing its end. In one final conversation we agreed that there was only one solution, a divorce. We knew that she could obtain a divorce in New Jersey if I deserted her for two years. And so I had gone alone to the Grand National. I was not returning to Albemarle, and this offer to go to Boston suited my plans perfectly. No one knew of my reason for going to Boston until two years later when Ray married my brother-in-law, Mal Clopton. Mal was the surgeon who had married my sister Lily and the one who had been in the Spanish race with me.

During that two years' interval both my daughters, Bunny and Lily, were married at Albemarle. Bunny, soon after my departure, married Stacy B. Lloyd of Philadelphia. Stacy had been in the Ivy Club and was its president. His father, with the same name, had before him been a member and president of the club. Lily married William Fleming, also a member of the Ivy Club. It seems to run in the family. The legal requirement that I should not return to Albemarle during the two years of my absence from home was waived for these two weddings. I crossed the state line, feeling as if I should be under heavy guard, changed into my striped trousers down at the Princeton Inn, gave my daughters away at the weddings, and departed immediately after the ceremonies. Except for these two trips to Princeton I remained constantly in Boston.

When I arrived in Boston after my talk with George Whitney, the South Station looked very much as it did when I backtracked from there to New Haven in 1904. I went immediately to the Ritz-Carlton Hotel and engaged a sitting room, bedroom, and bath. This became my home in Boston for the next four years.

I went to my first meeting of the directors of the Gillette Safety Razor Company. It was held in the awe-inspiring Board Room of Lee Higginson and Company, the Boston bankers. I sat at the end of the table, slouched in my chair smoking a pipe, something I always do except in church. Facing me was a group of very austere gentlemen, quite erect in their chairs and indulging in no nonsense. Among them was Charlie Codman, Buck Hallowell, and Phil Stockton. I was elected president of the company. The formality over, one of the moguls relaxed enough to ask me the question I had been dreading.

"Mr. Lambert," he said, "what razor do *you* use?"

"The Schick razor," I replied. "I think it is the best razor in the world."

Puzzled and angry looks appeared on their faces. They sat, if possible, more erect. Who was this creature they had put at the head of their company? I let them stew a moment and then added, "Don't worry, gentlemen, I have never used a bottle of Listerine in my life."

The ice was broken and even a smile or two crept over their faces.

What I said about the Schick razor happened to be true. It accounted for a most humiliating experience. Just before going over to the Grand National, I went to the Schick razor people three times. I said I had nothing to do, that I had acquired some merchandising experience, and that I would like to go to work for them without pay. On each succeeding visit they became colder, finally making it clear that they didn't want me at any price. I have often wondered what they thought when, several months later, I became president of Gillette. They probably suspected me of doing some spying.

Before my formal election as president, I had been through some elaborate negotiations with the directors of the company. I suggested the same plan I had used in organizing the Lambert Company and they agreed. By a strange coincidence the figures were quite similar. Gillette, I was told, was earning about $4.00 a share. If I got the earnings to a figure that would be $6.00 a share on the outstanding common, plus $6.00 on my deferred stock, those shares would be converted to common. In addition a salary was suggested, but I refused this.

In a month I called a meeting of the directors and pointed out to them that the company in fact was earning only about $1.23 a share. To put it mildly, they were dumfounded but agreed with my figures. They immediately asked me if I wanted to rewrite my contract, because it was clear that I could never attain the $6.00 figure. Gillette had many, many more shares of common outstanding than Lambert.

My reply was to say no. I tore up the contract, refused a large salary, and went to work.

Gillette was in a pretty pickle. For a long time a certain group of New York directors, with large stockholdings, had pressed the management to keep on showing higher profits each year. They had gone to great extremes, which I do not intend to tell about here, but those excesses had resulted in a lawsuit by stockholders against the directors. Not long after I arrived the directors settled this suit out of court for a very large sum. I feel quite sure that none of my friends in Boston who were on the Board had anything to do with these unethical actions.

But this intramural trouble did not bother me much. I was concerned about the condition of the company itself. The blades were bad and the public had lost confidence in them. The banking fraternity had little confidence in the company's statements, and I don't blame them after my experience. To add to this, the trade was hostile and unco-operative and at odds with our sales force. Bad as these things were, the competitive situation was worse.

I had arrived in 1931, early in the depression. Everyone in the country was trying to save pennies. These economies hit the relatively high-priced Gillette blades. The patents on the razor and blades, which had made the company fabulously rich, had expired. It seemed as if every cellar in America was being used to make off-brand, cheap imitations to fit the Gillette razor. Some of these blades were very bad, but it is astonishing the lengths to which humans will go to save a penny.

One answer to this problem was obvious. The blade had to be improved. I put in new machinery and within a year was able to reduce the cost of manufacturing to one third of what it had been. But the problem still remained. For years the company, in its advertising, had promised that it had a new product and a better one. The public found this was not so and refused to believe any Gillette statement.

When I knew we had a much better blade, the sharpest in the country, I asked one of our engineers to join me at lunch at the restaurant in the South Station where we generally ate. After lunch I asked him if he could color a blade blue. Certainly, he could do it. He would just put on a blue lacquer. I made it clear that I did not want a blade to look like blue steel, I just wanted a different color, something other than the plain steel. The engineer promised to make me some samples.

When I saw these samples, I knew we had something. They were beautiful. I ordered the factory to get into production on the Blue Blade.

Shortly before this I had repeated the question I had asked at the Lambert Pharmacal Company: which agency did our advertising? I was told it was Maxon and Company in Detroit. They immediately received an invitation to come to Boston to see me.

Lou Maxon is a very successful and nice fellow, and I hope he will not be offended if I tell what followed. He arrived with a large retinue and put on a great show of advertising for two days. I sat there during these typical sessions, saying nothing and merely nodding. I had seen many of them in my day. When they had shot every arrow in their quiver, I turned to Lou. "Mr. Maxon," I said, "that is the most perfect 'presentation' I have ever seen." I paused a moment. "Now," I went on, "when you get back to Detroit would you mind sending down one of the young men in your office—I want to talk *advertising* to him." Lou is a smart fellow. He didn't turn a hair. "Certainly," he said. "I'll do that."

The young man who arrived and settled in Boston has become one of my dearest friends. He is now vice-president of the Gillette Safety Razor Company. His name is A. Craig Smith.

I was then a doddering old man of forty-five and so I sat down and gave Craig a fatherly talk. I outlined to him all the pet ideas I had on advertising, telling him of my past experience. I asked him to be good enough to get in touch with his office in Detroit and to request Maxon to prepare some of the best ads they could on the new Blue Blade, all to carry a coupon. I didn't bother with test towns, because I thought I knew what would happen. The next day I took an old piece of yellow paper—I remember it very well—and, with Craig sitting beside me, wrote in pencil the ad I thought we should put out. The entire thing was put in type with no illustrations of any sort.

What Maxon thought of this ad I have never known, but I do know that it startled a great many people. We ran a few to test them against the ones prepared in Detroit. I won't hurt Lou's feelings by giving the results even if I remembered them, but I do know we decided on the yellow-paper ad for a campaign in New York.

The psychological principle I used was one that I later employed when helping to write a speech for President Franklin D. Roosevelt. It is as old as the hills and equally as solid. When there is a conflict of opinion between you and another human being, if you admit you are wrong, then he finds himself right. From my experience with people I have concluded that there is no joy so sublime, with the possible exception of the ecstasies of sex, that equals the admission by someone that you are right.

These full-page ads, which broke in the New York newspapers, carried in bold black headlines the caption:

A FRANK CONFESSION OF THE GILLETTE SAFETY RAZOR CO.

From this eyecatcher we went on to say, in effect, that our old blades had been bad and that we admitted it. But now there was a new blade and it was the sharpest blade ever made. The important thing, we added, was that there was no fear that the reader would get the old stock. This new blade could be identified at once by its blue carton and the Blue Blade inside. This new product was, we explained, a little more expensive than the old, but when they used it this fact would be forgotten.

The results were as we expected. Millions of shavers who had hated our old blade but couldn't do anything about it had been tirading against us. Now, to their joy, they found they had been right all along. Their hearts began to warm to us. After you have confessed, people are very tolerant. Jimmy says, "Mama, I was a bad boy." She pats him on the head and forgives him. And they were sure that there was no confusing the new blade with the old.

Sometime after these ads broke, I heard a yarn that tickled me. It seems that six brokers in Wall Street who were interested in Gillette stock came uptown after the ads broke and had dinner together. One fellow started to scold about me personally. This man Lambert, he ranted, is crazy. He will ruin the company. Just imagine admitting that a company has been all wrong! Then he asked each one at the table if he had by any chance seen the ad. It seems they all had seen it, but that was natural, they explained. They were interested in the stock, weren't they? Someone asked if anyone there had bought any blades. With various excuses and apologies they all admitted they had bought the new blades. The facts suddenly dawned on one of them and he spoke of it. The ad had 100 per cent attention value and had made a 100 per cent sale. Not a bad record. After a drink they decided not to tell their customers to sell their Gillette stock after all.

The Gillette job was a difficult one in many respects. In the early meetings some of the New York directors tried to persuade me to put out optimistic statements to help stock values. I was adamant on this and instead insisted on making understatements which we always exceeded in practice. It was a peculiar situation. I owned no stock except a few qualifying shares. I had no power over these men. But there was one thing that helped. As I had no salary, they could not whip me into line with threats of financial ruin. I was told one day that two of these men were overheard to say that they wished I could be persuaded to take a salary, then perhaps they could do something with me. The fact that I had no salary and was completely independent financially rendered them helpless. I do want to say, however, that a committee of other directors, who had nothing whatsoever to do with these nefarious procedures, approached me each year that I was there with an offer of a salary to range between $100,000 to $150,000 a year. But I never took it.

Try as we would, the competition remained a problem. We brought out a thinner blade at a lower price that helped somewhat. We owned a factory, clearly labeled a Gillette subsidiary, where we made cheap blades under other brand names, and we fought low-priced competition in that way.

One of the products of this factory did at least afford us a chuckle. It was a time when there were several so-called "consumer" organizations that made a very comfortable living advising the consumer how to save money. One of these outfits published its findings on razor blades. With its "elaborate" testing methods it reported the Blue Blade low in the list of comparative sharpness. It recommended the purchase of the brand "Tuxedo." We kept our mouths shut because we knew that "Tuxedo" was made by our off-brand factory and that it was really nothing but discarded "seconds."

Most of our competitors in the razor field had a one-piece razor. This bothered me because the old Gillette was made of three pieces which you must put together. I started to work on the problem and invented a one-piece razor. When I received the patents I immediately assigned them to the Gillette Company. My first models were very crude and our engineers had to do a great deal of changing and improving to produce the present finished razor that is in use today.

I get a big thrill every time Gillette puts on a television or radio program covering the World Series and sells millions of these razors, in spite of the fact that they are quite different from my early effort.

When I arrived at the Gillette factory I selected an office in the corner of the first floor. It was a small space with ordinary factory windows and brick walls painted white. I had an old-fashioned oak roll-top desk and a low partition that separated me from my secretary. I had chosen this simple spot because I do not believe in swanky official offices. When I see the president of a company sitting in Hollywood surroundings I sell my stock, if I have any.

My secretary was a remarkable girl. Her name was Miss Malmberg, and she was literal beyond anyone I have ever known. On arrival I had gone to Phil Stockton, president of the First National Bank, and asked if he could get me a truly trustworthy girl. In revamping a company someone from outside is preferable. He said he knew of just the gal and her name was Miss Malmberg. Besides being extraordinarily able, she was worthy of the utmost confidence.

I had the habit, when I didn't want to answer the phone, of saying to her, "Oh, tell 'em I'm in Sweden." After I had been at work about six months complaints began to come in to our directors from prominent stockholders. "What's the trouble with this new president?" they said. "He's always abroad." Miss Malmberg had conscientiously told everyone that I was in Sweden. Before I left she was married, and I hope she has been equally reticent about her husband's whereabouts.

For some reason the job I did at Gillette has never made me very happy. It is true that while I was there we paid off $20,000,000 of debt, that we produced the Blue Blade, now famous all over the world, and the one-piece razor, and that sales increased and the profits rose slightly. Furthermore, our relations with the trade became very friendly. At last our financial statements were as trustworthy as those of the Bank of England. But there was nothing of the spectacular results I had experienced before. I hope that the foundation I laid has made it easier for the company, in the last twenty years, to increase its earnings, as it has done lately under Joe Spang.

In retrospect, perhaps this was because I had absolutely nothing financial at stake, as in the old days when I had to pay off debts. Perhaps the competitive conditions of the depression, which do not exist today, were more than any man could lick. Could it be that subconsciously I felt I was up there exiled for at least two years, filling in the time until Ray could get her divorce? I really don't know. Probably the real reason is that I had been spoiled. I was used to skyrockets and not accustomed to mere pin wheels.

In the beginning of 1935 I went to my good friend Phil Stockton, who was also one of our directors, and explained that I was getting out. For the first time I told Phil the reason I had come. Not one line had appeared in the press about our divorce and Ray's subsequent marriage to Mal Clopton. Phil was startled but admitted that I had earned the right to go.

WITH THE ACQUISITION of almost unlimited funds all of the joy of getting new things disappears. Gone is the thrill of saving to get a new overcoat or even a new car. Jewelry means almost nothing. A present, so treasured when you have little, finds you wondering how you adequately can thank the giver. You are completely bored with the things for which those less comfortably off would give their souls. In desperation you seek new thrills through material purchases, but find them disappointing when you get them. It is like a Pyrrhic victory, better not achieved. Sometimes a small thing is exciting, like a new kind of fountain pen or a flashlight. In despair you try to get what money can't buy, the exhilaration of writing something that will be published, or painting a picture that will win a prize. In those cases you know that you are in competition with the rest of the world and what you do must stand on its merits. Wealth has a sort of Siamese twin, satiety, of which it cannot rid itself.

But also there is a happier side to having money. First, and I put it above all else, there is the knowledge that you and your family and your dependents may have adequate medical attention. I am glad to say that I have given a good deal of money to provide medical care for others.

Next in importance I put the ability to furnish funds for proper education. This, in my mind, is of great importance. Of course today public education goes quite far, but I mean the kind of education that a person's economic circumstances may not permit, such as studying for a profession, or taking some advanced courses. I have noticed that the gifts we all make are mostly to institutions: hospitals or medical-research funds, or to colleges and schools. So apparently in the public mind those two things come first.

And, too, it is nice to help a friend in trouble. The fact that I have loaned more than a million dollars to friends and have received back practically nothing has not made me sorry I did it. The only lesson I have learned from this experience is that the loan seldom pulls the person around the corner. They, in themselves, were hopeless in the first place. But there have been some cases where my loan has put them on their feet, in spite of the fact that I lost them as friends.

And friends, I have found, are important. I have very few close friends, but they remain friends, even if years pass when we do not see each other. I am the sort of person who hoards the affection I have to dispense, so that the dose is concentrated when it is given. I am unwilling to appear to spread it lavishly at dinners and cocktail parties so that, when it is really needed, the solution is so diluted that it has no potency.

I once overheard a conversation that shocked me. I was taking two men in Palm Beach out to a golf course and they were talking in the back seat. They were social butterflies. One of them, all excited, was saying that he had had the most *wonderful time*. The previous night he had heard of a party, got out of bed and went to it. Why, he said, there were forty people there! The other man was disappointed that he had not heard of it; he would have got out of bed too. They spoke as if it had been a place where there were forty head of cattle.

Even if I do not like groups of forty people I do enjoy being with my friends and my family. As you grow older, seeing your family becomes more important. But also as you grow older they present an approaching problem. In time they become heirs to what material things you have. In my mind the question that is answered with less definiteness than any other is whether your children should be left substantial sums of money, sums beyond their reasonable requirements. Statistically it is easy to show the tragedies that result from children inheriting too much money. The rare exceptions are pointed out to prove the rule. But we inherit, I think, like animals, the instinct to protect our young. Offhand I cannot think of a very wealthy man who has left his children with nothing. And so I say it poses a problem for all parents who are growing old. We know of the evils it will probably bring, but we prefer to think that in our case it will be different. In these days the tax situation will spread what you leave very thin, and in one more generation the problem disappears.

6.   *The Birth of the Car*

HENRY FORD (1863–1947) needs no introduction. A genius among tinkerers, who said that as a boy his tools were his toys, Ford, along with two others—Thomas Alva Edison and Alexander Graham Bell—changed the life of his country and perhaps of the world more than any other American. That in matters other than technology he was something of a nut can hardly, on form, be regarded as surprising. His social thought was a weird mixture of humanitarianism and reactionary individualism, including as it did liberal wage policies and union busting, anti-Semitism and fanatical devotion to peace. His autobiography—every word of which was surely committed to paper by the journalist he chose as his "collaborator"—is full of cracker-barrel philosophizing, to the exclusion of almost anything about his personal life after his childhood and early adulthood. (And the story of his middle and late years is a highly dramatic one, as we know from Allan Nevins and Frank E. Hill's *Ford* [Scribner, 3 vols., 1954–63].) Essentially, the chapter headings of Ford's autobiography tell its story: "How Cheaply Can Things Be Made?" "Money—Master or Servant?" "Why Be Poor?" "Why Charity?"

The passages reproduced here reflect typical Ford attitudes: his naïve (false-naïve?) view of corporate finance, based on his early business experiences; his view of technology as artistry—"dealing with higher laws than those of sound, or line, or color"; his defense of his invention, the production line, on the grounds that the workers *like* monotony; and his emphasis on service to the customer: "A manufacturer is not through with his customer when a sale is completed." How a contemporary car buyer may wish Ford had succeeded in transmitting that idea to subsequent generations of car makers, in his own company or others!

WHAT I LEARNED ABOUT BUSINESS

My "gasoline buggy" was the first and for a long time the only automobile in Detroit. It was considered to be something of a nuisance, for it made a racket and it scared horses. Also it blocked traffic. For if I stopped my machine anywhere in town a crowd was around it before I could start up again. If I left it alone even for a minute some inquisitive person always tried to run it. Finally, I had to carry a chain and chain it to a lamp post whenever I left it anywhere. And then there was trouble with the police. I do not know quite why, for my impression is that there were no speed-limit laws in those days. Anyway, I had to get a special permit from the mayor and thus for a time enjoyed the distinction of being the only licensed chauffeur in America. I ran that machine about one thousand miles through 1895 and 1896 and then sold it to Charles Ainsley of Detroit for two hundred dollars. That was my first sale. I had built the car not to sell but only to experiment with. I wanted to start another car. Ainsley wanted to buy. I could use the money and we had no trouble in agreeing upon a price.

It was not at all my idea to make cars in any such petty fashion. I was looking ahead to production, but before that could come I had

---

From *My Life and Work*, by Henry Ford, in collaboration with Samuel Crowther (Doubleday, Page, 1922), pp. 33–46, 103–7.

to have something to produce. It does not pay to hurry. I started a second car in 1896; it was much like the first but a little lighter. It also had the belt drive which I did not give up until some time later; the belts were all right excepting in hot weather. That is why I later adopted gears. I learned a great deal from that car. Others in this country and abroad were building cars by that time, and in 1895 I heard that a Benz car from Germany was on exhibition in Macy's store in New York. I travelled down to look at it but it had no features that seemed worth while. It also had the belt drive, but it was much heavier than my car. I was working for lightness; the foreign makers have never seemed to appreciate what light weight means. I built three cars in all in my home shop and all of them ran for years in Detroit. I still have the first car; I bought it back a few years later from a man to whom Mr. Ainsley had sold it. I paid one hundred dollars for it.

During all this time I kept my position with the electric company and gradually advanced to chief engineer at a salary of one hundred and twenty-five dollars a month. But my gas-engine experiments were no more popular with the president of the company than my first mechanical leanings were with my father. It was not that my employer objected to experiments—only to experiments with a gas engine. I can still hear him say:

"Electricity, yes, that's the coming thing. But gas—no."

He had ample grounds for his skepticism—to use the mildest terms. Practically no one had the remotest notion of the future of the internal combustion engine, while we were just on the edge of the great electrical development. As with every comparatively new idea, electricity was expected to do much more than we even now have any indication that it can do. I did not see the use of experimenting with electricity for my purposes. A road car could not run on a trolley even if trolley wires had been less expensive; no storage battery was in sight of a weight that was practical. An electrial car had of necessity to be limited in radius and to contain a large amount of motive machinery in proportion to the power exerted. That is not to say that I held or now hold electricity cheaply; we have not yet begun to use electricity. But it has its place, and the internal combustion engine has its place. Neither can substitute for the other—which is exceedingly fortunate.

I have the dynamo that I first had charge of at the Detroit Edison Company. When I started our Canadian plant I bought it from an office building to which it had been sold by the electric company, had it revamped a little, and for several years it gave excellent service in the Canadian plant. When we had to build a new power plant, owing to the increase in business, I had the old motor taken out to my museum—a room out at Dearborn that holds a great number of my mechanical treasures.

The Edison Company offered me the general superintendency of the company but only on condition that I would give up my gas engine and devote myself to something really useful. I had to choose between my job and my automobile. I chose the automobile, or rather I gave up the job—there was really nothing in the way of a choice. For already I knew that the car was bound to be a success. I quit my job on August 15, 1899, and went into the automobile business.

It might be thought something of a step, for I had no personal funds. What money was left over from living was all used in experimenting. But my wife agreed that the automobile could not be given up—that we had to make or break. There was no "demand" for automobiles—there never is for a new article. They were accepted in much the fashion as was more recently the airplane. At first the "horseless carriage" was considered merely a freak notion and many wise people explained with particularity why it could never be more than a toy. No man of money even thought of it as a commercial possibility. I cannot imagine why each new means of transportation meets with such opposition. There are even those to-day who shake their heads and talk about the luxury of the automobile and only grudgingly admit that perhaps the motor truck is of some use. But in the beginning there was hardly any one who sensed that the automobile could be a large factor in industry. The most optimistic hoped only for a development akin to that of the bicycle. When it was found that an automobile really could go and several makers started to put out cars, the immediate query was as to which would go fastest. It was a curious but natural development—that racing idea. I never thought anything of racing, but the public refused to consider the automobile in any light other than as a fast toy. Therefore later we had to race. The industry was held back by this inital racing slant, for the attention of the makers was diverted to making fast rather than good cars. It was a business for speculators.

A group of men of speculative turn of mind organized, as soon as I left the electric company, the Detroit Automobile Company to exploit my car. I was the chief engineer and held a small amount of the stock. For three years we continued making cars more or less on the model of my first car. We sold very few of them; I could get no support at all toward making better cars to be sold to the public at large. The whole thought was to make to order and to get the largest price possible for each car. The main idea seemed to be to get the money. And being without authority other than my engineering position gave me, I found that the new company was not a vehicle for realizing my ideas but merely a money-making concern—that did not make much money. In March, 1902, I resigned, determined never again to put myself under orders. The Detroit Automoble Company later became the Cadillac Company under the ownership of the Lelands, who came in subsequently.

I rented a shop—a one-story brick shed—at 81 Park Place to continue my experiments and to find out what business really was. I thought that it must be something different from what it had proved to be in my first adventure.

The year from 1902 until the formation of the Ford Motor Company was practically one of investigation. In my little one-room brick shop I worked on the development of a four-cylinder motor and on the outside I tried to find out what business really was and whether it needed to be quite so selfish a scramble for money as it seemed to be from my first short experience. From the period of the first car, which I have described, until the formation of my present company I built in all about twenty-five cars, of which nineteen or twenty were built with the Detroit Automobile Company. The automobile had passed from the initial stage where the fact that it could run at all was enough, to the stage where it had to show speed. Alexander Winton of Cleveland, the founder of the Winton car, was then the track champion of the country and willing to meet all comers. I designed a two-cylinder enclosed engine of a more compact type than I had before used, fitted it into a skeleton chassis, found that I could make speed, and arranged a race with Winton. We met on the Grosse Point track at Detroit. I beat him. That was my first race, and it brought advertising of the only kind that people cared to read.

The public thought nothing of a car unless it made speed—unless it beat other racing cars. My ambition to build the fastest car in the world led me to plan a four-cylinder motor. But of that more later.

The most surprising feature of business as it was conducted was the large attention given to finance and the small attention to service. That seemed to me to be reversing the natural process which is that the money should come as the result of work and not before the work. The second feature was the general indifference to better methods of manufacture as long as whatever was done got by and took the money. In other words, an article apparently was not built with reference to how greatly it could serve the public but with reference solely to how much money could be had for it—and that without any particular care whether the customer was satisfied. To sell him was enough. A dissatisfied customer was regarded not as a man whose trust had been violated, but either as a nuisance or as a possible source of more money in fixing up the work which ought to have been done correctly in the first place. For instance, in automobiles there was not much concern as to what happened to the car once it had been sold. How much gasoline it used per mile was of no great moment; how much service it actually gave did not matter; and if it broke down and had to have parts replaced, then that was just hard luck for the owner. It was considered good business to sell parts at the highest possible price on the theory that, since the man had already bought the car, he simply had to have the part and would be willing to pay for it.

The automobile business was not on what I would call an honest basis, to say nothing of being, from a manufacturing standpoint, on a scientific basis, but it was no worse than business in general. That was the period, it may be remembered, in which many corporations were being floated and financed. The bankers, who before then had confined themselves to the railroads, got into industry. My idea was then and still is that if a man did his work well, the price he would get for that work, the profits and all financial matters, would care for themselves and that a business ought to start small and build itself up and out of its earnings. If there are no earnings then that is a signal to the owner that he is wasting his time and does not belong in that business.

I have never found it necessary to change those ideas, but I discovered that this simple formula of doing good work and getting paid for it was supposed to be slow for modern business. The plan at that time most in favour was to start off with the largest possible capitalization and then sell all the stock and all the bonds that could be sold. Whatever money happened to be left over after all the stock and bond-selling expenses and promoters, charges and all that, went grudgingly into the foundation of the business. A good business was not one that did good work and earned a fair profit. A good business was one that would give the opportunity for the floating of a large amount of stocks and bonds at high prices. It was the stocks and bonds, not the work, that mattered. I could not see how a new business or an old business could be expected to be able to charge into its product a great big bond interest and then sell the product at a fair price. I have never been able to see that.

I have never been able to understand on what theory the original investment of money can be charged against a business. Those men in business who call themselves financiers say that money is "worth" 6 per cent. or 5 per cent. or some other per cent., and that if a business has one hundred thousand dollars invested in it, the man who made the investment is entitled to charge an interest payment on the money, because, if instead of putting that money into the business he had put it into a savings bank or into certain securities, he could have a certain fixed return. Therefore they say that a proper charge against the operating expenses of a business is the interest on this money. This idea is at the root of many business failures and most service failures. Money is not worth a particular amount. As money it is not worth anything, for it will do nothing of itself. The only use of money is to buy tools to work with or the product of tools. Therefore money is worth what it will help you to produce or buy and no more. If a man thinks that his money will earn 5 per cent. or 6 per cent. he ought to place it where he can get that return, but money placed in a business is not a charge on the business—or, rather, should not be. It ceases to be money and becomes, or should become, an engine of production, and it is therefore worth what it produces—and not a fixed sum according to some scale that has no bearing upon the particular business in which the money has been placed. Any return should come after it has produced, not before.

Business men believed that you could do anything by "financing" it. If it did not go through on the first financing then the idea was to "refinance." The process of "refinancing" was simply the game of sending good money after bad. In the majority of cases the need of refinancing arises from bad management, and the effect of refinancing is simply to pay the poor managers to keep up their bad management a little longer. It is merely a postponement of the day of judgment. This makeshift of refinancing is a device of speculative financiers. Their money is no good to them unless they can connect it up with a place where real work is being done, and that they cannot do unless, somehow, that place is poorly managed. Thus, the speculative financiers delude themselves that they are putting their money out to use. They are not; they are putting it out to waste.

I determined absolutely that never would I join a company in which finance came before the work or in which bankers or financiers had a part. And further that, if there were no way to get started in the kind of business that I thought could be managed in the interest of the public, then I simply would not get started at all. For my own short experience, together with what I saw going on around me, was quite enough proof that business as a mere money-making game was not worth giving much thought to and was distinctly no place for a man who wanted to accomplish anything. Also it did not seem to me to be the way to make money. I have yet to have it demonstrated that it is the way. For the only foundation of real business is service.

A manufacturer is not through with his customer when a sale is completed. He has then only started with his customer. In the case of an automobile the sale of the machine is only something in the nature of an introduction. If the machine does not give service, then it is better for the manufacturer if he never had the introduction, for he will have the worst of all advertisements—a dissatisfied customer. There was something more than a tendency in the early days of the automobile to regard the selling of a machine as the real accomplishment and that thereafter it did not matter what happened to the buyer. That is the shortsighted salesman-on-commission attitude. If a salesman is paid only for what he sells, it is not to be expected that he is going to exert any great effort on a customer out of whom no more commission is to be made. And it is right on this point that we later made the largest selling argument for the Ford. The price and the quality of the car would undoubtedly have made a market, and a large market. We went beyond that. A man who bought one of our cars was in my opinion entitled to continuous use of that car, and therefore if he had a breakdown of any kind it was our duty to see that his machine was put into shape again at the earliest possible moment. In the success of the Ford car the early provision of service was an outstanding element. Most of the expensive cars of that period were ill provided with service stations. If your car broke down you had to depend on the local repair man—when you were entitled to depend upon the manufacturer. If the local repair man were a fore-handed sort of a person, keeping on hand a good stock of parts (although on many of the cars the parts were not interchangeable), the owner was lucky. But if the repair man were a shiftless person, with an adequate knowledge of automobiles and an inordinate desire to make a good thing out of every car that came into his place for repairs, then even a slight breakdown meant weeks of laying up and a whopping big repair bill that had to be paid before the car could be taken away. The repair men were for a time the largest menace to the automobile industry. Even as late as 1910 and 1911 the owner of an automobile was regarded as essentially a rich man whose money ought to be taken away from him. We met that situation squarely and at the very beginning. We would not have our distribution blocked by stupid, greedy men.

That is getting some years ahead of the story, but it is control by finance that breaks up service because it looks to the immediate dollar. If the first consideration is to earn a certain amount of money, then, unless by some stroke of luck matters are going especially well and there is a surplus over for service so that the operating men may have a chance, future business has to be sacrificed for the dollar of to-day.

And also I noticed a tendency among many men in business to feel that their lot was hard—they worked against a day when they might retire and live on an income—get out of the strife. Life to them was a battle to be ended as soon as possible. That was another point

I could not understand, for as I reasoned, life is not a battle except with our own tendency to sag with the downpull of "getting settled." If to petrify is success, all one has to do is to humour the lazy side of the mind; but if to grow is success, then one must wake up anew every morning and keep awake all day. I saw great businesses become but the ghost of a name because someone thought they could be managed just as they were always managed, and though the management may have been most excellent in its day, its excellence consisted in its alertness to its day, and not in slavish following of its yesterdays. Life, as I see it, is not a location, but a journey. Even the man who most feels himself "settled" is not settled—he is probably sagging back. Everything is in flux, and was meant to be. Life flows. We may live at the same number of the street, but it is never the same man who lives there.

And out of the delusion that life is a battle that may be lost by a false move grows, I have noticed, a great love for regularity. Men fall into the half-alive habit. Seldom does the cobbler take up with the new-fangled way of soling shoes, and seldom does the artisan willingly take up with new methods in his trade. Habit conduces to a certain inertia, and any disturbance of it affects the mind like trouble. It will be recalled that when a study was made of shop methods, so that the workmen might be taught to produce with less useless motion and fatigue, it was most opposed by the workmen themselves. Though they suspected that it was simply a game to get more out of them, what most irked them was that it interfered with the well-worn grooves in which they had become accustomed to move. Business men go down with their businesses because they like the old way so well they cannot bring themselves to change. One sees them all about—men who do not know that yesterday is past, and who woke up this morning with their last year's ideas. It could almost be written down as a formula that when a man begins to think that he has at last found his method he had better begin a most searching examination of himself to see whether some part of his brain has not gone to sleep. There is a subtle danger in a man thinking that he is "fixed" for life. It indicates that the next jolt of the wheel of progress is going to fling him off.

There is also the great fear of being thought a fool. So many men are afraid of being considered fools. I grant that public opinion is a powerful police influence for those who need it. Perhaps it is true that the majority of men need the restraint of public opinion. Public opinion may keep a man better than he would otherwise be—if not better morally, at least better as far as his social desirability is concerned. But it is not a bad thing to be a fool for righteousness' sake. The best of it is that such fools usually live long enough to prove that they were not fools—or the work they have begun lives long enough to prove they were not foolish.

The money influence—the pressing to make a profit on an "investment"—and its consequent neglect of or skimping of work and hence of service showed itself to me in many ways. It seemed to be at the bottom of most troubles. It was the cause of low wages—for without well-directed work high wages cannot be paid. And if the whole attention is not given to the work it cannot be well directed. Most men want to be free to work; under the system in use they could not be free to work. During my first experience I was not free—I could not give full play to my ideas. Everything had to be planned to make money; the last consideration was the work. And the most curious part of it all was the insistence that it was the money and not the work that counted. It did not seem to strike any one as illogical that money should be put ahead of work—even though everyone had to admit that the profit had to come from the work. The desire seemed to be to find a short cut to money and to pass over the obvious short cut—which is through the work.

Take competition; I found that competition was supposed to be a menace and that a good manager circumvented his competitors by getting a monopoly through artificial means. The idea was that there were only a certain number of people who could buy and that it was necessary to get their trade ahead of someone else. Some will remember that later many of the automobile manufacturers entered into an association under the Selden Patent just so that it might be legally possible to control the price and the output of automobiles. They had the same idea that so many trades unions have—the ridiculous notion that more profit can be had doing less work than more. The plan, I believe, is a very antiquated one. I could not see then and am still unable to see that there is not always enough for the man who does his work; time spent in fighting competition is wasted; it had better be spent in doing the work. There are always enough people ready and anxious to buy, provided you supply what they want and at the proper price—and this applies to personal services as well as to goods.

During this time of reflection I was far from idle. We were going ahead with a four-cylinder motor and the building of a pair of big racing cars. I had plenty of time, for I never left my business. I do not believe a man can ever leave his business. He ought to think of it by day and dream of it by night. It is nice to plan to do one's work in office hours, to take up the work in the morning, to drop it in the evening—and not have a care until the next morning. It is perfectly possible to do that if one is so constituted as to be willing through all of his life to accept direction, to be an employee, possibly a responsible employee, but not a director or manager of anything. A manual labourer must have a limit on his hours, otherwise he will wear himself out. If he intends to remain always a manual labourer, then he should forget about his work when the whistle blows, but if he intends to go forward and do anything, the whistle is only a signal to start thinking over the day's work in order to discover how it might be done better.

The man who has the largest capacity for work and thought is the man who is bound to succeed. I cannot pretend to say, because I do not know, whether the man who works always, who never leaves his business, who is absolutely intent upon getting ahead, and who therefore does get ahead—is happier than the man who keeps office hours, both for his brain and his hands. It is not necessary for any one to decide the question. A ten-horsepower engine will not pull as much as a twenty. The man who keeps brain office hours limits his horsepower. If he is satisfied to pull only the load that he has, well and good, that is his affair—but he must not complain if another who has increased his horsepower pulls more than he does. Leisure and work bring different results. If a man wants leisure and gets it—then he has no cause to complain. But he cannot have both leisure and the results of work.

Concretely, what I most realized about business in that year—and

I have been learning more each year without finding it necessary to change my first conclusions—is this:

(1)   That finance is given a place ahead of work and therefore tends to kill the work and destroy the fundamental of service.

(2)   That thinking first of money instead of work brings on fear of failure and this fear blocks every avenue of business—it makes a man afraid of competition, of changing his methods, or of doing anything which might change his condition.

(3)   That the way is clear for any one who thinks first of service —of doing the work in the best possible way.

THE TERROR OF THE MACHINE

REPETITIVE LABOUR—the doing of one thing over and over again and always in the same way—is a terrifying prospect to a certain kind of mind. It is terrifying to me. I could not possibly do the same thing day in and day out, but to other minds, perhaps I might say to the majority of minds, repetitive operations hold no terrors. In fact, to some types of mind thought is absolutely appalling. To them the ideal job is one where the creative instinct need not be expressed. The jobs where it is necessary to put in mind as well as muscle have very few takers—we always need men who like a job because it is difficult. The average worker, I am sorry to say, wants a job in which he does not have to put forth much physical exertion—above all, he wants a job in which he does not have to think. Those who have what might be called the creative type of mind and who thoroughly abhor monotony are apt to imagine that all other minds are similarly restless and therefore to extend quite unwanted sympathy to the labouring man who day in and day out performs almost exactly the same operation.

When you come right down to it, most jobs are repetitive. A business man has a routine that he follows with great exactness; the work of a bank president is nearly all routine; the work of under officers and clerks in a bank is purely routine. Indeed, for most purposes and most people, it is necessary to establish something in the way of a routine and to make most motions purely repetitive—otherwise the individual will not get enough done to be able to live off his own exertions. There is no reason why any one with a creative mind should be at a monotonous job, for everywhere the need for creative men is pressing. There will never be a dearth of places for skilled people, but we have to recognize that the will to be skilled is not general. And even if the will be present, then the courage to go through with the training is absent. One cannot become skilled by mere wishing.

There are far too many assumptions about what human nature ought to be and not enough research into what it is. Take the assumption that creative work can be undertaken only in the realm of vision. We speak of creative "artists" in music, painting, and the other arts. We seemingly limit the creative functions to productions that may be hung on gallery walls, or played in concert halls, or otherwise displayed where idle and fastidious people gather to admire each other's culture. But if a man wants a field for vital creative work, let him come where he is dealing with higher laws than those of sound, or line, or colour; let him come where he may deal with the laws of personality. We want artists in industrial relationship. We want masters in industrial method—both from the standpoint of the producer and the product. We want those who can mould the political, social, industrial, and moral mass into a sound and shapely whole. We have limited the creative faculty too much and have used it for too trivial ends. We want men who can create the working design for all that is right and good and desirable in our life. Good intentions plus well-thought-out working designs can be put into practice and can be made to succeed. It is possible to increase the well-being of the workingman—not by having him do less work, but by aiding him to do more. If the world will give its attention and interest and energy to the making of plans that will profit the other fellow as he is, then such plans can be established on a practical working basis. Such plans will endure—and they will be far the most profitable both in human and financial values. What this generation needs is a deep faith, a profound conviction in the practicability of righteousness, justice, and humanity in industry. If we cannot have these qualities, then we were better off without industry. Indeed, if we cannot get those qualities, the days of industry are numbered. But we can get them. We are getting them.

If a man cannot earn his keep without the aid of machinery, is it benefitting him to withhold that machinery because attendance upon it may be monotonous? And let him starve? Or is it better to put him in the way of a good living? Is a man the happier for starving? If he is the happier for using a machine to less than its capacity, is he happier for producing less than he might and consequently getting less than his share of the world's goods in exchange?

I have not been able to discover that repetitive labour injures a man in any way. I have been told by parlour experts that repetitive labour is soul- as well as body-destroying, but that has not been the result of our investigations. There was one case of a man who all day long did little but step on a treadle release. He thought that the motion was making him one-sided; the medical examination did not show that he had been affected but, of course, he was changed to another job that used a different set of muscles. In a few weeks he asked for his old job again. It would seem reasonable to imagine that going through the same set of motions daily for eight hours would produce an abnormal body, but we have never had a case of it. We shift men whenever they ask to be shifted and we should like regularly to change them—that would be entirely feasible if only the men would have it that way. They do not like changes which they do not themselves suggest. Some of the operations are undoubtedly monotonous—so monotonous that it seems scarcely possible that any man would care to continue long at the same job. Probably the most monotonous task in the whole factory is one in which a man picks up a gear with a steel hook, shakes it in a vat of oil, then turns it into a basket. The motion never varies. The gears come to him always in exactly the same place, he gives each one the same number of shakes, and he drops it into a basket which is always in the same place. No muscular energy is required, no intelligence is required. He does little more than wave his hands gently to and fro—the steel rod is so light. Yet the man on that job has been doing it for eight solid years. He has saved and invested his money until now he has about forty thousand dollars—and he stubbornly resists every attempt to force him into a better job!

The most thorough research has not brought out a single case of a man's mind being twisted or deadened by the work. The kind of mind that does not like repetitive work does not have to stay in it. The work in each department is classified according to its desirability and skill into Classes "A," "B," and "C," each class having anywhere from ten to thirty different operations. A man comes directly from the employment office to "Class C." As he gets better he goes into "Class B," and so on into "Class A," and out of "Class A" into tool making or some supervisory capacity. It is up to him to place himself. If he stays in production it is because he likes it.

In a previous chapter I noted that no one applying for work is refused on account of physical condition. This policy went into effect on January 12, 1914, at the time of setting the minimum wage at five dollars a day and the working day at eight hours. It carried with it the further condition that no one should be discharged on account of physical condition, except, of course, in the case of contagious disease. I think that if an industrial institution is to fill its whole rôle, it ought to be possible for a cross-section of its employees to show about the same proportions as a cross-section of a society in general. We have always with us the maimed and the halt. There is a most generous disposition to regard all of these people who are physically incapacitated for labour as a charge on society and to support them by charity. There are cases where I imagine that the support must be by charity —as, for instance, an idiot. But those cases are extraordinarily rare, and we have found it possible, among the great number of different tasks that must be performed somewhere in the company, to find an opening for almost any one and on the basis of production. The blind man or cripple can, in the particular place to which he is assigned, perform just as much work and receive exactly the same pay as a wholly able-bodied man would. We do not prefer cripples—but we have demonstrated that they can earn full wages.

7. The Testing of
General Motors

HENRY FORD AND ALFRED P. SLOAN, JR. (1875–1966), may be taken to represent opposing halves of America's most significant business-industrial creation, the automobile industry. Where Ford personified the engineer, emphasizing a standard, unvarying product and technical service rather than high-pressure sales, Sloan embodied the modern "scientific" manager. It is he who gets credit for organizing the management system (centralized control with decentralized operations) that brought General Motors Corporation to leadership of its industry and, indeed, of American business as a whole; it is he who gets credit—some might say blame—for firmly establishing the annual model change with related intense promotion that made possible the annual sales of millions of automobiles.

Sloan was born in New Haven, Connecticut, in comfortable circumstances, graduated from the Massachusetts Institute of Technology in 1895, and then went to work for the Hyatt Roller Bearing Company of Newark, New Jersey. He soon became a partner in that enterprise through his father's investment of $5,000 in his behalf, subsequently built it up to many times its former size, and in 1916 sold it for $13.5 million to William C. (Billy) Durant's United Motors Corporation, which was to become the nucleus of General Motors.

In the panic of 1920 General Motors came close to bankruptcy, largely as a result of Durant's incautious expansionism and central management's inability to control the company's various divisions. That General Motors pulled through the crisis may be attributed chiefly to the efforts of Sloan and Pierre S. du Pont, who was serving at the time as president. At the start of 1920 the corporation adopted Sloan's plan of reorganization—"a happy medium," as Sloan described it, "between the extremes of pure centralization and pure decentralization." The plan came into full operation soon after May 1923, when du Pont resigned as president and was succeeded by Sloan; it is, essentially, the plan that governs General Motors' conduct today. Sloan effectively ran the company for more than thirty years, building up a virtually unchallenged reputation as the greatest of modern corporate managers. Peter F. Drucker has written of him: "Sloan set out deliberately in the early Twenties to break the traditional patterns of business organization, business management and business leadership. To do this . . . he literally had to invent almost everything that is commonplace in business today: the concept of the big business and its organization; the very idea of a systematic management which defined responsibilities and organized means of communications and decision making; management controls . . . Above all he had to invent a person: the professional executive who is both master and servant of his creation, the large organized institution."

It is appropriate that the section we quote from this paragon's own story of his business career is an account of a failure from which much was learned. Just before the 1920 crisis General Motors' young engineering genius Charles F. Kettering came up with the then-revolutionary idea of an air-cooled engine; he sold the idea entirely to Pierre du Pont, partially to Sloan, and not at all to the corporation's operating divisions. There followed a mammoth corporate tug of war that is described in the ensuing passage. We see the internal pressure against the controversial innovation gradually mounting; we see du Pont becoming more adamant as Sloan becomes more compromising. We get a bit of corporate comedy as executives try to defuse the controversy by abandoning the explosive term "air-cooled" in favor of "copper-cooled" (all but Kettering himself, who goes on saying "air-cooled"). We see the copper-cooled Chevrolet being introduced in January 1923, to great acclaim—but not great sales; only 759 were ever produced and only about 100 ever found their way into the hands of retail buyers. We see Kettering wanting to resign. It was an auto industry disaster comparable in many ways to the later one involving Ford's Edsel and in terms of corporate survival far more serious; Sloan says flatly that if the copper-cooled engine program had gone forward, there would have been no more General Motors. But the point is, it didn't go forward. (Much later, air-cooling would come to General Motors with the Corvair.) Out of the episode came a new rapport between centralized management and the decentralized divisions. Kettering did not resign; Sloan persuaded him to stay, and he went on to such key achievements as the development of tetraethyl lead, high-compression engines, nontoxic refrigerants, and the two-cycle diesel engine. In sum, modern management, based as it usually is on carefully considered compromise, triumphed and General Motors went on to glory.

Its glory, and that of its industry, is now largely faded, as we have lately been told persuasively by William Serrin in *The Company and the Union* (Knopf, 1973) and Emma Rothschild in *Paradise Lost: The Decline of the Auto-Industrial Age* (Random House, 1973). Gigantism and middle age have hardened the industry's arteries; Sloan's daring innovations have become shibboleths. There is still a thrill, though, in reading about the days when it was all new and General Motors was tested in the fire.

THE "COPPER-COOLED" ENGINE

LOGICALLY one might suppose that, upon the adoption of the concept of management and the concept of the car business, the new administration should have proceeded forthwith to translate them into

---

From *My Years with General Motors,* by Alfred P. Sloan, Jr., ed. by John McDonald, with Catharine Stevens (Doubleday, 1963), Chapters 5 and 6.

realities. Such, however, was not the case. Indeed, for the next two and a half years—that is, for most of the first definable period of the new administration—we departed from and even violated those first principles. In other words, the logic of the mind and the "logic" of history were not of the same order. This chapter is a painful one in the General Motors story, but I see no way to avoid it if I am to account for General Motors' progress. For, as often happens, the lessons of such experience are the best-learned lessons. The years 1921 and 1922 fortunately offered time to spare for a schooling that was to have a considerable part in shaping the future of the corporation.

The problem was one of conflict between the research organization and the producing divisions, and of a parallel conflict between the top management of the corporation and the divisional management. The subject of the conflict was a revolutionary car with an air-cooled engine of Mr. Kettering's design, which Pierre S. du Pont proposed as a replacement for the corporation's conventional cars with water-cooled engines.

The story begins in 1918 when Mr. [Charles F.] Kettering began experimenting with an air-cooled engine in one of his workshops in Dayton. An air-cooled automotive engine was not unknown. Earlier ones were then in use in the United States in the Franklin car and others. The principle of air-cooling as we knew it was to draw off the heat of the engine through its walls by attaching fins to the walls and blowing air over them with a fan. The Franklin tried to do this with cast-iron fins. Mr. Kettering proposed to use copper fins, the conductivity of copper being ten times that of cast iron, and to braze or weld the fins to the engine walls. This involved new technology both in engines and in metallurgy. Mr. Kettering found a number of difficult design problems in the area of expansion and contraction of the two metals, but he had in mind and under test, solutions to the problems of design; problems of production were still another matter and of course belonged to a later stage of development.

The air-cooled engine offered an attractive prospect. It would get rid of the cumbersome radiator and plumbing system of the water-cooled engine and promised to reduce the number of parts in the engine, its weight, and its cost, and at the same time to improve engine performance. If it fulfilled all these promises it would indeed revolutionize the industry. But it is a long way from principle to reality in engine design; one has only to observe the years and engineering man-hours taken to develop practical jet and rocket motors, or to note that the water-cooled internal-combustion engine had come to its 1921 level of efficiency after constant development by an entire industry since the late nineteenth century. Nevertheless, though he had been at it only a short time, Mr. Kettering's convictions regarding his new air-cooled engine were optimistic; and he had then a very considerable reputation in the automotive field because of his pioneering work on the self-starter and ignition and lighting systems, and in the aviation field where he was so far ahead as to have experimented with a pilot-less plane.

Mr. Kettering came before the Finance Committee on August 7, 1919, to explain the work he was doing on the air-cooled engine and on fuel research—to result later in tetraethyl lead for gasoline (ethyl gas)—at the Dayton Metal Products Company and the Dayton Wright Airplane Company. I had some part in the preliminaries of this meeting. I had known Mr. Kettering since 1916, when his Dayton Engineering Laboratories Company came into United Motors, and had kept in touch with his work. On the day before the meeting of the Finance Committee, Mr. Kettering had met with Harold E. Talbott, president of Dayton Metal Products Company, Mr. Haskell, Mr. Raskob, and myself to work out arrangements for General Motors to purchase the assets of the Dayton companies—Domestic Engineering Company, Dayton Metal Products Company, and Dayton Wright Airplane Company. The thing was wrapped up at the committee's meeting of August 26, 1919. There Mr. Durant and Mr. Pierre S. du Pont reported on the Dayton situation, saying, "that Mr. Charles F. Kettering . . . is the center of this situation; that the obtaining of Mr. Kettering's entire time and attention is of prime importance, it being desired to place him in charge of the new Detroit laboratory . . . and that in the opinion of Mr. Durant, Mr. Haskell, Mr. Sloan, Mr. Chrysler and others Mr. Kettering is by far the most valuable man known to this Corporation for the position . . ." The Finance Committee minutes then say:

The Committee was advised by the President [Mr. Durant] regarding the air-cooled engine which is being developed by the Dayton Metal Products Company and the possible future thereof, it appearing that this invention has as yet not progressed to the point where its success is absolutely assured but that its chances of proving successful are favorable and that in this event our investment will provide a splendid financial return.

So it was that we got Mr. Kettering's services, the Dayton properties, and the air-cooled engine; and a good deal of General Motors' history was set in motion.

More than a year went by and much water went under the bridge . . . On December 2, 1920, shortly after Mr. du Pont became president of General Motors, Mr. Kettering reported to him: "The small air-cooled engine of the Ford type is now ready to push toward a production basis." Mr. Kettering suggested that a few cars be made and tested, and that if they were satisfactory a number of cars, 1500 or 2000, might be made ready for the market in 1921.

A few days later, on December 7, 1920, a party of us made a trip to Dayton to look things over there. Pierre S. du Pont, John J. Raskob, J. A. Haskell, K. W. Zimmerschied, who was general manager of Chevrolet, C. D. Hartman, Jr., secretary of the Finance Committee, and myself, went down together. On the train to and from Dayton we discussed a number of things, among them the air-cooled engine. A record of the discussion says:

> After careful consideration it was the consensus of opinion that the new car being developed at Dayton should be tested in adequate numbers and under the most rigorous conditions before undertaking to exploit the type in any degree. When satisfied as to the merits of the product, it will be adapted for the Chevrolet line, and will replace the present 490 model.

The "490" was then the standard lower-priced Chevrolet in our line, potentially though not then actually competitive with Ford. The question of a new engine for it was a big thing, conceivably a decisive one for General Motors in the high-volume market.

It is not surprising, therefore, that on January 19, 1921, at one of its earliest meetings, the new Executive Committee agreed upon making a comparative study of the air-cooled engine and the existing water-cooled Chevrolet "490." It was the consensus of the committee that no material changes in the "490" were possible for the next model year, beginning in the autumn of 1921, "and that it would be well to await future developments in the air-cooled engine before deciding upon the changes to be made for the production year beginning August 1922." Thus we decided to "await" the air-cooled car and in the interim to do nothing to develop the old, water-cooled "490" model. I say "we decided," for the Executive Committee always made decisions as a body.

Two weeks later we moved to a firmer position, resolving "that it is our intention that the air-cooled engine be developed first for a low-priced car and that it be made in the Chevrolet Division, and that Messrs. Kettering and Zimmerschied be informed of this opinion." This was actually an order, and so far as Chevrolet was concerned the die was cast.

In another two weeks the Executive Committee expanded its position with a proposal to take a second car, the Oakland, into the air-cooled program with a new six-cylinder engine. The Executive Committee, however, noted "great uncertainty" within itself on the question and ordered a report on it from the Advisory Staff, of which I was then the head. If I am not mistaken in memory, the "great uncertainty" among the four of us on the committee was mainly in my mind. This will become clear later. But the committee was led with a firm hand by the president, Mr. du Pont. He pressed for the air-cooled program, upon the advancement of which he had by this time set his mind.

Another week later, on February 23, 1921, at a meeting from which I was absent, the Executive Committee moved on quickly to new decisions: "It was assumed," the minutes say, "that the 4 cylinder air cooled car now under study and development would occupy the lowest price field; that second to this would be a 6 cylinder air cooled car, selling in the neighborhood of $900. to $1000." Mr. Kettering was ordered to "proceed with the design and construction of the 6 cylinder air cooled car." But, the committee said, "no quantity production should be attempted until success had been established, by a thorough test of a few [trial] cars." Mr. Kettering, who was present along with Mr. Mott and Mr. Bassett, said he expected to know the merits of both cars by July 1, 1921, and that preparations for the manufacture of the air-cooled "4" could be started on August 1 with a view to bringing out the car about January 1, 1922. Mr. Zimmerschied of Chevrolet was called in and told about the program for his division. He demurred, saying he desired to prepare for production of the air-cooled "4" in August 1922. He said he had improved the water-cooled "490" and had designed a new body for it. The Executive Committee and the Chevrolet Division were thus revealed as moving in different directions.

Mr. Kettering had test cars of both types in operation in Dayton in May 1921 and reported that either the "4" or "6" could be first to come out. On June 7 the Executive Committee agreed that a small manufacturing section—a kind of pilot operation—should be created at the General Motors Research Corporation (later called our Research Laboratories) in Dayton, with a maximum production of not more than twenty-five cars a day.

About this time Mr. Zimmerschied's reservations regarding the air-cooled Chevrolet crystallized, and the divisional problem, so to speak, thereby came to the foreground, where it was to remain for some time. Circumstance had dictated that Buick, which was doing well, should be left for the time being more or less in its former, wholly decentralized state, and with its own program. But notwithstanding our concept of organization and directly contrary to it, expediency was permitted to centralize the affairs of other divisions. This trend was made emphatic by the decision of the top officers to impose a radical car design upon two divisions, Chevrolet and Oakland. The Executive Committee thus made both the policy and the program for these divisions on the most significant question that can come before a division, namely its engine and car design. The Executive Committee had that privilege, and in the circumstances it elected to exercise it. The difficulty lay not only in the question of whether the decision regarding the new car was sound, but in how to get it carried out where it had to be carried out, namely, in the divisions. In extenuation of what was done, I should say that this was the first time, to my knowledge, in the history of General Motors that intimate co-operation was called for between the Research Corporation and the divisions on an important problem and no established means existed by which this co-operation was to function. Since the initial production as well as the creation of the design was assigned to Mr. Kettering's research group in Dayton and the actual mass production was assigned to the divisions, the responsibilities were blurred. Mr. Zimmerschied wanted to know who was adviser to whom on production: Research to the car division or the car division to Research? Even if there had been no question as to the merits of the new design, this would have represented a problem in management. As it was, there was skepticism at Chevrolet about the new engineering design, and anxiety at the Dayton laboratories that the car divisions would change the design. Divisional engineers and the general managers traveled back and forth between their home bases and Dayton, and in the course of these visits Mr. Kettering observed that George H. Hannum, general manager of Oakland, was more sympathetic to the new car. Mr. Kettering also thought that he could have the air-cooled "6" ready for Oakland by the end of the year.

I was in Paris during the first part of July 1921, and on my return all four of us on the Executive Committee again traveled together to Dayton, arriving there on July 26. We met informally with Mr. Kettering and Mr. Mott, who was then group executive for the car divisions. Mr. Kettering's enthusiasm for the new car was stronger than ever: ". . . it is," he said, "the greatest thing that has ever been produced in the automobile world." Mr. du Pont left no doubt of his faith in this judgment. Mr. Kettering again noted the differences between the attitudes at Chevrolet and Oakland. Naturally he was anxious to work more closely with the division that expressed the greater sympathy, namely, Oakland. A transcript of the meeting in Dayton says: "It was finally recommended that the 6 cyl. car be pushed ahead and that the 4 cyl. car be held up for the time being as it was felt that they could profit by their experience on the '6' when producing the '4' . . ." Mr. Zimmerschied of Chevrolet, it was believed, could be sold on the air-cooled "4" engine after the validity of the "6" was established. Chevrolet anyway, Mr. Mott said, had an inventory of about 150,000 "490's" which still needed to be liquidated.

This temporizing attitude toward Chevrolet was not permitted to last long. A few weeks later Mr. du Pont presented to the Executive Committee a general review of the product situation in General Motors with proposals for a definitive corporation program. He reaffirmed the decisions regarding the air-cooled "6" for Oakland. When he came to Chevrolet, he wrote: "It [the '490'] is not to be continued in production beyond the time necessary to reduce inventories and commitments. Immediate decision upon a new car for permanent manufacture is necessary." The air-cooled "4," he said, was to be "the adopted standard for the Chevrolet Division unless a definite change of policy should be made," and it should be ready for production before May 1, 1922. The Executive Committee as a body concurred.

The development work on the new engine continued at Dayton through the fall of 1921, and at the same time studies were made concerning new plants, conversion of plants, and marketing programs for the air-cooled cars. As the time for the delivery of the first test car from Dayton to the Oakland Division grew near, there was a growing atmosphere of expectancy in the New York and Detroit offices. Mr. du Pont wrote to Mr. Kettering, "Now that we are at the point of planning production of the new cars I am beginning to feel like a small boy when the long expected circus posters begin to appear on the fences, and to wonder how each part of the circus is to appear and what act I will like best."

Specific dates for the Oakland schedule were officially set by the Executive Committee on October 20, 1921, as follows:

Production of the existing water-cooled car to be stopped on December 1, 1921.

New air-cooled cars, made in Dayton, to be introduced at the New York Automobile Show in January 1922.

Production of the new car to begin at the Oakland Division in Pontiac, Michigan, in February at one hundred a day and to increase thereafter.

No further questions on program remained, it seemed.

The first air-cooled car then was sent from Dayton to the Oakland Division for test. This was the first evaluation of the validity of the air-cooled car outside of the test cars operated by Mr. Kettering in

Dayton. There was a pause, and then shock. Word came that the car had failed its tests at the Oakland Division.

On November 8, 1921, Mr. Hannum wrote to Mr. du Pont:

With the changes that are necessary to make this a real job, it is going to be impossible to get into production in the time specified, in fact, to get this car to the point where, after all tests are complete and we are ready to put our O. K. on same, it will take at least six months.

To bridge the time when the present allotment of the old models are completed, which will be about Dec. 15th, and the time we bring in the Air Cooled Car, we are planning on bringing in a complete new [water cooled] line . . .

I want to say further the changes which we have in mind for the Air Cooled Job have not changed my views of the proposition in the least, as I believe, when we get the first job on the road, with the changes incorporated, there will be a great change in the test reports.

Thus in less than a month the adopted schedule of the corporation was overthrown and the whole situation with respect to Oakland and the future General Motors product line had profoundly changed. There was disappointment and alarm in New York and pessimism in Detroit, Flint, and Pontiac concerning the outlook for the air-cooled car. Between Dayton and the manufacturing divisions controversy and confusion arose over the testing of the new car; there was no meeting of minds between Mr. Kettering's designers on the one hand and the divisional engineers and general managers on the other. Mr. Kettering felt fatigue and was so discouraged that the Executive Committee, upon officially canceling the Oakland air-cooled schedule on November 30, 1921, sent him a letter of confidence, as follows:

Dear Kettering:—

It is most important in our opinion that your mind be kept free from worries foreign to the development of the air cooled car and other laboratory work.

In the development and introduction of anything so radically different from standard practice as the air cooled car is from the regular water cooled job, it is quite natural that there should be a lot of "wiseacres" and "know-it-alls" standing around knocking the development.

In order that your mind may be completely relieved as to the position of the undersigned with respect to the air cooled development, we beg to advise as follows:—

1st. We are absolutely confident in your ability to whip all problems in connection with the development of our proposed air cooled cars.

2nd. We will continue to have this degree of confidence and faith in you and your ability to accomplish this task until such time as we come to you and frankly state that we have doubts as to the possibility or feasibility of turning the trick and you will be the first one to whom we will come.

We are endeavoring in this letter to use language such as will result in complete elimination of worry on your part with respect to our faith in you and this work and if this language fails to create this result, then won't you kindly write us quite frankly advising in what respect we have failed?

Due to the fact that criticisms are bound to continue until the air cooled cars are in active production and use, would it not be well for you to agree with us that at any time you have occasion to pause and wonder about our faith and confidence in you and this development, that you will pull this letter out of your desk and read it again, after which you will write to us in consideration of our frankly stating that we will write to you first in case of any doubt?

The letter was signed individually by the four members of the Executive Committee and by C. S. Mott, who as I have said was the group executive for the car divisions.

The crisis passed. The president's faith in the new engine was restored, Mr. Kettering revived his interest and energies, and the scene shifted from Oakland to Chevrolet.

On December 15, 1921, the Executive Committee proposed a

strong effort to get the Chevrolet air-cooled "4" into production by September 1, 1922. To reconcile the divisions and research, O. E. Hunt, chief engineer of Chevrolet, and B. Jerome and E. A. De Waters, chief engineers representing Oakland and Buick, respectively, were sent to Dayton to collaborate with Mr. Kettering on the design of the air-cooled "4" and "6." Daily test reports were requested to be sent to the division managers and to the president.

The year 1921 closed with no definable progress in the General Motors product line.

These events bothered me to the extent that I attempted to raise them to a higher level in my mind with a view to taking them up with the Executive Committee. I did not feel strongly one way or the other about the technical question of an air-cooled versus a water-cooled engine. That was an engineering matter, for engineers. If I have any opinion today it is that Mr. Kettering may have been right in principle and ahead of his time, and that the divisions were right from a development and production standpoint. In other words, in this kind of situation it is possible for the doctors to disagree and still all be right. From a business and management standpoint, however, we were acting at variance with our doctrines. We were, for example, more committed to a particular engineering design than to the broad aims of the enterprise. And we were in the situation of supporting a research position against the judgment of the division men who would in the end have to produce and sell the new car. Meanwhile, obsolescence was overtaking our conventional water-cooled models and there was nothing in the official program to protect their position.

Late in December 1921, having in mind the breakdown of the test at Oakland and the problems that the proposed new car had created, I wrote some notes to myself to clarify in my mind the problems of the corporation, with a view to discussing them with Pierre S. du Pont. Regarding the Dayton situation, I said:

> I believe that considerable time has been lost in the development of the air-cooled car through lack of appreciation undoubtedly on the part of all of us, that certain fundamental facts do not, to any extent, subscribe to the contentions of Mr. Kettering—that everybody in General Motors must be sold on

the details of his proposed car. I believe that if he had developed a car and demonstrated its performance or it had demonstrated its performance in the hands of independent observers and that he had left the production of the car to others as a principle, that we would have been farther ahead. I think we have made a mistake in putting it all up to Mr. Kettering and not recognizing his particular and peculiar situation. I believe that the Corporation needs and the industry needs advanced engineering. We are not going to get advanced engineering from a mediocre mind such as the average of our engineers compared with that of Mr. Kettering. Advanced engineering always, like advanced everything else, brings down upon it the discredit of ridicule of minds who cannot see so far. For all this reason, such engineering must be demonstrated in such a way that the facts must be accepted rather than theories. I do not think that there would have been any trouble in Oakland or that any changes would have been suggested had Mr. Kettering waited until he had a car that would demonstrate a reasonable satisfactory performance. I fear that the way this is working will result in the loss of a great many of the ideas that we need so badly and can only accept from a man of Mr. Kettering's marvelous ability.

The writing of this memorandum served mainly to mark a turning point in my conduct concerning the air-cooled engine. I began then to pursue a dual policy: first continuing to support Mr. du Pont's and Mr. Kettering's hopes for the new car, and second, giving support to the divisions in the development of alternate programs of the conventional water-cooled type. And, incidentally, on the side, for a while Mr. Zimmerschied and I looked into a new "Muir" steam-cooling system, which never went into production. While Mr. du Pont had no enthusiasm for alternatives to the air-cooled engine, he did not forbid my taking this position. We simply worked along somewhat different lines. But such a situation between the two leading members of the operating organization was not entirely comfortable and could not last forever.

For the next sixteen months the air-cooled car continued to distract the corporation and to keep its leading officers in a state of tension over the question of what the future product of the corporation was to be.

At the beginning of 1922, the pressure on Chevrolet for the new car was increased, while that on Oakland was somewhat relieved. I took a first step toward the compromise which I felt was necessary to protect the corporation in the event of failure of the new program, and to bridge the gap that had opened between top management and the divisions. As vice president of operations I held a meeting in my room in the Hotel Statler in Detroit on January 26, 1922, with Mr. Mott (car group executive), Mr. Bassett (Buick), and Mr. Zimmerschied (Chevrolet), and reached an understanding that the official air-cooled program for Chevrolet was to be advanced, but with caution. The official program required that the experimental air-cooled "4" models under development at Dayton, "if proper, should be put in production by the Chevrolet Division as of September 1, 1922," that is, just seven months away, though the Chevrolet management had not yet received a test car from Dayton. We agreed, however, "that there is nothing before the Corporation or the Chevrolet Division at the present time to justify the positive conclusion that the air-cooled car should be put into production on the date specified," but that on April 1, 1922, after tests had been made, we could determine a safe program. At the same time we agreed that "a second line of defense should be prepared—this being only a conservative policy." The second line of defense was a parallel effort in the division to improve the existing water-cooled Chevrolet.

As to Oakland, on February 21, 1922, I reported to the Executive Committee and obtained approval to postpone a new schedule for the air-cooled "6," production of which had been canceled. For Oakland then we agreed:

1. To continue its recently established [water-cooled] models for a period of a year and a half, ending June 30, 1923.

2. To eliminate from consideration, as far as Oakland is concerned, the introduction of any air cooled model previous to that date.

3.   That any design that Oakland may develop in the meantime will be in accordance with the program of designs already established by the Corporation.

4.   That if the economic position of the Oakland models change[s] to the extent that the Division is unable to break even, steps will have to be taken at that time as seem best in view of all the circumstances prevailing at that time.

Since the Research Corporation at Dayton was the only substantial corporation-wide, staff engineering group in General Motors at the time, and it was occupied with the air-cooled-engine experiment, the advanced engineering for the water-cooled models devolved largely upon the divisions. All of the car divisions at that time were in need of advanced engineering staff work to make and keep their conventional cars competitive. At Chevrolet, Oakland, and Olds the need was acute. In other words, the divisions had to attend not only to their principal business of engineering, manufacturing, and selling current models, but to their own staff work on forward engineering as well. Not that matters had been any different in this area previously, but it was our intention to provide for comprehensive engineering staff work for the corporation. From the way in which the Research Corporation chose to operate—that is, as a long-range idea organization centering upon Mr. Kettering's unusual capabilities—it was evident that a gap had opened between his important function and the bread-and-butter type of advanced engineering. I did not then know that a historic distinction was being made in General Motors, but I saw the gap before me and on March 14, 1922, obtained approval of a policy of seeking outside engineering designs for the divisions. This policy would never solve the problem but it would help; many years would pass before the problem was entirely understood and met. Among those whom I consulted at that time was Henry Crane, who later came into the corporation as technical assistant to the president and contributed importantly to the corporation's engineering progress, especially in the design of the Pontiac car. O. E. Hunt had only recently—in October 1921—been brought by Mr. Zimmerschied into Chevrolet as chief engineer and I was not yet familiar with his fine capabilities.

The compromise between the air-cooled and water-cooled developments at Chevrolet was an uneasy one. It was soon accompanied by a change in management. On February 1, 1922, at Mr. Mott's suggestion, William S. Knudsen, who had formerly been Ford's production manager, was brought into the corporation's Advisory Staff and assigned as manufacturing assistant to Mr. Mott. Mr. Knudsen visited Dayton and on March 11 made a report on the air-cooled car, in which he recommended "that the car be put in production at once." He advised me, however, that he meant that production should be started in a small way to test the car both commercially and technically. On March 22 Mr. du Pont obtained the agreement of the Executive Committee to remove Mr. Zimmerschied from his post as general manager of Chevrolet and make him assistant to the president of General Motors; and to appoint Mr. Knudsen as vice president of operations at Chevrolet. Mr. du Pont also proposed to make himself general manager of the Chevrolet Division, while remaining chairman and president of the corporation, and it was agreed.

On April 7, 1922, at the president's request, we officially named the experimental development the "copper-cooled" instead of the "air-cooled" engine. Mr. du Pont wished to differentiate it from other systems of air-cooling. But Mr. Kettering continued to say "air-cooled."

Preparations for tooling up for production of the copper-cooled Chevrolet "4" began, with manufacture expected to start about September 15, 1922, at ten cars a day, increasing to fifty a day by the end of the year. The Canadian organization, too, was instructed to develop and introduce a copper-cooled "4." But the spring of 1922 passed without bringing any reality to the new programs. The copper-cooled engine remained under test at Dayton.

Spring sales of cars showed 1922 to be a year of fair recovery, and the Chevrolet "490," underdeveloped as it was in engineering design, was selling again. At a meeting in Detroit in May 1922—at which Mr. du Pont, Mr. Mott, Mr. Knudsen, Colin Campbell, then sales manager of Chevrolet, and I were present—Mr. Mott, with my support, proposed another compromise—namely, to put the new Chevrolet bodies, designed for the copper-cooled car, on the old "490" chassis in the fall, to make certain that we would have something new to sell for the next model year. Mr. Campbell opposed this, saying he was afraid to load up the dealers with "490's" during the winter and then give them copper-cooled cars in the spring of 1923. Again I tried to advance the policy of a dual program, saying: ". . . we should use the copper cooled car as an experiment until April 1st [1923]. Then, if it has become successful and is holding up in the field, increase production on the copper cooled jobs and on August 1st [1923] bring in the car as the sole product of the Chevrolet Division. If the car were not successful, we could continue to manufacture the 490s." The differences thus were laid on the table, but nothing was decided.

The parallel programs and proposals for programs created inevitable tensions in the corporation. Mr. Kettering continued to feel that the divisions were dragging their feet. Oakland, he observed, was now several months behind Chevrolet in the copper-cooled development, and Chevrolet plans, he said, were inadequate. He said in May of 1922 that he was working best with Robert Jack, chief engineer of Olds. Mr. du Pont supported Mr. Kettering's opinion of Chevrolet's plans and in June proposed a stiffening of the copper-cooled program at that division. Since chassis and body changes for the new engine were expected to be complete in the fall, and the change-over then would be concerned with the engine only, he recommended that production of the copper-cooled Chevrolet be scheduled for the forthcoming winter.

In September production had not begun, but the official expectations were optimistic. The plan for Chevrolet was to have a monthly capacity of 30,000 water-cooled and 12,000 copper-cooled cars by March 1923 and to convert the entire water-cooled production into copper-cooled by July or, at the latest, October 1923.

In November, Mr. Kettering noted a lack of interest in the copper-cooled car at Olds as well as at Oakland. I said to Mr. du Pont that I was fearful of the outcome of committing three main divisions to a new, untried engineering car design. Mr. du Pont pointed out to me that the decision had been made by the Executive Committee some months ago "and that the only decision left was the question of a change of front, or the abandonment absolutely of all experiments with water cooled and steam cooled cars." He agreed, however, that there would be no final determination with regard to Chevrolet until May 1, 1923. He then proposed that the Olds program be converted exclusively to copper-cooled.

Mr. du Pont's and my views were then expressed on November 16, 1922, in this compromise resolution of the Executive Committee:

RESOLVED, That the copper cooled program shall be as follows:

1. That the product of the Olds Division as of August 1st, 1923, shall be a six cylinder copper cooled car . . . All experiments and developments of water cooled motors shall be discontinued from this date (November 16th, 1922).

2. The Chevrolet Motor Division will proceed with the development of its copper cooled model cautiously, with a view to determining all factors involved, both commercially and technically, always recognized as being present in the development of any new product, in such a way that the hazard to the Corporation is at all times kept at a minimum.

3. The policy of the Oakland Division will be hereafter determined, but under no circumstances shall the Oakland Company put in production a copper cooled car of any kind or description until the position of the copper cooled car as a type is determined in a broad way by actual experience in the field of a sufficient number of cars, such experience being both of a technical and commercial nature.

Thus at the end of 1922 we were committed exclusively to the copper-cooled program at Olds, to a dual program at Chevrolet, and Oakland was exempted until the new car had proved itself. In December, Mr. Knudsen began to manufacture 250 copper-cooled cars at Chevrolet. The year 1922, like 1921, ended with uncertainty as to what the engineering design of the General Motors product was to be.

At the New York Automobile Show in January 1923 the copper-cooled Chevrolet—chassis and motor—was unveiled. It was priced at about $200 above the standard, water-cooled Chevrolet (now called the "Superior" model), and was the sensation of the show.

The schedule of the Chevrolet Division called for the manufacture of 1000 copper-cooled cars in February, with the monthly rate to increase to 50,000 in October. The only question that seemed to remain at the beginning of the new year regarding the water-cooled car was the exact date on which it should be abandoned. But troubles appeared in the course of production and Chevrolet copper-cooled cars failed to appear in February in large numbers.

Two decisive events occurred simultaneously during the months of March, April, and May 1923. First, we found ourselves in the greatest boom year up to that time in automobile history, the beginning of the industry's first four-million car-and-truck year. Second, difficulties in production had slowed the manufacture of copper-cooled Chevrolets to a walk, and the few copper-cooled Chevrolets that were on the road and being checked by the division produced a large number of reports of troubles, indicating that they were still experimental, unproved, and in need of further development. The question of what to do required no great act of mind. The only Chevrolet we had to sell was the old, conventional water-cooled model. Although it was not a high-performance automobile, even for those days, the Chevrolet water-cooled "Superior" model had been improved and it was a workable car. It ran up record sales that spring.

One could feel that a new era in the demand for automobiles had opened up, and it was imperative that the corporation settle upon its product program for a future that would present itself but once. On May 10, 1923, Mr. du Pont resigned as president of General Motors and on his recommendation to the board I succeeded him in that office. We continued to disagree on the merits of the copper-cooled program, but it was left to me as chief executive officer to make the decisions.

At Olds, in accordance with prevailing policy, all work on the water-cooled car had stopped; the inventory of cars was being sold off at a loss of about fifty dollars a car while the division waited to go into production of the new copper-cooled "6" on August 1, 1923. But the troubles with the copper-cooled Chevrolet clearly threatened the validity of this program.

As president I was of course chairman of the Executive Committee —which was enlarged to include Fred Fisher, head of Fisher Body, and Mr. Mott—and at the first meeting at which I presided on May 18,

1923, I took up the Olds question. I stated the facts about the Olds situation and said: ". . . the continued delay in producing the Chevrolet copper-cooled car is a constant reminder of the uncertainties and the difficulties in engineering and manufacture which would most certainly delay the program and might lead to serious embarrassment to the Olds Motor Works organization at the factory and throughout the world." After a discussion with Mr. Kettering, Mr. Knudsen, and Mr. Hunt, we appointed a committee of three engineers —A. L. Cash, general manager of Northway, an engine-producing division of General Motors, Mr. Hunt, chief engineer of Chevrolet, and Mr. De Waters, chief engineer of Buick—and instructed them to report on the status of the six-cylinder copper-cooled engine. They presented their report to the Executive Committee at a meeting on May 28, 1923, from which Mr. du Pont, Mr. Haskell, and Mr. Raskob were absent. The report was the main business of the meeting. The engineers said:

That the [copper-cooled "6"] engine pre-ignites badly after driving at moderate speeds in air temperatures from sixty to seventy degrees. That it shows a serious loss of compression and power when hot, though the power is satisfactory when the engine is warming up from the cold condition.

These major difficulties plus several minor ones which can be reported in detail, if you so desire, lead us to the conclusion that the job is not in shape for immediate production. We recommend that we set it aside for further development and it be left out of consideration as far as immediate production is concerned.

Upon hearing this report the Executive Committee canceled the prevailing copper-cooled program at Olds and instructed the division to proceed with the development of a water-cooled engine that would be able to function on the copper-cooled chassis. We expressed confidence in the principle of copper-cooling as a longer-range development, and assigned the copper-cooled "6" engine to Mr. Cash for development at the Northway Division.

At Chevrolet 759 copper-cooled cars had been produced, of which 239 were scrapped by the production men. Of the balance, 500 were delivered to the sales organization. Of these about 150 were used by factory representatives. Something over 300 were sold to dealers, of which about 100 went to retail buyers. In June 1923 the Chevrolet Division decided to recall all of these copper-cooled cars from the field.

On June 26, 1923, in a letter to me, Mr. Kettering proposed to take the copper-cooled engine out of General Motors. He wrote:

> We started out to do a perfectly definite thing, which has been done, and it is just the same now as it was a year ago, but in the transition stage certain factors have entered into this, which have confused the thing to the point where, unless things can be clarified, I believe the whole proposition should be dropped. If we cannot get some practical way of commercializing this product, in our own organization, I should like very much to discuss with you the possibility of taking this outside of the corporation and this is a thing which has come up within the last week. I am sure I can get capital and pretty much of an organization to go do this job the way in which I know it can be done.

It appears that he did not understand then that the copper-cooled Chevrolets had been withdrawn. Four days later, upon his learning of this decision, Mr. Kettering wrote to me again and proposed to resign from the corporation:

> I have definitely made up my mind to leave the Corporation unless some method can be arranged to prevent the fundamental work done here from being thrown out and discredited through no fault of the apparatus . . .
>
> I am perfectly sure that we can take any proposition and make out of it a 100% success, provided we do not have to overcome an organized resistance within the Corporation. This is impossible unless the Executive Committee can take it upon themselves to force through an Executive order when they know it is going to be of value to the Corporation.
>
> I regret very much that this situation has developed. I have been extremely unhappy and know that I have made you and

Mr. du Pont equally unhappy by my frequently discussing this matter with you. I am not temperamentally constituted where I can sit down and do nothing. I have never failed in any proposition that I have undertaken yet. The work here at the Laboratory, I realize, has been almost 100% failure, but not because of the fundamental principles involved. Enough may have come out of the Laboratories to have paid for their existence but no one will care to continue in Research activities as the situation now stands.

My only regret, in severing my connection with the Corporation, would be the wonderful association I have had with yourself, Mr. du Pont, Mr. Mott and others. There are many possibilities for work of the kind which I can do in industries where the problems which exist in getting new things over, are not quite as difficult as in the motor industry. Therefore, I hope, after reading this, that you can formulate some definite plan whereby either the situation within the Corporation can be cleared up or I can be relieved of my present duties. I would like to have some definite conclusion reached on this as soon as possible, as I would like to formulate definite plans.

Mr. Kettering was always very frank. In our forty years of friendship and association, he always spoke his mind clearly to me and I spoke the same way to him. I think that this was our worst moment. His biographer T. A. Boyd, has written: ". . . the discontinuance of the copper-cooled Chevrolet in the summer of 1923 was a staggering blow to him. It was then that his spirits reached the lowest point in his research career." I knew that. But I was as certain of the position I felt I had to take as he was of his, and of course we had different responsibilities. Management involves more than technical problems. I could not, as I saw it, in the face of an expanding market hold up the programs of the corporation for an uncertain development. If I had done so I do not believe there would be a General Motors today; we would have missed the boat. Furthermore, however sound the engine might have been in principle, it was not my policy then or at any time afterward to force on the divisions a thing of this kind against their judgment. On this question (though not on any other) there had unfortunately opened a wide gap in the corporation, with Mr. Kettering, his laboratories, and Mr. du Pont on one side, and myself and the divisions on the other. I was anxious to close it.

My problem was to reconcile Mr. Kettering's natural reactions and enthusiasm for his new idea with the realities in the case. The copper-cooled car had failed to meet the test of validity. It had failed at Oakland. It had been adjudged as needing further development by a joint study made by the chief engineers of Buick, Chevrolet, and Northway—a highly competent group. Sample cars produced by Chevrolet and sent into the field had been withdrawn because of various defects. The problem was complicated by the uncertainties of a new chassis as well as a new engine. We had to recognize that research engineers had little experience, relatively speaking, in chassis design as compared with the engineering staffs of the operating divisions. I had of necessity to respect all these facts and circumstances.

On July 2, 1923, I wrote Mr. Kettering a letter, from which I quote the following:

> 1.   You say that you learned the day before yesterday that all Chevrolet cars were to be taken off the market. Now, you recollect in Mr. du Pont's office in Detroit it was agreed that the copper cooled Chevrolet car would be discontinued so far as further assembly is concerned and assembly would not be started again until Messrs. Knudsen, Hunt and yourself reported to us that it was satisfactory to do this. You were a party to this you recollect, and it seemed after a very lengthy discussion in which many technicalities were brought up, that this was the right thing to do. At the same conference it was agreed that for the sales year beginning August 1st the copper cooled car would be continued and Mr. Campbell was authorized to write contracts both ways. You recollect that. Therefore, as a matter of fact, the Chevrolet position as agreed to at that conference is: first, that they would sell both cars during the sales year of 1923–4 and second, that no copper cooled would be assembled until it was further authorized. Therefore, you can see that they are in a rather embarrassing position. They are told that there will be two cars and yet they

can only produce one. I just mention this so that there will be no misunderstanding.

2.   It was called to my attention recently that there were 143 copper cooled cars out in the territory and it appeared to be desirable to withdraw them and reassemble them. In other words, it was thought desirable, in view of the fact that there were more or less complaints, not dealing with the engine particularly but dealing with the whole car, that they should be taken in and an adjustment made. There was nothing said that it was due to engine trouble or anything else. It simply seemed, all things considered, to be the desirable thing to do. You must appreciate that when these things are done the policy has to be worked out in detail and it is sometimes impossible to get all of the many people that have to carry out the thing to thoroughly understand and properly present the real reasons behind the policy.

I pass over matters which are not essential here and go on to the conclusion of my letter:

7.   I do not agree with you that the situation is in any sense hopeless. I have great confidence in our organization, speaking of it as a whole. I think they are entitled to the credit that is due them and they are also entitled to the discredit of their shortcomings, if I might put it so. The great trouble is that there is an apparent lack of confidence in this copper cooled car and notwithstanding that the executives of the Corporation and the Executive Committee have tried to do their best to get it across, the fact that our Divisions have not believed in it so far has made it practically an impossible problem. That, as I see it, is the real problem before us. It is not the merits of the case and days and weeks spent over it will not alter the situation. What we have got to do is to make our people see the thing as you see it and with that accomplished then there will be nothing more to the problem. I do not think that forcing the issue, is going to get us anywhere. We have tried that and we have failed. We have got to go at it in a different manner if we are going to succeed.

I have quoted from this letter at some length because of the various matters it brings up, most of which are self-evident, at least as to what my position was.

In an effort to relieve the tension I proposed a new development program for the copper-cooled car.

It appeared clear that one basic mistake was a divided responsibility. The Executive Committee, the operating divisions, and the Research Corporation, all with different viewpoints both within themselves and with each other, were trying to do an administrative job. It was clear that we now must get back to sound principles, concentrate the responsibility in a single place, and support that effort. My plan was to create an independent pilot operation under the sole jurisdiction of Mr. Kettering, a kind of copper-cooled-car division. Mr. Kettering would designate his own chief engineer and his production staff to solve the technical problems of manufacture, and his organization would market the copper-cooled cars. They would make a few, or many, as the circumstances dictated. Such a program would provide Mr. Kettering a free hand, without interference, to demonstrate successfully the validity of the concept in which he had so much confidence.

To appraise the new approach I called a meeting of Fred Fisher, Stewart Mott, and myself. We all were sympathetic to this proposed solution of the problem. I quote from a memorandum I sent to Mr. du Pont on July 6, 1923:

> Mr. Fisher, Mr. Mott and myself had a long talk yesterday regarding a policy that would be more constructive and more fundamental than the one we have been pursuing heretofore. We feel that in forcing the Divisions to take something they do not believe in and in which there are certain argumentative points yet to be demonstrated, is not getting us anywhere and with the divided responsibility between the Chief Engineer and Mr. Kettering we are not going to get anywhere unless the responsibility is positively assured in the hands of one or the other party. We are most anxious to practically demonstrate the commercial value of the proposition and believe that the

solution, practically determined upon subject to your approval, is the only way out.

We have discussed the matter with Mr. Kettering at some length this morning and he agrees with us absolutely on every point we make. He appears to receive the suggestion very enthusiastically and has every confidence that it can be put across along these lines. The plan is based upon the following principles:

1. That as we stand today our efforts to commercially develop the copper cooled have resulted in a total loss and we feel that we are worse off than we were two years ago on account of the resistance which has been set up on account of our repeated failures.

2. That the engineering responsibility for putting the job across must be definitely centralized in one man.

3. That we feel that the only way to get the desired result is to establish an independent Operation with the sole purpose of commercially demonstrating the copper cooled idea.

4. Therefore, we have decided to set up a new Division at Dayton using a part of the Research Plant, especially that part which is being vacated by the Aeroplane Division, and we will set up an organization there which will be more or less of an assembly proposition. Mr. Kettering will have complete charge of the engineering side of it, operating through a Chief Engineer whom he will appoint.

5. The new Operation will take over the four cylinder copper cooled engine and probably the six cylinder Olds and will market these two copper cooled jobs under their own name, starting with five or ten a day and building up as the demand increases.

6. All tool equipment and inventory already developed will be available except so far as Mr. Kettering may determine to make changes.

7. The Operation will be of a specialty nature, putting an extra long price on the job on account of the comparatively small production and special nature of the power plant, adding at-

tractive features to the body which we feel sure will get the job across.

Mr. Fisher, Mr. Mott and myself feel that this is the only way out and place the responsibility where it belongs and eliminate all confusion with the other Divisions who can go ahead about their business in their own way as they have very big problems to work out to maintain their present position for the future. I believe that it is useless to attempt to establish an agreement between Mr. Kettering and Mr. Hunt or Mr. Kettering and anyone else on these various technical points involved in the copper cooled development. They never will agree and one or the other must be required to work the thing out largely in his own way along lines that commend itself to his judgment.

Mr. du Pont did not approve of this plan to segregate the copper-cooled development from the divisions and their large sales organizations, but in the end he accepted it. With the burden of the copper-cooled development placed in Dayton under Mr. Kettering's jurisdiction, and the car divisions cleared to proceed on standard water-cooled programs, I wrote on July 25, 1923, a memo of review to the members of the Executive Committee, from which I quote the following:

Two and a half years have elapsed since the reconstruction of General Motors commenced and in that time, due to the jam we have got into on account of the copper cooled, the position of our Chevrolet car has not made the progress that I think it should have made. Certainly every step that has been taken has been carefully considered and many reasons could be ascribed to this result and probably there would be some difference of opinion as to what really has contributed to the cause, but nevertheless the fact remains, and the object of this memorandum is to simply point out certain advantages that would accrue had we an intensively developed model at this time or what we can expect to gain by getting such a model at the earliest possible moment. Undoubtedly all these advantages, or certainly the most important ones would be available if the power plant was copper cooled as well as water cooled because I do not think that the real difference between the two designs would be material other than that the copper cooled would eliminate water which, if all other conditions were the same, would undoubtedly be a step in advance.

This memorandum was not a mere expression of regret for lost time but a preamble to a new program of advance with new designs for the water-cooled Chevrolet that would be put into competition in the low-price, high-volume market in accordance with the product plan of 1921.

The copper-cooled car never came up again in a big way. It just died out, I don't know why.[1] The great boom was on and meeting the demand for cars and meeting the competition with improved water-cooled car designs absorbed our attention and energies.

Mr. Kettering and his staff went on to their great achievements in creating and developing tetraethyl lead, high-compression engines, nontoxic refrigerants, the two-cycle diesel engine which was to enable General Motors to revolutionize the railroads, and innumerable other inventions, refinements, and developments which are everywhere to be found in automobiles, locomotives, airplanes, and appliances.

The significant influence of the copper-cooled engine was in what it taught us about the value of organized co-operation and co-ordination in engineering and other matters. It showed the need to make an effective distinction between divisional and corporate functions in engineering, and also between advanced product engineering and long-range research. The copper-cooled-engine episode proved emphatically that management needed to subscribe to, and live with, just the kind of firm policies of organization and business that we had been working on. Altogether, the experience was to have important consequences in the future organization of the corporation.

---

[1] Many years later the state of the art of the air-cooled engine improved to the point where application of its principles to automobiles became practicable. An example of such an engine made of aluminum is in the . . . Corvair built by Chevrolet.

STABILIZATION

THE CHANGE IN THE PRESIDENCY of General Motors in the spring of
1923, when Pierre S. du Pont resigned and I succeeded him, marked
the end of the first period of the modern corporation. Despite the
delay in the product program, the corporation in this period achieved
general stability, which at that time represented its greatest need. This,
in part, was made possible by the passing of the slump of 1920–21,
but the foundation of the achievement itself belongs to Mr. du Pont.
To him more than to any other individual must be assigned the credit
for rescuing the corporation in its time of need and guiding it into a
broad position of strength. It was when he recognized that the management of the corporation was again able to continue on its own
feet that he made his own decision to turn the operating leadership
over to the automobile men. He took this action in the following way.

An annual meeting of the shareholders took place on April 18,
1923, and elected a board of directors to hold office for the ensuing
year. The next day, April 19, the directors held an organization
meeting and re-elected the same officers, including Mr. du Pont as
president, and the standing committees, to serve for another term. Almost all members of the board thought that we were set for a year.
I certainly did. But it was not so.

On May 10, after a regular meeting, Mr. du Pont called a special
meeting of the board and after asking Mr. Mott to act as chairman,
presented his resignation as president of the corporation. Thereupon
the board adopted unanimously the following resolution:

> On motion duly made and unanimously carried, it was
> RESOLVED, that the resignation of Mr. Pierre S. du Pont as
> President be accepted, and it was further
> RESOLVED, that in accepting Mr. du Pont's resignation as
> President the Directors wish to place on record their apprecia-
> tion of the invaluable services that he has rendered the Corpora-
> tion during the past two and one-half years, and also

to recognize the sacrifices that he made in taking over the duties of the presidency. During his incumbency of this office the affairs of the Corporation have been brought to a high state of prosperity and the Directors wish to express deep regret that he has decided to retire from this office. They are gratified to know that he is not in any way to disassociate himself from the Corporation, but is to continue active participation in the direction of its affairs as Chairman of its Board of Directors.

The meeting then proceeded to the election of a president to fill the vacancy. Mr. du Pont nominated me and I was elected. Subsequently, I was also elected chairman of the Executive Committee. Although Mr. du Pont's resignation at that time was not expected, it had been understood when he took office that it would be for a limited time, and that during his term he would transfer many of his operating duties to vice presidents. He had in fact done so.

No one can appraise Mr. du Pont's conspicuous service to General Motors in the critical period in which he served as intimately as I can. I was very close to him throughout his entire presidency; we traveled together, we attended meetings together, and we counseled together on all the problems that arose. Mr. du Pont had come out of retirement to become head of a complex enterprise which was in financial difficulties, and one in which he had little practical experience. The enterprise was decimated by resignations, its market position was declining, and its management's faith in itself and the future of its opportunities was shaken. Yet the mere fact that Mr. du Pont was there at the head of the enterprise changed the psychology of the whole situation, so to speak. The banks were reassured; the organization's faith in its future was renewed; the shareholders were encouraged; all of us in the corporation determined not only to carry on but to capitalize the vast opportunity inherent in the very nature of our business, and in this we were inspired by our faith in the new and distinguished leadership of Mr. du Pont.

His administration was an active one for him. He withdrew from his home in Pennsylvania, just outside Wilmington, Delaware, in which he took pride and satisfaction, and divided his time between New York and Detroit in alternate weeks. He made frequent trips into the field to inspect the properties and to discuss problems that could be better evaluated on the spot. Days were spent in inspection and observation, nights in discussion; and even then it was hard to keep up with the problems. Mr. du Pont's administration might be called one of evaluation and construction. As a result we were able to identify the elements of the business and, through the process of much trial and many errors, to construct the foundation upon which the modern corporation has been built.

Mr. du Pont's administration adopted in principle a sound scheme of organization and in principle a sound approach to the product line. At the same time, system was introduced into accounting and finance. A most comprehensive incentive plan was developed by John J. Raskob and his former du Pont associate Donaldson Brown, and it was supplemented by an opportunity for the more important executives to participate in the financial gains of the business. The plan for executive participation known as the Managers Securities Plan (described in a later chapter) was made possible by Mr. du Pont's belief in the validity of a partnership relationship between shareholders and executives. Mr. du Pont also liquidated unprofitable divisions, such as Samson Tractor, and guided a vast financial reorganization that put the corporation on a sound and solid basis.

An administration may also be measured by the caliber of the men brought in or retained by it. In or associated with the corporation in one place or another in 1923 was a large number of men who were to make a mark in American industrial history. Some of them had already begun to make it. There were the Fisher brothers, led by their dean, Fred Fisher. In Anderson, Indiana, as factory manager of the Remy Electric Division, was young Charles E. Wilson, who would one day be president of the corporation and afterward Secretary of Defense of the United States. James D. Mooney was vice president in charge of General Motors' overseas business. Down at Dayton, in charge of Delco Light, was Richard H. ("Dick") Grant, who would guide Chevrolet's sales through the twenties, and so become the top salesman in the United States. The comptroller of the AC Spark Plug Division was Harlow H. Curtice, who would be president during the great post-Korea expansion of General Motors. There was William

S. Knudsen, who directed Chevrolet for some years before he, too, served as president of the corporation. John Thomas Smith was general counsel; he was later to serve on the Executive Committee, and I might say that his advice and influence in the corporation were of a very high order in moral and public-policy matters as well as in the law. The manager of manufacturing for Chevrolet was K. T. Keller, later to be president and chairman of the Chrysler Corporation. Albert Bradley, who would one day be chairman of General Motors, was then a young and important member of the Financial Staff. And so on; these and many others, together with those I have mentioned earlier—notably Charles S. Mott, Charles F. Kettering, John J. Raskob, Donaldson Brown, and John L. Pratt, the latter three of whom came from the du Pont organization—were a great team of experienced or promising automobile and financial men.

As to myself, I recognized that my election to the presidency of the corporation was a big responsibility and a business opportunity that comes to few. I resolved in my own mind that I would make any personal sacrifice for the cause, and that I would put forth all the energy, experience, and knowledge I had to make the corporation an outstanding success. General Motors has been for me a dedicated activity ever since, perhaps to a fault. My becoming president involved few changes in the activities for which I had been responsible as vice president in charge of operations. The work flowed on without a break. I became president under the auspicious fact that many of my basic views had become the accepted policy of the corporation. The period of development lay ahead.

But to Pierre S. du Pont must go the credit for the very survival of General Motors and for laying the foundation of its future progress.

8. Union Guys

No AUTOBIOGRAPHY of American business would be complete without something from the point of view of a union man; and the great days of American unions, it is generally agreed, were those between the middle 1930s when the Magna Charta of organized labor, the National Labor Relations Act, was enacted and the greatest of industrial union combinations, the Congress of Industrial Organizations (CIO), was formed until the Korean War and the postwar boom. In those early days there were the great, trail-breaking struggles, like the one in 1937 between the United Automobile Workers (UAW) and the Ford Motor Company's strikebreakers led by Harry Bennett's goon squad, by which organized labor established once and for all its right to exist and to bargain collectively without violent interference. In those days union leaders, their heads often literally bloodied in clashes with company strikebreakers, were heroes to all workers and to much of the nation at large. In those days, too, militant and responsible labor men like Walter P. Reuther (1907–70) and his stanch supporter Clayton W. Fountain, often had to divide their energies between fighting their capitalist bosses and fighting Communist party members within their own unions, who sought to bend the unions to Communist ends.

Fountain was born in 1910 in upstate Michigan; by his own account, his paternal grandfather had been "either a full-blooded Chippewa Indian or so close to it that you couldn't tell the difference." As a young man he went to Detroit to work on the Packard production line. Beginning in 1931, as the great Depression approached its nadir, he was out of work for two and a half years. Finally back at work, he was sacked by General Motors in 1936 for union activity. In 1937 he joined the Communist party, but—like so many other union men of his time—almost immediately became disillusioned and resigned. He was a delegate to the 1937 convention of the UAW and thereafter was deeply involved in union leadership struggles and took an active part in the General Motors strikes of 1939 and 1946. In 1946 he became associate editor of the official UAW newspaper, *United Automobile Worker*. In view of his status as a professional journalist and of the fact that he names no collaborator, he may be assumed to have written his reminiscences entirely by himself.

In the following account of Reuther's election to the presidency of the UAW at its convention at Atlantic City, New Jersey, in the spring of 1946, we catch the full flavor of this great—perhaps the greatest—union in its great days: the flamboyance of its rhetoric, the brawling rambunctiousness of its manners, the sharp tinge of ideology suffusing everything it said and did. We hear a discussion of militant strike tactics. We watch the Communists scheming for control and the incumbent union president (as Fountain sees it) "trumpeting the Communist Party line." We see a fist fight on the convention floor—over a question of ideology.

Today, almost all commentators are agreed, the huge unions have left their great days behind, having submerged themselves in an almost pure market orientation that apes that of their employers, and, through systematic escalation of their demands for increased wages and pension benefits, have become major contributory factors in domestic inflation and overseas depreciation of the dollar. If Daniel Bell's thesis as to "the end of ideology" is questionable when applied to American society as a whole, it is persuasive as regards the unions. Of course, the decline of ideology and the concomitant reduction of intramural fights have probably served to make the unions more effective representatives of their members in wage negotiations; but that gain is surely balanced to some extent by a loss of the unions' former role as an exciting and generally responsible force in our society.

BOARDWALK BALLET

THE 1946 UAW-CIO CONVENTION, which opened March 23 in Convention Hall at Atlantic City, was probably the most rugged and rambunctious gathering in the history of the union. It convened just ten days after the settlement of the hard-fought General Motors strike. Newspapermen came from far and wide, their pencils poised to report the impending bid of Walter P. Reuther for the presidency of the union. Few observers in the know doubted that the tireless redhead would run for the top spot.

Reuther's decision to make the race was not nailed down officially until a mass caucus was held on the evening of the opening day of the convention. But some of his closest supporters had been trying to smooth the way for the contest for some time. For one thing, they tried hard to neutralize the opposition of George Addes, who was top man in the enemy caucus. First they worked on some of the more competent non-Communist members of Addes's staff. The argument used on these people was that, if Addes would keep hands off while Reuther challenged [Roland J.] Thomas for the top spot, there was nothing to stop Addes from being second top man for a long time to come. That would be the sensible way to solidify the union and eliminate factionalism, with a minimum of political hatchet-work, our people argued. Some of the Addes guys agreed with this thinking and said they would try to get their man to accept the proposition.

Addes appeared to give this offer his serious consideration. Some Reuther people, including myself, were impressed with the way Addes

---

From *Union Guy,* by Clayton W. Fountain (Viking, 1949), pp. 187–98.

responded. His conduct during the GM strike had been almost above reproach. Little incidents cropped up to fan our hopes that he was ready to make a deal. One such episode happened at a meeting of the Top GM Negotiating Committee in Reuther's office during the strike. On that occasion, when Charles Beckman, a CP-line committee member from Fisher Local 45 in Cleveland, tried to apologize for the conduct of the UE-CIO during the GM strike, Addes responded quickly and explosively.

"To hell with the UE," Addes said and proceeded to dress Beckman down with a tongue-lashing. Events like these encouraged us to think that he might be contemplating a shift away from his Communist allies.

When the chips were down, however, Addes came out openly in support of Thomas for president. His apparent strategy had been to play along with our offer of a deal based on a Reuther-Addes team in order to insure that we would not groom a candidate to contest his position as secretary-treasurer. But finally it became evident that all bets were off, and we junked the notion of ever cutting a deal with Addes.

The boom to make Reuther president of the union was kicked off in Detroit on March 10, while the GM strike was still in progress, by a committee of presidents of seventeen large local unions. In its statement to the press, the committee put itself on record as follows:

> A large majority of the union's membership feels strongly the need for a change in the administration. . . . The membership feels the need for a change to carry out a vigorous, intelligent and progressive program in order to eliminate the factionalism which has divided our forces for several years. . . . We know and respect Reuther's refusal to devote time to any activity other than fighting and winning the GM strike. It will not, however, be necessary for him to divert his attention from the strike to a political campaign. His acceptance of the candidacy will make his election certain, without further effort on his part.

After declaring that "The incumbent president [Thomas] has perpetuated himself in office only by fostering rivalry between Reuther and Addes," the committee declared itself as favoring the re-election of Addes as secretary-treasurer. This was done to woo the support and votes of certain non-Communists in the Addes faction, even though by this time Addes had already publicly pledged his support to Thomas. There was still a powerful bloc of independent rank-and-file members in the union who were fed up with Thomas and would vote for a Reuther-Addes team, no matter what Addes himself said or did.

Campaigning to elect Walter Reuther president of the union was an exciting experience for most of our people. There had never before been a real contest for the office. Francis Dillon, first UAW president, had been appointed by William Green under the AFL charter in 1935. In 1936, at the South Bend convention, Homer Martin had been elected by acclamation under an agreement worked out by the leaders before the election was held. Martin had had no opposition in 1937 at Milwaukee. R. J. Thomas got in through a compromise in 1939 and was returned to office by acclamation, or with only token opposition, at each succeeding convention. The only really sharp political fight for power, after the upheaval that blew Martin into oblivion, had erupted in Buffalo in 1943, when Dick Leonard came within seventy votes of trouncing Addes for the job of secretary-treasurer. Now, for the first time in eleven years, the union that bragged so loudly of its militant democracy was about to engage in a serious contest for its presidency.

There was little time that winter to carry out an extensive campaign in the delegate elections conducted by the local unions. I went out to my local union to vote for a pro-Reuther slate but did no campaigning. In a few key areas, where the membership was heavily concentrated, we did get out some literature and hold meetings to rally votes for our candidates. The bulk of the locals were touched only lightly, if at all, by the vote-gathering activities directed by the higher councils of the power caucuses. Reuther followers were too deeply involved in the GM strike to give anything but secondary attention to politics. It was no secret, of course, that we believed the winning of the strike would help Reuther's candidacy more than anything we could do.

Before the convention opened, it was clear that the Addes-Thomas-Leonard caucus, brain-trusted by the Communist party, was going to pick on the General Motors strike as the key issue. The *Daily Worker* harped away at the charge that Reuther had "jumped the gun" in calling the strike, that he had kept the workers out too long, and that he had settled for too little. Commie puppets in the local unions picked up this line and echoed it across the land. R. J. Thomas himself, while never expressing open criticism of the strike on the floor of the convention, supported the Commie attacks when he told newspapermen in Atlantic City that the strike was called too early and settled too late. We countered that one by publishing direct quotes from press releases issued in Thomas's name all during the strike, in which he stated his complete agreement with the strike strategy and its conduct. When the campaign got really hot, I spent hours in an Atlantic City print shop getting out leaflets supporting Reuther.

Oddly enough, an open discussion of the merits of the strike never came up on the convention floor. This hurt Reuther's candidacy. We would have welcomed a free-for-all debate expressing the views of the top officers and the delegates with respect to the strategy and conduct of the strike. The Addes-Thomas-Leonard strategists and the Communists were afraid to risk the outcome of such a democratic discussion. With Thomas in the chair, the anti-Reuther forces controlled the agenda. Secure in their control of the convention machinery, they kept controversial committee reports off the floor before the elections. Reuther's powerful oratorical ability was his ace in the hole—and they knew it. So they steered clear of a showdown. Reuther was thus prevented from speaking on any important issue, let alone defending himself against the charges of lousing up the strike.

In an effort to shame the opposition into an open discussion of these charges, we published a stinging pamphlet challenging Thomas to debate Reuther. Thomas ducked the challenge, refused to match himself against Reuther on the platform. Attacking on another front, one of our delegates made a motion to hold a night session for the purpose of staging a debate between Thomas and Reuther. Addes was in the chair at the time. He ruled that the motion would involve changing the rules and would thus require a two-thirds majority to carry. After a flurry of hectic debate among a few delegates, the vote was taken. It was evident to those of us on the platform that the delegates standing up in favor of the motion had a clear majority, possibly a two-thirds majority. But Addes, ignoring scattered demands for a roll call, ruled that the motion had lost for lack of a two-thirds majority. Despite the fact that a majority of the delegates felt Thomas should meet Reuther in an open debate on the charges made against the conduct of the strike, the opposition was afraid to meet this test. This refusal of Thomas to face his opponent on the platform may have alienated enough democratically minded delegates to lose him the election.

Unable to dispute the popularity of Reuther's program for dynamic unionism extending beyond the bargaining table into the community, and afraid to face his forces in a free discussion of union issues on the floor, the Commies and their stooges worked overtime their favorite weapon of character assassination. They spread the lie that Reuther was plotting with David Dubinsky, head of the International Ladies' Garment Workers, and John L. Lewis to take the UAW into the AFL. To attempt to prove this absurd charge, they cited the fact that Dubinsky had contributed several thousand dollars to the GM strikers.

R. J. Thomas toyed with this fairy tale in his report to the convention, but did not express the accusation openly before the delegates.

"There is a man in the American Federation of Labor who, during our General Motors strike, gave money to the workers of General Motors," Thomas bellowed. "And I say to you quite frankly I have worried about that situation. That same man, during the fight in our union when this union ousted Homer Martin from the presidency, that same man gave twenty-five thousand dollars to whip the UAW-CIO. And that man is none other than Dave Dubinsky. . . . I say to you I don't believe that the Automobile Workers can be whipped from within any more than they can be whipped from without."

Thomas was trumpeting the CP line in a last desperate effort to bolster his faltering fortunes as a labor leader. On March 27 the *Daily Worker* ran an editorial which said: "The enthusiastic response of the UAW convention to the speech of President Murray [who had just addressed the convention] reflected the concern of the overwhelming majority of the delegates over the threat to the unity of the CIO and its largest affiliate. This threat comes from those within the CIO who are allied to the Lewis, Dubinsky, Woll clique in the AFL."

The editor of the *Daily Worker,* in typical Communist fashion, had hung his editorial on the peg of a single paragraph in Murray's speech, which said: "Oh, I had a committee come over to see me in Washington last week and they said some people in New York were interested in splitting up this organization. I said, 'I don't give a damn who those people are in New York, they can't do it, they are not going to do it; whether they are alleged leaders of the American Federation of Labor makes no difference—they are not going to do it!'" Out of these two sentences the *Daily Worker* wove a fabric to disguise Reuther as a devil designing to take the UAW into the AFL. Of course the editor also heaped his blessings on Thomas and Addes.

It was difficult, as it always is in such strained political situations, to judge the impact of Murray's speech. There is no doubt that the word of the president of the CIO carries considerable weight with the average convention delegate. That the workers do not, however, regard the presidency of the CIO as a shrine of infallibility was demonstrated in 1940 when the Lewis endorsement of Willkie fell on deaf ears so far as the rank and file was concerned. Nevertheless, the UAW-CIO delegates in 1946 greeted Murray with an ovation, received his remarks with rapt attention, and applauded him with another ovation.

His every word was weighed for political implications. Would he endorse Thomas? Would he frown on Reuther's candidacy for the top job? What would he have to say about the GM strike and its relation to the over-all strategy of the CIO in the recent wage increase battle?

In his soft Scotch burr, gesturing dramatically and building involved sentences up to climactic conclusions, Murray led the delegates through a long oratorical hallway to the issue of the GM strike. Then, in angry, thunderous tones, he blasted at the rumor that he had had a hand in the decision of the President's fact-finding board to recommend only nineteen and a half cents for the GM strikers. He said:

> Another very erroneous rumor got afloat, due to a statement attributed to a high officer of the General Motors Corporation,

that I, Philip Murray, had done the detestable thing of going to the members of the GM Fact-Finding Board for the purpose of having that Board allegedly reduce the so-called recommended wage increase from 24 per cent to nineteen and a half cents, the contention being that Murray went to the Board for that purpose because he, Murray, did not believe, according to these rumors, that he could get a 24 per cent wage increase in the steel industry.

That, of course, was a diabolical, detestable lie, manufactured out of whole cloth by a high officer of the General Motors Corporation, and circulated throughout the union for the purpose of creating division among CIO workers. I detested that ugly rumor because it attacked the integrity of the President of the CIO and it also questioned the integrity of the members of the GM Fact-Finding Board—positively untrue, wholly preposterous and circulated by a defamer of defamers for the purpose of injuring the Congress of Industrial Organizations.

From this climax, he coasted down into an outline of the CIO program and purposes. Then he built his way upward again toward a carefully worded appraisal of the UAW-CIO political situation. Treading a tightrope between the different hopes and expectations of the factions that hung on his words, he admonished the delegates to guard the unity of their union. Nearing the end of his speech, he teetered ever so slightly and brought joy to the Thomas backers with these words:

Before I close, I wish to express also my appreciation to the officers of your International Union for the splendid spirit of support they have manifested towards me personally in the conduct of my work as President of the Congress of Industrial Organizations. That goes to Secretary Addes, Vice-President Reuther, Vice-President Frankensteen, and to this great big guy for whom I have a distinct fondness, the President of your Union, R. J. Thomas . . .

Thomas backers, reaching for straws to prop up their man, clutched happily at this "distinct fondness" for the "great big guy" and almost beat fence-riding delegates to death with it for the balance of the convention. The fact that Murray was distinctly fond of Thomas, they argued in a frenzy, was unquestionable proof that the CIO chief wanted R. J. voted back into the top UAW-CIO spot. In our camp, we felt that a few wavering delegates might slide over to Thomas as a result of Murray's quaint bestowal of a weak blessing on the incumbent president, but it did not worry us. We had estimated the support for Reuther and believed ourselves in possession of a slender but safe majority. Our job was to hold that majority and to work faithfully to add to it.

The Reuther forces were greatly outnumbered in the convention by the political workers for Thomas. Almost the entire International staff was present to campaign in accordance with the preference of various department heads. Reuther had the certain support of his own staff and that of seven regional directors; they could beat the bushes for stray votes. Two regional directors were on the fence, after a fashion, and their staffs were divided in loyalty between Reuther and Thomas.

Members of some minor organizations were working on Reuther's behalf, too. A few Socialists, most of them key leaders in local unions, were intensely active in the pro-Reuther caucus. Another group with considerable influence—but not nearly the weight attributed to it by the Communist press—was the Association of Catholic Trade Unionists. The ACTU is concentrated in Detroit, but has a few outposts scattered around the country. Trained and directed by the Catholic Church to build democratic unionism and to fight Communism within labor, the ACTU people have earned the violent hatred of the CP. Nor is the party the only group that looks with suspicion at the ACTU; most orthodox leftists, remembering historical incidents when the Catholic Church has fought on the side of reaction, do not trust the Catholic trade unionists. My own opinion is that this mistrust is out of place. From personal experience with ACTU unionists, I have come to believe that their loyalty to the union is unquestionable. Speaking for myself only, I would say that the ACTU has made an important contribution to the ousting of Communists and fellow travelers from the UAW-CIO leadership.

On Thomas's side, there were the staffs of the president, the secretary-treasurer, one vice-president, and nine regional directors. In addition, the Communists were there in force, from New York, Detroit, and all points of the compass. They threw in every stunt, gag, and trick they could think up to influence the voting. Not the least in their bag of tricks was the importation of glamorous female comrades who worked the swing shift in hotel rooms at night to convert delegates to the Thomas cause. Some of these babes got taken in by smarter and lustier delegates on our side, who pretended they wanted to be converted—both for the joy of it and for the practical purpose of wasting the time of the CP Mata Haris.

Intimidation was another tactic used widely by the Commies. There was one particular case that I personally know of in which the CP pressure boys browbeat a zealous Reuther follower into switching his vote. The delegate was from the deep South. I had made his acquaintance a couple of years earlier at a regional summer school in the mountains of Tennessee. He was a bright young Negro, unschooled, but filled with instinctive intelligence, eager to work for the cause of labor. I talked to him early in the convention and he swore that Reuther was his man forever. About a day before the voting took place I happened to notice that a Negro member of the opposition staff had that delegate in a corner and was really laying down the law to him. I hung around until the confab broke up, then got the delegate off to one side. Believe it or not, he just wouldn't talk to me about Reuther. His eyes were sad and full of misery. Nothing I could say would induce him to confide his troubles to me or to indicate what had been said to him. Later, during the roll calls, he voted straight down the line for the Thomas slate. Thomas Starling, Director of Region Eight, told me later that he had found out that the delegate had switched because of threats of physical violence.

At another point in the convention a fist fight broke out on the floor while Local 669 was voting on a vice-presidency. R. J. Thomas, acting under power granted to him by the rules adopted earlier in the convention, appointed a committee to investigate intimidation of delegates. In the months that followed, this committee became a kind of traveling sideshow. Thomas and Addes sent it into pro-Reuther locals to harass and bluff the local officers. It spent many thousands of dollars of union funds for expenses and was still going strong when the pro-Reuther majority at the 1947 convention stopped its activities. Once, while reporting to the International Executive Board, the committee admitted coyly that it had discovered one delegate who had been intimidated. Pressed for details, a committee spokesman said that a delegate from Local 669 had said that he was pro-Reuther but had been pressured into voting for Thomas!

The roll-call election for the office of president of the UAW-CIO on March 27, 1946, was probably as tense and dramatic as any political crisis that will ever occur in a labor union. A delegate from Local 1, carrying one vote (for the workers of the Buchanan Steel Products Corporation in Buchanan, Michigan), cast his vote for Reuther. Thereafter, the voting went down the roll call from local to local for several hours. Whenever a large local voted in a block for either candidate, partisans burst into long, loud cheers. As the cheering subsided, the voice of the chief teller droned the number of the next local on the list. Hundreds of people sat hunched over their roll-call tally sheets, figuring furiously to compute the accumulating totals to three digits past the decimal point.

Suddenly a group of Reuther supporters surrounding their candidate on the platform picked him up, hoisted him to their shoulders, and began shouting hoarsely with joy. He had a mathematical majority—even if the rest of the locals voted against him, he was in! The largest union in the world had finally elected a leader in a close and hard-fought contest waged on the basis of programs and philosophies. Flash bulbs illuminated the platform as press photographers worked their shutters madly. A few Thomas backers muttered that it was all a trick to influence the locals which were still to vote. But when the adding machines stopped clicking Reuther had won by the scanty margin of 124 votes out of 8,765 votes cast—each vote representing a hundred dues-paying members.

George Addes, as acting chairman, introduced the new president to the convention. The delegates erupted into a wild uproar of applause. I stood at the end of the press table, weary and with all my nerves tightened by emotion, as Reuther began to speak. Tears ran down my face and trickled onto my shirt, and mine were not the only wet eyes in the hall.

"There is much work to be done in the world," Reuther said, in tones vibrant with feeling. "We won the war. The task now is to win the peace. We have the job of mobilizing America, the labor and progressive forces, so that we can be certain that there will be just as determined a fight on the home front to make the peace secure as was demonstrated by our boys on the battlefront to make victory possible.

"I stand here humble—humble at the great task that you have given me. Let us go home when this convention is over motivated by the same spirit that motivated us back in 1936 and 1937 when the only thing you could get for belonging to the union was a cracked head. Let's be motivated by the simple loyalty we have in our hearts. Let's be guided by the sincere desire to place the union's welfare above any personal consideration or any personal differences."

The end of the fighting, however, was not yet in sight. [Secretary-treasurer] George Addes was re-elected by a unanimous vote. Then, out of the bigness of their hearts, the unpredictable delegates blessed R. J. Thomas with a vice-presidency. On the next ballot, since Dick Frankensteen had two months earlier announced that he did not choose to run, Richard T. Leonard defeated John W. Livingston, the Reuther candidate, for the second vice-presidency. In the regional elections for International Executive Board members, all incumbents but one were returned. Melvin Bishop was replaced in Region One (Detroit) by Emil Mazey, a leader of Briggs Local 212, who at the time was an Army sergeant in the far Pacific and did not even know that he was a candidate. The Briggs delegates, who held the balance of power in Region One, ignored all persuasions and used their power to get the Reuther caucus to approve Mazey's candidacy.

Some people said that in the election of Reuther as president we had won a battle but lost the war. He was surrounded by three hostile top officers and could count on only seven of the International Executive Board members, out of a total of eighteen, to support his policies. It looked like tough going until the next convention. The Communists would not give up. There was to be no rest for those of us who wanted to build the UAW-CIO into a force pledged to fight for security and liberty, against both the commissars and the capitalists.

9. New Dealer to Businessman

DAVID E. LILIENTHAL was born in 1899 in Morton, Illinois; graduated in 1920 from DePauw University (where he was an amateur boxer) and in 1923 from Harvard Law School; practiced law in Chicago for the next eight years; and then, after a short stint on the Wisconsin Public Service Commission, served memorably as one of the leading lights of President Franklin D. Roosevelt administrations—as a director of the Tennessee Valley Authority (1933–41) and as its chairman (1941–46). From his capacity as a leader of the New Deal's most categorically socialistic undertaking, he gained a reputation as a philosophical opponent of free enterprise. Then, after a further term of public service as first chairman of the United States Atomic Energy Commission (1946–50), he quit government and went into private business himself. He became a consultant to the investment-banking firm of Lazard Frères & Company, and that firm's senior partner, André Meyer, set him the task of taking the lead in reorganizing a small, troubled company in which Lazard had a large stake, called Minerals Separation North American Corporation. Lilienthal replaced its longtime president, the nonagenarian Dr. Seth Gregory, as chief executive, helped guide the company through a series of mergers (with Attapulgus Clay Company and Edgar

Brothers, among others), and saw its stock become a popular market favorite. As part of his compensation, Lilienthal was granted stock options; by 1960, he held over 40,000 shares in the company and the shares were selling at more than $25, so Lilienthal was not just a businessman but a millionaire businessman.

Not surprisingly, this change of career direction prompted some of Lilienthal's old New Deal associates to accuse him of being a turncoat, and, since he is a man of moral sensitivity, the charge caused him some anguish. He argued that he had never been "against" free enterprise, only against its abuses. His book *Big Business: A New Era* (Harper & Brothers, 1953) is a paean to big business and its accomplishments and possibilities in the cause of bettering the general human lot.

At any rate, Lilienthal's background, combined with his sensitive yet combative character, gave him a fresh view of business and the moral dilemmas attendant upon engaging in it. He entered it like a man—a celebrated and accomplished man—from another planet; on his first visit to the floor of the New York Stock Exchange he found it as strange, mysterious, and fascinating as a zoo. In the following passages from his journals, about his first big business venture, we see him chafing at the loss of the status that public service had conferred on him; worrying about being "sold out" or about others thinking that he was; suffering for the first time the inconveniences and frustrations of business travel; experiencing the thrill of being at last hot on the trail of business success; and, finally, having the satisfaction of succeeding in business and gaining the unfeigned respect of his new colleagues. Needless to say, few people enter business with the advantages Lilienthal had, and few indeed have the luck to hit a bonanza on stock options (which many regard as a mere tax loophole). But besides making money, Lilienthal brought to the practice of business a unique perspective as fresh as morning dew, from which others may learn.

MAY 12, 1951

Week in New York—the first round in the effort to learn how to be a banker.

The big event of the week was a real case of funk, which seems normal enough, I suppose, when starting out to do something you are skeered about, because you don't know how you'll do. . . .

Tuesday afternoon, for two and a half hours, [Albert J.] Hettinger, a partner, gave me a long and intensely interesting review of the firm of Lazard Frères. This was reassuring—a sense of history and continuity about the business itself and revealing about "Hett" himself, a scholarly, relaxed man, shrewd as hell and competent, utterly devoted to André Meyer for his business ability but especially for his character.

Thursday afternoon George Murnane [another Lazard man] spent an hour and a half with me. "I've got a world of confidence in you," he said as he left, "but I know how unhappy you are right now." Very considerate and comprehending man. They all want to "make something of me," and though they have somewhat inconsistent ideas about how this happens, it helps.

Lunch, for two hours on Wednesday with André Meyer and Pierre David-Weill, the principal owners of the firm here and in Paris, and with a big stake in the London house. I said: you advised me to be in New York if I wanted to engage in business; I'm here, what do I do? How do we get down out of the general—"how does the world look to you in Washington?"—to concrete situations?

We took up some examples, especially Bob Uihlein's flirting with me to see how the Schlitz Brewing Company (if they should get down to cases with me) would fit into the Lazard picture and mine. From

From *The Journals of David E. Lilienthal,* Vol. III: *Venturesome Years, 1950–1955,* by David E. Lilienthal (Harper & Row, 1966), pp. 158–59, 164–67, 186, 197–98, 232, 244, 249–50, 348–51, 526–27, 542–43, 590–91.

this I learned that one of the things Pierre wants of me—André too, but less so—is to bring new people into the range of Lazard's influence and possible services in a financial sense. Whether I can actually do this, without huge luck, seems doubtful, but one thing is clear: I can't make my future there depend on that. Whether they will get me into the grist of things that they work on, or put me onto things they themselves already have a finger in—on this hinges my prospects in the next trial months (to Jan. 1) and in longer perspective.

André discouraged the "consulting retainer" idea with outsiders for me; I'm not so sure. I can see that it means nothing much to them as a firm; but I certainly have to do some tall hedging at this point.

During the week lunched with Bernard Baruch (who has aged a great deal since I saw him six months ago) and the banker, Thomas McKittrick (with him Edward Love, a senior vice president of Chase National).

Getting up a list of names of people I ought to get in touch with, or renew acquaintances, people who might have ideas that fit into the Lazard picture. I do know a very great number of people, when I sit down to write their names down; in business, I mean. But most of them are ruled out—like Charley Thomas of Monsanto or Oliver Buckley of Bell—because their businesses are huge ones with well established financing channels; besides, says André, corporate officers of large companies are very much like civil servants—meaning they have so many people to whom they are responsible and who must consent to their action that the idea of enterprise is not feasible for them; whereas the owners of capital or business (like the Uihleins, or the Houghtons of Corning) can deal on an entrepreneurial basis. . . .

MAY 24, 1951
44 WALL STREET, NEW YORK

Looks as if I am in the minerals business. In a small way, that could become a big way. Anyway, it is something specific at last, after a year of vagueness.

Have just returned from my first visit with the fabulous Dr. Gregory, president of Minerals Separation North American Corporation. We got along fine, reiterated what he had said to Jim Adams of Lazard, that he welcomed my coming into the picture. Remarkable man: 93 years old, has very recently had two major operations from which he has completely recovered. Has a fine head, a full gray neat beard, and the shrewdest pair of blue eyes I have seen in a long time.

The office of the corporation gives about the most spectacular view of New York harbor I have ever seen. In an old building right on the Battery, at 11 Broadway. Just below the window is the old aquarium, scene of childhood visits to the fish; the whole busy to-and-fro of the harbor lies right out there and you can practically touch the Statue of Liberty herself. But the office is an old-fashioned one, completely untouched (including the help) by anything that has happened in 40 years. Made me grin to myself contrasting it with my Washington office in the American Security Building, or the one I had with AEC, except that in this funny old office this old wizard, with hardly a lifted finger, has been turning in a fortune in royalties. His patent on copper ore separation brought in $13½ million from John Ryan, the old copper king, before the patents expired, and the present patents on potash and phosphate separation bring in half a million of net a year, with prospects for the future bright.

My interest, of course, is in the process for concentrating low-grade iron ore by a flotation process they have developed and tried out in a pilot plant operation. I will start digging into it right away, beginning with a meeting with Mead, secretary of the company, this afternoon. May want to travel up to Michigan and to Lakeland, Florida (where their lab is) and then see if I can figure some way of beginning negotiation with some big companies, like M. A. Hanna or U.S. Steel, for a joint venture in building a plant using the process. This is either not worth bothering with at all or it is very big.

MAY 31, 1951
44 WALL STREET, NEW YORK

Had an hour with Dr. Gregory—11 to 12.

His conclusion was that I should do anything my business judgment prompted me to do about the iron ore thing, and that he would do nothing without consulting with me about it first. This was a pretty broad "vote of confidence" from him.

He is "fully satisfied" that the iron ore flotation process is a real success, and that it is the best in the field.

I asked whether he was averse to a joint venture with others in which we put in the flotation patent plus a plant as our contribution. He said definitely not. Anything I thought workable was all right with him. . . .

(Later)

New York has really taken me today. Stepped out this morning to a sight that made me gasp—the great towers of mid-town New York, the most glamorous bitch of all the cities man has ever raised as a monument to his imagination, greed, sense of beauty, lechery, and gregariousness. Then I had a good day in business, companionable, full of the fencing and test of wit, the personal decision and the excitement of the game of money-making. After everyone left tonight, I wandered down along the waterfront just a few blocks from my office. There I saw the tugs, smelled the strange mingling of roasting coffee, stale beer from the waterfront bars, and the whiff of the sea, which is, I suppose, the most potent and most disturbing smell in all the world.

Then I came back to the hotel just in time to see the glow of sunset over Central Park, on a warm, friendly, city night, when everyone is out.

The day was an important one in giving me the beginning of a sense of confidence. I could feel the blood circulating through me again, as I talked to old Dr. Gregory about iron ore separation, or with André Meyer and his partner Jim Adams, about a consulting contract to look into the iron ore flotation process, and what could be done with it. It is like learning to walk after a bad accident or a long illness, I suppose. At first you have to *think:* move the right foot, move the left foot, etc. Then you are walking without thinking, and then, once more, walking is something one does with unconsciousness and utter confidence. This latter state, as to business, has yet to come, but I had the first touch of it today, after a year of having to discipline myself to keep from running—not literally, of course, but in a real sense.

What came out of the day was that Dr. Gregory is all for me, much to my satisfaction and the surprise and relief of the Lazard people; people are "afraid" of the old man. Adams said Mead, the old man's eyes and legs, reported after our last meeting that the Dr. liked and trusted me more than anyone whom he had seen in years. We got along even better today, meeting alone. I fired a series of simple questions at him, which he answered beautifully, but with decreasing vigor as the hour wore on. He looked his age today at the end of the hour, but he certainly is a shrewd and interesting old man. He concluded by saying: "As to all these matters you ask about, you have had more experience than I have had; whatever you decide to do is all right with me; consider yourself in charge of the iron ore process."

If he sticks to that, things should not be too bad, but he may change his mind—he *is* terribly old and infirm—and the corporation is in bad shape and needs a great deal of activation. It is earning *net* nearly a million dollars a year before taxes, with no risk whatever, which is not a minor operation. And this it is doing with no management whatever, no driving, no one in charge. Fantastic. The number of opportunities that must be all over the place, not developed.

JUNE 21, 1951

NEW YORK

André came in, beaming as I have not seen him, ever, extending his hand. "The Minerals Separation matter is settled; the report from the meeting was that the word of your taking hold was greeted, from Dr. Gregory on down, as if China had suspended shooting in Korea." So I am in business at last. André explained that even if the ore separation matter does not succeed there is no reason why I should not have the company and its one and a half million dollars of surplus to work with on other things; "and other things will come, just you see."

JULY 24, 1951

WASHINGTON

. . . Dinner at the Cosmos Club, in the garden. Ran into Dave Coyle and Lowell Mellett.[1] Lowell kept remarking on how *"healthy you look and young; is that the way it goes, getting out of public service and going down the path of private enterprise?"* Rather a re-

[1] Coyle, a writer and economist, held several Federal agency positions in the 1930s and '40s; Mellett was the former editor of the Washington *Daily News,* and administrative assistant to President Roosevelt.

proach that I look healthy and happy, which I sure am. Then Coyle said he had heard rumors that I was making money, etc., and therefore I had gone to the dogs. I am very fond of Lowell and Dave and admire them greatly, and I didn't take this as more than what it was, a bit of kidding. But they had better keep it that way. . . .

OCTOBER 5, 1951
NEW YORK

. . . The big news of the day . . . was advancing Minerals Separation a bit farther. Yesterday was a dismal one, for having served notice that I would not go farther without a stock option, Jim Adams convinced me that this could not be done now.

André bowled me over with his concern about protecting my interest, which I think is honestly his chief concern at this point. He disagreed that the stock option matter should be put over until the company was going along under the new management, on the grounds that the owners would or might say, later, "Why should we give Lilienthal all this stock? We're doing all right now." He wanted it all in a single package. All in all I found him most friendly and keen. I have been having doubts again about the Wall Street business and this helped greatly.

OCTOBER 19, 1951
LEAVING NEW YORK BY TRAIN

Rough time. Had to wait to see André, couldn't make my plane, managed to get out to the airport in the Friday night crush to find that there wasn't even a waiting list for a place until Saturday A.M. Then a taxi back to Penn Station in time to stand in a huge crowd of my fellow countrymen and finally board the 7:30 (at 7:50, of course). Nothing to eat, but the line waiting in the diner is longer than my appetite. No seats in the parlor car, which I don't really mind. But it doesn't look like any food, and an after-midnight arrival.

But a rugged day in every way. Didn't sleep well last night—had a third-floor room on the street. [Joseph] Volpe and I talked like mad all afternoon getting our report in shape, getting the Minerals Separation story ready for consideration by the London stockholders. He and I could do a good job on that bunch of antiques. We might have to get rid of the 23-year-old "protégé"—Adams says she is quite a gal. That old bearded doctor, he is a wonderful story.

Standing in the station, or riding pell-mell from here to there this evening, I had the strangest relaxed feeling, a feeling of love of country, of people. Curious how it is. Sometimes so many, many people, in throngs, is oppressive. Today it was quite otherwise. . . .

OCTOBER 28, 1951
SUNDAY
AT HOME

Perspective. I keep saying that this is what we need most of all. But maintaining it, in my own personal affairs, is something I am having trouble sustaining.

But what I really *want* is to try to *understand*. To try to understand those things in the world that, to me, seem most important to understand. The movement of events, today's events, fitted into the texture of the past, measured against what may come.

I have long felt that it takes experience, action, being in the middle of moving things, really to understand and to explain and persuade and teach. That's the source of my impatience with most academic people. They have the opportunity, the function, the mental equipment, the time; they lack being in the middle of the going concern, and so what they come up with so often lacks validity.

Businessmen, on the other hand, and most administrators, are in the middle of things, but they lack the time or the desire to try to put things together. It is hard enough to get through the next day, the next appointment, the next Congressional hearing, or the next financial reporting period.

What I am reaching for, perhaps, is to have my cake and eat it, too, but in a way that is not wholly senseless nor futile. That is, I can have enough actual contact with the affairs of business to keep a sense of reality, or develop one. How otherwise can I explain the pleasure I get in visiting a copper mine or talking to operators of an electric furnace, or a coal research project, or watching how André Meyer or George

Murnane work? I want to continue to do this. It puts real flesh on the bones of how things actually happen, how they work, what they look like. It provides the episodal, or anecdotal, or illustrative substance without which understanding is most difficult, and communication and persuasion and teaching out of the question.

But along with that I want to be free enough (of time, responsibility, etc.) to think and write about what these things mean, free enough to read outside the immediate field of interest. This requires not taking a big "status" full-time job (the absence of which I know makes me vaguely unhappy). By this I mean being a "consultant," a kind of economic free-lance. But "status" would tie me down much more than I am now tied down, and what I would gain in feeling "attached" I would more than lose, I fear, by confinement.

DECEMBER 8, 1952
HOME

What is it that Wall Street investment bankers do for their money? Well, I have certainly had my eyes opened, as to the amount of toil, sweat, frustrations, problems—yes, and tears—that has to be gone through. The most recent is the registration statement in connection with the marketing of Filtrol stock. If everyone who has something to sell had to be as meticulous and detailed in his statements about what he is selling as those who offer stock in the market are now, under the "Truth in Securities" law, darn little would be sold, in time to be useful at least.

I was to have dinner with André Meyer and Jim Adams last evening, to discuss the future of Attapulgus [Clay Company]. About six André caught me on the phone to say that the entire evening had to be given over to a powwow (part of it on the long-distance phone with the West Coast associates) talking over questions concerning the revised SEC registration statement. Those fellows out there, particularly the lawyers, have been working night and day, *and* all day Sundays, just as people have been working here, for weeks now. And the responsibility assumed is considerable. I am signing the registration statement, as a director of Filtrol, but not knowing too much about these things, I must pretty well take the word of responsible cosigners. But it is all a new picture of a sector of business about which I have known only, heretofore, from the Government side.

DECEMBER 20, 1952
WOODLAND RISE, REDDING RIDGE, CONNECTICUT

I wanted the experience of private business and I am certainly getting it, with the trimmings.

A week ago yesterday I took the sales figures given me by the management of Attapulgus, as forecast for 1953. They were considerably lower than had been forecast for 1952, even lower in results than achieved in 1952—which went into the doldrums in the last quarter. André came into my office (he'd had them overnight) and he was in a lather. I'd never seen a man more upset, or who expressed his distress and chagrin in such an extreme way. I had myself been disappointed with the estimates. I had sent them to him saying they seemed "conservative." He said they were not only bad in the sense that they indicated a soggy business (in which case we had all been misled and stupid) but a management that was more interested in justifying its estimates than in making a hard effort to do a bang-up aggressive job.

I had to admit, to myself, that he was right; but fear that this sort of scolding would be repeated until I would lose *my* temper, as I had already lost my taste for the whole business—this fastened itself in my mind, and I couldn't get it quite out the *whole* weekend. If you ever saw a man who had lost his peace of mind, I was that guy last weekend, with a feeling of "to hell with the whole idea" strong in the fore. Along with it, though, was a feeling that if I ever got firmly in the saddle of the new company, I could work it out. Not by following André's advice that I hammer these fellows and make them understand what's what (he was quite intemperate on this line) but in my own way, which is different, perhaps too vague and easy-going, but which has been fairly effective in other managerial crises.

Great doubts came over me. "What am I doing here?" Thoughts of alternatives. Mental pictures of walking into André's office and telling them all what they could do with this clay. And so on. I was sorry for Helen to have to put up with me in this frame of mind.

Monday I went to Philadelphia. Streander[2] had been out all last week, pretty depleted by the rapid turn of events; a rather frail man anyway. I started in on the estimates, making a speech to the effect that they seemed defeatist to me, and not the mark of a company that thought it was going places. There were the usual explanations, some of them not unreasonable. But after wearing away at it, alternatively expressing my own conviction that we could do much better, and trying to explain that a budget estimate is not a contract nor an estimate of what *surely* can be attained, the clouds began to roll back, and by Wednesday the sales manager walked in with new estimates, representing an increase of about 15 percent over the earlier figure.

Then I explored the question of expense savings, and found some that had not been taken into account, i.e., some automatic packaging machinery that would save $75,000 a year in labor costs (and eliminate a very dusty and unpleasant chore for men to handle); then I asked about prices, should some of them be increased, if controls were taken off. Well, by Thursday late I came home with new figures; yesterday André and Jim Adams thought they were "fine." Now we have to make them come true. But it was a *week*.

My purpose in this Attapulgus venture is, of course, to make a good deal of money. But there is another purpose, and one that really induced me to try the role of businessman before I really believed any such opportunity as this one was more than a come-on.

The real reason, or a chief reason, is a feeling that my life wouldn't be complete, living in a *business* period—that is, a time dominated by the business of business—unless I had been active in that area. What I wanted (I write as if this were in the long-time past, whereas in fact it is current, and only dates in its origins to less than three years ago) was to be an observer of this fascinating activity that so colors and affects the world's life, but not an observer from without (as a writer, teacher) but from the arena itself. I still have this feeling, and when I get low and glad to chuck the whole thing (as I have from time to time), the sustaining part is that even the bumps and sore spots are experience within the business world.

[2] L. R. Streander had been president of the old Attapulgus Clay Company. He became president of the new Attapulgus Minerals & Chemicals, and I became board chairman.

I've had a number of careers; why one more? If I am collecting careers, why not become a trapeze artist or a fight manager, too; because a man wants to see how the world moves, does he have to be part of everything he finds interesting? There is something nonsensical about the craving to be in on everything that looks interesting.

Perhaps part of the answer is in the picture I have of myself as wanting to interpret my times. That is the kind of "memoir" I'd like to write. And to do this, about a time when business is so important, and an understanding of men of business so essential, the thought seems to be that you must associate with them, get to know all kinds of the species, and yourself share the life, or what you say won't be authentic.

Then, too, I want to be able to make a valid *comparison* of the managers of business enterprises—their tensions, their motivations, etc.—with the managers of public, governmental enterprises, and this requires actual experience in the business world comparable to my experience in government.

I don't kid myself that I will ever be accepted as a businessman, not after those long years when I wore horns, in the opinions of businessmen outside the Tennessee Valley, at least. Even my Big Business book [*Big Business: A New Era*] won't admit me to the lodge; and in it (as distinguished from the articles) I rather rubbed in things that will stick in the craw of many businessmen, such as extolling organized labor (rather than accepting it as a necessary evil) or saying good words about the new expanded role of Government arising out of the New Deal, or the frequent adoring references to TVA. . . .

JUNE 30, 1954
60 SUTTON PLACE

These past two days have confirmed so clearly the growing conviction that I have found a new kind of satisfaction and, in a sense, fulfillment, in a business career. I really never felt that the "consultant" thing was being a businessman, or engaging in the realities of a life of business. Too remote from the exercise of judgment and decision that, in running public enterprises, I found, alternately, so interesting, exciting, frustrating, and on the whole so deeply satisfying.

But in the new enterprise I am helping to build, I am beginning to find a repetition on a quite different scale, and with quite different goals and motivations, I suppose, of the joy of building something, that I found in the TVA and AEC, particularly the TVA.

In this company, as we are evolving it, there are so many of the elements of fun. I might try to set some of them down, tired as I am—it is now almost 11 P.M. and I have had two long and hard days.

I started with almost nothing, in this process of building. The newspapermen in the earliest days of TVA used to say that "TVA is something that Dave Lilienthal carries around in his briefcase"; that was almost literally true, too. And it was certainly true with old, broken-down, antiquated Minerals Separation North American Corporation.

The building of the business began with a theme—a kind of principle—and the theme has been working out to a remarkable degree as I envisioned it. A lot of this is luck, but luck or not, there it is, a case example of building upon a "central and unifying idea."

The story includes its prime example of what not to do—the old Minerals Separation company, without a pension system, without communication or confidence between the central office and the people who were doing the work. Litigious. Depending upon patents alone.

It has a financial side: acquisition, mergers, stock issues, proxy statements, the methods of financing internally and by bank loans, laying the groundwork for making it a "public" company and going to the public with a stock issue, etc. The story includes the way stock prices are made, the silly and almost childlike basis upon which grown-up men decide when a stock should be bought, and at what price—a kind of burlesque of the Wall Street wiseacre.

The merger with Edgar, a family business that had gone to the dogs, then was rejuvenated by the desperately hard work of a few young men; then the merger with Minerals, the combining of forces, the process of negotiating a basis of agreement, the great rise in the price of their stock (from 8 to 33 in a few months, on the strength of the merger).

The accession of Wright Gary, and how he left Filtrol. The breath of fresh air when a real man comes in. The drive and energy and imagination; the nights and days (in the lab until 2 A.M. night after night); and finally the beginning of a new business.

The careful working out of procedures so Edgar might *know* their costs. The discussion, by me, of why higher prices may be the wrong answer; the importance of remembering the public interest as well as our own private interest, in increasing production at lower costs and consequently lower prices.

Health hazards, union problems, incentives to executives; the growing evaluation of the importance of research.

And a great many *pictures*, not the least being that around the table the last two days—all the elements of a successful enterprise being represented there, in terms of interesting and capable and decent men —men different as different can be, but each representing, in his person, some of the elements necessary, and some of the many human traits of temperament and inclination often very different, but capable of being put together into agreement and harmony and action, through leadership.

It will be quite a story.

AUGUST 12, 1954
60 SUTTON PLACE

As we (Ferd Eberstadt, Jim Adams, and I) got into our car to leave the Minerals & Chemicals Executive Committee meeting at Metuchen today, Ferd (not one who is easily satisfied in business matters) said: "That was a sweet meeting; that was one of the best business meetings I have ever attended in my life. *What* a group of fellows!"

That pretty well says it. As Jim said: "That's the way business should always be—but isn't."

We made decisions, rather than sweep the difficult or touchy ones under the rug, where they might, hopefully, be forgotten or perhaps just disappear on their own. I knew that Jim Adams is a good and experienced management man, but I never fully appreciated how good until today. When he saw an organization chart that represented a deferring of a decision by calling someone a "Coordinator," he would say: "This won't work. It won't work for three months or six months. We might as well make the hard decision now, rather than later." When he found six or seven people "reporting" to Gary, the president, he said: "That's too many. That just won't work." When there was a disposition to duck or defer a question of naming one man director of research, because this would hurt the feelings of the men who had been there longer, we walked right up to it, and made the decision, after some of the best and most discerning discussion on management I have heard in a long, long time.

These are not the average quality of men, this team of Deshler, Gary, Blake [executive vice president] and Nielsen [treasurer]. And to find them all in one company, and a little company at that, is just a miracle, a piece of good fortune beyond price. It makes the job so much more fun. And as Eberstadt says: "With that kind of a team you just can't fail." And we won't; that's pretty clear. The market's value put on these shares, which for so long has seemed absolutely crazy to me, turns out to be smart.

We dealt with a lot of important matters—organization, sales, and sales organization—rather fundamental propositions concerning the comparative value and cost of distributor versus direct sales; the building and financing of a new office building; research, its management and direction. A serious challenge to our phosphate patents and royalty income. A new retirement system. Policy about labor negotiations that are just coming up. And so on. Right down the line of important matters. Clearly presented, intelligently discussed, courageously faced and promptly decided.

This is a rare lot. I doubt if there is more management talent (sans Sarnoff and Folsom) in the whole of RCA, big as it is. And there won't be any drones or deadwood in this outfit very long.

DECEMBER 18, 1954
NEW YORK

. . . What counts in acquiring a business reputation is not sitting on boards but making money. This is the test; this I can see clearly now. That is one of the reasons why I am so anxious that Minerals & Chemicals make a great success, and particularly in this critical year of 1955.

I certainly wanted a business career in order to acquire independence, if I could. But again and again it was clear that what I wanted at least that much, perhaps more, was to be able to demonstrate that

I could succeed in the business world, by the measures and standards that the business world itself sets up. Making money is certainly the predominant measure. It has taken me quite a while to get that completely through my noggin.

Last week "Bobby" Lehman and Paul Mazur, senior partners of Lehman Brothers, were leaving after a session with André. We met in the lobby and walked out together. In the past eight months or so Lehman Brothers have taken an active interest in our stock. Now they want to be the ones who underwrite a public offering—and considering their high standing, this would be a great thing for M & C.

But the point of my comment is the different way in which these bankers greeted me the other day, compared with a year or more ago. I get more than my share of the credit for the minor miracle of M & C; and I am, by their estimate, going to make a lot of money out of it. So I'm no longer David Lilienthal, the "controversial" public servant, but am becoming someone who succeeds in *their* own game, and so an almost respectable and possibly even respected individual.

Well, what I was able to do in public service is so far more important than this that it isn't worth a thought; but not according to the standards of businessmen *when they are thinking business*.

I don't know why this isn't a perfectly sensible viewpoint, come to think about it.

A musician, now, might have great respect for a public figure; but if the latter set himself up to become a musician, the thing that is important is not what he did as Ambassador to the Netherlands or whatever, but how good he is on the fiddle.

The fact that money-making as the prime objective in business doesn't in itself seem an important objective really doesn't affect the point. Important or not, in and of itself, it is the measure of achievement in the game.

"Game" isn't just a figure of speech, either. Even so scholarly a man as Hettinger will come in now and then at Lazard, beaming, chortling, to say: "Isn't it fun?" He is more boyish and naïve about it than some of the others, perhaps, but that is the way he feels about seeing such a thing as the remarkable progress of the once defunct Minerals Separation North American Corporation. Eberstadt enjoys the "hunt"; his eyes take on the intense look of a man in the midst of an absorbing game. André takes it in still another way: he meditates, sitting way back in the corner of his big room, his chair tilted back, and he sitting practically on his spine; or getting quite excited as he plans things, tries to find the answer to difficulties, appraising risks, trying to see ahead, letting his sense of "feel" tell him when is a good time and when is a bad time to go to the market, and so on. None of these men has any need either of money or of glory, and they all have had a great deal indeed of both. But theirs is the pattern of motivation that ends by measuring what they are trying to do in business and what they have done by: "Did we make money?"

10. Zeckendorf Rampant

OF THE VARIOUS WAYS of earning a living in America, real estate is one of the few in which one may build monuments to oneself and still end up broke, and that is what William Zeckendorf did. During the two decades in which he flourished prior to his bankruptcy in 1966, he was certainly the most celebrated real estate man in the country and probably the most important one.

Born in Paris, Illinois, in 1905, descended from pioneers who had helped develop the Far West in the middle of the nineteenth century, he went into real estate as a young man and in 1938 joined Webb & Knapp, a then-staid New York City real estate management firm. Within a decade, he had bought out the other partners and transformed the firm into the wildest of thin-margin plungers in the field. His first great success was his role in bringing the United Nations to New York City, but subsequently he also built the Mile High Center in Denver, the Place Ville-Marie in Montreal, and dozens of urban redevelopment projects. At one time, Webb & Knapp owned 8,000 hotel rooms, and for a number of years, in New York City the name "Zeckendorf" was all but synonymous with huge dealings in real estate. Always mortgaged to the hilt, he liked to live dangerously, and he and his firm paid the price for their daring in the money squeeze of 1966.

In the first of these excerpts, Zeckendorf is upstaged by another character—quite a feat, but then the other character is the legendary Howard Hughes. Indeed, this is one of the best of the few authentic first-hand pictures of Hughes in action as a businessman now extant. Zeckendorf, with a letter of authority from a New York banking consortium in his pocket and with his son William, Jr., Laurance Rockefeller, and Spyros Skouras in his retinue, flies to the Coast in 1954 to try to buy nothing less than the entire Hughes empire. After their arrival at Beverly Hills and some fine cloak-and-dagger feints and parries in the Dashiell Hammett-Raymond Chandler tradition, the visitors are whisked in a villainous jalopy to a seedy hideout where Hughes actually manifests himself. The bidding begins almost immediately at $350 million, but after Hughes has routinely expressed disdain and the figure has risen a couple of hundred million, Hughes suddenly becomes depressed by the surroundings and suggests moving the conference to Las Vegas, whereupon he flies everybody there (except Rockefeller, who decides things have gone far enough) in his own Constellation. When the haggling resumes, it develops that Hughes had apparently never planned to sell but was only trying to get a market appraisal for tax purposes. A fine anecdote of high-style dealing, told with spirit in the best Hollywood hugger-mugger tradition.

The second excerpt concerning what Zeckendorf calls his "Wall Street maneuver" in the middle 1950s—a maneuver designed to keep New York's financial district from moving uptown, and incidentally to make Zeckendorf some fat commissions—shows him at the top of his form as to both influence and egotism. In it, he "moves" the Chase Manhattan, Chemical, and Morgan banks, giving some abrupt instructions to *David* Rockefeller and explaining to an astonished Morgan president that J. P. Morgan & Company will shortly be involved in a merger (it was). He also tries unsuccessfully to "move" the New York Stock Exchange, in the course of that endeavor taking occasion to explain the steel business to Roger Blough, chairman of United States Steel ("You are archaic and reactionary, and it's time you fellows woke up"). But while we are laughing or wondering at Zeckendorf's sheer nerve, we must be admiring his accomplishment; his "Wall Street maneuver," more than any other single force, was responsible for preventing the financial trade from leaving Wall Street for uptown.

Zeckendorf is ultimately a poor businessman and not all of his projects win the approval of urbanologists, but he cannot be dismissed as a mere promoter and deal maker. As I wrote in the New York *Times Book Review* in August 1970 when his autobiography was published, "In his good days he showed heart enough for ten men. Some primal energy drove him, and one feels that he played for money simply because that was the only game in town. Had he lived in medieval times, he would surely have built cathedrals by the dozens for no purpose but to proclaim the glory of God."

DEALING WITH HUGHES

HOWARD HUGHES, an industrial genius and paradoxical man, has been phenomenally successful. He has also produced some disastrously costly movies. He was known as a famous Hollywood Don Juan who collected and discarded beautiful women the way boys collect and discard model airplanes. For the past twenty years he has also managed to live as a traveling recluse, a sort of peripatetic Trappist. He deals with his various company managers only intermittently, sometimes through handwritten notes, at other times through obscure intermediaries, midnight phone calls, or summonses to secret, out-of-the-way meeting places.

The last time I saw Howard, he had already surrounded himself with the phalanx of competent, honest, and thoroughly humorless young Mormons who served as the gate-keepers, errand boys, and

From *Zeckendorf: The Autobiography of William Zeckendorf,* with Edward McCreary (Holt, Rinehart and Winston, 1970), pp. 155–62, 264–82.

contact men. Through them he wards off and deals with much of the rest of the world.

The first time I met Hughes, in the early 1950's, was in Florida, where we had talked about his buying the 63,000-acre Indian Trail Ranch that Webb & Knapp controlled. At one point, I also offered to swap our 12,000-acre Mountain Park property in Los Angeles for his RKO Theatre stock. Nothing came of these brief encounters, all of which had taken place in motels, beachside shacks, and the like. These meetings, I presume, helped set things up for the following episode.

It started in October, 1954, with a telephone call from Spyros Skouras, suggesting we have lunch. I had met Spyros, a stocky, gravel-voiced Greek, when he was chief of Twentieth Century-Fox during my earlier California reconnaissances. Spyros, who had long been a friend and, as much as anyone could be, a confidant of Howard Hughes, hoarsely announced at our lunch: "I've been talking with Howard Hughes, and he is ready to make a change. He wants to retire from business and devote his time and money to medical research. . . ." Spyros continued for a time building on this theme and the vast extent of Hughes' holdings. Finally he said, "You are a man who is always dealing with money people. Can you find a group big enough to handle this thing?"

I immediately replied, "It sounds like a Rockefeller proposition . . . they have the money. They would also be interested from the standpoint of their own foundation work, Laurance Rockefeller especially. They are backing lots of research in cancer. Do you want me to try it?"

He said yes, so I called Laurance Rockefeller for an appointment. We met, and I told him the story. He asked, "Do you think Hughes really means it?" I said I thought Hughes meant it because Spyros thought he meant it, and it was the kind of thing an eccentric like Hughes might do. The only way to know for sure, however, was to go to California and find out. Rockefeller agreed to come along, and through Spyros I arranged for a meeting, while quietly lining up some other backers who might have a special interest in some part of Hughes' holdings.

Rockefeller, my son, and I flew out to Los Angeles. There we met Spyros. The four of us lunched in the terrace dining room of the Beverly Hills Hotel, where, I suppose, we were all scrutinized by Hughes or his agents. In any event, we found ourselves programmed into a script that only the members of various undergrounds, portions of the CIA, the NKVD, and perhaps the Minutemen would normally take seriously. At precisely 1:30 Spyros was to get up and take a taxi-cab to a predetermined place, where he would be met and then taken to the rendezvous. At 1:50 Rockefeller and I were to go to a certain intersection, where a man wearing a red shirt with an open collar would contact us and drive us to the rendezvous. The meeting was to be attended by Spyros, Rockefeller, and me. There was no provision for my son's being there, but I thought I'd bring him along for the experience.

At 1:50 Rockefeller, my son, and I got up and walked over to the nearby corner. A man with a red shirt, open at the collar, came up, looked us over, and said, "Follow me." We did, for about a block, where he climbed into a 1932 Chevrolet jalopy, something the Okies might have used on the trek west twenty years ago. The car was dusty blue in color, some of the windows were cracked, the fenders looked as if they had been battered in and hammered out more than once, and the rugs in the back had been worn through. It was quite a sight to see the immaculate Rockefeller get into this wreck. It wasn't a very large car, and maybe my squeezing into place amused him as well. At any rate we got rolling, and after a time found ourselves in a seedy section of town. We stopped in front of a four-story building, a one-time private home that looked as if it had been converted into a flop-house, except that the building was now being patrolled. Four or five young, neatly dressed, rather good-looking men, all with crew-cuts, continually walked around the place. These were Hughes' Mormon entourage, and as we pulled up one of them came over and said, "Mr. Hughes has called the meeting off."

I said, "Why?"

"Sir, just you and Mr. Rockefeller were supposed to come to this meeting. You have a third party here, and Mr. Hughes feels that is a breach of the understanding."

"The third party is my son."

"It doesn't make any difference who he is."

I turned and said, "All right, Bill, you go back to the hotel, and we'll carry on."

The young guard said, "Wait a minute, I have to find out if Mr. Hughes will still go through with the meeting." We sat out in the hot sun till our native guide came back to say that Hughes would see us. We then climbed up to the top floor of the building and down to the end of a long hallway, where our escort rapped on the door with a distinct pattern of knocks. The door opened, and there stood Howard Hughes, looking exactly as he has often been shown in newspapers and magazines: six-foot-three, slender, youthful-looking, he had a three-day growth of beard, wore a V-neck shirt, soiled sport trousers, and dirty tennis shoes. The only thing neat about him was his hair, which was combed straight back, covering a balding head. He was around fifty-two years old at the time. As we stepped into this hideaway office, I introduced Rockefeller and joshed Howard a bit about his not buying the Webb & Knapp Mountain Park property, which was fast rising in value. We all seated ourselves. Hughes, who wore a hearing aid, pointed the speaker at whoever was talking. After a bit, and in the most casual way, he asked, "What do you fellows want?" Since it was Hughes who had approached us through Spyros, and since polite indirection had done nothing for me in previous meetings, I decided to be blunt, saying, "Howard, you know damn well what we want. We didn't come three thousand miles to admire your old trousers and sport shirt, or because we like this part of town; we came here to buy. I was told by Spyros that you were ready to sell."

"Oh," he said, "I told Spyros I'd *listen* to something."

I said, "If that is the way things are going to go, we've wasted our time. Either you are talking in good faith or not. Spyros says that you want to sell out and devote the rest of your life to science and the interests of humanity. Is that true? If it isn't, we may as well leave."

"I said something like that to Spyros."

I turned to Spyros and said, "Before we go any further, suppose you tell Howard what you told me."

Spyros, hoarse voice, Greek accent, and all, has tremendous charm and is very persuasive. He soon got the meeting on a much better footing, and it began to go along more easily. Rockefeller, who up to this time had said very little, now spoke up, saying that he had come there only because I asked him to. If a deal required capital financing, he would be interested in helping, but he did not come out there just to make money. He was interested in getting new money for cancer research. Hughes replied that he was interested in backing a great research foundation and that he had already established one foundation which was doing great things in medical research and would do more. Then, turning his hearing aid toward me, he said, "What do you have in mind for buying me out at . . . as long as you are here?"

I said, "Let's analyze what we are talking about, and I'll make you an offer. We are talking about Hughes Tool Company and Hughes Aircraft. We are talking about RKO, your real estate in Tucson, plus the brewery in Texas, and we are talking about TWA. That's your portfolio, isn't it?"

He said, "Generally speaking, that's it."

I said, "I'm recommending that we pay three hundred and fifty million dollars for all that."

"You don't know what you're talking about."

"Maybe . . . maybe I don't know anything about it. Let's assume I don't. But you do know all about it. Will you take three hundred and fifty million dollars? You can have a check for it."

"Where is the check?"

"Well, I have a letter and a check. I have a cashier's check for nineteen and a half million, plus a letter from Sloan Colt, who is chairman of the board of the Bankers Trust Company, stating that the check is for the purpose of making a down payment for the acquisition of your holdings. The amount is nineteen and a half million not because it bears any relationship to a price that might be negotiated, but because it is the maximum the bank can lend in one single transaction, being ten percent of their capital. Here it is," I said, and reached over to hand him the letter. He put up his hands, saying, "Don't give it to me, don't ask me to touch it."

"I didn't ask you to touch it, I want you to see it."

Hughes is the most suspicious man in the world. Maybe he was afraid that taking the letter might be tantamount to acceptance, or perhaps it was his morbid fear of bacteria that kept him from touching the letter. Up until this time he had been slouching on the edge of the couch, sometimes crossing his legs, occasionally leaning forward to shift his weight, but with never a change in facial expression. Now he leaned forward to read the letter I held out to him.

Finally he said, "I won't take it."

"Why not?"

"It's not enough."

"What is enough?"

"I won't tell you."

"*Do* you want to sell?"

"Under certain circumstances."

"What circumstances?"

"If the price is right."

"What price?"

"The price that you might offer me. If it is enough, I'll sell."

"Now you are getting me to bid blind. . . . I'm willing to match a bid of table stakes, but I don't like to shoot blanks. Are we fifty million dollars apart?"

Hughes said, "No."

"Do you mean it's less?"

He said, "No, I mean more."

For a man who supposedly wanted to get down to serious business, Hughes was acting like the original coy mistress, but I kept trying. I said, "Are we one hundred million dollars off?"

"Are you offering it?"

"No, I am asking."

He said, "I told you . . . I won't tell you."

"All right, I'll find out. I am offering you four hundred and fifty million; will you take it?"

"No. . . ."

"Howard, just exactly what do you want?"

"I won't tell you."

"Howard, take it or leave it, five hundred million."

He said, "I leave it."

"Howard," I replied, making no effort to hide my exasperation, "I think you invited us out here to give you a free *appraisal*. I don't think you were ever sincere."

He said, "Think what you like," then added, "I'll tell you what we'll do. I don't want to talk anymore today. We'll all go down to Las Vegas and talk down there."

Rockefeller said he couldn't go to Las Vegas, he had to get back to New York. Spyros said that he and I would go.

"Can I bring my son?" I asked.

Hughes agreed to this. And then, as if we were ten-year-old members of the latest Post Toasties secret membership club with "super" clues and passwords, four grown men who among them commanded or could influence a significant share of American wealth, sat there with never a smile, as Hughes programmed a properly secret rendezvous.

Spyros, my son, and I were to meet Hughes at midnight at a semi-abandoned airport on the outskirts of Los Angeles. He would fly us to Las Vegas, but would arrange that we be driven to town in separate cars. Once in Las Vegas, we must go directly to our rooms. Under no circumstances were we to leave them during daylight, when we might be seen and start rumors.

At midnight we arrived at the deserted airport, which was entirely dark. A Constellation, a plane which Hughes had helped design, bulked in the gloom, and a guard with a flashlight told us to wait. We waited till Hughes, accompanied by another young guard, drove up in a little car. Guided by flashlights, we climbed into the darkened Constellation. Hughes checked her out, revved her up, and we took off. He did the flying. In Las Vegas we were met by several Hughes cars, driven by another group of Daddy Warbucks' monosyllabic young men, and taken to our hotel, where we had already been checked in. At this point, if Orphan Annie (accompanied by her dog, Sandy) had now shown up offering drinks, I would not even have blinked. Nothing of the sort happened, however, and we had to order our own drinks. It was late, and with Spyros' remonstrances to "humor" Howard still ringing in my ears, I went to bed.

The next day at about one o'clock Hughes called. We met in his suite, and he began our discussions by saying, "I am willing to review the situation further only if you offer more cash on the barrelhead."

"What kind of money?" I asked.

"Oh, perhaps one hundred million dollars more."

"Well, that casts quite a new light on this thing. We'll have to get backers into it. I'll have to return to New York and let you know."

Then he said, "Never mind, we'll just forget it. The deal is off."

I told him this was a very shabby way to treat people. We exchanged some more words, but the deal was kept alive by Spyros, and after I returned to New York a number of other negotiations went on. By the time it wound up, the list of supporting characters included the chairman of General Electric, the chief of Lockheed Aircraft, one of the heads of Blyth & Co., the head of Allen & Co., a senior partner of Lehman Bros., and a senior partner of Lazard Frères. Spyros, however, fell sick about this time and had to undergo an operation. That delayed things. Lehman and Meyer, of Lazard Frères, eventually did go out west on their own for a meeting with Hughes, but they were interested only in part of his kingdom. They offered, I think, to buy Hughes Tool. Eventually the whole deal died away. I was not surprised. After those first meetings with Hughes, I never thought he was serious. I think he was trying to find out what he was worth for tax purposes, perhaps in order to make gifts to a foundation. One of the best ways to determine the value of vast holdings is to have someone make you a bona-fide offer for them. However, Hughes' TWA situation was already getting a little sticky, Hughes Aircraft had been having management troubles, and his bankers at Irving Trust had found themselves way overboard on loans to TWA and were pressuring for changes. Hughes may have been checking out a financial countermaneuver. We'll probably never know exactly what he was up to. . . .

WALL STREET MANEUVER

ALTHOUGH PRIVATE BUILDING complexes, urban-redevelopment projects, and massive land deals constituted the visible bulk of the Webb & Knapp empire, we had never given up our original business of assembling properties and packaging deals. In the 1950's and 1960's we continued buying and selling lots and buildings as we had in the 1940's, except, where we had once dealt in thousands of dollars, we now dealt in millions. We were the most noted and trusted dealer in the business, and it was through a reputation built up over the years that we were led into the single greatest project or series of projects of all, the Wall Street Maneuver.

In 1954 I was invited to a special meeting at the old Chase Manhattan Bank headquarters at 18 Pine Street. Arriving there, I was led down a paneled corridor to a deep-carpeted conference room where David Rockefeller and a group of his distinguished colleagues were gathered. I stepped into the room with these distinguished gentlemen, and we began to discuss the Chase's dilemma within a general Wall Street dilemma.

The Chase, like every other New York bank, was growing. Its offices were inefficiently scattered through eight separate buildings in the area. Their immediate problem was: should they build a new building downtown to bring everything under one roof or should they abandon their downtown holdings in favor of new quarters in midtown?

The Chase, like every other major financial institution downtown, was living with its hat on, ready to jump uptown. Mid-Manhattan was enjoying an office-building boom. More and more important corporate headquarters were being established in the midtown section. Nothing had been built in the financial district since the Depression. The decision was in balance. No one wanted to make the first move. No one wanted to guess wrong about what the other boys might do; so no one was doing anything. All it would take was for one major bank to make the leap, and the others would follow. The result, for midtown Manhattan, would be phenomenal congestion. The result in the old financial district would be nearly disastrous. Values would drop. By just how much values would drop would be anybody's guess. The deserted stock markets and investment community would come under pressure to move. In time, residential construction would creep into the area, but first there would be a period of relative decay.

When the gentlemen from the Chase said that they would like to preserve their thirty-seven-million-dollar investment in the area, I replied that while this saving was important, the real question was, could the Wall Street community be saved? If it could be saved, this would call for a truly bold maneuver. When everyone nodded, I said, "The whole community can be saved only if enough major banks agree to stay here, if not all of them, then a substantial number."

"Agreed."

I said, "The trick will be to stabilize Wall Street. You can't do it alone, but you can start. You have to start in a way that the others will follow. What you need is a musical chair, a place to move into. . . .

"There is only one logical musical chair open and available to you" —I pointed out the window—"and that is the Mutual Life site on the corner. Guaranty Trust was going to build a new home there, but they changed their minds and are restoring their old building at 140 Broadway.

"The Mutual Life site is under negotiation for sale, and you have no time. You have to bid for it today."

Somebody interjected, "What are you talking about, today?"

"Today is the day."

"What is the price?"

I said, "It is $4,670,000."

"We'll have to take that to the board."

"There is not a man in the room who cannot commit the bank to a maximum loan of fifty million dollars. Any one of you can lend the limit without consultation from your board. I'm not talking about ten percent of your maximum lending power, just one percent. Your whole future is at stake; you can't wait to go to your board with a silly thing like that. Here's what you do. I suggest you call Guaranty Trust and verify that they are about to sell off the property."

The call was made and it was verified that Guaranty were about to close.

All this time David Rockefeller had been quietly directing the meeting. He did this *sotto voce,* because that is his manner and because many of the older men in that room were more powerful than he within the bank, but it was David who personally guided Chase's gamble on the stabilization of Wall Street. The Chase now owned a musical chair. I undertook to liquidate their surplus buildings and to persuade other banks to stay downtown by providing them with proper quarters.

Some of the Chase properties adjoining the Mutual Life site became part of the new project, but I promised to get the thirty-seven-million-dollar book value of all their properties from sale of the remaining properties. We wound up getting sixty million. It was these other properties, which the Chase would vacate, that would create the open chairs in the game of musical banks I was planning.

To find the next player in the game, I called Harold Helm, chief of the Chemical Bank, and said, "Harold, I would like to see you and your colleagues for an important discussion of a relocation idea."

He said, "Fine. When?"

"At your convenience."

"Let's say tomorrow at ten."

"I'll be there."

The next day Harold Helm and three other heads of Chemical were waiting for me at their offices on 165 Broadway. I sat down, put the flat of my fingers on the edge of the table, and said, "The idea is that you should move to 18 Pine."

Helm said, "That's the Chase Bank."

"Yes."

"We move there, let them go uptown, and we're left holding the bag!"

"No, Harold, you move there, and we will have it written into your contract that you are not bound to that property unless the Chase puts up a building that does not cost less than sixty million dollars in the immediate neighborhood. They have committed themselves to buying the Mutual Life site to do this."

The Chemical Bank agreed to a deal in principle, and now we began talking price. The Pine Street building, I told them, would cost 17.5 million dollars. This was acceptable, but in part payment they wanted us to take two properties that were surplus to their needs. One was on William Street and the other across the river in Brooklyn Heights. Now we were in the used-bank-building business, but that is what makes deals. I agreed, took the proposition to the Chase, and our first step was set.

We had successfully popped the first olive out of the bottle. Everyone was delighted at how smoothly it had gone. Then, two weeks later, I got a call from Helm: "I'm sorry, Bill, but the deal is off. We are

on a very short lease here at 165 Broadway; we have three years to
go. The Chase won't get their new building up for at least six years.
Our landlord is a very tough guy named Norman Winston, and he
won't give us a lease of convenience. In fact, he is aware of the situation, and he wants to hit us for a twenty-one- or thirty-year extension,
or it's out in the street for us.

"This puts us in a terrible bind," he continued. "Should we stay
here for twenty-one years? That wouldn't be very good. Should we
go uptown? Should we do something else? We don't know yet, but
we can't make that deal with the Chase. We'll have to move before
they can give us 18 Pine Street."

I said, "Give me a little time, I'll see what I can do."

Ten days later I called Helm: "I've got you a lease of convenience."

"How did you do it? We couldn't."

"Well, I just did it."

"How?"

"I'm your landlord."

I had gone to Winston and bought him out. We had to pay more
than the building was actually worth, but I figured a wash on one
deal might be overcome by profits on others, and we went ahead.

The next place in the mosaic was 40 Wall Street, the tallest building
in the financial area, a typical product of the crazy, hectic financing
of the 1920's. It was built with speculative bond issues, the common
stock thrown in for free, and very ingeniously dovetailed out of three
properties. There were actually three fees. One fee, or piece of the
land, was owned by the Chase, because it had originally been the
site of the old Manhattan bank, which the Chase absorbed. Another
fee was owned by the Iselin estate. The third fee belonged to the building corporation that put up 40 Wall Street. The ground rent payable
to the Chase for its ownership of one of the fees was $500,000 per
year. The Chase had a bank and offices in the building, for which
they paid one million dollars a year in rent. The Chase wanted to be
relieved of paying that rent and also wanted to get back the cash value
of $500,000 land income. I promised the Chase that at current rates
of five-percent interest I would get them ten million dollars for their
fee. (Actually, by the time of the sale, interest rates had climbed to
six percent.) That $500,000 income was worth only 8.35 million

dollars, but I had said ten million, and I kept my word. The next job was to get our money out by selling that fee to someone else. Now, selling only part of the fee of a great building would be very difficult to do. There was only one way to turn the trick: we would have to pour in more money in order to buy the other two fees from the Iselin estate and from the publicly held company that owned and leased the building.

The first move was to buy from the Iselin estate. My contact here was Graham Mattison of Dominick & Dominick. He had once been a member of the firm of White & Case. The trustee of the Iselin estate was Robert Youngs, chairman of the Louisiana Land & Exploration Company, who was also a one-time White & Case man. Mattison brought us together. I met Youngs in Paris for dinner. We supped at the Au Caneton, a fine restaurant near the French stock exchange, and there we sealed an agreement. Next came the job of buying up the shares of the third company. Most of the two classes of bonds and bonus stock of this company was in the hands of Wall Street secondary-money types, scavengers who had picked up the property during the Depression. We gradually bought up close to half of the shares from the larger holders, then opened market purchases for the balance. We knew that we could not get more than two-thirds of the stock, but under New York State law, if two-thirds of the stock-holders of a company vote to sell the assets and liquidate, they can do so. When we had two-thirds, I moved for liquidation that would put the property up at auction, with the highest bidder taking it. I knew we could outbid anyone, because two-thirds of almost anything we bid was our own. We had a lawyers' holiday, however, getting this thing through. Every strike lawyer in town, and some lawyers that were not supposed to be strike lawyers, hurried to get his oar in, in hopes of getting a little extra money through an out-of-court settle-ment designed to buy his cooperation. Finally, however, the court gave us the right to auction, and the affair was held in the main hall of the Wall Street Club, which was a tenant in the building. We won our auction, against competition, at a price where the old bonds were paid off one hundred cents on the dollar and the stockholders got twenty-two dollars per share for bonus stock it had cost them nothing to acquire. Our total cost of this acquisition was ten million dollars to the Chase, 4.25 million to the Iselin estate, and some 17.75 million for the remainder of the property, for a total of thirty-two million.

The Chase was now free to move out. Meanwhile, there was an excellent building at 15 Broad Street which the Chase would also be emptying, and I had to find a buyer. I called on Henry Alexander, president of J. P. Morgan & Company, explained what we were trying to do with this total Wall Street maneuver, and how the ideal part for Morgan would be to take over 15 Broad.

Henry wasn't buying. He said, "We're not real-estate people. We already have this beautiful little corner here. We play a special role in finance; we are not big, but we are powerful and influential, we have relationships. Furthermore, we don't want to be big and don't need the space."

I said, "Henry, you are going to get married."

"What?"

"Someday you are going to merge with another bank, a big one. When you do, this property will be in the nature of a dowry coming with a bride; you will be able to make a better deal with your new partner."

"Morgan will never merge."

"Well, that's just my prediction," I said, but I kept pointing out to Alexander the advantages to Morgan of the new property, and eventually they decided to buy it for 21.25 million dollars.

Five years later I called Alexander and congratulated him on Morgan's coming merger with Guaranty Trust Company. He said, "You know, I've often thought of that conversation we had and how right you were."

"I wasn't right, Henry, I was wrong."

"How so?"

"You're not the bride."

Having moved the Morgan and having moved the Chemical, I was beginning to run a little low on possible tenants for the vacant slot we would have for a bank at 40 Wall Street. In fact, this situation was becoming crucial.

Metropolitan Life was interested in 40 Wall. Fred Ecker said they'd buy it for twenty million dollars.

I said, "Fine, we'll lease it back at six percent, and that means we now have only twelve million in the building in the form of a lease-hold."

"But," Ecker said, "you'll have to find a tenant to replace the Chase Bank. That million-dollar-a-year rent is too important for us to take it on speculation."

I went down to see my friend Jeff McNeill at the Hanover Bank and said, "Jeff, how about moving over to 40 Wall?"

"What about my buildings here at 60 and 70 Broadway?"

"Jeff, you know we are the biggest dealers in slightly used bank quarters in America; we take them in like secondhand cars."

"My book value is six and a half million dollars."

"What are you telling me?"

"That's what I've got to get."

"Oh, Lord, that's a terrible rabbit warren. God only knows what we will do with it when you get out."

"Bill, I can't give you anything better than that. If we take the lease over at 40 Wall for one million a year in rent, that's the deal."

We argued a little and bargained a lot, but on basic price McNeill was unshakable; he had to get book value for his buildings, so finally I said, "You've made a deal," and we shook hands.

McNeill made a memo of the meeting. I never make memoranda —I try to use my own memory and rely on people's word. Sometime later the bank drew up preliminary papers; I looked them over, and the price read 6.8 million dollars.

I told Jeff he'd made a mistake in the papers.

He said he was sure they were right.

There had been a lot of conversation that day, and it was entirely possible he was right. I told him if that was how he remembered it, it was O.K. with me. The business of drawing up the papers then went on, but after a few days I got a call. It was Jeff McNeill: "Bill, I got that memorandum out. You were right. It is six-million-five, and I'm changing it. And I'm telling you right now, you are a wonderful sport."

The Hanover then passed title of the building to us, took back a mortgage and a lease of convenience. That gave us three years to move the property, but there were problems. The buildings were old, there were three different floor levels in what were actually three

buildings. In fairness to the Hanover, they were beautifully maintained, but the interiors were a Minotaur's maze of offices and hall-
ways that only the Hanover or somebody like them could use. What's
more, they were down at the end of things, near the tip of Broadway.
The Wall Street area was still shaky. Number 2 Broadway had not
yet been built, and few companies would want to move in down there
at the perimeter. The only logical and possible buyer was the Irving
Trust Company, whose offices at 1 Wall abutted the Hanover properties.

The Irving Trust already had a beautiful building, a well-designed,
soaring tower. This great tower was not efficient; because of its great
height and small ground area, it was really a test tube; you were running up and down all the time. So I tried to sell Irving Trust on the
idea of buying the Hanover buildings, using them, or putting up a
new structure on the site. They showed interest from time to time as I
talked with them, but I was asking something over nine million dollars
for the properties. There are no secrets on Wall Street, so they knew
we had paid over 6 million for the Hanover properties and balked at
my figure. I took the position that our cost had nothing to do with
what we would sell for. After all, I still had the problem of selling
off our lease at 40 Wall. I still didn't know how I'd get out of 40 Wall.
If we sold the Hanover properties at cost and had to take a loss on
selling 40 Wall, we would be in trouble. Nobody cares too much
whether it is profitable or not for the other fellow, but I had to look
out for our interests. We were not a nonprofit foundation dedicated to
putting out our capital for the benefit of the banking industry. Finally
Irving Trust offered us seven million, then seven and a half million,
and I was advised to take it, but I said no, I was asking nine and I
was going to get nine.

"How are you so sure you will?" I was asked.

If the Irving Trust had already crossed a certain bridge in their
own minds and were planning to go uptown, I could offer them the
properties at a fire-sale price and not get a nibble. But when they
began bidding 7.5 million dollars, I knew they had crossed a different
type of bridge; they were not going uptown. I knew then they would
have to pay the nine million or change their policy, and 1.5 million
dollars was not enough to force a change in that kind of policy; 1.5

million in the total land cost might have constituted five percent of the total cost of a new building and I felt this was pretty good ground on which to stand pat. I stood my ground, and we got nine million.

The negotiators for the Irving Trust handled themselves beautifully. In that sense it was a classic series of negotiations, but after a certain point they knew and I knew what the land was worth to them, and we settled at a worthwhile figure; land values are only a relatively small portion of the total cost of a new structure. For instance, take the new Chase building: it ended up costing 120 million dollars. The original land cost $4,670,000 (more land was added later). But, if the original land had cost eight million, this would not in the long run have mattered. Once a course of action is set, a wise negotiator knows what its parts and pieces are worth to him. If he can get it for less, fine; but he will not scuttle his plans on a matter of minor increments. You can lose that much money in the door knobs for a new building.

The Irving Trust deal was concluded in June, 1961, but I still had to find a buyer for the twelve million dollars we had tied up in the lease we held on 40 Wall Street. We got a ten-million-dollar mortgage on this lease from the Chase. This left us with two million in equity on a profitable property, but I needed a buyer to get out our sorely needed cash, and in time one came to me. A London-based real-estate financier named Charles Clore was merging with another Englishman, Jack Cotton. They were starting an American real-estate company. I had previously talked with Clore about 40 Wall Street, with no success, but now the phone rang; it was Clore in London.

"Do you still have 40 Wall?"

"We do."

"Do you want to sell it?"

"Yes."

"What will you take for it?"

"The same price."

"What's that?"

"Fifteen million for the leasehold."

There were more talks and conferences, but eventually he bought it. The 40 Wall Street chapter was closed, and our game of musical

banks was ended with a grace note. Seven years had gone by. We
had moved the Chase. We had moved the Chemical and Morgan
banks. We had moved the Hanover Bank. We had persuaded the
Irving Trust to take over the Hanover properties and sold off a half-
dozen ancillary properties on the side. Webb & Knapp's profit of perhaps ten million dollars from these combined deals amounted to little
more than music teacher's pay for our efforts. The Chase Bank financed many of our moves, but we put up Webb & Knapp assets over
and beyond those of the subject properties as collateral; we were the
prime risk-takers. The total volume of business involved directly and
indirectly amounted to some 250 million dollars. Considering five
percent is the average broker's commission, with no risk involved, our
take at four percent was indeed modest. We were in business for
profit, so why did we do this? We did it because it had to be done,
and nobody else could do it. There is a tremendous satisfaction to
individuals and corporations alike in leaving an important constructive mark in their trail. There was excitement and fun in putting the
puzzle together, but, second only to our United Nations deal, the
Wall Street Maneuver was the most important thing we ever did in
the New York community, and we were happy to do it. Expanding
the effects of these maneuvers, David Rockefeller and his associates
have sparked an imaginative renaissance and reformation of downtown Manhattan which Webb & Knapp tried to further make use of
and accelerate.

Throughout our Wall Street Maneuver the very first building we
had purchased, the Chemical Bank headquarters at 165 Broadway,
had been burdening our books. We had had to pay Norman Winston
such a surcharge for his stock in this fifty-story structure that the
return on investment was negative. Over the years, however, land
values in the area promised to rise, thanks to our maneuvers, and,
thinking in terms of land values instead of building costs, I began
to sense a possibility. If I could buy everything south of 165 Broadway
for two blocks, including 111 and 115 Broadway, we would have
a tremendously valuable plottage. Other buyers and sellers were thinking in terms of return on investment on existing buildings. But if we
could buy the whole sweep of land, we would have enough underlying

value to make it worthwhile to tear down the existing buildings, seal off or overpass the existing streets, and create a new superbuilding. West of this site, near the Hudson River, the Port of New York Authority, guided by Rockefeller, was planning an enormous World Trade Center. Our plottage, lying directly between the Trade Center and the new Chase Plaza, would become a people-magnet between these two areas. The more I thought about it, the better it looked. The New York Stock Exchange needed new quarters and would sooner or later have to move. The slot between the Chase Plaza and World Trade Center would be wonderful for them.

Actually, we had not bought full ownership of 165 Broadway from Winston, only a controlling interest. As in the case of 40 Wall Street, we then had to buy up two-thirds of the rest of the stock and bonds, go to the court requesting a reorganization, and in that way take over the whole property. This took about three years. This done, I set about buying adjacent properties. The biggest was the Singer Building, into which the company had just put 1.5 million dollars in automatic elevators and a general modernization. For reasons of his own, Donald Kircher, the chief at Singer, liked the idea of moving. He was in the process of trying to spark up and revive this old dinosaur of a company, and a move to new quarters might loosen some of the encrusted tradition that still befuddled the company. However, he wanted eight million dollars for his building; after all, there was all the money he had spent on elevators. Since we wanted to tear the structure down, the elevators, to us, represented a waste of money, but Kircher had his books to think about and was adamant. I argued and bargained again and again, getting nowhere, and we finally agreed to pay his price. Now we had two big buildings and respectable plottage, but because of the high cost of both structures, our average costs per square foot of land were still prohibitive; we had to buy more. I began buying in the next block south of the Singer Building and west to Church Street.

Though I negotiated earnestly and long, we never did get to purchase 111 and 115 Broadway. These buildings were owned by a man named Benjamin Miller, one of the most unreliable and difficult people in New York to deal with. He was an incorrigible delayer. He was trying to hold us up, and succeeded. I finally decided to go ahead without him. We had enough property, what with street closing and overpassing, to give us plenty of land at two hundred dollars per square foot of cost. We could put up our building and let him go his own way. In all, we spent twenty-eight million dollars acquiring 165 Broadway, the Singer Building, and other properties, but while all this was going on, of course, I had been working on the New York Stock Exchange as future tenant.

The man I went to see was John Coleman, who, though little known outside the Street, is one of its most influential members. He is head of the firm of Adler Coleman, who are specialists and probably have more seats on the Exchange than any other firm, except Merrill Lynch. Coleman's father was a policeman, and John Coleman had started as an office boy working for a man named Adler. He finally became a partner, and the firm became Adler Coleman. When Adler got in trouble, Coleman, who had an excellent reputation, carried on. He was a central figure in the Exchange, which is generally run by and for the specialists, and as we drove downtown in a cab one morning, I said, "John, here is a sketch of where I think the Stock Exchange should be."

"You mean we can buy all that property?" he asked.

"You can buy it or lease it, I don't care which. I'll give you everything from 165 Broadway down to 115 Broadway, and I can even buy 111 and 115 Broadway and bring you all the way down to Trinity Place.

"There will be the new Trade Center to the west. You have Chase Plaza to the east. One-forty Broadway will be replaced by a new building. The axis between the Trade Center and Chase Plaza, with its access to parking and subways, will make for a year-round people-passage. We will have covered walks, malls, shops, and restaurants. Set the Stock Exchange on our site, and it will be the very heart and core of the entire financial district."

We talked further in his office, and Coleman finally said, "O.K., Bill, you deliver those buns, and we'll buy them."

I figured that conversation was enough to move the Stock Exchange. I thought Coleman did business that way; it is the way I did business. I walked away from his office and soon after agreed to pay Kircher his eight million for the Singer Building. Webb & Knapp then began buying south of the Singer Building. We formed a new corporation called Finance Place and set our architects to designing the greatest possible column-free area for a new Stock Exchange trading floor.

It is simple enough to build a giant auditorium or theater, which is what the Stock Exchange floor is, but it is something else to put an office building three-fourths the size of the Empire State over such a manmade cavern. I turned the task over to Pei and his partners, and Henry Cobb came up with one of the most ingenious building designs I have ever seen. One solution to the problem would be to create our "auditorium," then put a giant 25,000-ton, 270-foot-long truss or bridge of steel over the open space to support the skyscraper. This would be a brute-force and very expensive solution. What Cobb did, instead, was design a building that was seemingly conventional in all but two respects. First, the building would be sloped inward from a 270-foot width at the base to a 90-foot width above its forty-fifth office floor. In a sense, it would be something like a beautifully tapered Mayan temple. Across the 90-foot-wide top of the building, however, we would have a series of 28-foot-deep steel trusses. During the construction phase, the building would be put up with conventional steel girders rising through the center section to support the framework above. However, when the 28-foot-deep trusses were finally placed across the roof, all the great girders cluttering up the bottom-floor space where the Stock Exchange would go would be cut out with acetylene torches and carted away. Instead of being held up by center-floor girders, the office floors above this "auditorium" would hang down from the roof trusses, much as a nonmoving elevator hangs by its cables from a building's roof. The Stock Exchange area would therefore be entirely column-free.

It is dangerous to design a speculative building with only one prime tenant in mind, but I had decided to do so. We had a fabulous and distinctive design, and an ideal location. We also had, or thought we had, unofficial but powerful backing within the Exchange, so we went ahead. More accurately, we tried to go ahead—but didn't get very far. In fact, we lost out. As to the details of this story, I must be vague. I was, unfortunately, never entirely privy to what was actually going on. What I do know is that during the time of our planning of and assemblage for Finance Place, Keith Funston, president of the

Stock Exchange, had been negotiating for a new site with another real-estate group headed by Sol Atlas and my friend John McGrath, a fellow trustee of Long Island University. Down close to the tip of Manhattan, near the Battery, Atlas and McGrath had a five-acre site, part of which they had offered to the Stock Exchange. The site had started out as an urban-renewal project, and the original assemblage was very cleverly done and neatly dovetailed. There had been some quite adroit use of city planning and street widening, so that by street-widening condemnation, original owners who might have held out against the assemblers were easily swept up and away at a relatively modest cost. Then, at the proper time, there had been a rezoning of the area, so the assemblers could charge top rates for later sale to the city. The area had originally been intended for some kind of housing project which the Wagner administration was increasingly attacked about. Therefore, the plot was turned into an office development. Moving the Stock Exchange to the Battery site would very neatly get the Wagner administration off an uncomfortable hook, so the whole thing was deep in local politics. Coleman was very close to the Wagner administration. Perhaps he was, or thought he was, tied into something he could not get out of. As I say, I still don't know the full story. I thought I had backing, but at the crucial moment it turned out not to be there. By this time, the infield who were running the Exchange had their own deal lined up and wanted no inside comment, and certainly no outside suggestion whatsoever. However, the logic of the situation spoke so strongly for Finance Place that I kept trying. I made calls, made presentations, argued and pleaded my cause. In time, individual Stock Exchange members also began to argue against the foolishness of moving the Exchange so far south. Even *The New York Times* wrote a strongly worded editorial to the same effect. Over many months the ensuing dialogue generated a great deal of heat. It also brought a certain amount of light on a matter that the Exchange managers would have preferred not to debate, and for which they gave me no thanks.

One immediate result of all this was that Webb & Knapp and Finance Place lost out: the Exchange managers flatly refused to consider our site.

Part of what happened was that the Stock Exchange, a free-ride monopoly controlled by a small group of insiders, is a very sensitive and defensive institution. Like the old-time barons in Europe who charged a handsome toll for all boats using the stream by their castles, the Stock Exchange membership charge fees out of all proportion to the services they actually perform. Aware of and nervous about this, they habitually overreact to any outside interest or criticism of their situation. As a case in point, when Mayor Lindsay suggested a transfer tax on Stock Exchange transactions, the reaction was an immediate threat by Funston to move the Exchange out of town. The truth of the matter is that in spite of Funston's thundering, no Exchange members ever thought seriously for more than half a minute about moving the true heart of their operation out of New York. However, as happens at a time of pressure, politics, and propaganda, the Exchange, which officially was still committed to move to the Battery site, used this situation to extricate itself from the Battery move which so many of its members were now opposed to. Claiming the need for flexibility of action in their contest with Mayor Lindsay, they publicly rescinded the planned move to the Battery.

Shortly after the above incident, Funston left the scene. That the Stock Exchange might yet decide to move to the site we suggested to them was a very faint possibility, but the loss here was to the Exchange and not to Webb & Knapp. By then we had sold off that property, at a modest profit . . .

During our assembly of the Finance Place properties and earliest wooing of the Exchange, the cash demands of the assemblage were relatively low. But, come law day, when we would pick up the various deeds and pay out over twenty-four million dollars for our purchases, we would need cash. The assemblage was good enough so I could borrow eighteen million dollars on the properties. If I could sell, lease, or borrow another ten million, we could get all our cost out, and some profit; if not, we would have one more potential disaster nipping at our heels. The difficulty was in finding a big enough and strong enough buyer or combination of backers to come into the thing with us. For months I had been casting about in my mind, and finally came up with the name of the single, most logical one of all possible entrants: the U.S. Steel Corp.

U.S. Steel, in spite of its size and ramifications, is an introspective company with very few outside interests. They might not immediately recognize that they were the logical buyers of Finance Place, but I planned to remedy that. By now we were working very closely with Alcoa on a great many fine projects. I called Leon Hickman, Alcoa's executive vice-president and chairman of the finance committee, and asked him if he knew Roger Blough, head of U.S. Steel.

It turned out that Hickman and Blough were great friends. As a matter of fact, it was Hickman who proposed Blough to the United States bar.

That phase of the bar is much like proposing a man's name to an exclusive club, and when Hickman said, "Would you like to meet him?" I replied, "I would, very much."

A few days later I got a call, and a voice announced, "This is Roger Blough. I understand you want to meet me."

"I do, Mr. Blough."

"Well, I'll be in town Saturday. I'm officiating at a Pennsylvania Society meeting; we are going to give Jim Symes of the Penn Railroad a medal as 'Man of the Year in Pennsylvania.'"

Blough then said, "I could be in your office at twelve o'clock."

"Would you like me to call on you, Mr. Blough?"

"No, I'll be there."

I had our architects and staff alerted. We had a beautiful model of Finance Place set up in our upstairs conference room, and at twelve o'clock the next Saturday, in walked Mr. Blough, accompanied by one other gentleman. Blough introduced the second man, Tyson, as chairman of Steel's finance committee. I thought to myself, "That's the guy I really want to see." We shook hands all around, and we took them upstairs to see the model.

Though other metals had lately been entering the picture, steel's great competitor in construction was concrete. Steel, however, had great advantages over all its competition, and one advantage I wanted to point out right then was its use in the truss. Only the truss, by overpassing the streets, could free architects from the design limitations imposed by city street patterns. Most architects, I remarked, are little more than zoning lawyers. The truss, however, could help architects break into new areas, I said, and pointed to the intriguing detail of our model as a lively example of what I meant.

Blough and Tyson were quite interested and pleased by the idea (we all like to see our product well used), and as this little exposition came to a close Blough said, "I want to thank you very much, for showing us all this."

They both got ready to leave, and I said, "Gentlemen, I didn't exactly go through this for my health or because we are running a school; I had a purpose in telling you what I did.

"The purpose of this discussion was to point out that the concrete industry is taking the cream of the building business right away from you.

"When I was a boy, all these buildings around here were going up with nothing but steel. Concrete was for one- and two-story structures only. Today, structural concrete is doing the job in sixty- and seventy-story structures. In fact, it is becoming the rule to use concrete and the exception to use steel. You people are dying in the high-rise market. You are losing ground every day to concrete.

"I'll tell you what your real difficulty is: you've got mastoid trouble."

They were turned back and listening now, and Blough said, "What do you mean by that?"

I said, "Think of this: when you were a boy, mastoid disease of the inner ear was very common—it was a threat to every child, and a most important specialty in the surgical profession. As a matter of fact, a hospital known as the Manhattan Eye, Ear, Nose, and Throat Hospital, of which I am a trustee, was built around the mastoid operation. It was the hospital to go to for mastoid, just as some other hospitals are the place to go for cancer, open heart surgery, or some other specialty.

"But the mastoid operation has gone out of style; penicillin has put it out of business. The number of surgeons familiar with this operation has been cut by at least ninety-five percent. The mastoid specialist has retired somewhere along with the horse and buggy. . . . God forbid there should be a sudden new kind of mastoid epidemic; you would have no people around to handle it. Nobody studies it anymore.

"In building, it's the engineers and architects who determine what materials and techniques will be employed on a job. In years gone by, all structural engineers studied structural-steel design—in great depth; it was a primary course. Today, the only fellows who do that are the bridge builders. Young doctors don't bother studying the mastoid operation; they have penicillin. In your case, the engineers have concrete. The schools are turning out more and more brilliant young designers in concrete, and this is a self-feeding thing. I'll grant you, steel can't go all the way out of business like the mastoid operation has. And your industry is so big and such an important buyer that you can persuade a lot of companies always to choose steel over concrete—but you can't persuade enough of them. You are losing the market!"

Up to this point I had encountered nothing but stunned silence, and I kept right on talking.

"What you've got to do is go out in the field and develop some imaginative uses that show how steel does jobs concrete can't even begin to match. I will name some for you right now. Steel is unexcelled for overpassing. It can be used in treacherous subsoil conditions. Steel is quicker to erect. Steel lends itself to a design change of pace, where, for a change of horizons, you may want an open auditorium at one point, a closed theater in another, or apartments or offices in juxtaposition. With steel you can create flying bridges at the upper levels of high-rise buildings. Steel has so very many advantages, that I don't believe you really need to lose relative position to concrete. But nobody is going to pull your chestnuts out of the fire; you've got to do it for yourself.

"And it will take ten million dollars," I said.

"Ten million for what?"

Pointing to the model, "That's how much we need to take title to this property."

Tyson said, "We're not in the banking business, we're in the steel business."

"You are in the steel business, all right, but you are archaic and reactionary, and it's time you fellows woke up. All you have to do is look over beside you and see the trail that's being blazed by the aluminum companies. The whole aluminum industry have gone out into open-field demonstrations of their product by going into real estate. Other industries are doing the same thing. But I didn't see the steel industry doing anything that counts. The cement industry is far more progressive. Gentlemen, you've got to take some steps to get in line and get up there with the best."

This frank discussion of what their best friends wouldn't tell them was new to my visitors, but if I was being harsh, I was also being sincere, and they knew this. They also knew I was the man who had put Reynolds and Alcoa into real estate and construction, so I spoke as far more than a visionary. We talked a bit more, and then they left. They left making no promises, but about ten days or so later they agreed to put up the ten million dollars we wanted to buy our land, and that got us out of our problems at 165 Broadway and points south. Finance Place was not built as we first visualized it. U.S. Steel designed a most conventional structure. The First National Bank of Chicago did later put up a building very much like our Finance Place conception. They wrote us a letter of apology, saying that this was purely coincidental, they had arrived at the idea on their own, but since our conception was written up in every technical journal in the country years before their project started, none of us took this protestation very seriously.

By now we were through with the Wall Street Maneuver. We were out of the woods with 165 Broadway, but the tie-in of one deal to another in a city like New York can, in time, spread out like a network of roots in a rose garden.

11. The Birth of Life

ROUTINE COMPANY HISTORIES have been rigidly excluded from this compendium on grounds that they are not corporate autobiography but rather biography (and often subsidized and therefore untrustworthy biography at that). Robert T. Elson's history of Time Inc. (a second volume, bringing the story up to 1960, was issued in 1972) is the exception. The book was personally decreed by Henry Luce, founder and head of the company (who lived to read only the first half of the manuscript); the author, Robert T. Elson, had been a Time Inc. employee for a quarter century before undertaking the project and remained one while completing it; the editor, Duncan Norton-Taylor, was another company employee, as were the three archivists, four researchers, and various advisory editors who participated in it. Structurally, then, this book has no more pretensions to objectivity than any subsidized corporate history. But in this case the journalistic standards of the compilers, themselves part of the company, tend to transcend their corporate bias. Professionally skilled in getting the needle into others, they cheerfully or compulsively plunge into themselves. This book is almost in a class by itself in being corporate autobiography in pure form, and at a high level of both candor and writing quality.

Time Inc. is in many ways the quintessential American publishing venture of this century. Founded in 1923 by two brilliant, genteel-poor, success-crazy young Yale graduates, Henry R. Luce and Briton Hadden, it made an instant and lasting success with its first product, the brash, cocksure, high-handed news magazine *Time*. A decade later, having successfully launched the business magazine *Fortune* the very year of the stock market crash, 1929, the company, flourishing through a great depression, was more than ever expansion-minded. The following passages tell the edifying and hair-raising story of the founding and launching of the third jewel in Time Inc.'s crown, the weekly picture magazine *Life*. Clearly, the idea of such a magazine was one whose time had come, and here we see the brilliant, nervous, vital, quarrelsome people with whom Luce liked to surround himself, first conceiving the idea, then developing and testing it (and, for a while, thinking of naming the new magazine "Dime"), and finally, with hope and trepidation, launching it. We then see the new enterprise flourishing so quickly and so mightily that success nearly kills both it and the parent company, because initial advertising rates had been guaranteed for a year and could not immediately be raised to meet the huge costs of wildly increasing circulation.

In its heyday—say, about 1940 to 1955—*Life* was a sort of model product, perfectly meeting the wants of its vast audience with its up-to-the-second picture coverage of news events, its tone of controlled sensationalism, and its fillip of artistic and intellectual interest. After that, it began mysteriously to decline in popularity, perhaps because of the rise of television, perhaps in conformity with the old theory that popular magazines run their course in a generation. At any rate, by 1970 *Life* was operating in the red, and in 1972 Time Inc. decided to discontinue its publication, thus ending an era in American magazine publishing.

THE STAFF OF TIME INC. was excited by rumors of the new project. In March, C. D. Jackson tried to quiet these with this memo: "The current activity on the 51st floor may give rise to the query, what's up? Something is up, and until further notice it should be considered an office secret. The Experimental Department is working on the idea of a picture supplement for *Time*. The less said about it, the better." His memorandum was very obviously a diversionary tactic. Some hint of Time Inc.'s intentions had appeared in the newspaper columns because of the company's increased activity in picture procurement, an interest that obviously outstripped the immediate requirements of *Time* and *Fortune*. In March, for instance, Time Inc. had signed a reciprocal agreement for use of the full pictures services of the Associated Press; and Time Inc., through a wholly owned subsidiary, Pictures Inc., became the sales agent for non-newspaper rights to Associated Press pictures. The real purpose of Pictures Inc. was to acquire for the Time Inc. magazines the rights to pictures from all foreign and domestic agencies. At the same time there was set up a central picture-procurement bureau within the company. All of this was to ensure that the editors would have unlimited access to the output of news photographs from every available source.

In June 1936 Luce made a formal presentation to the directors. The magazine would have a page size approximately that of the *Illustrated London News,* be printed on "shiny" (coated) paper "much better than *Time*'s, not quite as good as that of the most expensive magazines," contain 40 to 48 pages of editorial matter to be supported by 20 pages of advertisements. The contents were to be "a bigger and better collection of current news photographs than is available in all the current events magazines plus all the Sunday gravure supplements combined. Altogether about 200 photographs with full explanatory captions." The tentative price: ten cents on newsstands,

From *Time Inc.: The Intimate History of a Publishing Enterprise, 1923–1941,* by Robert T. Elson, ed. by Duncan Norton-Taylor (Atheneum, 1968), pp. 274–303.

or $3 a year. The name: *Dime, The Show-Book of the World.* (Within the office the staff called it "Uncle Harry's Show-Book.")

The basic premise was that "people like to look at pictures . . . but nowhere are all the best . . . pictures brought together and printed clearly on good paper in logical, coherent sequence so that you can enjoy and study them in one comfortable sitting." *Dime,* said Luce, would not be a "mere selector" of pictures; it would edit as well as select, and would

> seek to advance the art and function of pictorial journalism. It will have its own staff of four or five outstandingly good camera men [and] be a ready purchaser of the best product of the best free-lance camera men. . . . *Dime* will be the complete and reliable *record* of all the significant events which are recorded in pictures [and] will seek to reveal more of the current events . . . and more of the contemporary life of the world . . . than has hitherto been revealed in pictures.

The financial outlook for the magazine was admittedly uncertain, inconclusive on the prospect for profit:

> It is easy to imagine how millions can be made out of *Dime.* Since it is by far the biggest and best package of pictures for the money, and since "everybody" likes to look at pictures, it will achieve millions of circulation and, having achieved five or ten million circulation, it will be the most potent advertising medium in the United States. Result: profits sufficient to pay off the national debt.
>
> But alas, short of this dream bonanza, it is difficult to find a logical profit formula. Truth is that *Dime* is not an investment —or even a speculation—which is likely to appeal to an unimaginative Scotsman. For example, here is a budget for 500,000 circulation with an advertising rate of $2,000 a page:

Income

1,000 pages of advertising @ $1,700 net	$1,700,000
500,000 circulation @ 5 cents per copy	$1,300,000[1]
	$3,000,000

[1] Figure represents not gross but net returns from newsstand sales.

Expenses

Paper and Printing (plus some allowance for replacement of circulation)	$2,200,000
Editorial	250,000
Selling Ads	250,000
Circulation Promotion	200,000
General	100,000
	$3,000,000

A magazine which cannot make money on 500,000 circulation and a $3,000,000 turnover is not one which is calculated to separate a Scotsman from his whiskey.

Dime was set up on a financial pattern radically different from that of *Time* and *Fortune.* Those magazines had relatively low break-even points; by reason of their high subscription prices, nearly all the cost of printing and publishing could, theoretically, be paid for by a small number of subscribers. To apply the same principle to the new magazine would require a price of 25 cents a copy, "which would put it out of the reach of the middle-class American [and] thereby deny one of the chief characteristics of pictures, which is that 'everybody' likes them." *Dime*'s circulation would pay only for the cost of printing and paper for its 40 to 48 editorial pages and the cost of maintaining circulation. The advertising revenues had to cover: the cost of printing the advertising pages, and of selling them; the cost of putting together the editorial content; any increased costs of circulation; and all overhead. The margin of profit rested entirely on the sale of advertising, which meant that "the gamble is largely on the question of whether or not *Dime* will prove to be a popular advertising medium."

The publishing plan envisaged publication in early autumn 1936 in order to take advantage of the Christmas gift subscription season, which it was hoped would enable the magazine to establish a circulation base of 200,000 (not the 500,000 in the imaginary budget) for 1937; the basic page rate for advertising was to be $1,200, or $6 per thousand. The goal was to sell 1,000 pages in 1937. On this basis, the presentation concluded:

Investment in 1936 will be between $250,000 and $400,000. If all goes well, *Dime* will theoretically break even in 1937. But if all goes well, *Dime* must drive on to bigger circulation, which will require an additional $300,000. If things do not go well, the $300,000 will be needed for repair and for retreat purposes. That comes to a total of $700,000 indicated outlay. Add to that another $300,000 for bad (or good) luck and it can safely be assumed that $1,000,000 will see *Dime* safely through to a break-even 500,000 circulation or to an honorable grave.

The directors voted to proceed.

Luce's associates had mixed feelings. [Charles] Stillman, an enthusiastic supporter of *Fortune,* was lukewarm—possibly, he admitted, "because the subject matter of *Fortune* was of more intense interest to me." Allen Grover wrote: "The sums involved, the long odds against success, the small return to the company from anything except an enormous circulation, make it a gamble which puts Wall Street and Broadway to shame." But he was for the venture because he felt the company should invest in publishing.

The staff was virtually unanimous that the name *Dime* would not do. [Manfred] Gottfried wrote: *"Dime* is a swell name but it will soon rival syphilis as a cause of insanity—among telephone operators, office boys, newsstand boys, newsstand buyers, advertisers and everyone who has to use Dee-ime and Tee-ime in a business way. . . . You might even call it 'Tent'; it covers everything." Another argued, "I don't like *Dime;* after all, you might want to change the price some day." Nick Wallace wrote from Chicago: "When I visualize the countless errors in handling which are sure to result from a name that sounds and looks so much like *Time,* I start picking me out a nice, comfortable sanitarium. One of our worst bug-bears is the illegible writing of most people. We can now pick out the word *Time* without much difficulty, but when that is complicated by deciding whether it is *Time* or *Dime,* we will all be dizzy. . . . Call the new magazine (1) Scene—or Seen (2) Pictures (3) anything but *Dime!* Please!" [Roy] Larsen was for the name: "It strikes me as crazy enough to make sense."

Between June 8 and 29, Luce produced a prospectus for the new magazine that has seldom been surpassed as a piece of promotion:

> To see life; to see the world; to eyewitness great events; to watch the faces of the poor and the gestures of the proud; to see strange things—machines, armies, multitudes, shadows in the jungle and on the moon; to see man's work—his paintings, towers and discoveries; to see things thousands of miles away, things hidden behind walls and within rooms, things dangerous to come to; the women that men love and many children; to see and to take pleasure in seeing; to see and be amazed; to see and be instructed.

> Thus to see, and to be shown, is now the will and new expectancy of half mankind.

> To see, and to show, is the mission now undertaken by a new kind of publication, *The Show-Book of the World,*[2] hereinafter described.

The need and opportunity for *Show-Book* existed because while there were many pictures in a week's harvest of news, nowhere could be seen at one comfortable sitting "the cream of all the world's pictures," and almost no attempt had been made to

> edit pictures into a coherent story—to make an effective mosaic out of the fragmentary documents which pictures, past and present, are. . . . And, more than that . . . reveal to us far more explicitly the nature of the dynamic social world in which we live.

The magazine promised to scour the world for the best pictures, to edit them with feeling for form, history, and drama, and to publish them on fine paper in a "complete and reliable record." The magazine's content would be built, the prospectus promised, on two cornerstones: the Big Newspicture Story of the Week—"the biggest news that is best recorded by the camera"—and the Big Special Feature, "some subject of major current interest and significance." As distinguished from the News, the function of the Feature

[2] A footnote said, "Actual name will appear on Vol. I, No. 1."

will be Revelation—taking you intimately into the life of a famed personage, be it Shirley Temple or the Pope; or intimately into the inner workings of a celebrated institution, such as The Jockey Club, The Japanese Army, Alcatraz, Vassar or Father Divine's Heaven. . . .

The rest of the contents would vary as pictures vary, but at least two or three "great photographs" were promised, and pictures recording "the shifting mores and fashions," Broadway openings and Hollywood movies; and *Show-Book* undertook to "crash the Party-of-the-Week." Finally, the prospectus promised to produce the unpredictable,

> so that while *Show-Book*'s readers will usually know what to expect they will never be quite sure that they will not get a whacking surprise. . . .

All in all, *Show-Book* promised to be quite a package. The editor of *Advertising and Selling,* on reading the prospectus, commented: "The fine promissory glow, conviction of success and siren seductiveness which Luce wraps up in a prospectus is lost on a publication, but would make millions for an enterprising pre-SEC underwriting house. . . . Seems sort of a shame that they have to get out a new magazine and can't just sell the prospectus."

THE CREATION of a new magazine, Luce wrote in describing the launching of *Life,* is "a compound of hundreds upon hundreds of decisions, varying in importance from agreement on an editorial point of view, frequency of issue, schedule of prices, etc., to style rules on the use of commas. These decisions are based upon innumerable individual experiments, mock-ups, make-ups and make-believes—trial copy, trial photographs."

It was a far from orderly process, extending over eight months in 1936, and before the first issue appeared the nerves and physical resources of the company were stretched to the breaking point. The decision to publish was taken before any number of essentials had been determined. The first sales staff was hired before a dummy had been prepared . . . They made their first calls on the trade before the date of publication had been set, a circulation guarantee established or the page size chosen—and the magazine had no name. (In the office, *Parade* was a working title.) Yet such was Time Inc.'s reputation in advertising circles that some agencies were willing to take a chance. And, of course, the Luce prospectus, circulated to the trade, became a powerful persuader. Ben Duffy of Batten, Barton, Durstine & Osborn immediately signed a space contract. Dr. George Gallup, of Young & Rubicam, predicted the magazine would be successful because Time Inc. "had the intelligence and initiative to grasp an idea which has been a natural ever since pictures were born. . . ." On the basis of a series of test mailings in late spring the circulation guarantee was set at 250,000 and the advertising rates at $1,500 for a full page, inside color at $2,250 and the fourth cover in color at $3,000. Advertisers who signed contracts prior to publication were guaranteed these rates for the first twelve months—as it turned out, one of the greatest bargains in the history of periodical advertising, and a near-disaster for Time Inc.

The circulation guarantee proved to be conservative, because prior to the first issue the new magazine had 235,000 charter subscriptions. The first major mail solicitation, a letter over Luce's signature, went to 755,000 subscribers to *Time* and *Fortune*. It consisted of a description of the magazine and concluded with a direct personal appeal:

> . . . before we take our final plunge, before we risk upwards of $1,000,000, we need some friendly assurance that you and people like you—the alert, newsminded audience for whom we are planning our new venture—are willing to risk with us the price of a year's subscription.
>
> We must reach our final decision this month—to publish or not to publish.
>
> So if you think we are right—
>
> If you have faith that we can create with pictures a new magazine you would value as you now value *Time* or *Fortune* . . . if you are willing to join us in the venture as an Original Subscriber—
>
> Then may I ask you—please—to help us to our decision by signing the enclosed card today and rushing it back to me airmail.

It was one of the most successful mailings in Time Inc.'s experience; 26,151 cards were returned in a single day, 72,955 in the first week (almost 10-percent return).

Financial and production planning was enormously complicated. Pierrie Prentice, who had succeeded as over-all circulation manager after Larsen moved to *The March of Time,* prepared a series of budgets based on a variety of plans—"for a 25¢ fortnightly at 100,000 circulation," for a weekly of the same circulation and "one last shot at a 10¢ quality magazine" at 100,000, 200,000 and 500,000 circulation. By mid-May fourteen production and distribution budgets had been produced for magazines with a circulation of 200,000 and a 280,000 print order. They included page sizes ranging from 9⅜" x 13⅜" (*Parade*) to 10½" x 14" (*Illustrated London News*), and a variety of qualities of paper. In the absence of firm decision there was an air of unreality about much of this budgeting.

In the preliminary stages the production planning was handled by a committee, which apparently added to the confusion at the Chicago end. There Nick Wallace was rapidly running out of patience. He remarked that things were being done the way Baptists prepare for a picnic, with "no allowance for rain, and it always rains." On his own initiative Wallace came to New York to confront Stillman with the situation and to demand that Stillman take charge of production. Stillman did so with the help of the company's assistant treasurer, David W. Brumbaugh.

Brumbaugh, a man of rising importance, had been hired by Stillman in 1933 through a want ad in the New York *Times* which brought hundreds of responses. Among these was a letter from a Dr. Seay, who said he knew just the right person and hoped Time Inc. would make no final choice until his nominee could be interviewed. Stillman did not know Dr. Seay, or that his candidate was his prospective son-in-law. Purely on a hunch, he took Seay's advice and interviewed Brumbaugh. In advising the directors of his choice, Stillman wrote that the new man was "a native of Virginia, where he worked his way through Roanoke College, emerged with an A.B. and a scholastic average of 90. He then borrowed the money to go to Harvard Business School, specialized there in Accounting, was graduated with Honors in 1931." His starting salary was $3,000 a year.

It was Brumbaugh's memorandum, entitled "Recording of a Decision of Major Importance," that justified the adoption of the large page size. The choice had narrowed to a *Vogue*-size page (9¾" x 12¾"), which offered the prospect for greater profit, or the larger *Illustrated London News*-size page, which the editors preferred. The decision was to settle on the 10½" x 14" page size; this was slightly larger than that of the *Saturday Evening Post,* offered excellent display for photographs but at the same time would accommodate advertising plates made for either *Vogue* or the *Saturday Evening Post.* An appendix to the memorandum reflected the philosophy that still guides Time Inc. management:

> Never in our history have we come out of any tight spot by a choice of conservatism or economy *in the usual sense of those words,* but always by expenditure of more money and more effort to gain greater income at greater expense. This will always be the right choice as long as the ideas and the vitality are flowing freely to keep pace with the increased outlays. This has produced profits which must be considered the result of the most effective and hence the most economical use of an enviable concentration of manpower, an element in success far scarcer than gold, no matter what price per ounce.

It was relatively easy to decide on a page size; it was far more difficult to fulfill Luce's prime specification—the quality reproduction of photographs on coated paper. The technology required in both printing and paper-making was far from perfected when Donnelley delivered to New York their first experimental samples. Prior to 1936, for instance, coated paper in rolls was not readily procurable because there was little demand for it. Magazines which used coated paper were printed on sheet-fed presses and therefore the paper was delivered in the form of sheets rather than rolls. The Mead Corporation, which supplied paper for *Time,* would supply coated paper in rolls on demand, but it was produced by a costly and cumbersome method, each side of the paper being coated separately. While patented processes did exist for coating paper on both sides of the sheet in one continuous operation, they had not been developed. One of Stillman's first problems was to determine whether an adequate supply of coated paper could be guaranteed. The Mead engineers went to work on the problem, came up with a paper which they called Enameline, offered at a tentative price of $98 a ton, well within the budget projections for the new magazine. While the Mead production was limited, Stillman felt that sufficient progress had been made so that he could gamble that additional supplies would be made available if a market developed.

There was a problem in printing; the experimental pages Donnelley had shown in New York were produced on makeshift equipment specially converted to accommodate the new quick-drying ink. The ideal procedure would have been to design and engineer new presses, the construction of which would have taken a year or more. The men at Time Inc. were determined not to wait. The men at the Donnelley plant therefore took two presses which had previously been used to print mail-order catalogues, equipped them with gas-fired heaters needed to speed the drying of the ink. They had many misgivings about this equipment. A few weeks before the first issue went to press, T. E. Donnelley recalled, he told Zimmermann, "We may have overestimated our ability to deliver. The foreman just told me he has yet to get a satisfactorily printed sheet out of those converted presses." The two presses alone were not adequate to handle the job; pending the delivery of new machinery, the magazine had to use, as standby and auxiliary equipment, a rotogravure press and outmoded sheet-fed presses.

The Luce prospectus seemed to provide a coherent and clear editorial blueprint; it proved more difficult to translate into a printed magazine than was at first anticipated. The earliest surviving dummy was produced—so the editors said—"from the 5,000-odd pictures that came into existence or were for the first time available to U.S. magazines during the week of May 18–23 . . . selected and arranged experimentally to demonstrate our conviction that, while the camera has achieved high efficiency as a reporter and recorder of our time, a journalistic job remains to be done in articulating a language of pictures." It was, by common agreement of all who worked on it, a failure. It lacked taste and distinction and was too sensational. Among the pictures were those of a lynching, brutally captioned

"Nigger Hunt," a murderer strapped in the death chair and a nudist colony at the San Diego fair. "One nude is nude," [Archibald] Mac-Leish hooted on seeing this spread, "twenty nudes are just bare."

A printed effort, entitled *Dummy,* was produced in midsummer; it went to press in twelve days under conditions intended to simulate actual publication. A good deal of confusion prevailed; Thomas Cleland, the designer of *Fortune,* had been hired as a consultant, but complained to Luce that he had been ignored: ". . . I was never even consulted . . . or given any opportunity . . . to correct or revise any of my own part of it. It appears to have been immediately subjected to the criticism and suggestions of all the Toms, Dicks and Harrys except the particular Tom engaged for that purpose by the particular Harry who engaged him." The editors, well aware of *Dummy*'s shortcomings, asked its readers to "please pretend . . . a magazine like this has been coming to the house every Thursday. This is no special issue—indeed it is below par and suggests that the regular editorial staff had gone on vacation leaving this issue to be put to press by inexperienced juniors."

The selected audience to which *Dummy* was shown was not impressed. "It was a complete flop, as far as we were concerned," said [Daniel] Longwell. While Director Robert Chambers objected that the pictures were "lurid—reminiscent of the graphics [the tabloids]," former director Harry Davison told Luce he doubted that the magazine would interest "the average straphanger."

Luce agreed with both of them. To Chambers he wrote: "Most of the criticisms were on the other side of the fence. . . . The point is, of course, that we do not intend to appeal to the mob, but we do hope that the magazine will appeal to a million or more people who are not all of them high-brow." And to Davison: "The dummy was a disappointment. . . . I hope it proves we can't do any worse. . . . We are now setting out to get the job done right."

Another critic was Paul Hollister, a friend of Luce and Larsen and one of the most creative advertising men of his generation. When *Dummy* appeared he was executive vice-president of R. H. Macy & Co. in charge of advertising. He wrote Luce: "It is inconceivable that even an avowed dress rehearsal just for 'fun' should have turned out so far short even of where you intended. . . . Great God, that a

LOOKS paper should make even a tentative *peek* looking like this.
. . . The dangerous thing is you have good raw material; it must not
be 'bootchered.'" He added that he was taking off for a vacation at
Manchester-by-the-Sea in Massachusetts, but that for $1,000 he
would rework *Dummy* and show how it should be done. He did not
expect this offer to be taken up, but Monday morning in Manchester
his telephone rang. As he remembered the conversation:

> LUCE: "I got your note. It is very intriguing."
> HOLLISTER: "Oh."
> LUCE: "What do we do now?"
> HOLLISTER: "What do you mean, what do we do now?"
> LUCE: "I mean what do you do next? I want your comments."

Hollister asked to have twenty copies shipped to him; he then drove
to nearby Gloucester, bought a drawing board, a can of rubber
cement, scissors, art gum and a T-square. For ten days he holed up,
forgoing beach, tennis and golf, re-making *Dummy.* Longwell went
up to see the result—a new dummy, pasted up accordion-style so it
could be spread out on the floor. Longwell said it was "fine."

That was all Hollister heard for several weeks. Finally he wrote
Luce: "Was it that bad?"

Next day he was invited to lunch in New York with Luce, Longwell
and Ingersoll. Luce described to Hollister the work-in-progress, then
turned to him and said:

"Now we have an editorial prospectus. Now we have a basic format. . . . Now what do we do?"

"What you do," replied Hollister, "is to get an art director and put
him at a drawing board. Put tape over his mouth, because whatever
he has to state should drain off through his fingers onto paper. Never
let an art director talk. On a table at his left put your basic format
dummy for reference. Onto a table at his right, feed him batches of
photographs with a note saying you want 1, 2, 3, 8—any number of
pages you need, for each batch, and any suggestions you have for
playing up any particular angles of the picture story.

"So he makes layouts from the pictures. If they are right, you pat
him on the head. If they have strayed from the mood of the basic
format, you take a small hammer, rap him smartly on the skull, point

severely to the dummy and cry 'No, no, no! Naughty!' He then repents and makes the layout right or you get yourself a new art director."

"Fine," said Luce. "Will you get us an art director?"

In September, Hollister recommended his own art director at Macy's, Howard Richmond, for the job.

Luce designated himself as managing editor "for an unstated term of months or years." His alternate, he said, would be John Martin, who, when the magazine was successfully under way, would take over, enabling Luce to "retire to his sinecure as General Editor of Time Inc. publications"; Longwell became picture editor, "supremely responsible for the flow of pictures. . . . Every nickel spent for pictures and all work of photographers must be regulated by him. . . ." There were three associate editors (writers): Joseph Kastner, drafted from *Fortune;*[3] [Joseph] Thorndike, who had been with the Experimental Department from the beginning; and David Cort, transferred from *Time.* The first staff photographers listed were Eisenstaedt and Stackpole; the names of McAvoy and Bourke-White were added within a few weeks.

Miss Mary Fraser, designated by Luce as copy chief, would, he said, "be in the unhappy position of having two bosses, but as between the two she is more responsible to the Picture Editor than to the Managing Editor."[4] "Fra" (Wellesley '23) was outstanding among many dedicated and resilient women who played an important role in Time Inc.'s development. On graduation she had joined the company as a circulation-department typist, then become secretary to [Briton] Hadden. She resigned in the summer of 1924 to get some newspaper experience on the New Brunswick (New Jersey) *Home News,* then returned to *Time* in November 1927, where she became

[3] Kastner, who had had to resign as copy boy when *Time* moved to Cleveland, had been hired back in 1930 after his graduation from Yale. According to Eric Hodgins, Luce demanded one day at lunch: "Is there anyone on your staff who can be concise?" Hodgins replied that Kastner had been writing the "Off the Record" department for *Fortune* and managed to keep it within four columns. " 'Joe Kastner,' said Luce, 'that's the boy I want.' That afternoon I had to tell Joe that I had apparently and inadvertently sold him down the river."

[4] This turned out to be true in her personal life. She married Dan Longwell in December 1938.

head of research and copy chief until drafted temporarily for this new job.

This staff was largely responsible for the second printed dummy, *Rehearsal,* which was printed in September. The content, the editors said, was "suggestive" of the magazine to be; it carried some sample advertising pages, although advertisers were warned that the make-up was "not to be considered as an ultimate guide to advertising positions available" in the actual magazine. In format and content, *Rehearsal* closely approximated the magazine that appeared on the newsstands six weeks later. It had good spot-news photographs—the fall of Irun in the Spanish war; the Nazi rally at Nürnberg; a "biography," in Soviet paintings, of Stalin "as Communists *must* see him." But the photograph that caught all eyes was Paul Outerbridge's full-page color study of a seated nude, entitled (presumably because her face was averted) "Modesty."

This was long before the day of *Playboy,* in whose columns "Modesty" today would scarcely raise an eyebrow. In 1936 the editors knew all too well that so explicit a nude would not be acceptable in a magazine of general circulation. In a dummy printed for limited circulation, directed to the trade, they obviously enjoyed being a little naughty. The alarm bells sounded. The head of the American News Company warned that "while the picture will undoubtedly create sales, it would be better not to print a picture of this type in a magazine published by a house that has the wonderfully fine standing of your company." From Chicago, Nick Wallace wrote that he did not want his subscription agents to see *Rehearsal* because "it would rub them the wrong way." A *March of Time* crew, dispatched to Hyde Park to film a sequence on the Roosevelt family, took along a copy; when the President's mother's eye fell on "Modesty," she announced firmly that it was not the kind of magazine her family would wish to have in their home. T. E. Donnelley wrote Luce, "You will lose no subscribers by leaving such pictures out, and you will keep a great many more if you do." Luce replied, "As to the nudes, I'll agree. . . . Of course, I had in mind the fact that actually this dummy was not for general publication—I thought the Outerbridge color (with or without nudes) would be of special interest to advertising men."

The over-all reception of *Rehearsal* was somewhat mixed. Dorothy Thompson, the columnist, wrote Luce that she and her husband, Sinclair Lewis, thought it "curiously unmodern, a combination of Bernarr Macfadden and the *Illustrated London News.* In fact, Henry, the magazine does not look like you. I should expect from you something handsome, dramatic, speedy. . . ." Prentice was also disappointed, commenting, "If the magazine we turn out is going to be anything like that, I do not believe we will hold more than 50% of our prepublication subscribers. . . ." But Longwell was enthusiastic and told Luce: "Encouraging is the attitude of . . . people like Larsen, Billings, Hodgins. . . . They criticize [details], yet with publishing-editorial imagination enough to see what we are aming at and how we are approaching what we shall be. Frankly, they think we could go right on the stands." Luce decided that the period of experimentation was over. "We won't experiment any more," he said to Longwell. "We'll learn how to do this in actual publication."

Some months before the first issue of *Life* went to press, there occurred an incident that had a lasting influence on the relations of Mrs. Luce to the Time Inc. magazines. Apparently neither she nor her husband had taken too seriously his promise, when he was courting her, to make her co-editor of the new picture magazine. But throughout the pre-publication period he had constantly discussed the project with her and she had been most enthusiastic. One afternoon Luce called her and, as she remembered it, said that [Ralph] Ingersoll and Dan Longwell had invited them to dinner, adding with a chuckle, "I think I know what's coming." "I said, 'What?' He said, 'I think they want to offer you a place on the magazine.' I said, 'Oh, that's wonderful!'"

At dinner at Voisin it soon became evident, at least to Mrs. Luce, that her hosts had no intention of making her an offer. Toward the end, Ingersoll asked if they could go back to the Luce apartment at River House. There, he began talking about how well Luce had handled *Time.* Then, according to Mrs. Luce, Ingersoll turned and said, "Harry, you have got to make up your mind whether you are going to go on being a great editor or whether you are going to be on a perpetual honeymoon. When you edited *Time* you stayed in the office until ten and eleven o'clock every night. Now you catch the 5:10 back to the country. You clear out of that office at five o'clock every afternoon. Clare, if she really loves you, won't get in the way of the success of this magazine. And what I have to say to her is that you cannot publish a great magazine with one hand tied behind your back."

Her husband, Mrs. Luce recalled, was thunderstruck. She said to Ingersoll, "Mac, I have something to tell you, and I hope you'll remember it and Harry will remember it. Harry Luce can publish a better magazine with one hand tied behind his back than you can publish with both of yours free." And with that she went upstairs "to have a little cry."

When Ingersoll and Longwell had left, Mrs. Luce said to her husband: "'I've been hoping and thinking of how I could be of most help to you and it's perfectly clear the way I can help you most is to set about my own business. And for some time I have been thinking what I'd like to do is to write another play.' And I did, and it made a million dollars." The play, *The Women,* produced in December 1936, ran for 657 performances on Broadway, was twice made into a movie, and has been many times revived in summer theaters.

The prospectus said that the name of the new magazine would not be announced before publication. Charter subscribers and the staff were invited to submit suggestions; the list covered several pages: *Affairs, Candid Camera, Graphic, News-Views, Pageant, Scene, Show, Witness, Sight, Eyewitness, Picture.* Paul Hollister called Luce in great excitement one morning, saying he was coming over with the ideal name. He appeared with a drawing of an eye with the word *See* superimposed. *Look* was actually used in some cover mock-ups. Larsen argued that because of the broadcast and movie, *The March of Time* should be considered.

The name finally chosen was the one Mrs. Luce had mentioned in her memorandum to Condé Nast several years before; it was also suggested by James A. Linen, Jr., the father of the present president of the company and an old family friend of Luce. On reading the prospectus, he wrote, "The name *Life,* if it were to be preempted, would appear to me to best typify the proposed publication." A month later, when Luce had finally decided to buy the old *Life,* he wrote Linen, "We have been trying to get the use of the name *Life* and I had hoped [to] write you before this that we had been successful. . . . As you can see, I agree with you fully that it is the perfect name. . . ." As the prospectus said, "To see life; to see the world; to eyewitness great events . . ."

The old *Life* was in its fifty-fourth year. Founded by three young Harvard men, it had reached the peak of its circulation (a quarter million) and influence in World War I years. After the war its longtime contributor, the famous illustrator Charles Dana Gibson, acquired a controlling interest. *Life*'s pages were graced by the writing of Franklin P. Adams, Robert Benchley, Dorothy Parker and Frank Sullivan, and the drawings of Gibson himself, Gluyas Williams and the great political cartoonist Rollin Kirby. One of its editors was Robert E. Sherwood, later to become a distinguished playwright and a personal assistant and ghostwriter for Franklin D. Roosevelt. But *Life* failed to keep up with changing modes and manners; it lost ground to *The New Yorker,* was changed from a weekly to a monthly. In 1932 its ownership passed to a trio of advertising men, Clair Maxwell, Henry Richter and Frederick G. Francis. By 1936 circulation had declined to 70,000.

Was it for sale? When Luce decided on a Friday afternoon in August that *Life* was the name he wanted, he called in *Time*'s advertising manager Howard Black, a friend of Maxwell: "I practically whispered the name to him, and then asked him if he thought we could buy it. I never spent such a long, nervous weekend. It was Monday before Black reported back. 'The answer is yes,' he said, 'if you'll give jobs to the small staff.' " The matter was settled immediately; the price was $92,000.

The intention was to keep the sale secret until Time Inc. was ready to launch the new magazine, but Walter Winchell broke the story on the day of sale. However, the last issue of the old *Life* was not withdrawn from the newsstands until the day before the new *Life* appeared. The sale of *Life* touched off many sentimental tributes, among them H. I. Phillips' verse in the New York *Sun:*

Life takes time, I always knew
In this drab world of strife,
But truer is the headline still
That tells me *Time* takes *Life.*

Prior to the publication of *Life* the management of Time Inc. was aware that another picture magazine was about to be published. In fact, as a hedge against the possible failure of *Life,* it invested in the venture. John Cowles and his brother Gardner, publishers of the Des Moines *Register* and *Tribune,* were friends and stockholders of Time Inc. With full knowledge of Time Inc. plans, they showed Luce, Larsen and company a dummy of *Look.* It was planned as a monthly, printed in rotogravure on cheaper paper, aimed at a mass audience, with production costs budgeted so low that newsstand sales could produce a small profit in the first year. No advertising was to be solicited in the first year, pending the establishment of a circulation base.

The Cowleses felt there would be no competition between the two publications; they therefore offered Time Inc. a 20-percent interest in their magazine—50,000 shares for $100,000. John Cowles wrote Larsen: "Although it is an extreme gamble, we think it is a chance worth taking. . . . Circulation might conceivably go to 600,000 or 800,000 the first year. . . ." Larsen and Stillman recommended the investment, arguing that "if our plans for *Life* prove to be top-heavy with overhead and bigness, as they might, the modest scale of operations proposed by the Cowles brothers is so much the opposite extreme that they might well succeed where we might fail."

The Executive Committee agreed to the investment, taking note of a reservation by Luce, who was "afraid their journalism would prove to be too 'yellow' for us to be in entire sympathy with it." However, Larsen noted that the Cowleses "feel that they will be able to become less 'yellow' as they go along, as did the *Daily News.*" The Time Inc. investment, at the Cowleses' request, was reduced to 45,000 shares before publication started. In July 1937, with both *Life* and *Look* in operation, the Cowleses requested that Time Inc. resell them its interest, which the company did for $157,500, a profit of $67,500.

Six months before *Life* went to press Luce took [John Shaw] Billings aside and said, "There is going to be a lot of talk about this picture magazine. Everyone is going to want in on it. I want you to be the one person who doesn't bother his head about it. Just keep *Time* going." Luce knew his associates only too well; before the magazine appeared the company executives, with the exception of Billings, were almost wholly involved in one way or another. There was a good deal of confusion as to who was doing what, as is evidenced by a small aberration on the part of Longwell a few weeks before publication. He wrote to Ingersoll, the general manager: "May I shift off onto you lettering for the *Time* cover and stationery? Will you see that no stationery is printed until you have the final lettering for the cover?" To which Ingersoll replied acidly, "The lettering of *Life*'s (not *Time*'s) cover is your problem, not mine. When Harry and you have chosen the lettering, I shall be happy to take on matters of masthead wording, etc. . . . Stationery will not be printed until it is necessary. But in view of the tardiness of the editors, it may be necessary—in the interest of collecting money—to print stationery without benefit of cover type."

The cover design is attributed to artist Edward Wilson; his idea, said Longwell, was "to get the best damn picture we can find every week and slap *Life* on it wherever it fits on top and agrees with the design of the picture." The lettering and distinctive red background of the logotype and the red border band below were contributed by Art Director Howard Richmond. It was first proposed that the color should vary from issue to issue, but Luce and Larsen, on the basis of their experience with *Time,* decided to stay with red.

Then, only weeks from the publication date, *Life*'s editorial management underwent a shake-up. John Martin's erratic personality had begun to have a corrosive effect on everyone. He handled Longwell roughly, criticizing him before an embarrassed staff, and arbitrarily rejected pictures and layouts. He was at odds with Luce; at one luncheon he shouted down all of Luce's suggestions as "buckeye." On October 23, Billings recorded in his diary:

At 5 o'clock Luce called me to his office, shut the door, and proceeded to tell me that a great crisis had arisen on *Life*—a crisis due to Martin's behavior. Luce and Martin just don't pull together as a team. As a result *Life* is still badly disorganized and nowhere near ready to go into publication. . . . Now Luce wants to put Martin back on *Time* and make me Managing Editor of *Life*. He thinks he and I could work well together, and so on. I was surprised and startled at this proposal. I know nothing of the philosophy of *Life* and am devoted to *Time,* which is clicking along well. . . . Yet *Life* is a new job with fresh excitement—and much harder work, I suppose. My answer to Luce was: I am ready to do whatever he thought best for the organization.

Luce wrote Martin:

> . . . You and I have not been enough of a success to date as collaborators. . . . Perhaps, without alibi, I should take most of the blame, since it was my job to organize *Life* including the "collaboration." But I must also express candidly the opinion, which is shared by others, that you are a most able editor and an equally difficult collaborator. Roy and I . . . are agreed . . . that there is one obvious good solution—namely, that you should forthwith take post again as Managing Editor of *Time* and that Billings should come to *Life* as my collaborator-in-chief. . . .

Billings took over his new assignment just seventeen days before the first issue was scheduled to go to press. "I had so much to learn in so little time," he recalled. "The staff was green and Longwell was out with the flu. . . . Everything had to go to Luce for a final yes or no. When he wasn't squinting critically at layouts or editing captions, he was filling me full of *Life*'s principles and purposes. *Life* would inform, but it would also entertain. There was to be a lot of show business about it. It would have unity in flow, pace and change of pace, charm and shock—phrases that persisted for years."

Typical of the confusion, not to say near-chaos, attending the birth of *Life* was a curious episode involving Ingersoll, who withdrew from current operations, retired by himself to a hotel room and produced a seventy-four-page memorandum re-examining the whole project. He handed this massive document to Luce on November 2, just two weeks before the first deadline. Luce dropped it into his desk drawer unread. Ingersoll felt that he was being slighted. Luce then had to take time out to mollify him, writing:

> Your work is neither lost nor wasted nor unappreciated. . . . If I am petulant, I am sorry and will try to reform. Meanwhile, what is most on my mind is *getting things done*—and for the next few weeks the emphasis should be on volume rather than quality of work. By quality, I mean whether I cause the right or the wrong thing to be done. If my instincts are wrong, it's too late to change them or me now. . . . Right now I'm afraid, alas, it's got to be the spirit of the Light Brigade—disastrous as that proved to be. Here's hoping we survive!

The cover for Vol. I, No. 1, was Margaret Bourke-White's picture of the massive Fort Peck Dam being built by the WPA in Montana. The frontispiece, captioned "Life Begins," showed an obstetrician holding a newborn baby by its heels. The news section began with further pictures of Fort Peck, showing the workers at a Saturday-night jamboree and the frontier shanty towns where they lived. There were pace and variety in its pages—the first aerial photograph of Fort Knox; Fort Belvedere, Edward VIII's country residence; a spectacular shot of the newly opened Bay Bridge linking San Francisco and Oakland. There were scenes from the Broadway hit *Victoria Regina,* with a family album of the star, Helen Hayes, and from *Camille,* about to open with Greta Garbo and "today's Great Lover of the Screen," Robert Taylor. The magazine offered a three-page color portfolio of the paintings of John Steuart Curry, the first of many which would acquaint *Life* readers with America's contemporary artists. The magazine closed with a party—a hunt given in honor of the British Ambassador to France. The last picture in the magazine was the enormous bag: row on row of dead hares.

Editorially the first issue made a pleasing impression, giving no indication of the infinitely complicated process of putting it to press. With the exception of one advance form, *Time* had a single deadline. *Life* had to be put to press in sections, which meant that the editors had to meet a succession of deadlines. The *Life* editors had to assemble a layout with the original photographs and captions and ship these to Chicago nightly by the Twentieth Century Limited. In an emergency, substitute pictures could be sent by wirephoto and corrections teletyped, but this added a further complication best avoided. Thus the struggle to keep pace with the production schedule and current with the news imposed a constant strain on the editors, writers and artists. The pictures for the lead in the first issue did not arrive until twenty-four hours before the final deadline; Luce and Billings were so swamped with detail at that moment that they had to turn them over to Ingersoll for layout. He drafted MacLeish from *Fortune* to write the captions.

The deadline was Saturday night, but Stillman, who had gone to Chicago to oversee the first printing, reported that on Monday morning when he arrived,

> Wallace had just sent through some changes on two pages that had come by teletype. At around 10:30 a.m. Chicago time (11:30 a.m. New York) Ingersoll telephoned four more changes.
>
> There were four rotary presses supposedly all made ready and set to go, but it wasn't until 4:30 p.m. that the first press started turning out acceptable work. The rest followed along, but it didn't make much difference how fast they turned over, as the bottleneck of the operation proved to be the collating of the twelve sections.

The sections printed in advance had to be assembled with the later pages and fed into machines—stitchers—to bind the magazine together. Crews of girls did the collating:

> There were four gangs working. But the paper being slippery and the sheets larger and heavier and the line longer than they were used to, they made very heavy going. Futhermore many of the girls were green. . . . Desperate efforts were made to speed up, including taking two crews off the *Farm Journal* and putting them on *Life*. . . . They averaged about 7,000 an hour and with all available girl power on the job, they were just barely keeping their heads above water, running about 50,000 copies behind schedule.

When Luce saw the first proofs from Chicago "he thought the whole issue had gone sour on the press," Billings recalled. With the actual delivery of finished copies the mood changed. "As the congratulations and cheers began to roll in, we all felt better," wrote Billings. "Of course there were always the jokers who were quick to write, 'You stink!' [But] we seemed to have a success on our hands. But one issue does not make a magazine, and we had to push on and on."

On Thursday morning, November 19, 1936, some 200,000 copies of the first issue of *Life* were placed on sale, 475 of them in Worcester, Massachusetts. These 475 copies were sold out in a few hours, as were copies in other cities; scores of telegrams from news-dealers poured into the headquarters of the American News Company asking for additional magazines. The orders could not be filled because the press run of 466,000 had already been exhausted. Gratifying as was the demand, management partially discounted it, attributing the initial sellout to curiosity. The following week the magazine sold out again, and again in the third and fourth weeks. The press run could not keep up with the demand. Management was totally unprepared for a situation unparalleled in the history of periodical publishing. Until 1936 the largest circulation ever attained by any magazine in its first year of publication was 500,000, a figure *Life* had apparently surpassed in weeks. A Time Inc. executive, asked how the new magazine was doing, replied, "Having *Life* isn't like having a baby. It's like having quintuplets."

In an attempt to gauge the market, management decided to flood the newsstands of Worcester. The test began with the December 4 issue and a shipment of 2,000 copies; they disappeared as quickly as the original 475 copies. In successive weeks the shipments were raised to 3,000, then 4,000. After 9,000 copies of the March 8 issue were sold, the Worcester distributor telegraphed: "Send 12,000 next week." Another sellout. This figure—12,000—projected on a national scale, indicated that the potential demand for *Life* was between five and six million copies, an all but incredible figure in view of the fact that the biggest newsstand sale for any national magazine was one million—at a per-copy price of five cents v. ten cents for *Life*. Tests in other cities confirmed the figure.

In publishing the story of the Worcester experiment as a two-page house advertisement, *Life* said: "There are many reasons why the Publishers . . . cannot feed endless freight trains of smooth stock paper into the maws of innumerable presses. The demand for 5 or 6 million copies a week is the kind of demand we can *not* follow. So we can only settle down to producing our 1,000,000 a week now and gradually raise production to 1,500,000 by the end of the year. Meanwhile our principal efforts will be devoted to making *Life* a magazine of continuing pleasure and profit to the millions of people who will read each issue this year."

The result of the Worcester experiment precipitated a debate on the magazine's long-term objective. The immediate decision—to limit circulation for the time being to a million copies, then to increase to 1,500,000—was of necessity. It was impossible to produce any more copies. In fact, it was only by prodigies of effort on the part of the Donnelley company that *Life* was able to deliver a million copies each week. The pre-publication plans called for weekly production of 400,000 increasing slowly to a million over a three-year period to permit the orderly introduction of new equipment. The delivery of a million copies weekly was achieved by running the presses around the clock, shutting down only to change plates for the next issue. During the first months there was literally no print order; Publisher Larsen took all the magazines that could be printed. The circulation department was never certain how many copies would be available. The equipment was not geared to such a demand and the weekly runs were subject to many hazards. The early heaters used to dry the ink were gas-fired and as the web was exposed to the heat a thin sheet of flame could be seen spreading across the paper as the volatile solvents were released. If for any reason the web slowed or the press stopped, the paper was liable to catch fire. One visitor to the Lakeside Press was told that fires were so frequent that there was no time for fire drills. But, by some miracle, there were only two damaging press fires in the first year of production.

Production was also endangered by shortage of coated paper. Prior to publication, Stillman had contracted for 10,000 tons from the Mead Corporation; he estimated that *Life* in its first year, with 350,000 circulation, would consume 11,000 tons and that consumption would increase gradually to 35,000 tons in 1940. Within six months *Life* was consuming more than three times the pre-publication estimate. There were no facilities in existence for producing such quantities. Stillman and his associates bought the best paper they could at whatever price in the open market, much of it of inferior grade. The day-to-day supply was so precarious that in Chicago members of the *Life* production staff could be seen leaning from their office windows counting the incoming freight cars being shunted onto the Donnelley siding, hoping the day's delivery would be sufficient to keep the presses going.

As the circulation increased, losses skyrocketed and very soon were running at the rate of $50,000 a week; the original estimate of $1,000,000 to see *Life* break even or to "an honorable grave" proved a major miscalculation. As early as December 1936 *Life* announced that in February 1937 advertising rates would be doubled; even the new rates did not fully reflect the actual delivered circulation. Moreover, the holders of pre-publication contracts had the privilege of ordering additional space at the original rates, and many were quick to make the best of a bargain. The more circulation and the more advertising, the greater the losses.

The losses could not be avoided ad interim. But the urgent long-range question concerned *Life*'s future. Should facilities be expanded to meet the demand indicated by the Worcester experiment—expansion which would require the company and/or its suppliers to make capital commitments running into millions of dollars? Pushing *Life*'s circulation into the millions also meant that *Life* would be entering direct competition with long-established mass-media magazines like the *Saturday Evening Post* and *Collier's*. As Ingersoll put it, a race with them was one in which "there is a big cash purse for the winner and only a silver-plated cup with your name engraved on it for the runner-up." Stillman, who had long since overcome initial reservations as to the wisdom of the new enterprise, was now for going all out. On the back of a place mat from the Hollywood Palace Hotel in Los Angeles he wrote Larsen: "I believe we have got the chance of a lifetime. . . . We should have a set statement which we all make about the money we are losing and why we are losing it. Then we should proceed to lose it without hysterics in an atmosphere of *complete and serene confidence* that we know what we are doing and that we are building a great property for the advertiser and ourselves. Any limitation policy smacks of hysterics—an admission that we are taken by surprise by our own creation instead of exuding confidence, which is what will sell the big-time advertisers a year from now."

Larsen was in agreement; he argued for a policy based on

(1)   Recognition of *Life* as a *Satevepost* with circulation of 2,500,000–3,500,000.
(2)   Recognition of possible short-lived business boom to 1939–41.
(3)   Recognition of necessity for leadership in weekly mag field once we pass 1,500,000.
   (a)   Leadership can ask and get highest price; runners-up take lower than leader's price.
(4)   1938 profits must pay '36–37 losses.
(5)   1938 must be another stepping-stone year.

Luce was not wholly persuaded; he still wanted to move more slowly, not get the company too much involved with capital expenditures, paper plants, etc., and avoid a direct confrontation with other magazines. His answer to Larsen:

Yes, as to the unabashed recognition that a well-edited *Life* may be destined to have and to hold 2,500,000 or more circulation. But *No,* as to direct comparison with *Satevepost* as advertising medium. . . . Let us recognize that *Life* may develop into as *"different"* a thing advertisingly as it is editorially. As a matter of fact, *Life* has to be defined editorially before it can be defined advertisingly. . . . It will take at least one year to see what our editorial definition will lead to for better or for worse. . . . In 1938 we have to determine whether *Life* is a sound and profitable advertising medium. If *Life* is a good advertising medium, it will be good at 1,500,000—without any reference to whether it will go to 3,000,000.

He did not agree with Larsen on the necessity of "leadership" (i.e., being top dog in circulation):

The more we concern ourselves with the leadership angle, the more we have to fight the price battle—until we have achieved sound leadership. We need a higher price. But I don't think we need leadership to get it. I am for having a pretty low price in 1938—to make unmistakably sure the advertiser gets his money's worth. . . .

However Luce tried to skirt the idea, his decision meant that *Life* was going to head for a mass circulation and rigorous competition. Years later Howard Black recalled that in 1937 a million dollars was bandied about rather freely. He remembered being at a meeting in the Cloud Club with Luce, Larsen and Stillman. Luce asked those assembled, "Shall we lose another million dollars on *Life* this year?" All agreed they should.

12.   The Rise of Xerox

LARGE-SCALE COMMERCIAL application of xerography—"dry writing" —was perhaps the most important of all the business-equipment advances of the nineteen-sixties, and Xerox Corporation, the company that had developed it during the preceding decade and exploited it during that one, was the most successful American company of the time, making millionaires by the hundreds out of its early brave or lucky investors. As for the invention itself, it added a word to the language, revolutionized commercial and bureaucratic paper handling, and, some would argue, brought about a permanent alteration in the use and impact of the written word itself, as the telephone did of the spoken word.

The story of the rise of Xerox is pure nineteenth-century business melodrama: how in 1938 in Queens, New York City, an obscure inventor working in an improvised laboratory hit upon an entirely new process; how he spent years trying without success to peddle it to some manufacturer; how at last, in 1944, Battelle Memorial Institute, a nonprofit research organization, agreed to undertake its development; how in 1946 the Haloid Company, a small Rochester, New York, photographic equipment firm, took over development rights in exchange for royalties; how Haloid in the succeeding decade gradually made a life-and-death commitment to xerography, the firm spending $75 million, some of its executives taking their pay in stock and even committing their home mortgages to the cause; how, in 1960, the venture came to a triumphant climax with the public introduction and instant acceptance of the 914 copier. In sum, a better mousetrap had been built, and a path beaten to the builder's door.

John Hans Dessauer, a chemical engineer who came to the United States in 1929 from Germany, began working at Haloid (later Haloid-Xerox and eventually Xerox) in 1935; he became head of research in 1938 and in that capacity presided over the technical aspects of the development of xerography into a marketable product. In the first of these excerpts from his book (written with the help of Oscar Schisgall) he tells something of the company's hopes and fears in the early days of the trail-breaking 914—which, as millions have come to know, was a desk-sized machine that made black-and-white copies at a rate of about one every six seconds. In recent years, faster and more sophisticated copiers have all but made the 914 obsolete; the fact remains, though, that in its heyday it may well have been the most successful commercial product in history.

Many things about the Xerox story are almost too good to be true, and one of these is the fact that the original inventor, Chester F. Carlson, ended up rich. Part of the Battelle-Haloid deal was that Carlson should get stock and royalties, and by 1968 his Xerox stock was worth so much that *Fortune* listed him among the sixty-six richest people in the country. (Carlson's original assistant, Otto Kornei, did not participate in these arrangements, but as we learn from Dessauer, Carlson found a way to reward him.) Alas, Chester Carlson died without writing his own memoirs. We learn how fascinating they might have been from the second Dessauer excerpt, in which we see the inventor during the nineteen-sixties, withdrawn now from the company's affairs but living not far away, crippled by arthritis but apparently glowing in spirit, trying to teach spiritual contemplation to young xerography engineers working on refinements of what Carlson —or God—had wrought.

THE INCREDIBLE 914

A TELEVISION STATION in New York, having heard [presumably in 1959] about the wonders of xerography, invited Haloid-Xerox to demonstrate its machine [the 914 copier] before TV cameras. Our sales force and public relations department quickly endorsed the idea. It was a wonderful opportunity to exhibit our product, free of charge, to millions of viewers.

Moreover, the public relations men, headed by David Curtin, urged Joe Wilson [Haloid-Xerox's chief executive] himself to make the televised speech of presentation, and he agreed.

A copier was transported to New York. On the scheduled day it was assembled in the TV studio, ready for an 8 P.M. performance. In the afternoon Joe Wilson dutifully rehearsed his speech. This was a dress rehearsal during which a copied page was to be exhibited in front of the cameras for all the world to see.

At the rehearsal, when the copy was raised for inspection, it was so faint as to be useless for TV exposure!

In consternation our engineers found that something had gone wrong with the toner. It was now almost 5 P.M., and you could not find any other such toner in New York. Joe rushed to a telephone to order a fresh supply immediately flown down from Rochester by chartered plane. "In a hurry!" he pleaded. "We go on at eight tonight!"

All might have gone smoothly had not a heavy fog chosen that day to settle over New York City. The plane with the toner was kept circling and circling around LaGuardia, unable to land. Finally it was diverted to Newark. There a frantic messenger, carrying the toner, raced for a taxi.

In the TV studio the entire Xerox staff watched the wall clock as

From *My Years with Xerox: The Billions Nobody Wanted,* by John H. Dessauer (Doubleday, 1971), pp. 129–54, 185–89.

the hands crept nearer and nearer to eight. The anguished producer of the show kept daubing a handkerchief over his sweating forehead.

At precisely five minutes to eight the man from Rochester rushed in with the toner. He was disheveled. He was breathless. But he was in time.

The performance went as scheduled.

One of the millions of people who watched it that evening was Thomas J. Watson of IBM. He became fascinated by the demonstration. Setting aside all the advice his company had in the past received to shun xerography, he telephoned Joe Wilson the next day, suggesting they get together to talk about a joint program.

"By that time we had gone so far on our own," Joe later said, "that there was no stopping. We were pleased and honored by Mr. Watson's interest. But we could not turn aside now from the course we had taken."

So we followed our course alone.

It was a bumpy course and still full of obstacles. Whenever I am asked to explain the 914's prenatal troubles I am tempted to ascribe many of them—perhaps too many—to the wide prevalence of what we termed "shim stock."

The word "shim" is defined as "a thin segment of metal or wood for driving into crevices, or between machine parts to compensate for wear." The process originated, I believe, with handcraftsmen who could not make every part of a machine fit smoothly into the others. They relied on plugs and filings to fill gaps or to even out rough edges.

I have said that we purchased most of the 1260 components of the 914 from outside sources. We therefore had to rely on the expertise of these suppliers. We had also to trust our local tool-makers, die-casting firms, sheet-metal cutters, and so on for equipment. Most of these people, excellent and painstaking as their work might be, were accustomed to accepting mechanical tolerances not nearly as tight as those we required.

For example, there was a highly regarded desk manufacturer from whom we ordered the 914's cabinets. The desks this supplier constructed were beyond criticism (which was why we selected him). Naturally, when he turned out a *desk* whose drawers slid easily and that stood four-square on the floor without tilting, he knew he had done a good job. He did not have to concern himself about making the various parts of this desk *interchangeable* with the parts of thousands of other desks.

When this manufacturer sent us his first cabinets for the 914, they looked very good. They were made up of separate panels fitted together—rear, sides, front, top, all in the striking fawn color we had selected—and they certainly had an irreproachable appearance. Then somebody accidentally dented one of the side panels. When we tried to substitute another, we stared in dismay. There was no tight, smooth fit. The panel was unsteady in its new spot.

What was true of the desk manufacturer was equally applicable to many other suppliers. They were simply not attuned to our exacting needs. Some of them, given to mass production, were primarily interested in keeping costs down, in taking short cuts that would save dollars not only for themselves but for us.

We could not accept parts that failed to meet our specifications. Only precision-built parts could be interchangeable. It fell to me to see that those that were unsatisfactory were rejected and returned. The manufacturers, faced with heavy losses, all but screamed their protests. In the old Haloid and Rectigraph days, when they sold us parts for cameras, we did not insist on such undeviating precision; we could generally adjust parts to fill our needs. But now, when we planned to market thousands of copiers, we could not risk the slightest laxity in meeting tolerance specifications.

Many a supplier declared that we were asking the impossible. They pointed to me as to an unreasonable taskmaster who had lost his mind. The outcries became so outraged that we finally had to call a meeting of suppliers, and Joe tried to make them understand our plight.

"We *own* the machines we lease," he explained. "We bear the cost of repairs or of replacing parts. That's written into the contracts we sign with our customers. A single service call, we have figured, will cost us between fifteen and thirty dollars, depending on how far our serviceman has to travel, how long it takes him to make repairs, and how much it may cost to replace malfunctioning parts. We estimate we face an *average* of twenty-five dollars a service call. If we eventually place five thousand machines on the market and have to make just one service call a month on each machine, it could cost us $125,000 a month, or $1,500,000 a year!"

Here and there a man whistled in astonishment. Others blinked at one another. Apparently few people among our suppliers had thought in these terms.

"It's the kind of expense we just can't afford," Joe went on. "We must have copiers that are not only as near perfect as we can make them; *they must have interchangeable parts*. We will have to send spare parts to every one of our regional offices, and they will have to fit every 914 around the country. This means every part will have to be manufactured to the tightest possible tolerances, tighter than anything we have so far attained. I know it will mean retooling for many of you, and added expense for us all, and I know it will cost us all more at the outset. But the expenditures we make now will soon be recovered through the savings we make on service calls. We ask you gentlemen to meet our needs."

We had some defenders, but most suppliers were shocked. The room was clamorous with objections. One man declared that we were *already* getting the tightest tolerances that could be obtained. He had the testimony of his own engineers.

Notwithstanding all this, we simply had to have better workmanship. And though the remonstrances of the holdouts continued for months, we had no alternative but to remain adamant. How else could we market a machine profitably?

We urged the suppliers to use our own staff for consultation and co-operation. "Our men have developed many ideas along these lines," we said. "They are perfectly willing and ready to work with your people."

Horace Becker, Paul Catan, and a few others personally went to suppliers' plants, sometimes with several of our men, and after days, even weeks, of work helped achieve the tight tolerances we had to have.

Of course, most suppliers ultimately co-operated. This was a matter of good fortune for us all, for the cumulative result was the obliteration of the "shim stock" weakness. Manufacturers began giving us tools and parts refined to what one observer called "man's utmost capacity for precision."

His words were kind, but one hopes man will never reach his "utmost capacity" for precision or anything else. If ever he does he will have attained a tragic apex from which there is no path save that of retrogression.

In any event, once our suppliers delivered equipment that met our tolerance specifications, many of the 914's birth pangs subsided, leaving us a copier that worked with gratifying smoothness.

ROCHESTER IS A LONG WAY FROM STOCKHOLM, and the twentieth century is a long way from the eighteenth. Still, I should like to connect them with a curiosity of Swedish history.

In the eighteenth century, Sweden was glorified, at least in scientific circles, by a scientist named Karl Wilhelm Scheele. He made a considerable number of important contributions to human knowledge, among them the discovery of chlorine and barite. Because of the many papers he published the results of his research became internationally celebrated among scholars.

There was a time when His Majesty, Gustavus III, King of Sweden, made a state visit to France. A deputation of French scientists came to pay their respects and to congratulate the King on the fact that Sweden had produced so great a man as Scheele.

King Gustavus was puzzled. He had no idea of who Scheele might be. He knew Sweden's military leaders, its statesmen, its political figures. But research scientists? They lived in a world apart. His Majesty, like most of his subjects, had scant knowledge of that ivory-towered world.

Nevertheless he felt that if one of his subjects had attained such obvious renown abroad he should certainly be honored in his own country. By courier he sent orders back to his Prime Minister, saying, "Scheele is immediately to be raised to the dignity of a count."

The Prime Minister was as baffled as the King had been. Who was this Scheele? Clearly the message was urgent, and His Majesty's commands had to be obeyed. The Prime Minister instructed an aide to investigate at once.

Within forty-eight hours he had the information from his exhausted but triumphant emissary: "Your Excellency, Scheele is a lieutenant in the artillery, a capital shot and a first-rate hand at billiards."

No one could blame the aide for having sought information in military and diplomatic circles. Who would have dreamed of turning to the mysterious realm of scientific research? The Prime Minister promptly acted on the report, and His Majesty's orders were obeyed. The following day an obscure Swedish artillery lieutenant—more baffled than anyone else in his country—was elevated to the rank of count.

I relate the incident only as a reminder of how enormously scientists and engineers have grown in public esteem, especially in our own century. Ours has been called The Era of the Engineer, and assuredly there is ample technological evidence to substantiate the phrase. We can apply it to events on earth, under the sea, and in the heavens. This had truly become the most rewarding of all ages to be an engineer. Government agencies, private corporations, research laboratories—so many organizations had been seeking engineers (even those fresh out of technical colleges) that the competition for their services had become keener than ever in history. For a comparatively small company like Haloid-Xerox, whose future was far from certain in 1958 and 1959, it was a difficult challenge to recruit the kind of men we needed. We had to seek them throughout the United States.

Our search was for specialists who could contribute the kind of knowledge, skill, or experience that those already on our staff had not had the opportunity to acquire. I make the point because we tried, for the sake of morale, never to downgrade any capable man by making him feel his work would be duplicated, superseded, or overshadowed by a newcomer. Instead we were providing him with help. Engineers can be as temperamental as opera stars—particularly those among them who have vision and never hesitate to deal with imaginative ideas. Their sensibilities have to be respected.

At a scientific conference in Anaheim, California, I was once asked to discuss the major qualities we at Haloid-Xerox looked for in the engineers we hired. I thought of imagination, of broad experience, of a spirit of co-operation with one's colleagues, of past achievements —all of which would have been true. But the most important requisite I finally settled on was creative people.

At this a gentleman in the audience rose to say, "I understand what one means by creativity in a composer, an artist, a novelist, an architect, a poet. But how do you define creativity in an engineer? Do you expect every engineer to be an inventor?"

He was closer to the truth than he knew. At Haloid-Xerox we did expect our engineers to supply innovative and imaginative answers to the problems we posed for them. Much of modern industry operates this way—telling its technicians exactly what needs to be invented. Then, as a team, they go to work on the challenge. When Dr. Mervin Kelly of Bell Laboratories told his engineers that he needed a certain contrivance, they responded by producing the invention that later became known as the transistor.

"You tell us what you require; we'll provide it," seems to be the modern engineer's code of operation.

One must remember, however, that the same temperament that makes some of these men gravitate toward invention and innovation can also make them non-conformists, born revolutionaries, people dissatisfied with the past. Some brilliant engineers may become revolutionaries simply for the thrill of doing things that are radically different. *The challenge to management is to channel the efforts of the revolutionary into productive deeds that will advance group objectives.*

Conversely, one often finds a well-trained engineer who is so timid as to be his own enemy. He is afraid to take chances because he dreads the stigma of failure. In cases like this, management's task is to protect the timid one from himself, to *encourage* him to take risks, to make it plain that management *wants* him to venture forward. It should assume, as we tried to do at Haloid-Xerox, that the only possible stigma in creative engineering lies in the failure to take courageous action.

One day I heard a "veteran" engineer (he had been with the company eight months) warn a new colleague, "You're going to attend more conferences here than you ever attended before. Might as well be prepared for them."

"What kind of conferences?" the new man asked.

"The kind that tell you *why* you're doing what you're doing."

I was pleased to hear this because it confirmed company policy. We had found that in order to motivate people to do their most intelligent work, it was essential that they understand management's aims and problems. They had to be told of such corporate concerns as present and anticipated competition, the results of market surveys, target dates for reaching the public with new products, and the required resources. Since we had a large number of machines on lease, we wanted them to understand the financial needs for capitalizing the machines we would produce; and this capitalization applied to the cost of tooling in our plants as well as to the funds necessary for the acquisition of added space and facilities.

Frank communication with personnel, we had learned, established a high level of confidence in the company and in its management. Giving engineers—and others, too, of course—the knowledge that they were sharing management's hopes, problems, and plans helped beyond measure in increasing our staff's dedication to the tasks it undertook. I have always felt that the clearer the comprehension the creative engineer has of what the company requires of him, and why, the better the relationship, the enthusiasm, and the probability of success.

Also, we became aware long ago that among technical people, as among educators and physicians, the desire to be identified with outstanding professional accomplishments often overshadows all other considerations, even monetary demands. Engineers, we knew, had to be given the opportunity to talk about their successes with their peers—which is to say with other engineers and scientists.

We tried to make this possible not only in many internal seminars and meetings; we also encouraged our men to read original papers before professional groups and to publish them in scientific journals.

This kind of corporate atmosphere (now evident in many aerospace and electronics organizations) is an important factor in stimulating creativity, in getting the very best out of inventive people. It need hardly be added that financial reward is another key element in eliciting their maximum capabilities. Technical experts, like everyone else, see in financial rewards a yardstick of corporate appreciation of their contributions.

Haloid-Xerox management realized that the personal success of the individual was closely allied to the total success of the company. So our pay system included bonus plans, stock options, and pension programs, all designed to attract new employees, especially technical people, and to keep those already with us happy in their work.

As long as I can recall, we have regarded engineering as a form of pioneering. We *had* to pioneer, since no other company had ever worked in the realm of xerography. And because Americans have an historic admiration for the pioneering spirit, ours was one of the factors that enabled us to recruit and retain the extraordinarily creative people we so sorely needed.

IN APRIL OF 1959—ten months before the 914 began serving American business—Joe Wilson was invited to address the Philadelphia Securities Association. No doubt he was expected to discuss fiscal affairs, market potentialities, investment prospects, and other such matters of interest to stockbrokers and bankers. He did discuss them. He could have based his predictions for the future on our last planning meeting. For years the heads of departments, about a dozen of us, had gone off annually to the seclusion of a remote island. There we were expected to fix a calm look at what our company could and should do in the next twelve months and the next five years. Each of us wrote a plan. We discussed our ideas, debated them; and later Joe Wilson selected those he liked best. These became company policy.

Joe could have talked of these projects to the analysts. Instead he began his talk with a few remarks that eloquently asserted his personal philosophy in the promotion of xerography. They also described the corporate motivation of Haloid-Xerox aside from its normal desire for profits.

"The mark of man, the characteristic which distinguishes him most from the beasts," Joe told his audience, "is his ability to communicate with his fellows in the present, and through time by means of recorded history. We build on the treasures of other's minds, present and past. Intellects of other centuries and from other lands contribute to our progress now because we can make use of their ideas. Work and thought are never lost when they are recorded.

"The basic art of communications, which has grown from pictures in caves, from hieroglyphics on papyrus, from smoke signals, to the present electronic miracles of radar, television, photography, and multicolored high-speed printing, is one of man's most precious material possessions.

"It is an exciting, challenging role for us to be the first to bring to men a fundamental new way of visual communication, the process called xerography."

After reminding his audience that xerography had existed only "a brief moment in time," he predicted that it must become a big industry because it could serve man in so many ways. It would make every conceivable type of information more readily available.

His prognostications did not include estimates of actual revenues in the next year or two. There was no reason to tell the analysts that we had again been privately informed by our market researchers— and by some of our sales people—that we might expect to lease about five thousand machines in 1960 and about seventy-five hundred more in 1961.

In Rochester these projections brought a quick repercussion. Men like Clyde Mayo, then Director of Development and Product Engineering, Kenneth Dennis, in charge of manufacturing, and Merritt Chandler, who had been hired to co-ordinate the 914 task force, had some firm ideas of their own. One day Chandler strode into Joe's office.

"Low estimates like those you received," he protested, "restrict the orders we can place with suppliers for future needs. They limit our budget for motors, cabinets, everything else. In my opinion—and Clyde and Ken agree—we should be prepared to lease at least fifteen thousand copiers in 1961. And we've got to order ahead on that assumption if we plan to be ready to meet the demand."

Joe looked at Chandler thoughtfully. He had a profound respect for Chandler's opinions. Still, planning for fifteen thousand copiers in 1961 seemed a wild flight into astronomical numbers. Purchasing materials for so big a volume meant committing the company to heavy debt. Joe did some serious thinking as he toyed with a pencil.

Chandler added, "If we can't make it big with xerography we're fooling around with the wrong product."

This was true. We had been counting on copiers to be the very foundation of Haloid-Xerox's future. It seemed unreasonable now to undermine our own faith. Beyond that, what could possibly happen if we prepared for sales of fifteen thousand in 1961? Surely we would still be dealing in copiers in 1962 and 1963. The unused supplies could be utilized in those years if they exceeded the requirements of 1961. Joe finally promised to discuss the figures with the sales department.

Before long Merritt Chandler *was* empowered to plan and purchase for fifteen thousand copiers in 1961. (In view of what later happened—the overwhelming volume of orders that came to the company, increasing 1961 revenues by $22,400,000 above those of 1960—the early insistence on higher estimates proved to be an important service to Haloid-Xerox. It helped to prepare us for the unexpected.)

In late 1959, as we drew nearer to the target date of January 1, 1960 for delivery of the 914, the pace of operations quickened for every man in the company. Yet we were still in an innovative stage, creating a new kind of mechanism, and even now not everything we designed or built worked as we hoped it would. One could record page after page of failures, all of which caused delays. Chandler finally had to tell Joe Wilson that the first 914 copiers—twenty of them —could not possibly be ready until February. "But you can count on February," he added.

By February they were indeed ready, and a spirit of triumph pervaded the entire Haloid-Xerox company.

Jack Hartnett, who was then serving as Chairman of the Board, was accorded the honor of producing the first 914 copy before an audience of sales people and engineers. "You fellows," he said in his welcoming speech, "have finally built a machine even I can work!" He put a document on the plate, closed the cover, pushed the requisite button, and waited with the smile of a magician about to astonish the world with a miracle. The paper came out of its slot, and Hartnett began to raise it for all to see.

Then his expression changed. He blinked in dismay and disbelief. *The sheet was blank!*

Through a few seconds of dreadful silence nobody stirred. Was the 914 a failure?

David Curtin, head of the public relations department, was white of face as he stepped close to the machine to see what had happened. In a daze he lifted the cover off the platen—and uttered a gasp of amazement.

"For heaven's sake, Jack," he cried, "you put the document in with its blank side down!"

Curtin turned the paper over, pushed the button again, and this time a perfect copy flowed out of the 914.

Jack Hartnett stared. Then he shook his head. "This company," he said, "should never trust its Chairman with an engineering problem."

EXACTLY HOW SUCCESSFUL was the 914 in its first two years? "The sales and rental of our xerographic products rose 98.8 per cent in 1961," Joe Wilson reported to an amazed group of shareholders. "This was due in large part to the success of the 914 Office Copier."

For the machine was welcomed so enthusiastically, with orders coming in so fast, that the 914 can truly be called the foundation of the Xerox success. As I have indicated, many publications and sales experts have regarded its skyrocketing record as one of the outstanding successes of American business.

Actually it became more than that. It became the very bedrock of the copier's international acceptance. If its popularity amazed the financial world, I must confess it amazed many of us in Rochester, too. In the sales of the 914 we were witnessing a miracle so far in excess of anything we had anticipated, that production could not keep up with demand. From the start, in 1960, we operated with a backlog of orders waiting to be filled.

In retrospect one finds it hard to believe all the things that occurred in 1960 and 1961. *Total* revenues (including what we were earning from the old Haloid and Rectigraph products) rose from $37,074,-374 in 1960 to $59,533,105 in 1961, an increment of more than 60 per cent of this total volume. Xerographic equipment contributed 80%—an increase of 98 per cent over 1960. As for the total assets of the corporation, they soared in that year to $97,166,538, or $40,-739,249 more than they had been in 1960—not at all bad for what we in Rochester still thought of as "our small company."

Had there been nothing else to report about those two remarkable years, they would still have constituted an historic period. There was, however, much more that happened.

To begin with, the Board of Directors informed all stockholders:

"Xerox Corporation is the new name chosen for our company. We shall recommend it to the shareholders at the annual meeting. There is a fundamental and compelling reason for the recommendation. In 1961 more than 75 per cent of our sales and a still higher percentage of our earnings will come from xerographic products.

"Since the fifty-five-year-old name 'Haloid' is widely known and respected in the photographic and photocopy industries, we will henceforth describe this part of our business as the Haloid Photo Division of Xerox Corporation."

At the same time it was evident that our four-floor rented facility on Orchard Street, where the 914's were being assembled, was inadequate. So architects were instructed to intensify the development of the Webster site [on farm land a few miles from Rochester]. Construction there was soon proceeding so rapidly that to drive through its maelstrom of activity was a stunning experience. Bulldozers, cranes, trucks, concrete mixers, and armies of men filled the area. My own headquarters, the Research and Engineering Center, had recently been completed. Nearby, the original factory for the production of xerographic plates and drums was being enlarged. On other sites builders were putting up a toner and developer plant, a machine manufacturing plant, a collection and distribution center for raw materials as well as for manufactured products, a general services building, and an administration headquarters. Despite the pressure of all these simultaneous projects, we insisted that the architects and builders speed up their work in order to meet the demands for the 914.

I remember pausing one day beside an aged man who was gazing over all this activity in awe. "It just don't seem possible," he said. "Here I stand, after living all my life on the edge of this land, and all of a sudden I can't even recognize it!"

Curious about local reaction to change, I asked, "Do you object to what's happening?"

He drew a long breath. "Mister, I guess nobody likes to see familiar things taken away. Nobody likes to see a quiet farm turned upside down, if you want the truth. On the other hand—" He paused, and said, "My son's gone into the building supply business, and he's making himself quite a bit of money out of all this. When I think of what it's doing for him and his family I guess I ought to be thankful instead of complaining. So, to get back to your question—no, sir, I don't mind what's going on. It's just that it makes me feel sort of sad."

I suspect he reflected the feelings of many people in Webster. Don't we all hesitate to accept change? Don't we all regret seeing familiar sights disappear even in the cause of progress? Happily Joe Wilson had taken the precaution, in a number of speeches he made before Webster audiences, of assuring everyone that the new installation would incorporate beauty and spaciousness; it would have a campus-like atmosphere; our architects had been instructed to adopt all the best features of the modern industrial park—wide lawns, trees, a sense of airiness everywhere. Joe insisted on making the area attractive in every possible way, and I must say he succeeded.

Whether or not the new complex pleased everybody in Webster aesthetically, its economic impact was powerful. It created thousands of jobs. It poured millions of dollars into the community. It produced a new taxpayer, one that became the largest taxpayer in town. As time went by, the Xerox plant became a kind of local showplace and a source of community pride. Though Webster had to expend more on civic services like additional police, sewers, streets, and schools, a large portion of these costs, everyone knew, would ultimately be defrayed by the corporation's tax payments.

I dwell on the year 1961 because it set a new pace for the company in many ways. In the matter of financing, for example, we needed a considerable amount of additional capital, not only for the development at Webster but for the manufacture of the machines that were being leased. Kent Damon flew from city to city around the country, talking to bankers. The outcome of his trip was an eloquent tribute not only to his personal abilities as treasurer but to the respect Xerox Corporation was beginning to command in the financial community. Nine of America's largest banks joined in a revolving bank credit that made loans up to twenty-five million dollars available to the company . . .

In another area of funding, one of the nation's most prestigious investment bankers, The First Boston Corporation, underwrote in 1946 the sale of one million dollars in securities to a group of financial institutions. "We wanted Joe Wilson to explain his operation to possible investors and answer all questions," said . . . Charles Glavin of The First Boston Corporation. "At a meeting in New York I was dumfounded when Joe arrived without a single note or document. Usually, at such meetings, company officials come armed with a hundred booklets and papers. Joe brought nothing except a pleasant smile. He talked easily, informally, for the better part of an hour. It was not a speech; it was a bit of conversation. When he answered questions I sat fascinated and amazed. He had every figure in his head, every fact at the tip of his tongue. By the time the meeting ended and the men shook his hand, the million dollars was as good as delivered."

On the wall of The First Boston's New York office there are now two framed documents that present breath-taking evidence of Xerox growth. The first is a clipping of a 1946 newspaper advertisement offering one million dollars in securities. The second is a similar newspaper clipping published exactly twenty years later. This one underwrites securities for *one hundred million dollars!*

The finance department was by no means the only branch of the company that was displaying ability to meet the challenges of rapid growth. Other groups were our researchers and engineers and our Patents Department. We now owned over two hundred patents relating to xerography, thirty-three of which were issued in 1961. In this patents area we called upon the long experience of Chester Carlson to help us, and his guidance was invaluable. He once observed with a laugh, "Remember, I'm really a patent attorney. Inventing was something I did in my kitchen after hours."

Meanwhile, overseas (where Rank-Xerox seemed to have become as enthusiastic about xerography as we were in Rochester), a different kind of progress was taking place. Our Board of Directors reported to American shareholders:

"One of the most significant accomplishments during the year was the successful completion of negotiations (by Rank-Xerox) for the formation of Fuji-Xerox in Japan. This new firm, which will manufacture and market xerographic products for the Far East, is jointly owned by Rank-Xerox and the Fuji Photo Film Company, Limited. It is Japan's leading manufacturer of photographic products."

The report went on to say that Rank-Xerox had also added sub-sidiary companies in Mexico, Italy, Germany, France, and Australia. And so, through our British alliance, our "little" Rochester firm was reaching out into every part of the earth. Our growth was being de-scribed in business publications as sensational.

"But this is only the beginning," was the prediction in the annual message to stockholders. "Our goal is to be a leader throughout the world in the field of graphic communications, concerned particularly with copying, duplicating, recording, and displaying images. Today our machines work from visible characters. Tomorrow they may work, at great speed, from electronic impulses and invisible signals.

"So long as there is need for man to send information and either to copy directly or to convert the language of computers or other elec-tronic devices into a form which other men can understand, there will be a great need for making images.

"This is our field."

It was a high-sounding, prophetic pronouncement. Words like that could be quoted in scientific, technical, industrial, and even socio-logical journals. University students, reading such lines, would know that ours was the kind of forward-looking industry that would offer vast opportunities.

In all candor, however, I must confess that we who were laboring to produce enough 914's to fill current orders had little leisure to contemplate the lofty message. The 914 crowded our lives. We worked at it all day in the plants and talked about it all night at home.

But we were not supermen, and we were subject to making some mistakes that could be called downright silly. In the main they were the fault of simple oversight. To illustrate: We sent five early models of the 914 to Rank-Xerox. We dispatched them with a feeling of pride and accomplishment. Our British associates received them with equal admiration. They decided to test them in their own offices. And then they made an appalling discovery.

Our best engineering brains, and theirs too, had overlooked the fact that British doors are narrower than American doors. The 914 could not be moved into the typical British office.

Rank-Xerox rushed several of its best engineers to Rochester. There they worked with our men to reduce the size of the machine's cabinet, and eventually, by cutting down a few inches, they were able to produce a model that could be delivered to an English office.

In our excitement we were also overlooking another fact: Rank-Xerox had long ago been assured that it was our aim to produce a small copier that would fit on top of an ordinary desk. Now, every time a British representative came to Rochester, we heard the same question: "Where is that desktop machine?"

At the beginning we accepted this query with a smile and a nod that meant, "Be patient." It was something we hoped to undertake in the misty future. But before long more serious pressures were applied to the research and development staff. The demands now came not only from England. Our own sales force insisted that there was a considerable American market for a small machine.

These urgings concentrated on my department. They also assaulted the ears of Joe Wilson. We all began to realize that despite our absorption in producing the 914 we would have to apply ourselves just as vigorously to producing a desktop copier. "England and Xerox," as one rather too enthusiastic engineer expressed it, "expect every man to do his duty. We will now produce something we don't yet know how to produce."

THE IMPOSSIBLE DREAM COMES TRUE

ALMOST EVERY TUESDAY evening [in the later nineteen-sixties] a small group of friends visited the suburban home of Chet and Dorris Carlson. Sometimes there were ten or twelve guests. Occasionally there were as many as fifteen. What they did would have mystified observers. They sat on flat cushions scattered around the room. Eyes closed, they remained silent. The stillness lasted undisturbed as long as the guests stayed, usually one or two hours. To speak at all in the semi-darkness would have been as unthinkable as to scream blasphemies in a church.

Dorris Carlson, tall, dignified, dark of hair, serene, sat on a hassock. She wore a long beautiful gown. Impassive and silent, her beautiful face vague in the shadows, she offered her visitors no entertainment, no conversation. She provided only the cushions, the pervasive odor of incense, and peace.

Chet sat on another cushion, his graying head bent. Unlike his wife, who managed always to sit regally erect, he allowed his shoulders to droop. He always looked tired. Because of his arthritis, which was worsening year by year, he was usually in pain, though he never mentioned it. His wife knew because it was reflected so starkly in the lines of his face.

Sitting like that, he meditated. What his secret thoughts were, no one ever knew. He often revealed them not even to Dorris, for such revelation would have destroyed the profound privacy of soul, of mind, he had learned to cherish as a precept of Zen Buddhism.

These weekly sessions were devoted to reflection and self-examination. Dorris Carlson had become a leader and sponsor of this cult in Rochester. She brought an aura of nobility to her beliefs, a quiet conviction that sought to enlist disciples not by persuasion or argument but by example.

A pragmatic young engineer at Webster once asked Chet what on earth he saw in Zen Buddhism. Chet answered with a smile that what he saw was not "on earth" but rather in Nirvana.

"And what do you mean by Nirvana?" the young man persisted.

"It's not easy to explain," Chet said, "I'll send you a description."

The following day the engineer received a note in which Chet had written:

Nirvana? In the words of Chang-tao Ke:

> Like the empty sky, it has no boundaries.
> Yet it is here, ever profound and clear.
> When you seek to know it you cannot see it.
> You cannot take hold of it.
> But you cannot lose it.
> In not being able to get it, you get it.
> When you are silent, it speaks.
> When you speak, it is silent.

However vague the Zen Buddhist philosophy may have seemed to the young engineer, it appeared to bring Chet the same sense of peace and meaning it gave to Dorris.

Also, it brought him an extraordinary attitude toward all of life. He was wealthy now. In 1964 his share of xerographic royalties amounted to over 3 million dollars, and it was increasing at the rate of about a million dollars a year beyond that figure. (In 1967 it rose to over six million dollars.) "If he had kept everything he earned," his wife said in 1969, "he would have had well over one hundred fifty million dollars. But of course he gave away what is now worth about 100 million dollars."

Giving his money away, philanthropy, became Chet Carlson's major activity. He gave millions to his alma mater, the California Institute of Technology, for a new laboratory building. He gave to other institutions of learning and to unusual groups—for the promulgation of Zen Buddhism, for studies in extrasensory perception, for psychical research. There were at least sixteen major beneficiaries of his gifts, and scores upon scores of minor recipients.

With so much money pouring into his life, so much to manage and dispose of, he found himself compelled to seek the counsel of bankers and investment brokers. The daily inundation of letters asking for donations made it necessary to hire a secretary. He spent hours every day in studying requests for money and in deciding which to honor and which to decline.

One morning he called in his secretary, Mrs. Mary Laurino, and dictated a letter to a man who was now working for IBM in California. To the new secretary the man's name was unfamiliar: Otto Kornei.

"He and I," Chet said, "worked together in Astoria. Without his help I might never have had all this." He motioned to indicate his home. "I'm sending him a block of Xerox stock in gratitude."

In the same manner he expressed thanks to those relatives of his and his wife who had helped him buy 40 per cent of Battelle's interest in xerography.

In spite of his affluence, Dorris Carlson said, he remained the simplest of men. He had no desire for magnificence. "We enlarged our home, yes, but this was done to accommodate the office he used for his philanthropic work. But we never owned more than one car— Chet saw no reason for that. We never bought homes on the Riviera or in Florida or any place else. What we had here was all he desired."

He spent most of his time at home now, though he loved to take long walks with his dog. When he was in the house he generally carried a straw basket—the kind women fill with garden vegetables—and in the basket he kept the reading matter he wanted to scan. At night the basket lay beside his bed. When he went out into the garden, it sat next to his chair.

What he loved most was the new freedom he found in being able to live exactly as he wanted to, Dorris said. In fact, freedom was almost an obsession with him.

In New York they were once strolling beside Central Park when they passed a man selling children's balloons. On impulse Chet bought one. Dorris watched in amusement. What could he possibly have in mind?

A moment later Chet released the balloon. He stood looking up, following its course as it soared high above rooftops and out of sight.

"What made you do *that?*" Dorris later asked.

"I just wanted the pleasure," he whispered, "of seeing something go free."

Yet total human freedom, he often maintained, could be achieved only in a world that was liberated from the plague of war. He saw the rule of military force as the antithesis of personal freedom. That was why he gave liberally to the causes of peace. He also gave to those agencies of the United Nations concerned with health and to other organizations whose purpose was the amelioration of human misery and bondage.

"Chet and I," Mrs. Carlson explained, "found greater satisfaction in giving his wealth to worthwhile causes than he would have found in any other use of it."

As might have been expected, his generosity brought many rewards in the form of citations, honorary titles, and medals. He usually smiled over these and put them out of sight. Dorris attributed this to his innate shyness. "He was never one to flaunt his honors. In fact, there were a few of which even I didn't know. Some notification would come in the mail, and he would put it into a desk drawer. Perhaps weeks or months later I would learn that he was being invited to this or that college or institution to receive the award in person."

At the time of the Brussels World's Fair, Chet's cousin, the distinguished scientist Dr. Roy Carlson, persuaded him to come along on a leisurely trip through Europe. The two men went together. Dorris had never liked traveling and had urged Chet to go without her. She truly preferred staying at home.

At the Brussels Fair the Carlson cousins were startled to come upon an exhibit of Xerox copiers sponsored by Rank-Xerox of England. A young man was lecturing a group of sightseers on the wonders of xerography. As he demonstrated the machine he spoke of its brilliant American inventor, Chester F. Carlson. He went on to praise Chet's genius in the most elaborate terms. In embarrassment Chet tried to get out of the crowd. But Dr. Carlson held his arm and made him stay to the end. Then he said, "Chet, you ought to let that young fellow know who you are. He'll remember this moment the rest of his life."

"No, no," Chet answered as he motioned to the crowd pressing around the young speaker. "This is *his* stage. He is the star here. Let's not take away from that."

The words were merely an excuse, Dr. Carlson later told Dorris; Chet left that place because, in spite of wealth and renown, he was still one of the shyest men on earth. He still prized privacy above acclaim. The Brussels lecturer never knew he had been face to face with the subject of his praise.

13. Safari Training
on the Charles

Now THAT WE HAVE HEARD the testimony of a gallery of American business figures, past and present—some more celebrated than others, but all, at least for a time, successful—it may, paradoxically, be appropriate to look at business education through the eyes of a student. The Harvard Business School (more properly, the Harvard University Graduate School of Business Administration) is indisputably the West Point of American business education, producing far more top executives of huge corporations than any rival institution and commanding such respect that its untested new graduates walk into starting jobs with salaries higher than many less favored businessmen will ever attain. Indeed, some bosses look on these very attributes as liabilities. In Robert Townsend's backhanded tribute: "Don't hire Harvard Business School graduates. This worthy enterprise . . . trains its students for only three posts—executive vice president, president, and board chairman."

Peter Cohen, a young Swiss who attended Harvard Business School in 1968–70 and in the latter year was awarded its coveted degree, Master of Business Administration, presents in diary form the only first-hand account of student life there that I have ever seen in print. His is the somewhat appalled perspective of an elegant

young European taking safari training preparatory to a hunting expedition in the American (or European) business jungle. He repeatedly stresses the existence of a calculated (as he believes) officers-
training-school atmosphere of pressure and fear and the brutalizing
effect of this atmosphere on sensitive students. Nor is the faculty
immune; Cohen tells of a young instructor's suicide, precipitated, he
suggests, by unpopularity with students, brought about by the instructor's strictness, which is obligatory under the "system." Cohen's
years at Harvard coincided with the heyday of the so-called "youth
counterculture," which set out (for that short time) to overthrow the
ethic of competition and success and replace it with one of co-
operation and love; and in the little world of Harvard, the two ethics
were beautifully symbolized by the liberal arts-oriented undergraduate college on the west side of the Charles River and the bottom
line-oriented "B School" on the east. There is no mistaking where
Cohen's sympathies lie.

Undoubtedly, he is unfair to the Harvard Business School, which
exists, after all, to train leaders of the business system rather than
to revolutionize the system's ethics and objectives, and therefore is
entitled if not obliged to foster an atmosphere that mirrors that of
the "real" business world. My personal observation is that social
objectives as opposed to the bottom line of the financial summary are
given considerable attention at the Harvard Business School. Yet to
say that is to beg the question. Cohen's vivid sketches of life in the
incubator of tycoons throw into vivid relief the great questions facing
contemporary American business: Can competitive conditions and
the desire for personal success be mitigated and tamed without re-
moving the raw incentives that produce great business results? Can
corporations learn or be forced to serve their communities, their
consumers, and their society as much as their employees and stockholders without losing the primal drive that makes them go? Are
other values in business, after all, as important as, if not more important than, legally acquired profit?

SEPTEMBER 19:

The case method is to the Harvard Business School what the crooked tower is to Pisa. The Harvard Business School invented the method; the Harvard Business School succeeded with it; the Harvard Business School swears by it, and we have to put up with it, every grinding minute of every grinding day. There are no lectures, no labs, few textbooks even. Only cases, cases, and more cases.

In its outward appearance, a case is a bundle of mimeographed pages—some thirty to forty on the average—written in a heavy-handed, lumbering prose that creaks from an overload of nouns. It describes a real event (although the names may be disguised) that happened in the course of some real business campaign, at times giving a general's grand view, at times a corporal's blurred impressions; it reports on the conditions in the trenches and bunkers of the business front; on the progress of armies of salesmen marching against each other, of supply convoys steaming down channels of distribution. It is a factual listing of men, money, and materials risked; of brilliant victory, of losses beyond imagination.

It often begins with grandiose flourishes: "For J. Hamilton Peacock, chairman of the board of the First Haverhill National Bank, planning was not a luxury . . ." Invariably it ends with a question that is beginning to haunt us in our sleep: "What would *you* do?"

These aren't the "case histories" people get in law or medical school. You know, and here is what the judge said. Or here is what the doctor ordered. Our cases have no ending. They just kind of dump the whole mess into your lap—tables, columns, exhibits, and all—and you can't run away from it because tomorrow ninety-four people—the entire Section—will be waiting for your decision. You may not be the guy the professor calls on "to lay out the case," but then again you may, which makes for a lot of motivation.

From *The Gospel According to the Harvard Business School,* by Peter Cohen (Doubleday, 1973), pp. 16–17, 23–24, 34–35, 124–25, 131–33, 326–29.

Three cases a day; sixty, maybe a hundred, maybe more than a hundred pages a night. You almost read yourself to death, just to find out what the *problem* is. And then, of course, you need a *solution*.

Here you are, a strapping production manager, or financial vice-president, or marketing executive, alone in a jungle of unfamiliar terms and technology, with no lecture notes, no fundamentals, or formulas to go by; with, perhaps, a reading list and a textbook and an equally confused, dry-mouthed roommate. And if you haven't done so already, you do a lot of growing up in a hurry, because you've got a problem. And no time. And little help. And something like your life depending on your finding a solution.

OCTOBER 10:

On its way through Cambridge the river Charles is a smelly, unpleasant fellow, rolling its waters back and forth through numerous bends like a Sunday sleeper, unwilling to get out of bed. In fact, because of its many bends, the Charles seems like the only river in the world that you can cross and end up on the same shore.

Following the border between the townships of Brookline and Cambridge, it gently bends around the Business School, cutting it off from the rest of the Harvard campus—if you can call it a campus. Sure, across from the Business School, there is Harvard Yard, guarded by a heavy, wrought-iron fence, dotted with undergraduate dorms and class buildings. But the Yard measures no more than about five walking minutes in breadth and length. All the rest of the university is tucked away in the maze of narrow Cambridge streets, amid businesses and barbershops, boutiques and boardinghouses.

Aside from the Yard, the Business School is the only part of Harvard that you could really call a campus. Built on the riverbank opposite the rest of the school, it sits at the edge of a small plain, worn into the landscape by the Charles. Surrounded by athletic fields, a huge parking lot, and farther to the rear, by storage houses, car dealers, and gas stations. An elegant front for a sprawling commercial area that is crisscrossed by multiple lane highways and throughways.

Still, for all the complicated local geography, back "across the river" isn't a place, it's a state of mind.

From the Business School, as we are beginning to find out, across the river means the hippies, the "kids"—the emotional people, the shouters. Those who discuss problems instead of solving them.

From the Business School, "across the river" is a threat. Something stirring up fears that the crowds from over there—the daydreamers, the self-righteous idealists, the critics blinded by their own enthusiasm, the fools who mistake a flash of insight for the light of truth—might try to smash the whole intricate apparatus of which we very much want to be a part.

But across the river also is where the girls are, the coffee houses, the subway trains into Boston, and an ice-cream cone with jimmies in one of the greasy spoons around Harvard Square.

And, although they never admit it, across the river for many of us is the slightly bitter taste of a dream only partly come true. Of an undergraduate education spent at a small, obscure place where the work was just as hard but the prestige infinitely smaller. The view of the Harvard Yard. The realization that we, as graduate students —and especially as graduate students of business—are kind of stepsons of this prestigious family.

"Abolish the B School," someone has written on a wall, over in the Yard. That's what across the river seems to mean to them over there: a subsidiary of IBM. A farm club for the CIA. A machine spewing out briefcase-carrying tin soldiers—mercenaries in the battle for higher profits; little schmucks who are willing to sell their left hand for the right to build a new Coca-Cola factory in outer Swaziland.

And so, when somebody says, "across the river," it isn't which but whose side he is on. Though there are two convenient bridges, each side has neither the time nor the interest to cross over for anything other than football, sex, or ice-cream cones.

OCTOBER 24:

When you read about it in the school catalogue, this thing called a "study group" sounds like the ideal cure for all possible ills of the Business School. It seems like a human haven made of shared misery and joint effort. A point from which to stem the tide of losing, of trying to cram ten or twelve hours of work into six hours of evening. A way of putting an end to the silly catch-up game that forces you to tackle tomorrow's cases with yesterday's barely mastered techniques. And when you hear McKay saying that people who are in a study group have a greater chance of making it, then the study group becomes more than a convenience, it becomes a necessity.

Thus, although nobody is forced to join and although they aren't organized formally, everybody is eager to be part of one. What started as brief, exploratory chats during the first couple of weeks is turning into an eleventh-hour, often desperate behind-the-scenes struggle. What could have been a group of guys working together, sharing their experience (which seems to be rich and varied in Section B) is turning into just another source of pressure and anxiety. "Now Reddick," you begin to calculate, "he seems to know a lot about accounting . . . with his experience in accounting and my experience in marketing . . ."

But what if, like some of the guys, you don't have any experience in accounting, have never worked in marketing? What if you're left to face those overly long cases alone? Alone to face the larger than life figures of the professors. A thought that sends people scurrying for shelter, willing to risk rejection and insult. For at this stage, even the illusion of belonging is better than the certainty of being on your own. And so the strong, as they get together, become stronger while the weak, afraid of dragging one another down to defeat, stay apart.

Our own fault? A fault of the school? A mirror of the real world? Comparing people to diamonds, some sloganeer in the Section exclaimed that "diamonds are made of pressure." Diamonds, yes. But not the light that gives a diamond its fire.

MARCH 24:

On this day, a perfect spring day, David Rosen shot himself in his office.

He was to have started a new course with us today, LOB (Laboratory in Organizational Behavior). At eight-forty he was to have been here for the first class of the course.

It was a class to which we looked forward with apprehension. Our troubles in HBO (Human Behavior in Organizations) have not really been cleared up but instead faded away in a mutual withdrawal of forces. Indifference, a sort of compassion that sought to prevent further injury, and the inability of some concerned students to get through to Rosen had left the issues in suspension.

And so it was all here today—the questions, doubts, mistrust, hanging over our heads like a sultry Boston summer afternoon. To make things worse, there were rumblings of discontent stirred up by some of the inexplicably harsh grades which Rosen had handed out in HBO. A number of people were bitter and it seemed just a matter of time before there would be new confrontations.

But David Rosen didn't show up.

At nine o'clock McGrady, our SA representative, went to give him a call. Rosen had left his home late, McGrady said, and would be here shortly.

He didn't come.

After Rosen's class we had Finance, and halfway through Finance, McKay showed up and then Dean Kellogg. They left and came back and people looked at one another, trying to figure out what was happening. At the end of Finance, the dean turned toward the Section: "I have bad news for you," he said and his voice was shaking. "David Rosen took his life. You . . . you can go home. There will be no more classes today."

It was completely unexpected. The violent blow sent the mind spinning, tumbling out the same message over and over: "Rosen is dead. Rosen is dead. . . ."

It is peculiar how the soul protects the thin flame of consciousness against the violent gusts of emotions. How in moments of great triumph and tragedy alike, it shuts and bolts its windows, keeping the little flame in stillest darkness with nothing but a distant echo of the agitation outside.

And so it was today, as this shot resounded through Aldrich 108. No more than a faint "thump" could be heard in the shuttered, locked confines of our minds.

WENDY BURGESS REFLECTS ON THE EVENTS
LEADING UP TO ROSEN'S DEATH:

"When I thought about it, afterward, I realized that the people I disliked, whom I had heard gossiping and saying nasty things, did not participate in the attack on Rosen. The people who led it were actually sort of dark horses. You know, I think it was that which made me feel: 'My God, even these sweet, quiet guys are seething with this kind of nasty I don't care who gets in my way . . . kind of I don't care what I say, I'll say anything because . . .'

"They weren't doing it with any malice. It was just complete obliviousness. And I felt, you know, that . . . the maggots had come out of the walls. Not only were there these . . . these vocal detractors of Rosen who were silent on that day, but were absolutely vicious in their cutting down of him outside of class. And sat there in stony silence, not participating. But all of a sudden, these, you know, these gentle creatures had come out and said: 'I hate your guts.'

"Looking back, there were very few individuals that I can honestly say I disliked. But sometimes I took out on the Section at large a kind of hostility I had for certain individuals that I felt were . . . just not nice people. They created some situations and said things in class, and they said things out of class, about other people—I think that was the thing—they were so catty. So brutally catty that I was really surprised.

"I've gone to girls' schools all my life but I never heard anything like the opinions that some of the guys had about other guys in the Section on, you know, one day's viewing.

"Perhaps it's a natural reaction to attack when you feel threatened, but that whole thing got to the point . . . you know, it gave me a kind of a turn. Even in our study group we sort of divided into the . . . the commie bastards and fascist pigs and fought it out every time something came up.

"Everybody in the Section always talked about what a close group we were and so forth, but I think, very early, I got a sense of, you know, this is no group. This is a . . . an enforced intimacy that is only making . . . is bringing out the worst in everybody. Anytime I got to the end of a day, I wanted to just run from everyone in that room and get as far away as possible and not have to see them again until the next day. And it wasn't really because anybody had done anything to me. It was just a feeling

—the way everybody was reacting together. I felt the Section . . . there was something of . . . of a mob spirit in the air. People were out to do something to somebody.

"The people I talked to in the first year, a lot of people, were very, very frightened by the whole thing. I mean, even though a lot of us could joke about it and so forth, fear is a strong emotion and it has different effects on people. I think there were times when the circumstances combined in such a way as to bring out people's fear . . . in the aggressive way, in the destructive way. The whole first few months there was a lot of tension and pressure and 'this is boot camp' and 'this is serious business' and 'you've got to measure up' with very sort of unclear—it was unclear exactly what was expected of one.

"Everybody was eating up the rough, tough cream-puff stuff that McKay was dishing out and they were all in awe of him. McKay was the strong man who fulfilled their wildest dreams and nightmares of what a . . . what an executive could be brought up to be. That they could be supermen. He was an intimidating personality and he did, you know, a sort of Pavlov thing. One day he was cutting everybody down and the next day he was saying: 'Well, I'm really your friend and I'm here to help you.'

"I do not find fear a valuable motivating force. Yes, possibly to save my life or something like that. But to get people to learn? It just doesn't make sense. I don't think I really started listening to what was going on for at least the first couple of months, until, you know, the initial shock wore off. I was in a state of . . . of paralysis. I think even with all the things people had told me, I wasn't prepared for the . . . the sort of emotional reaction I had to the whole thing. You know: 'My God, what is this? We can't be *real* inside that classroom.'

"And all kinds of really funny little paranoid reactions that I never thought myself capable of came out in those early couple of months. Like that day McKay called on me and I blanked. I have never in my life, before or since, blanked like that. I just completely drew a blank. Could not think or speak. And I have no memory of what I said. Because it was just, you know, it was one's worst fears realized. The day you *really* hadn't prepared the case, he calls on you. The funny thing was that after that I still didn't read the cases. I still went to class, almost every day, having, you know, glanced at it once over breakfast. The fear . . . the fear was enough to paralyze me. But it was not enough to make me do something about it.

"I think part of it was the feeling—this sort of group feeling, the feeling that this is a mob, not a group. We are people when we're outside of class, talking to each other. And, suddenly, when we walk in there and sit down, we're all transformed. We become lions . . . lions and Christians or something."

DECEMBER 15, EVENING.
CAMBRIDGE, MASSACHUSETTS:

Terner and Terner's wife, who had been staying in Cambridge through summer and fall and into yet another winter, were sitting on one of those beat-up benches on the left bank of the Charles. He held her close to keep warm, their bodies—with the heavy coats and scarves—forming a kind of cozy, tangled heap; their breaths curling into one another in white ribbons.

The woosh of the rush-hour traffic from the big highways on both sides of the river blurred their words, and behind the Business School, the yellow sun, like a burning log, cracked on the sharp edge of the horizon, sending up a flight of brilliant sparks to light the shapeless, seamless pit of coming night.

Only high up, on the gables of Aldrich, did some of the light linger —a kind of dark-red vapor, rising from the cool silver of the tiles— making the dark that wrapped up the building seem darker, hiding its massive walls, reducing their brutal proportions to a very far and light and almost pleasing shape.

As usual, the snow has turned gray early, from the traffic, and over at the School, all the lights are going, as if we had forgot to turn them off. The withered pretense, the false airs lie out there, along the two years, like the glittery debris of a costume party. The ticky-tacky fronts we had put up are razed; a lot of myths have been exploded like balloons.

If the Business School is great and daring, it is in its ambition to help people make sense of the million little problems which make up the big one—life. To acquire those basic habits, that undefinable mix of thought, intuition, and faith in one's basic abilities that people, for lack of a better word, call "common sense." That even the longest voyage must start with the first step, and that once you understand a problem, you have half its solution.

This is the ambition. And then you remember Stahl, who went into the Army. And Rosen. And Leroi, the SA rep. And the Saturday WACs. And what went on in class. You know that something went wrong. Yeah, you did pick up some of that common sense, a surprising lot of it. It helps, and you are sincerely grateful. But no matter how you look at it, the price seems unreasonably high.

As in college and in high school, throughout your education really, they started out by saying how education is to make you a better man or woman. How you have to question everything and not accept anything at face value. How they have faith in man and his goodness. And then they turn on the pressure. They expect 200 per cent out of you. And you realize they haven't got faith in anything except pressure, fear, and terror.

And that is what the real game was at the Harvard Business School. Only this time the promises were even grander and the reality even further away. Students, professors, even the secretaries—it was as if everybody were fighting to get out of some corner, and they were not worried too much about habits of thinking and questioning anything, but content to accept *that the maximization of long-range profit is why God hath created the earth*. They were living the shortest of all possible short-range strategies, the only object of which was to survive.

It is surprising how long the Business School has been able to continue on in this way, miraculously untouched (or only lightly touched) by dissent and demonstrations; amid mounting proof that its way, the American way, was leading the nation into a heap of trouble. The American way, that outworn, hilariously twisted and disfigured ethic which urges people to compete for the sake of competing, achieve for the sake of achieving, win for the sake of winning, and which honors him who does all this without pause or letup—the fastest, the richest, the smartest, the nicest, the sportiest, the artiest;

because things wouldn't be the way they are unless God meant them to be.

The school doesn't want to hear the tumult outside. That the American way of death is about to poison, shoot, and burn America. That something is going on out there—a second reformation which is preaching *love* and *togetherness;* which doesn't want anything to do with the idea that man is the enemy of man, and which is repudiating the ultimate American belief, *that in all things the individual is supreme.* A reformation whose long-haired apostles proclaim that to put the individual above society is to be asocial. *That America is an asocial society.*

All this the Harvard Business School can't hear because it is up against the worst obstacle to progress—success. It is producing too many millionaires, too many presidents and chairmen, too much fame for itself to need to change substantially. True, it accepts more blacks and women; it keeps putting in cases on pollution and social responsibility. But it isn't really doing anything to change the mood, the attitude, of the place. The professors continue to be more interested in sharing than in harnessing business' power; the school remains more concerned about placing its graduates and getting business' financial support than about whether business is using the nation's productive resources for the good of the nation.

The really disquieting thing is that other business schools, the nation's law and medical schools, the whole so-called professional establishment seems to be doing much the same thing. How else could you explain that those most in need of medical attention have such trouble getting it? That those most in need of justice can't seem to get it? That the majority of those who produce a factory's profits have no say in the disposition of them; those whose entire lives are tied up with a business have no influence over its objectives? How can you explain all this other than by concluding that the first concern of medical schools is with the health of doctors; the foremost concern of law schools with the rights of lawyers; that what business schools are after is promotions, not production.

14. *Trying Harder*

ROBERT TOWNSEND tells his business autobiography obliquely, in the form of a set of carefully rambunctious precepts based on his experience. For three years during the nineteen-sixties he served as chief executive officer of Avis Rent A Car, and it was during his term that Avis launched the famous "We Try Harder" advertising campaign (conceived by the Doyle Dane Bernbach agency) that put the company on the national corporate map and raised its profits from nothing to $5 million per year. The precepts, part put-on and part iconoclastic good sense, would appear to apply specifically, and in some cases exclusively, to a certain type of company—a comparatively small one oriented to advertising and engaged in offering services rather than producing goods: that is to say, a company just like Avis. In spite of, or because of, Townsend's breathless air of one who has just invented corporate management as if it were the wheel, his little book became a big best-seller and undoubtedly helped jolt many executives out of their familiar ruts. However, his precepts considered as autobiography must be taken—as must so many autobiographies— with a grain of salt. He did, as he explains, operate without a secretary and step aside before he had worn out his welcome; but contrary to his advice to others, at Avis he did not fire the company's public relations, personnel, or purchasing departments.

Although not yet fifty at the time, Townsend retired—"cashed in his chips" might be a better way of putting it—in 1965 when Avis was sold to International Telephone & Telegraph Corporation.

ADVERTISING

Fire the whole advertising department and your old agency. Then go get the best new agency you can. And concentrate your efforts on making it fun for them to create candid, effective advertising for you. Unless you've just done this, the odds favor that you have a bunch of bright people working at cross purposes to produce—at best— mediocre ads. We started at Avis by asking a few people for a list of the hottest agencies. Then we called on the creative heads of those agencies and tried to interest them in the rent a car business. Ultimately we stumbled on the right question: "How do we get five million dollars of advertising for one million dollars?" (our competition has five dollars for each dollar we have, and yet we have to pay the same price for cars, insurance, rent, gas, oil, and people).

Finally, Bill Bernbach heard the question and answered: "If you want five times the impact, give us ninety days to learn enough about your business to apply our skills, and then run every ad we write where we tell you to run it. Our people work to see how effective their ideas are. But most clients put our ads through a succession of Assistant V.P.'s and V.P.'s of advertising, marketing, and

---

From *Up the Organization,* by Robert Townsend (Knopf, 1970), pp. 19–20, 49–52, 104, 115, 116–17, 148–49, 159, 168–72, 196–97.

legal until we hardly recognize the remnants. If you promise to run them just as we write them, you'll have every art director and copywriter in my shop moonlighting on your account."

We shook hands on it.

Ninety days later, Bill Bernbach came out to show Avis his recommended ads. He said he was sorry but the only honest things they could say were that the company was second largest and that the people were trying harder. Bernbach said his own research department had advised against the ads, that he didn't like them very much himself—but it was all they had so he was recommending them. We didn't like them much at Avis either, but we had agreed to run whatever Bill recommended.

The rest is history. Our internal sales growth rate increased from 10 per cent to 35 per cent in the next couple of years.

Moral: Don't hire a master to paint you a masterpiece and then assign a roomful of schoolboy-artists to look over his shoulder and suggest improvements.

DIRECTORS, BOARD OF:
THE BACK-SEAT DRIVERS

The huge, successful company is a dinosaur, but it has one decisive advantage over the middle-size outfit that's trying to grow public; also over the established company that's in trouble enough to be ready for change. The advantage: most big companies have turned their boards of directors into non-boards. The chief executive has put his back-seat drivers to sleep.

This achievement has to be understood to be admired. In the years that I've spent on various boards I've never heard a single suggestion from a director (made *as* a director *at* a board meeting) that produced any result at all.

While ostensibly the seat of all power and responsibility, directors are usually the friends of the chief executive put there to keep him safely in office. They meet once a month, gaze at the financial window dressing (never at the operating figures by which managers run the business), listen to the chief and his team talk superficially about the state of the operation, ask a couple of dutiful questions, make token suggestions (courteously recorded and subsequently ignored), and adjourn until next month.

Over their doodles around the table, alert directors spend their time in silent worry about their personal obligations and liabilities in a business they can't know enough about to understand. The danger is that their consciences, or fears, may inspire them now and then to dabble, all in the name of responsibility.

Two simple tactics have been devised and time-tested in large organizations to head off this threat.

First, make sure that the board is composed partly of outsiders and partly of officers. Since all the important questions relate to the performance of key men and their divisions, no important questions will be asked. To do so would be a breach of etiquette, an insult to somebody at the table. Nor will any officer-director with an instinct for self-preservation (and a modicum of respect for the ignorance of the outside directors) ever bring a new or controversial idea before the board.

Second, be sure to serve cocktails and a heavy lunch before the meeting. At least one of the older directors will fall asleep (literally) at the meeting and the consequent embarrassment will make everyone eager to get the whole mess over as soon as possible. Caution: let sleeping directors lie.

If one ever finds out that you rely on his somnolence, he will come to life with fierce and angry energy.

Unfortunately, smaller/newer companies often have directors who are investors or lenders able to exert the power of ownership. These directors are generally disastrous in their effect upon young managements. If not firmly under the thumb of the chief executive, they indulge a nervous impulse: they keep pulling up the flowers to see how the roots are growing.

Directors and the like spend very little time studying and worrying about your company. Result: they know far less than you give them credit for. What they know you can get best by a phone call. It is dangerous to take their formal advice seriously, or be too earnest about their casual questions. If they can ask important questions that the chief executive hasn't already thought of, he ought to be replaced.

Directors have one function, other than declaring dividends, which is theirs to perform: they can and must judge the chief executive officer, and throw him out when the times comes.[1] So the manager of a small/new company must come to these terms: he must make it clear from the outset that he accepts without question the right of the directors to assemble whenever they want and decide to replace him. Having in effect signed a resignation datable at their pleasure, he must meet with them quarterly for a whole day and report to them on the state and trend of the business. These four meetings and the monthly statements should enable the directors to judge him and fulfill their one significant function when the time comes.

Replacements for retiring directors should be other chief executives in completely unrelated businesses or experts active in related fields of knowledge. But suppliers of

[1] Since this task is painful, it is rarely performed even when all the directors know it is long overdue.

goods and services—like lawyers, accountants, bankers and investment bankers—should be kept off the board if at all possible. Give one of these a seat, and you shut off healthy competition from his profession to serve your company.

MANAGEMENT CONSULTANTS

The effective ones are the one-man shows. The institutional ones are disastrous. They waste time, cost money, demoralize and distract your best people, and don't solve problems. They are people who borrow your watch to tell you what time it is and then walk off with it.

Don't use them under any circumstances. Not even to keep your stockholders and directors quiet. It isn't worth it.

Many organizations who've been through it will react promptly, thoroughly, and effectively to the threat: "If you fellows don't get shaped up in thirty days so you're a credit to the rest of the company, I'm going to call in Booz, Allen."

MISTAKES

Admit your own mistakes openly, maybe even joyfully.

Encourage your associates to do likewise by commiserating with them. Never castigate. Babies learn to walk by falling down. If you beat a baby every time he falls down, he'll never care much for walking.

My batting average on decisions at Avis was no better than .333. Two out of every three decisions I made were wrong.

But my mistakes were discussed openly and most of them corrected with a little help from my friends.

Beware the boss who walks on water and never makes a mistake. Save yourself a lot of grief and seek employment elsewhere.

MISTRESSES

It's interesting that otherwise competent businessmen, capable of budgeting a complex operation, can't figure out that the cost of maintaining two women is twice the cost of one plus certain fringes. An early symptom of the mistress is a sudden surge of creativity in an executive's expense account. I once had a personnel vice-president who had taken up with one of our executive secretaries. If it had been outside the company I wouldn't have minded unless it interfered with his work. But a personnel man with his arm around an employee is like a treasurer with his hand in the till.

Having nothing but persistent rumors to go on, I was dragging my feet until all of a sudden all the executive secretaries got a raise (Thank heavens, somebody said later, he wasn't sleeping with a key-punch operator). But how do you get proof? I'm against using shamuses. Finally it came to me. Suppose it were me. Suppose my boss called me in and told me I was fired and why. If I were innocent, I'd go off like a roman candle. If I were guilty, I'd sheepishly ask, "Who did you hear that story from?"

That afternoon I called him in and told him. He lowered his eyes and asked, "Who told you that story?" He was a good man. I helped him start again a little way from temptation in another company. When I cut all the executive secretaries back to their previous pay levels, not one raised the voice of righteous indignation.

P.R. DEPARTMENT, ABOLITION OF

Yes, fire this whole department, too. If you have an outside P.R. firm, fire them too.

Most businesses have a normal P.R. operation: press releases, clipping services, attempts to get interviewed; all being handled, as usual, by people who are embarrassingly uninformed about the company's plans and objectives.

We made many mistakes at Avis, but we were at least smart enough to realize that the professional P.R. operation was as dead as the button-hook industry. We knew too many editors had trigger mechanisms that acted automatically to wastebasket anything starting off: "For release."

So we eliminated the P.R. staff. And we called in the top ten or so people in the company and the telephone operators and told them they were the P.R. department.

The telephone operators were given the home phones of the ten people and asked to find one of them if any of the working press called with a question.

The ten people were given the following framework within which they could be themselves and talk freely:

1. *Be honest. If you don't know, say so. If you know but won't tell, say so.*
2. *Pretend your ablest competitor is listening. If he already knows your latest marketing plan, you use the call to announce it; if not, shut up. (This mindset also prevents knocking the competition, which is always bad for everybody.)*
3. *Don't forecast earnings. If asked why not, tell them we don't do in public anything we can't do con-*

*sistently well (and believe me, nobody can fore-
cast earnings consistently well).*

This system worked well. Example. One day Ford Motor
Company announced they were going directly into the
rent a car business through any Ford dealer that wanted
to. The *Wall Street Journal* phoned and was put through
to the general manager of our rent a car division. Next
day the front-page left-hand column was heavily salted
with quotes from their conversation.

Far down the page our competitor's V.P. of Public Relations had pulled off this coup: "A spokesman for the
Hertz Corporation said they were studying the matter."

Hertz was older and twice our size, but who looked like the
industry leader that morning?

PURCHASING DEPARTMENT

Yes, fire the whole purchasing department.

They cost ten dollars in zeal for every dollar they save
through purchasing acumen.

And that doesn't count the massive unrecorded disasters
they cause. Let's say somebody has persuaded a young
Edison or Steinmetz to go to work for General Conglobulation, Inc. By the time he's found out that there's no way
to get that $900 desk calculator through the purchasing
department he's lost all respect for General Conglobulation
("They'd hire Einstein and then turn down his requisition
for a blackboard.").

So let's be sensible. Fire the whole purchasing department.
The company will benefit from having each department
dealing in the free market outside instead of being victim-
ized by internal socialism. And don't underestimate the
morale value of letting your people "waste" some money. If

you must, have a one-man "buying department" for those
who want help in the purchasing area and ask for it.

SECRETARY, FREEDOM FROM A

For years I had the standard executive equipment—a
secretary. Most of them very good. Then I used the Man
from Mars approach. Then I didn't have a secretary.
Here's my analysis:

Telephone

Before

Jane took all my calls
and made all my calls
(it really has to be all
one or all the other). Two
of the many games we
played: "How long shall
I let it ring before I
decide she's not there?"
"Shall I interrupt his
meeting with this
call?" (How many meet-
ings, finally at the
nitty-gritty, are inter-
rupted by your secretary
asking if you want to
take a call, and you never
seem to get back on the
track whether you take
the call or not?)

After

The telephone operators
took all my calls until
eleven in the morning
saying, "May I have Mr.
Townsend call you back?"
Then at eleven, they'd send
all the call messages in,
start putting incoming calls
through, and I would do
the dialing myself. Result:
Nobody mad. (Note, no
offense because when she
offers to have me call back,
she hasn't asked who you
are.) My calls were con-
centrated in a forty-five-
minute period. I'm on the
phone first (one-up). Same
thing from lunch until four
o'clock, when the afternoon
call messages were sent in,
and incoming calls were put
through again.

Before   After

Appointments

I'd come back from a
one-day trip or even a
long lunch to find my
calendar cluttered with
appointments with my
own people.

Since there was no one to
make an appointment with,
people would stick their
heads in. If I wasn't there,
they'd come back later, or
change their minds. Interruptions? A few. But that's
what I'm there for.

Mail

Jane would read it first.
What with interruptions
it was generally the next
morning before I got the
replies back for signature.

Had two sets of note pads.
One with just my name. The
other, for strangers who
wrote to the office, had my
name, title, address, phone
number. Handwritten
replies.
Advantages: Impressed
the recipients. No files. Can
be done on trips, weekends,
early morning, evening. Lots
faster. The infrequent letter
that needed typing was done
by staff services. If I wanted
a Xerox of my note, I'd say
so in a note to staff
services.

Files

Jane filed copies of everything. Just to be sure.
Spent a lot of time at the
Xerox machine or in
transit. Finally had to
have more space for her

Emptied all three file
cabinets. What I kept filled
half the file drawer in my
desk. When that filled up,
I'd weed it back to half. If
you ever get a serious

Before   *After*

third four-drawer file   antitrust action, the thing
cabinet.   that will hang you (even
                                        if you're innocent) will be
                                        Jane's files.

Trips

One of my close associates   When I called in the
had a great secretary.   telephone operators had
Whenever he called in   my messages. The mail-
from out of town to get or   room also had a rubber
leave messages, she was   stamp: "I'm away. Please
"away from her desk."   handle this in your own
And when he came back,   style and don't tell me what
she would have all the   you did. Thanks. R.C.T."
mail and memos and   They'd open the mail, stamp
appointments spread out   it, route it appropriately.
so he couldn't find his   When I got back—clean
desk for two days.   desk.

Morning coffee, in-box, out-box, Xeroxing, and other
matters were handled by staff services. An important thing
I learned was that my secretary had been acting like an
assistant-to. Helping me where I didn't want and couldn't
be helped. Playing favorites with my associates. I got much
closer to the people who reported to me when I didn't have
a buffer state outside my office.

Working without a secretary depends on a good staff-
services operation. And making friends with the telephone
operators, which is a breeze when they find out you're
going to can your secretary. Telephone operators and
executive secretaries are natural enemies.

Build a good staff-services setup and then try to persuade
your executives to give it a good fair try for a month
every time somebody's secretary quits, or for however
long she's sick or having a baby or on vacation. In my
case, unloading a secretary worked out like finding an extra
four hours a day.

WEARING OUT YOUR WELCOME

Nobody should be chief executive officer of anything
for more than five or six years. By then he's stale, bored,
and utterly dependent on his own clichés—though they
may have been revolutionary ideas when he first brought
them to the office.

Also, decisions aren't based on consensus, but on one
man's view of what's best for the organization. And that
means even the best decisions make some people
unhappy. After five or six years a good chief will have
absorbed all the hostility he can take, and his decisions
will be reflecting a desire to avoid pain rather than to do
what's right.

In 1940, when Sewell Avery had completed eight years
as chief executive of Montgomery Ward, that company's
common stock was valued in the stock market at
$200 million compared to $500 million for competitor
Sears Roebuck. Avery stayed fourteen more years and
a race became no contest. In mid-1967, before Montgomery Ward disappeared from the stock market by
merger, its common stock was valued at $400 million—
a double in twenty-seven years. Sears Roebuck in mid-
1967 was worth $9 billion—up 1800 per cent.

**Lesson for stockholders and directors: If the chief executive
doesn't retire gracefully after five or six years—throw the
rascal out.**

15.   Madness Avenue

WITH THIS SELECTION we move into the wild, swinging world of a part of American business in the nineteen-sixties—what I have elsewhere called "the go-go years." We also move into that characteristically American form of enterprise, the advertising business. Various novelists—in particular, Frederic Wakeman in *The Hucksters*—had previously given highly colored fictional versions of the business and private lives of advertising men, and various well-known advertising men—in particular, Rosser Reeves and David Ogilvy—had written about their business in such a way as to make it seem sober, serious, professional, in the traditional sense "businesslike." Jerry Della Femina, who in the nineteen-sixties came out of nowhere to found his highly successful firm, Della Femina, Travisano & Partners, when he had barely turned thirty, goes to the other extreme. He stimulates, indeed confirms, the fantasies of those outsiders who imagine advertising as a "business" not remotely like any other—a wild romp of madmen in a gamy Madison Avenue jungle where employers whimsically massacre their staffs in mass firings, parents casually forget their child-model offspring, "creative" men ogle girls in neighboring windows and settle their disputes with fists or ball-

point pens, account executives steal each other's best lines in meetings and each other's accounts on the telephone.

Undoubtedly, the truth lies somewhere between—or, perhaps, between and at both poles too. There are advertising shops as sober
and businesslike as the offices of General Motors, and there are advertising bigwigs as personally dignified and as community-conscious
as a Rockefeller. But as the following short takes show, we have
Jerry Della Femina's word that the other kind of advertising man and
business exists in fact as well as in legend, and perhaps, in the
nineteen-sixties, it was the more characteristic kind. At any rate—
a layman can hardly help feeling—considering advertising's best-
known contemporary product, the television commercial, it seems
logical and appropriate that the product should have come out of
such a vulgar and vital setting as Della Femina describes rather than
out of one of efficiency, sobriety, and restraint.

I AM VERY POOR ON DATES and it is a good thing I'm in the advertising business where they don't worry too much about how accurate
résumés are. I was born in 1936 and in July I will be thirty-four
years old. I got married when I was twenty years old but I really have
been married all my life. I graduated from Lafayette High School in
Brooklyn in 1954 and I went to night school at Brooklyn College for
one year. That's it with regard to education. My first job was as a
messenger boy for *The New York Times* and I really didn't do anything much beyond that from 1954 to 1961. In 1961 I finally got a
job with a real advertising agency, Daniel & Charles. I started with
Danny and Charlie as a copywriter at $100 a week, and when I left in
1963 to go to Fuller & Smith & Ross I was making $18,000 a year. I
didn't last too long at Fuller & Smith—no more than nine months or so
—and the next place I worked, which was Ashe & Engelmore, was an

From *From Those Wonderful Folks Who Gave You Pearl Harbor:
Front-line Dispatches from the Advertising War,* by Jerry Della
Femina, ed. by Charles Sopkin (Simon and Schuster, 1970), pp. 19–
20, 55–59, 70–72, 76–77, 106–8, 180–81, 213–15, 247–48.

even shorter time. In 1964 I went to work for Shep Kurnit at Delehanty, Kurnit & Geller and I lasted there a couple of years. From Delehanty I moved over to Ted Bates in 1966, making $50,000 a year plus all the grief they could give you. We started our own agency in September of 1967 after Ron [Travisano] went out and practically raised $80,000 all by himself. I knew very few people with $800, much less $80,000. This September we will celebrate our third anniversary in business and of course we will have a big party. I really don't know what we're billing, but it must be someplace around $20 million a year, which is not bad at all. We've got fifty-three people working for us and we're paying some of these people $40,000 or so a year, which is not too bad, either. We have never been fired by one of our accounts. We resigned a couple of small ones because of some trouble with them, and one account, *The Knickerbocker,* just disappeared. We have a company car, a Lincoln . . .

Last summer, one of our clients mailed us a check for $400,000, which was to cover a lot of television buying, and Ron and I took a look at that check and started to giggle like kids. It is a very weird feeling to hold a check in your hand for that amount of money and not think about skipping town to Brazil. When we go to the Coast to shoot a commercial they are very nice to us at the Beverly Hills Hotel, and it's great to sit at the pool and get paged. Our banker is nice to us, too, and we even have a line of credit. Guys call us up and try to hustle us to go public, which I hope we will never do. We have terrific offices at 625 Madison Avenue, a full floor, and the day we moved into the place we ran out of space.

When I was working at the Daniel & Charles agency, we had to do a commercial for a children's toy called Colorforms. Because we couldn't afford to go and do the commercial on location, we had to settle for Central Park in the dead of winter. We got the kids into polo shirts and short pants and went out to the park. It must have been like maybe ten or fifteen degrees above zero and there was snow all over the place. We managed to shovel off one patch where the kids were going to play with the toy. The kids were turning blue and screaming; the mothers were screaming at the kids because they didn't want the kids to blow the job. It was terrible.

Once an agency was shooting a commercial on Fire Island, and there was the usual pack of people at the shooting—the kid model, the kid model's mother who was hanging on to the agency producer's ear, the director, the assistant director, prop men, grips, cameramen, script people, agency people, account people, the usual tremendous mob. Anyhow, they shoot the commercial, and it comes off okay and everybody packs up and starts walking to the dock to get the next ferry back to New York. The mother is still putting on the producer, telling him what a great actor her kid is; the cameraman is telling the director what a terrific job of camera work the commercial is; the copywriter is telling the account man what a great script he wrote— the usual nonsense from everyone concerned. Everybody gets to the ferry and they're starting to get on when somebody turns around—and it wasn't the mother, either—and says, "Hey, where's the kid?" Well, everyone starts looking high and low for the kid and it turns out they had left the kid back on the beach. Just left him there, playing in the sand.

When I worked at Daniel & Charles there were so many going-away parties for guys who got fired that I figured out a way to ease the financial burden on those people who had to kick in five or ten dollars every week for the party. I decided to sell insurance. I went around to the creative department and said, "Give me three dollars out of your paychecks every week and I'll book it. The next time somebody gets it I'll pay for the party."

There was a copywriter there named Marvin who was doing quite nicely with his accounts. One day he got into a conversation with some other people in the creative department who said, "Marvin, you're being underpaid. You're doing a hell of a job and they're killing you when it comes to bread. Frankly, Marvin, you're worth a lot more."

Now they weren't egging this guy on, they honestly thought that the guy was doing a job and deserved a better deal. Marvin says, "Holy shit, you're right, I'm going to go in there and talk to Charlie." Charlie Goldschmidt was one of the two owners of the agency and is the chairman of the board. Well, he went in to talk to Charlie and Charlie says, "Marvin, that's very funny, I wanted to talk to you." And then Charlie fired Marvin. Marvin was going to be fired all along; if he had kept quiet he would have lasted a few more weeks.

Charlie was doing a lot of firing those days. On one day there were account assignments coming out and Charlie had to pencil in assignments for everyone. He pencils in a lot of names and then when he comes to a guy named Dennis, he doesn't pencil Dennis's name in but rather he puts down "Mr. X" to work on such and such an account. In his mind, of course, he was about to fire Dennis. The only problem is that on the list are Dennis's accounts and next to Dennis's name is "Mr. X." Of course he hadn't gotten around to tell Dennis that he was out and "Mr. X" was coming in. And of course his secretary, she doesn't know anything, so she goes ahead, types the list out, and the account list is circulated throughout the agency. The next scene: Charlie running all over the agency trying to grab back these things from everybody including Dennis. Well, he wasn't fast enough—the legs go first on an agency president—and when Charlie gets to Dennis's office, there's Dennis, white, looking at the list. "I'm sorry," said Charlie, "I'm sorry you had to find out this way." Charlie had not been able to find a replacement for Dennis and didn't want to fire him until he did.

Charlie liked me and when I told him I was leaving he was quiet for two weeks. On the next to the last day he came into my office and said, "Kid, can't you change your mind? Kid, what can I do for you? Kid, you could own this place someday." Last day, he's in my office again. I shook his hand and said, "Goodbye, Charlie." "Goodbye, kid," he says. "I wish you luck, but you're making a mistake."

I went downstairs for a going-away drink with everybody. A guy comes running down saying, "You got to go upstairs again. Charlie's gone berserk; he's firing everybody. So help me. Go upstairs."

And he was. Charlie had simply gone into the office of a fellow named Mike Lawlor and said, "Mike, are you going to follow Jerry?" Mike says, "No, Charlie, I wouldn't do anything like that." Charlie says, "Mike, are you going to take your book [meaning portfolio] up to Fuller and Smith and Ross?" "I might," says Mike. Lawlor felt that the Bill of Rights allowed a guy to show his book around town. "Get out of here," says Charlie. "You're fired. Pack up your things and get out." He then went into the office of a guy named Bert Klein and said,

"Bert, you're Jerry's friend, aren't you?" "Yeah." "Are you going to follow him?" "Gee, I don't know." "Did you ever have your book up to that agency?" "Yeah, I've had my book up there." "Get out," said Charlie, "you're fired." Still another friend of mine, a guy named Bob Tore, was coming out of the men's room. He was a little wobbly because he had heard that Charlie was going from office to office firing people. Charlie grabbed this guy Bob and said, "You're Jerry's friend, aren't you?" Poor Bob. He starts to stammer, "Uh, uh, yeah, I know Jerry . . ." Charlie got compassionate: "Never mind. You got two kids. I won't fire you."

Charlie, who now is a good friend of mine, really did a job that day. I don't know what the final head count was, but he put in a good day's work. The next day he had four free-lancers working up there to take up the slack. And the guys he fired were no slouches. Mike Lawlor went to Doyle, Dane, Bert Klein to Wells, Rich.

One of the reasons for all the chaos is that, suddenly, an account can pull out of an agency. An account has to give an agency ninety days' notice before it pulls out. I swear there are some guys on Madison Avenue who hide in the bathroom on Friday. Friday is kill day because it's the end of the week—killing is done on Friday for book-keeping reasons. What's so sad about it is that the wrong guys get fired. Management calls in some poor guy and says, in effect, "As you know, we've just blown fifteen million dollars worth of billing, and your one hundred and sixty bucks a week stands between us and survival." It's almost ludicrous. Agencies net 15 percent of the account's billing, plus a little extra from things like production charges. Agency blows $15 million in billing, which adds up to like $2,500,000 to the agency and they go to the guy who's making eight or nine grand a year and they tell him, "Look, things are very bad and we're going to have to let you go." The guy who's saying this, by the way, is making forty or fifty big ones a year and he's usually safer. There seems to be a rule of thumb, written somewhere, that the guy making thirty thousand or better is much safer than the guy making eleven.

It's a terrible system and one of the results of it is the guy who makes that thirty or forty grand a year is a very nervous cat. Although he really is safer, he has so much more to lose. He cries a lot at night. During the day you can spot him breezing out of the agency for a fifty-minute pick-me-up from his shrink. God knows how many people on Madison Avenue go to the shrinks, but the number and percentages must be enormous. You see everyone zipping out on Wednesday afternoon, two to three, for a fix. They come back and they're acting like real people again. They're O.K.

In 1961 Daniel & Charles was like a school, except all the kids in the school seemed to be crazy. It was my first real job in advertising, I mean my first legitimate job. I had been out of work for seven months before going there and before I was out of work I had been writing hernia ads for a small outfit called the Advertising Exchange. I was living in Brooklyn and had no bread whatsoever. My relatives used to have my wife and me over to dinner. Sitting around the table, some uncle would say, "Hey, kid, I see by the *Chief* [the Civil Service newspaper in New York City] that they got some openings coming up in the Sanitation Department. Why don't you forget this advertising bug and get yourself a job?"

I really didn't have the heart—or the stomach—for the Sanitation Department. So I sat around in my apartment in Brooklyn and tried to get something going. I decided that Daniel & Charles was the agency for me. I had been going through a book called the *Advertising Agency Register,* which lists all of the agencies in the business, and I was down to the *D*'s. I started sending them in roughs of sample ads. I just sent them in to Danny Karsch, one of the agency's partners, but without a name, just my initials, J.D.F. Anyhow, I kept sending those ads in and one day I called Daniel & Charles and asked for Danny. When the secretary asked who it was, I said, "I'm J.D.F." Danny had me come up for an interview and he hired me at one hundred dollars a week.

I found that the whole place was filled with young guys who suddenly discovered that somebody was going to pay them a lot of money for the rest of their lives for doing this thing called advertising, and all of us got caught up in the insanity of it and went crazy. A whole group of people slowly went out of their skulls.

The first day I was at work we were sitting around in an art director's office and a guy came running into the office, screaming, "Channel Eight, Channel Eight, there's something on Channel Eight."

With this the room, which was full of guys, emptied. They literally ran over me. They ran down the hall and I followed them and when they got to the end of the hall they opened the doorway that led to the stairwell. Daniel & Charles was located on Thirty-fourth Street, about ten feet away from an apartment building. It was almost as if they were connecting buildings. From the stairwell these guys were able to look right into the apartment building, and they had designated the various apartments as Channel One, Channel Two, and so forth. Channel Eight was a very *zaftig*-looking young girl who happened to be walking around in her bra at the time—and nothing else. And like everybody was standing there, you know, commenting on the chick, throwing lines like, "I don't think she's as nice as Channel Five." This was my initiation into advertising.

I wouldn't want to give the impression that all the creative guys in town are crazy. I actually know of only one stabbing that ever took place . . . An art director named Angie once got into an argument with an account man over an ad and they started yelling at each other so Angie simply stabbed the account guy with a ballpoint pen. Oh, I guess there was a lot of blood and screaming, but the account guy lived. The agency decided they had to do something to Angie, so he was officially censured at a Plans Board meeting, which is composed of the most influential people in an agency. The account guy recovered nicely and then took out a Major Medical policy. I see Angie every now and then. I ran into him just the other day on Fifty-ninth Street, looking very strange. He was carrying his coat under one arm, his shirt was not tucked in his pants, he had a three-day growth of beard, and I don't think he had been home for a while.

On the whole, there's not that much violence. Once, on the New York Central, an agency president got into an argument about politics with the guy sitting next to him, and the next thing you knew, the president hit the guy a good shot in the mouth.

George Lois was involved in a small brawl with a friend of mine, Bill Casey. Casey had been working at Papert, Koenig, Lois and he was leaving. There was some kind of stock dispute about his leaving and so they scheduled a reconciliation meeting. Casey was the kind of guy who might have a couple of drinks in a bar and all of a sudden a brawl seems to erupt around him. Something went wrong at the reconciliation meeting and the first thing you know Lois vaults over a table and tries to take a punch at Casey. Secretaries were yelling, the usual chaos. It wasn't the greatest example of a guy leaving an agency. Casey then sued Lois, Julian Koenig, the whole bunch of them, on the grounds that "an atmosphere of physical violence" kept him from doing his work at the agency.

He might have had something, because back in 1965 there was a terrific fight at PKL during which an account supervisor named Bert Sugar slugged another guy, leaving blood all over the place. They used to call PKL "Stillman's East," after the old fight gym.

THERE ARE TALENTED PEOPLE all over New York today who are capable of turning out advertising that doesn't drive people crazy and does sell the product. Problem is whether the people can sell their advertising to their agencies and their accounts. Within every big agency there's a pocket of good people who for some reason manage to save the situation, make the advertising and do it well. Within every agency. When I went to Bates my team was, I modestly believe, that quality pocket of advertising. We turned out some excellent advertising at Bates. In one year, we literally turned the Panasonic Electronics account around.

It took some doing. My title was Creative Supervisor when I went to Bates. But I was part of the zoo. Bates had to form a zoo so that they could take their clients to it and show me to them: "Hey, look, he's creative, he's won awards, he dresses funny, he does all those mystical things that you hear about." What they were saying was: "Like we're in on it, we know exactly what it's all about. Don't worry, baby, you're going to get the same kind of work that you've been reading about other people getting." Somebody once described it as Operation Judas Goat. I was supposed to come in there and pull in a lot of people from the outside. The idea was that other writers and art directors would look at me and say, "Gee, if Della Femina is going in there, maybe it's worthwhile. Maybe I ought to take a shot at it and forget all about those crazy hammers inside people's skulls pushing aspirin." I had something of a reputation among creative people in town for doing good work. At that point they might want to try a place like Bates. So the notion was that hiring me was going to upgrade their entire image. This is the way they planned it. It was not the way I planned it. The first thing I decided to do was to make a declaration of my intentions, sort of to say, "Look, this is what it's going to be like and I'm not going to put up with most of the pompous crap that goes through the agency."

The first day they had a meeting on the Japanese electronics company Panasonic, and there must have been six or seven guys there: the account supervisor, the account executive, the executive art director, and a couple of others. I figured I'd keep my mouth shut for a few minutes, like it was my first morning in the place. One guy said, "Well, what are we going to do about Panasonic?" And everybody sat around, frowning and thinking about Panasonic. Finally, I decided, what the hell, I'll throw a line to loosen them up—I mean, they were paying me $50,000 a year plus a $5,000-a-year expense account, and I thought they deserved something for all this bread. So I said, "Hey, I've got it, I've got it." Everybody jumped. Then I got very dramatic, really setting them up. "I see a headline, yes, I see this headline." "What is it?" they yelled. "I see it all now," I said, "I see an entire campaign built around this headline." They all were looking at me now. "The headline is, the headline is: 'From Those Wonderful Folks Who Gave You Pearl Harbor.'"

Complete silence. Dead silence. And then the art director went into hysterics, like he was hitting the floor. To him it was funny. One of the account guys who was smoking a pipe—well, his mouth opened up at the line and his pipe dropped all over him, and he spent the next five minutes trying to put out the sparks. The rest of them looked at me as if to say, "God, where are we, what did we do?" They looked very depressed. I was pretty pleased. I thought it wasn't too bad a line. Later in the day I repeated the line to the guy who hired me, did the same bit for him. The feeling wasn't spontaneous as all that the second time around but it served its purpose. I know why I do these things: it sets the pace, it really tells people who I am, what I feel.

The meeting keeps going on. This year, it's fashionable for one guy to say we got to have a Wells, Rich, Greene commercial, and then the other guy knocks that notion off as soon as he rings in tradition, the history of the agency. Maybe the president has an early lunch date and he's had enough of the meeting. So he might suggest a compromise. He keeps the radicals happy who want a little Doyle, Dane ethnic humor and keeps the traditional guys happy by suggesting, "Oy, Fights Headaches Four Ways." Or something just as silly.

Do you think I'm kidding? I'm not. I'm dead serious. This kind of thing goes on all the time. They held this type of meeting at Fuller & Smith & Ross many years ago when the agency was trying to get the Air France account. The $60,000-a-year creative supervisor was trying to impress the $90,000-a-year creative director, and they all were throwing lines like, "What if we say . . . ?"

Sitting out of the main line of fire was a poor guy making $20,000 a year and he knew eventually he had to put his two cents' worth in, even though all the other people would dismiss it. He was a copy supervisor of some sort, but pretty far down the rung.

He spots a break in the conversation and says, "You know, I thought of something. Air France, like it's French. Why don't we say something like 'Come Home with Us to Paris'?" The meeting stopped dead in its tracks; the line struck them as great. Before the meeting was over the $90,000-a-year creative director was spouting the line as if it was his. He started by saying, "Let me tell you, that is a good concept because we could . . ." It was armed robbery the way he grabbed the line. The $20,000-a-year guy wasn't heard from for the rest of the meeting. He kept raising his hand—you know, he had scored something and he might be making $25,000 by the end of the year. The guy had a heart condition—he later died of a heart attack. But he really was dead at that meeting. They ran over him. Nobody wanted to know he was there any more. Everybody went for that bandwagon as fast as they could. The creative director, being the heaviest at $90,000, got there first. The $60,000-a-year guy saw what was happening and he tried to take a shot at the line, he was trying to score too, and he's saying, "Well, it's good, but what if we took part of the line . . ." The creative director beat off that attack quickly. "Look, nothing is going to beat 'Come Home with Us to Paris.'"

The creative director moved so quickly that before the meeting was out, people were convinced that the line was his. Each time somebody tried to bomb the line, the creative director would say, "I insist that this is the way we've got to go." People thought he came up with the line, he was defending it so much. Well, they got the Air France account and then things were even bigger and better for the creative director. I've seen it in different advertising trade papers crediting the creative director not only with the line but with pulling in the account. That creative director was making maybe $100,000 a year and riding high. The guy who came up with the line is dead and gone. The creative director was a hero at Fuller & Smith for a long, long time, just on the strength of that campaign. The only thing is that the creative director knows who came up with that line. He knows that he didn't; that he had to grab it off some poor guy. He has to know this and very late at night that guy must shake just a little bit.

Corum Watches is one of our oldest accounts and truly one of the best. Good success story for us. One of their watches is an old American gold piece split in half, with a watch movement inserted in it. We sell that thing very big in Texas. We heard about Corum originally from a guy at *Look* magazine who said they were looking for an agency and we ought to pitch it. After I got the call I got out the phone book and couldn't even find Corum Watches. I got back to the guy on *Look* magazine who knew the account. "Sure, Corum, know them well. Guy by the name of Jerry Greenberg is in charge of the whole business. He really is a great guy." I asked him about Greenberg. "Well, Jerry is a Cuban refugee, and he speaks with a heavy Spanish accent. He's a very gentle guy, very nice guy, but he likes ballsy things."

I picked up the phone, got Corum, and said, "Hello, Jerry Greenberg, I hear your account is loose. I'd like to come in and talk to you about it." At that point there's no sense saying we should get together and have a little talk. He's already talking to other agencies and I might have been too late. He had never heard of me. We had been in business for three months and things were bad. We were running out of bread, two of our partners had decided to pull out and things were very tight. I went to see him, showed him the stuff and got the account, just like that. I practically got it while I was there. When we took over the account Corum was advertising in the *Times* Magazine and spending something like $65,000. The account now bills close to a half million dollars with us. It's a major account with us —and pretty soon he's going to be all over the lot. His sales are fantastic—on that watch made out of a gold piece he's backed up with orders, two or three months' worth. The guy has a watch company now. When you're able to spend close to $500,000 in promotion and advertising, you've got to be making a lot of bread.

Let's say you track down a rumor and you're asked to make a pitch. You can do it two ways. You can have a standard regular pitch which you make to every prospective new client. Or you can do a lot of work on spec, showing the guy what kind of campaign he should have. Mostly the new and younger agencies feature a standard pitch. They don't believe in freebies—for anybody. The older agencies—the establishment, which is running scared—will do anything for new business and they'll go to any lengths, like preparing a whole campaign on spec. Like the TWA thing, which is the great example. One thing good that did come out of the TWA pitch was a growing reluctance on the part of all agencies to do free work.

There is still a third way to get an account, but it is really going out of style fast. What happens is that the chairman of the board of an old-fashioned big agency learns that an account is loose and remembers that he went to school with Bunny or Snoopie or whatever, who now is chairman of the board of the account. The advertising chairman of the board calls his friend at Chase Manhattan and the banker quietly sets up a discreet lunch for the two chairmen of the board. They have a terrific lunch, which is featured by the lack of talk about advertising. Maybe they'll talk about their mutual friend Stinky who was a big man because he stole the town bell one night after the senior hop. You've got to understand that the two chairmen of the board really can't discuss advertising, because they don't know a thing about it. After the lunch, if the account chairman is feeling good, he'll give the account to the agency chairman on the spot because he trusts him and "he's our kind of person." However, with so much more money at stake these days, this kind of pitch is going out of style. Only once did I ever run into a guy *I* knew when

I was a kid in Brooklyn. We were pitching a radio station and this kid who used to hang around the same street corner as I did turned out to be the account executive of the radio station. It was the first time I ever had a common background with a potential account. We sat around talking about old times, you know, things like "Hey, whatever happened to Baldy?" "I don't know." "What happened to Louie Nuts?" "Well Louie Nuts is doing three to five in Dannemora." "And how about Whacky?" "Whacky?" "Yeah, you remember, Whacky was the guy with the funny pointy head." "Oh, yeah, Whacky." It turns out that out of the first twenty years of his life, Whacky spent ten in various prisons. I'm not very good on pitches that depend on schoolboy chums.

Presentations are like an opening night on Broadway. It's very big, it's the make-or-break moment for an agency, and there is a lot of very tough pressure on everyone. You've got thirty-six minutes and your audience is sitting there, and like who knows what's going to happen? Sometimes you barely get the presentation off the ground before disaster strikes. Ron Travisano and I made a pitch not long ago to a very nice guy named Jerry O'Reilly, who handled the Evening in Paris perfume business. We walked into the offices and they were the slickest offices I've seen in a long time. We gave our names to a receptionist and this guy comes down this great long hall. This guy is Mr. O'Reilly's assistant. He leads us to this great big room where we are to meet Mr. O'Reilly. I was carrying the regular ad case and Ron was carrying the projector, which is a big thing and must weigh sixty or seventy pounds. Mr. O'Reilly walks in and I extend my hand and say, "Mr. O'Reilly, I'm Jerry Della Femina." He shakes my hand and then Ron turns to him and says, "Hi, I'm Ron Travisano." What Ron didn't remember as he turned to O'Reilly was that he was carrying that projector. When he turned, so did the projector, and the thing caught O'Reilly right on the kneecap. The sound of the projector hitting his kneecap was a sound I used to hear when I was a kid going to watch the Dodgers at Ebbets Field. You would listen to the crack of the bat and you could tell from the sound when it was going to be a home run. Same sound from O'Reilly's knee. I had my eyes shut when I heard that sound, and I could have sworn that his knee was going to end up in the left-field stands. O'Reilly went down to the floor immediately.

Ron turned to me right at the crack of the bat and said, "This is not going to be such a good presentation." And like I flipped when he said that. We both went into hysterics. Tears were coming out of my eyes. The guy, he went down and he had a little trouble talking for a few minutes. Ron and I went into such hysterics that we couldn't move—we were useless for the rest of the presentation. O'Reilly was very nice about it, considering that he might have been crippled for life by the shot. I'm sorry to say we didn't get the account . . .

16. Living It Up in Geneva

THE LARGELY SELF-CREATED LEGEND of Bernard Cornfeld is well known and can be summarized briefly. (The story is told in great detail, and the legend debunked, in *Do You Sincerely Want to Be Rich?* by Charles Raw, Bruce Page, and Godfrey Hodgson [Viking, 1971].) Raised in Brooklyn and educated at Brooklyn College, Cornfeld served for a time as a social worker and in 1957, at the age of thirty, founded Investors Overseas Services out of his apartment in Paris, to sell U.S. mutual funds to U.S. servicemen in Europe. Almost from the start there were troubles with local government authorities and with the Securities and Exchange Commission in Washington; quite soon, IOS moved its headquarters to Geneva, where its ostensible principal business came to be selling mutual funds to foreign nationals rather than to U.S. servicemen; its real business appeared to be providing a way, often illegal, for persons holding large amounts of weak currencies to convert their money into dollars. Not surprisingly, IOS or its subsidiaries were expelled from one country after another—Iran, Greece, West Germany, and eventually Switzerland. (An IOS director later told the authors of *Do You Sincerely Want to Be Rich?* that "You must never forget that the company developed out of illegal areas.") In 1970, caught in a stock market collapse in the United States and in the consequences of such improper acts as the arbitrary up-valuation of fund assets and a series of huge company loans to company officers, IOS had to suspend redemption of its customers' shares—the mutual-fund equivalent of a bank failure; there were two unsuccessful attempts to "save" it, the first by John King of Colorado and the second by Robert Vesco, who, as this is written, stands accused by the SEC of looting the company of hundreds of millions of the assets it had left. Raw, Page, and Hodgson concluded with some justification that the whole operation had been "an international swindle."

In 1969, though, when IOS was in its heyday, it managed $2.5 billion of other people's money. Cornfeld had amassed a personal fortune on paper of $150 million. His company seemed to have opened up a huge, previously untapped source of venture capital for American enterprise and to have helped the United States balance of payments at a time when such help was sorely needed (mostly by taking advantage of foreign investors, it now appears). Cornfeld, meanwhile, had become internationally famous for his "life style" (indeed, he seems to have been one of the first persons to whom that odious expression was applied)—moated castles, fleets of high-powered automobiles, all-night parties, a corps of miniskirted and complaisant girls, all mixed up in an aura of unabashed hedonism and insouciant contempt for bourgeois morality. As such, he was doing something to change the modal style of American business. He made it sound like fun and thereby dealt a blow to the age-old alliance between capitalism and Calvinism.

Bert Cantor, who for a time had been an IOS vice president in charge of publications and sales training, wrote the passages quoted here when IOS was trembling on the brink between triumph and disaster. They are concerned not with Cornfeld's methods of doing business (which were original in setting but not in structure) nor with his company's illegalities (which are amply documented in the Raw-Page-Hodgson book) but with his celebrated "life style," which is his only legacy to the business world. Now that IOS has fallen, the investors rich and poor have lost their money, and Cornfeld has languished in jail in Geneva for months before being released on huge bail, his antics do not seem so funny any more. But they are part of his time—and in the usually austere world of international finance are an equivalent in light-heartedness of Jerry Della Femina's capers on Madison Avenue.

LONDON, 1958

IN 1957 I WAS LIVING IN LONDON and attending the London School of Economics on a Fulbright grant. Although a Fulbright isn't the best-paid grant in the academic world, I wasn't the best academic so it was pretty much a stand-off. I got my $150 a month and the United States government got a Chicago newspaperman as one of its representatives abroad.

The grant was due to end in June, 1958, and my plans for the future were hazy. I had no real desire to return to Chicago and felt that I would like to see more of Europe than I had managed up to that time.

One of the acquaintances I had made in England was an American named Victor Herbert. We lived near each other in a transient section of London's West End, and over the course of a year we had got to know each other through meetings in local snack bars and pubs. Victor was already a seasoned expatriate and overseas survival expert, and had been the source of a good deal of help to me as a newcomer abroad. Verbal help only, since he had learned early in the game to be very close with a dollar and tended to fade out slowly like the Cheshire cat when I tried to negotiate a loan between government checks. It was through Victor that I first met Bernie Cornfeld.

The meeting took place in Victor's apartment. I had never thoroughly understood what he did for a living other than that he was some kind of salesman, but when he invited me to a cocktail party to meet his boss, I enthusiastically accepted the invitation. Even

---

From *The Bernie Cornfeld Story,* by Bert Cantor (Lyle Stuart, 1970), pp. 13–18, 145–60.

in 1958 the price of liquor was formidable enough in Great Britain to make the prospect of a free drink worthwhile.

The party wasn't impressive. Drinks consisted of a bottle of tax-free airport Scotch that disappeared early in the evening, followed by a few bottles of Spanish wine. The food was comparable in quality and quantity. The guests were nobody special—an American photographer from Detroit who specialized in pictures for nudie magazines, a sprinkling of students mainly preoccupied with getting money from home, and a few Scandinavian and German *au pair* girls anxious to practice their English or whatever else was going.

Bernie Cornfeld made his appearance about 9:30—long after the cocktail hour and well after most of the refreshments had disappeared. By this time I had learned that he was founder, president, and sole owner of a company called Investors Overseas Services—IOS—a sales organization that specialized in selling mutual fund investment programs to Americans abroad. Victor had written me off as a poor fund prospect shortly after our first meeting, and had never bothered to explain his business any further until the evening I first met Cornfeld.

IOS, at that time less than two years old, was headquartered in Bernie's Paris apartment and consisted of himself, a part-time secretary, and about fifteen salesmen, all Cornfeld-trained and of greater or lesser efficiency depending on the season of the year. While the mutual fund business isn't a particularly seasonal one, American salesmen in Europe at that time were.

This was before the period of European expansion by American industry and business, and most U.S. citizens living overseas, with the possible exception of the well-off film colonies in Klosters (Switzerland) and Rome, were either government employees or servicemen. Businessmen were a definite minority.

The biggest IOS market was the U.S. military, which numbered about 250,000 troops in Germany, another 100,000 or so in France, and about 30,000 in Great Britain. Others were the personnel of a few naval bases in Spain and scattered garrisons in Italy, Greece, Libya, and North Africa.

The salesmen were a considerably different breed of cat from the market they serviced. Most had come to Europe out of restlessness as students or would-be writers or painters. Some had come as tourists and decided to stay on and try their luck at earning a living in a relatively relaxed atmosphere. Some were avoiding the unpleasantness of the Joe McCarthy era in the States.

Life for expatriates those days wasn't easy and required great single-mindedness of purpose and determination just to survive. It was almost impossible to get work or residence permits in such desirable places as London, Paris, Rome, or Geneva, and most maintained a precarious existence on tourist visas. A kind of cautious camaraderie existed, based on residual memories of baseball, home cooking, and dated American slang.

The original IOS crew included a Harvard graduate in Spanish language and literature; a Canadian computer designer; a Ph.D. in mathematics from UCLA; a Yale M.A. in literature contemporary to Shakespeare; and a Washington, D.C., newspaperwoman who earned her living in Paris through a most extraordinary method of analyzing people's characters by mail. Others on the IOS sales staff were a ballroom dance team from Chicago, a cartoonist from New York, a former dealer in rare musical manuscripts, and an ex-trombonist from the Sammy Kaye band. The last was considered a man of great good fortune, since he had been badly enough wounded in World War II to draw a full-disability pension. Cornfeld's part-time secretary then was a graduate student in mathematics at the Sorbonne.

Bernie did not project the image of future tycoonship at the London cocktail party. At that time he was thirty-one years old. An experienced clothing salesman might have placed him as a short and portly size 36. His voice was so soft that it was necessary to pay strict attention in order to hear what he had to say, and his speech was peppered with interjectory phrases that covered his tendency to stutter.

As the evening wore on, most of the guests wore out and left, until just the hard core—mostly IOSers—remained. Bernie suggested that we all go out to have something to eat, and on the walk to the restaurant he turned to me suddenly and said: "Hey, do you know the difference between a philharmonic and a symphony orchestra?"

This question hadn't occurred to me before, but no reason not to answer it.

"I guess a symphony orchestra plays symphonies and a philharmonic orchestra plays everything else," I replied.

"Yeah, that's probably it," Cornfeld said. "Look, why don't you stop screwing around with this Fulbright nonsense and come to work with us? You'll make more money than you ever made in your life and you'll have a lot more fun."

I pointed out that my grant still had a couple of months to go and that I had never considered myself a salesman anyway.

Bernie then launched into the monologue on salesmen and salesmanship that has marked his company and everyone associated with it from the beginning. It goes something like this:

"Don't kid yourself about selling and salesmanship. If you know what you're doing, it's the easiest job in the world. Good salesmen are just good listeners. It's a matter of listening to a guy tell you what he wants and then you telling him what you want him to do. People are motivated by two things: fear and greed. They are afraid to lose what they have and they are greedy to get more. People want to own things, and everything worth owning has a price tag on it. Our job is to listen to a lot of basically unformulated desires and then show people how to get the money to realize them. Everybody considers himself unique and different, but in essence everyone is the same.

"Let me show you what I mean," he continued. "I was making a presentation to a girl for a monthly program. I wanted her to put away $50 a month for ten years—that's $600 a year—$6,000 in ten years. The amount wasn't too much for her, but she wasn't interested. She said she couldn't save money—she was different from other people. How was she different? Well, it turned out that she always bought new clothes in the spring and fall, so she could only save during the winter and summer.

"I told her that we had a special program for people like her. It was called the 'Summer-Winter Savings Program.' All she had to do was spend like a maniac during the new clothes season and put away $100 a month the rest of the time. That added up to $600 a year—$6,000 in ten years—right where we started, and I made the sale."

My response was impulsive but not entirely irrelevant. "Did you go to bed with her?" I asked.

"Yeah, but not until after she signed," Bernie replied.

"What about a guy who doesn't want anything?" I asked. "What do you do about him?"

"Once in a while you meet a guy like that," Cornfeld said almost wistfully. "Usually he's very nice—a poet or an intellectual. He drives an old car, or maybe has no car at all. He's happy wearing the same suit year in and year out. He's not concerned with what people think of him. He doesn't want to own a home and, if his kids want to go to college, they're on their own. He's probably a peaceful, happy person. If you happen to meet a guy like that—and you probably won't—leave him alone."

I was sold. The next day I went to work for Investors Overseas Services.

From college socialist to social worker to marginal salesman to billion-dollar jet-set tycoon, Bernie Cornfeld used his gut understanding of the dreams of the middle class to build his marvelous moneymaking machine.

THE NEW BERNIE [1968]

I WAS SITTING AT A TABLE in Allen's restaurant at 73rd and Third Avenue in New York. It was about 11 p.m. and I was tired and hungry. My flight from Switzerland had arrived a few hours earlier and the six-hour time difference between the two continents was beginning to wear on me.

Across from me, having a cup of coffee, was a girl I knew from Geneva. She had been sitting with friends when I came in and had left them to join me for a while. It was a nice combination of circumstances; after almost fifteen years of living outside the United States, I don't know too many people to call when I arrive, and I don't have much to say to those I do call after the first five minutes of greetings have been exchanged.

But it was pleasant to sit facing a pretty girl and make what passes for bar conversation on the Upper East Side. We chatted about her job, my job, the weather, and, of course, IOS in Geneva, where she had worked for a couple of years as a secretary. I glanced out the window.

A dark blue custom-built Continental limousine drew up to the curb and the chauffeur got out and opened the back door. A slim young man wearing Edwardian clothes with a lace jabot and lace showing at the cuffs got out. He walked over to the window and, cupping his hands to his face, shut out the light so he could peer inside. I waved. It was Bernie Cornfeld.

That is, it was the new Bernie Cornfeld.

Ever since he reached the age of forty, Bernie tended to wear costumes, not clothes. His sense of style developed somewhat late. The new, post-millions Bernie handles himself like a life-sized Barbie doll and puts on and takes off costumes which tell the story of what he is thinking, feeling, or doing at any time of the day. All of his costumes look good when he is telephoning—an activity which takes up a good part of Bernie's waking hours.

Bernie had a lot of help in developing his style: London hairdresser Vidal Sassoon worked over his creeping baldness and arranged what hair was left; Paris tailors Pierre Cardin and Guy Laroche, who make at least twenty suits a year for Bernie, have made him clothes that range from a frilly Regency style to semimilitary riding outfits; New York fashion designer Oleg Cassini, a regular guest at Bernie's homes around the world and a partner in Cornfeld-backed boutiques, has helped out with neckwear and accessories. Toshi, Bernie's valet and man of all work, who spends most of his time at the town house in London's Belgrave Square, was a top hair stylist in his native Japan, and backs up the original Sassoon hairdo with endless bottles of exotic hair nutrient. He also offers free-of-charge hair hints to such visitors as seem either to want or need them, and doubles as an excellent chef.

To go with his new look in clothes, Bernie had to develop a matching new figure. The old Bernie was a short, plump, generally rumpled man wearing conservative, off-the-hook, business suits, white button-down shirts, and Ivy League neckties. He usually looked as though he had slept in his clothes—often he had, since his late hours in the office generally made it easier to knock off a couple of hours of sleep on the couch there than go back to an apartment or hotel room to bed.

Aside from work in those formative days, a favorite hobby was eating. After a late night's work in the office, he loved to go to the last open restaurant in town and tuck into a full meal, washed down with plenty of ice-cold Coca-Cola and usually topped off with a whipped-cream-smothered ice cream dessert. Daytime eating was often sandwiches made of corned beef which Bernie had flown in from New York. When you are five feet six, a few meals like those can add the poundage—they could even make Twiggy look like Zero Mostel.

Since the major calorie-burning exercise Bernie got was the little that can be picked up from yelling at subordinates—still a favorite form of relaxation and exercise—he grew like the green bay tree. He was short and portly with a 17-32 shirt size.

"You're looking great," I said, and I meant it. "How did you lose so much weight?"

"It's really very easy to do," Bernie replied, "and no real inconvenience at all. All you have to do is just continue your regular eating habits—eat all you want of anything you want—but when you are through with a meal, you go into the toilet, stick your finger down your throat, and throw it all up. In that way you never gain an ounce."

(This was not Bernie's first dieting effort. Some years earlier, he had imported case-lots of Metrecal from the United States. His battle of the bulge failed then, because he used the Metrecal as a between-meal snack while continuing to pack away his usual trencherman's meals.)

The following day, Bernie said, he was going down to Philadelphia to speak to graduate students in business courses at the Wharton School of Finance, and would I like to come along for the ride and hear his talk? We arranged to meet at his place, the permanently rented five-room suite in the swank Carlyle Hotel on Madison Avenue, at 9:30 a.m. From there we would be driven down to Philadelphia in his limousine, arriving in good time for lunch at the faculty club as guests of the officers of the business fraternity and some of their professors.

I arrived at the hotel the next morning and noted some coolness on the part of the front desk staff when I asked for Mr. Cornfeld's room.

Later the lack of warmth was explained when I was told that Bernie had recently arrived at the hotel accompanied by a rather odd assortment of girls and his pet ocelot.

Since the suite was actually rented in the name of IOS's Wall Street broker Arthur Lipper, and served as a message center for IOS in Geneva through a direct open telephone wire, the Carlyle management indicated to Lipper that they were considering terminating the important rental agreement not only because of Mr. Cornfeld's colorful guests, but also because of his choice of language in the lobby when he was informed that the hotel didn't cater to wildcats.

Bernie was in the middle of a series of seemingly interminable phone calls when I found him, and by the time he finished them, we had breakfast, and he went on a shopping expedition to get a new belt—he was still losing weight and his pants tended to sag—it was nearly 11:30 and our lunch date was less than an hour and about ninety miles away. We loaded the IOS corporate film and a portable projector into the trunk of the car and took off.

We were just about an hour late for lunch and, by the time we got into the dining room, the other guests had already finished dessert and were restlessly watching out for their star speaker.

Bernie zipped through his lunch and announced that he was ready to speak. By the time we entered the auditorium it was packed to overflowing with students anxious to get a look at the Geneva tycoon. With his longish sideburns and elegantly cut Cardin-styled double-breasted suit, Cornfeld stood out in the crowd. The student revolution had by-passed the Wharton School of Finance by the looks of things, and his audience were almost to a man short-haired, clean-cut, and dressed in a mode certain to reassure the heart of any nervous dean, or corporate recruiter.

Bernie was introduced, to a sprinkling of applause; this was not a particularly pro-Cornfeld group and the running battle IOS was having with the U.S. Securities and Exchange Commission was being reported in the press, pretty much to the company's detriment.

Bernie acknowledged his introduction, and then excused himself to go out and lug in his portable projector, which he set up himself, fed the film into, focused, and then operated after a couple of false starts. This action endeared him to the students. The image of a super-slick international wheeler-dealer was wiped out by his fumbling and final triumph over the machine.

After showing what he called "our movie," pointing out that he had left courses at the university there in Philadelphia after a disagreement with an important professor in the department of social work—"If I had gone on to get a degree here, I would more than likely be out either teaching or practicing in the field instead of being in the investment business," he said—Bernie made a short presentation for international mutual funds, and agreed to answer any questions from the floor. A typical question: "How are your relations with the SEC?" Bernie's answer: "About the same as the relations between Liz Taylor and Eddie Fisher."

A couple of hours later in the car on the way back to New York Bernie was beaming. He had shown his favorite movie, talked about his favorite subject, basked in the intense reflected love that only budding businessmen can bestow on one who has made it, recruited a couple of likely-looking seniors—and he was on his way back to his favorite city.

LIFE AT VILLA ELMA [1969]

AT 218 RUE DE LAUSANNE, just a five-minute walk from the IOS main store in Geneva, is the Villa Elma. Nestled down on the Geneva lakeshore and surrounded by a stone wall which was recently doubled in height to insure privacy, the house—really a small palace that Napoleon built for Josephine—is flanked on one side by a private beach, and on the other by another mini-palace estate which now serves as the headquarters for the city botanical gardens across the road.

The four-lane highway that the house fronts on used to be the main commercial road between Geneva and Lausanne; now it feeds traffic into the freeway that links these two most important cities in Suisse Romande.

Although it's small by palace standards, numbering only about twenty rooms, the Villa is imposing, well-constructed, and beautifully maintained. Built in classic French eighteenth-century style, it fits the image of a mansion an emperor would give to an empress he loved. Its last tenant but one was a member of the Cartier diamond family.

Today, the Villa Elma houses Bernie Cornfeld; his mother, Sophie; a random number of Bernie's mini-skirted protégées; a staff of servants, which includes a couple of footmen who as the day progresses seem to change their livery from dark red in the afternoon to starched white after nightfall; a couple of not-so-tame ocelots which no one has ever bothered to name; a basset hound named Winthrop; and a flickering panorama of Bernie's guests that varies from old friends from Brooklyn to the international discotheque set.

In common with every other place Bernie has occupied in Geneva, the front door is seldom locked and people come and go at all hours of the day and night, lending a hotel-lobby or airport-lounge feeling to the establishment. This public-room atmosphere has caused a form of nervous anxiety on the part of some of the guests and most of the servants, since it's not unusual for Bernie to show up, well after midnight, with anywhere from five to fifteen people in tow, and expect everyone to be served and to eat a complete meal.

Bernie's personal life is really public, and his home reflects his life style. His theory seems to be that if a thing is worth doing, it doesn't make much difference who sees it—or, for that matter, who doesn't.

In his former residence, a 1960s-built suburban bungalow half a mile or so from the Villa Elma, the front reception mall featured a slot machine and a bowl full of Swiss francs (a coin about the size and value of an American quarter). Guests were invited to play Bernie's machine with Bernie's money. If they won, they kept their winnings. If they lost, they weren't really losers, since they were playing with their host's money. The machine got little play. By eliminating the chances of real winning or real losing, Bernie had reduced slot-machine playing to an arm-building exercise.

When Bernie traded up the housing ladder in 1967 and got a real palace to match his new wealth, the slot machine had to go. His new reception hall is a more formal place, with a collection of large paintings covering the walls. These copies of seventeenth- and eighteenth-century French and Italian masterworks were assembled by Serge Moreau, Bernie's favorite interior decorator, who can also take credit for the layout and furnishings of the rest of the house. Moreau's work is never done. Besides the Villa Elma, he is also occupied with the castle in France, the Belgravia town house in London, the Paris apartment just off the Etoile, the brownstones on New York's upper East Side, and whatever other houses Bernie has managed to acquire since he began collecting.

Moreau's over-all style for his patron is opulence—tending to the Oriental side. This may be accounted for, in part at least, by the fact that his former major clients, before he decided to concentrate on his job with Bernie practically to the exclusion of all outsiders, were members of the Saudi Arabian royal family.

Off the reception hall, to the right on entering, is a seldom-used formal drawing room. It is dominated by a massive Middle Eastern chess set, displayed on an inlaid table, illuminated by a concealed spotlight. The pieces are rarely moved. Backgammon is Bernie's parlor game when he's not engaged in his real game of international tycooning.

The living room of the house, and the center of social activity, is to the left of the reception hall. Decorated in soft colors, it is furnished with comfortable couches and chairs grouped around a large coffee table. Bernie's favorite spot in the room is on a couch next to a table holding his telephones.

Bernie seldom issues formal dinner invitations, yet he never seems to eat alone. When he says, "Why don't you drop by for supper tonight?" it can mean a plate of sandwiches in the company of Bernie's girls, Bernie's stockbrokers, and Bernie's friends and hangers-on, or it can mean a black-tie affair in the company of Bernie's girls, Bernie's stockbrokers, and Bernie's friends and hangers-on. In the 1960s Bernie's executives and their wives were sometimes included on the guest list and were usually the most apprehensive people in the room. Who really knew if the guy in the corner talking to their host hadn't already been tapped for a top job in the company with a higher salary and a bigger stock option than their own?

Usually the guests arrived before their host. Since there was no real hostess to make newcomers comfortable, guests were left on their own. The hardier ones introduced themselves, and the ones who knew the house found drinks. (Conversation is minimal, and the talk that does go on is cautious.) Since most people who came to Bernie's house either worked for him or did business or wanted to do business with him in one way or another, no one wanted to tip his hand too early in the game in case competitive strangers were present.

In the spring of 1969, I attended a party in Geneva. The purpose of the affair was to launch a new English pop group on the local scene, and Swiss television was there to cover the event. About half of what passes for the "hip" population of Geneva was present. During the course of the evening, I spoke to a healthy-looking, pretty, young blonde girl. She seemed completely out of place in the surroundings, and I asked her why she had come to the affair.

It turned out that she was a friend of the host—an amateur pilot— and had met him at Geneva's airport. Her appearance of healthy out-doorsiness wasn't deceptive. She was a qualified jet pilot, and kept in training much as an athlete does.

"Who do you fly for?" I asked.

"No one," she replied. "No one wants to hire a girl jet pilot."

"I may just possibly have a solution for you," I said.

In common with many other people in Geneva, my solution to offbeat problems is usually tied up with Bernie Cornfeld. I dialed his number.

The phone rang and rang. Finally, a sleepy voice answered.

"Bernie," I said, "who designs your pilot's uniforms?"

"Do we have to talk about this now?" Bernie said. "It's four o'clock in the morning."

I apologized for ringing so late, but insisted on a reply.

Bernie good-humoredly excused my call and said: "Pierre Cardin."

"I just happen to have someone here that will make anybody else you have in a Cardin uniform look like a bum," I said, and went on to describe my new acquaintance.

"You're a real innovator, and you have to act like one," I said. "Here's an opportunity for you to show that you believe in equal rights for women, get a good-looking and highly qualified chick on your payroll, and keep up your reputation for doing the unexpected—how about it?"

"Why don't you bring her over for dinner tomorrow night?" he said.

The next evening, Dominique (that was her name) and I went

to the Villa Elma about 8:30 p.m. As expected, Bernie wasn't home yet, but lots of other people were. They included: a top Geneva attorney who specializes in setting foreigners up with Swiss residence and tax arrangements; a representative of Time Inc., there to discuss a possible publishing venture with Bernie; a young, blonde American girl who wanted to sell him an interest in a soul group at that time working in Rome; two sisters from the Midwest, former Bunnies in Hugh Hefner's Chicago Hutch Number One of the Playboy Club; a French model and film actress, also blonde—the Bunnies were brunettes; Bernie's personal photographer; and Bernie's personal assistant, a young man in mod clothes who was, outwardly at least, the only relaxed person in the room.

The girls were all house guests and dressed in varying styles—a couple wore mini-skirts, the others wore pants suits. No one said anything.

We sat down and I ordered a drink from a passing footman. Dominique, due to fly the next day, refused hard liquor, but asked for an orange juice. It was very quiet.

"It must be nice for Bernie to have all you girls home from college at the same time," I ventured. There was no response.

"If this is a Christian Science Reading Room, where are the magazines?" I demanded. The silence was unbroken.

By this time it was 9:30 and Bernie still hadn't put in an appearance. An ocelot came in and peed in a silver bowl full of salted almonds on the coffee table. No one noticed. The ocelot clawed playfully at a bowl full of long-stemmed roses on an end table and knocked them over, denting the silver vase and spilling water on the floor. No one paid any attention to the accident, so I called a servant over and pointed it out to him. He came back and mopped up the water and led the ocelot away. It remained very quiet.

At 10:30 Bernie came home, and there was a sudden flurry of excitement. The girls came to life.

"Why don't we have dinner?" he said.

Then the real jockeying for position started. In Bernie's house, the one seated next to him at dinner has the best chance to make a sale, since that's one of the few times that he sits still and is relaxed enough to listen and make conversation. The only interruption allowed at mealtimes is the telephone. It's almost as though Bernie were Yehudi Menuhin and Alexander Graham Bell were Stradivarius—when an artist finds an instrument that fits him, he allows nothing to stand in the way of its use.

Bernie led us into the dining room and made his seating arrangements. Dominique sat next to the lawyer; I was placed between the Bunnies at Bernie's right with only one Bunny between me and him; the *Time* man sat at the end of the table with the soul girl and the photographer. The rest, including a couple of unidentified latecomers, filled out the group. It was very quiet.

Bernie's dining room is one of the most beautiful and restful rooms in a beautiful home. The floor is marble and the table is "faux marbre," a mammoth affair that can seat at least a dozen people comfortably. The sideboard, built of real marble to match the table, is massive and carved and, in addition to the food and drink for the diners, always holds a large flower arrangement. Marble busts of Greek gods and long-dead kings of France fill the corners of the room.

The service matches the furnishings. Somehow or other, Bernie has managed to put together a staff of servants who are devoted to him and to their work—this in spite of the comings and goings of the numerous live-in guests, the odd meal hours, and the other heavy demands made on their patience and good humor.

At dinner that evening, Bernie was pensive and more inclined to silence than to discussions of business. He shrugged off all references to pop music, publishing, and other investment possibilities that were dangled in front of him.

"How about Dominique?" I asked. "Wouldn't she make a great addition to your aircraft division?"

"The idea of a girl pilot really doesn't do much for me," he said flatly. "But maybe we can find something else for her to do around the place."

I explained that she was intent upon flying, and he lost interest immediately.

Dinner itself that evening was nothing special. Bernie's chef is Italian, but the food served at that meal was strictly American. That night it was southern-style fried chicken, mixed salad, and chocolate sundaes for dessert. The guests were served Bernie's standard table wine, an expensive, chateau-bottled Rothschild Bordeaux. Bernie himself stuck to his favorite drink: Coca-Cola in the family-sized bottle, served to him by one of his footmen with all the aplomb of a wine waiter in a top restaurant decanting a fine vintage.

After dinner, Bernie became all business again. While most of the guests went back into the living room for brandy and coffee, he retired with the lawyer and his assistant for a private conference in the paneled bar just off the dining room.

Bernie uses this L-shaped bar as a kind of ideal office. He places people on the stools and then gets behind the bar himself. In this way, he can pour drinks and carry on three or four different business discussions at the same time, much as a real bartender does, by going from client to client. Naturally, the room is equipped with a speaker phone.

Conversation in the living room lagged, and no one seemed anxious to liven it up. The *Time* man and the photographer spoke tiredly of mutual acquaintances in New York.

When Dominique and I left at 1:00 a.m., Bernie was settling down to a game of backgammon with one of the late arrivals. The girls were sitting in the same chairs and couches, in the same order, maintaining the same silence, as they had at the beginning of the evening.

I never saw Dominique again. Bernie hasn't either, as far as I know. In any event, his pilots are still all male.

But it isn't always like that at Bernie's house. On one of the occasions he has called me in recent years, he invited me to come over for dinner. Since it was already after 9:00 p.m. when he called, I declined politely but added that, if he wanted to talk to me about something special, I would come over the next afternoon, a Sunday, at any hour that was convenient for him.

"Come on over about 4 o'clock," he said.

When I arrived the next day, close to the appointed hour, it looked like a traffic jam in his parking lot. Guests were coming and going at a rapid clip. Just as I arrived, Eileen Ford of the New York model agency was leaving, and Bernie was arranging for one of his chauffeurs to drive her to the airport. It turned out later that this was the time when Bernie was negotiating to buy the two top model agencies in Paris and was talking over the business with Miss Ford—certainly one of the leading experts in the field.

Entering the foyer, passing the paintings, and the chess set, and going into the living room was a repeat of my previous experience. The same girls—or a group that resembled them in an uncanny way—were sitting around the room. Winthrop, the bassett hound puppy, was bouncing around the rug.

Bernie was busy with meetings going on in various parts of the house. Finally he came into the living room.

"Want to see a movie?" he asked.

"Not really," I said. "I don't much feel like driving downtown and looking for a parking place, and besides I'd kind of like to get home early."

"Oh, we don't have to go downtown," Bernie said. "We can see the film right here. Come on upstairs."

Bernie's bedroom may very well be Serge Moreau's masterpiece. At any rate, it will be hard for Moreau to top it no matter where or how long he stays in the interior decoration field.

The room is large and high-ceilinged. In the center of the ceiling is a gold crown with velvet draped in folds from this central point to the corners of the room. An emperor-sized double bed, with a fur spread that touches the floor all around, dominates the room. At the foot of the bed, against the far wall, are two large electronic devices—one, an oversized television screen, and the other, a forbidding-looking box that turns out to be the video tape player.

"This is a marvelous invention," Bernie said. "You ought to have one."

"What does it do?" I asked.

Bernie explained that the machine played tapes of television shows.

"A lot of the guys in the company here have these now," he said. "I gave a lot of them for Christmas presents last year. We've got a guy in New York who tapes all the TV shows for us and sends them over, and then we trade the tapes around. If you get one, you could have the tapes too, and it's a lot better than looking at French or Swiss television."

"How much do the playbacks cost?" I asked cautiously.

Bernie lost interest—like Louis Armstrong once said, "If you gotta ask, you ain't never gonna know."

"I don't know, a couple of thousand bucks, I guess," he said. "Anyway, anything special you'd like to see?"

"Have you got a Western?" I asked.

"Coming right up," Bernie said. He went over to a closet and began sorting through what seemed to be miles of video tape in tin cases. He threaded up the machine.

Four of the girls had come up to the room with us. Bernie and one of them, accompanied by the bassett puppy, got under the fur cover on the bed. The rest of us sat on the floor at the foot of the bed.

"Anybody hungry?" Bernie asked. "I could send down for a plate of sandwiches." No one replied, so Bernie called down to the kitchen and asked for the sandwiches to be sent up.

The film was undated, and my memories of it are vague. It was a story of a Western outlaw who faked a case of smallpox to escape from the U.S. cavalry. Occasionally, a long-outdated bulletin on the Vietnam war would flicker across the bottom of the screen. None of the girls at the foot of the bed said anything. Bernie and the girl under the fur cover moved restlessly. The dog bounced from the bed to the foot of the bed, begging for his share of the sandwiches.

It lasted an hour. Somehow it seemed much longer. When the film was over, Bernie got up, turned on the lights, and we all straggled downstairs.

"It's really nice to see you," Bernie said. "We really ought to get together more often. Why don't we?"

"I guess because we never invite each other," I said. "By the way—did you want to talk to me about something?"

Bernie looked blank. "No, nothing special," he said as he led me to the door.

As I was leaving, four or five people walked in. I don't know what kind of a movie they saw.

17. Youth Marketeers

NATIONAL STUDENT MARKETING CORPORATION (NSMC) was one of the highest-flying, and then hardest-crashing, of all the famous "concept" stocks of the late nineteen-sixties. It was the brainchild of Cortes Wesley Randell, a strapping young Virginian who, having attended the University of Virginia and served brief terms with General Electric and International Telephone and Telegraph, founded it in 1965 to exploit the "youth market," which was said by marketing experts to have something like $45 billion a year to spend. It was, of course, a time of youth-consciousness and, to some degree, youth-worship in all aspects of American life, not least in business and finance; under-thirty portfolio managers in Wall Street were drawing astronomical salaries for swinging their mutual funds in and out of the hot new stocks (of which NSMC was a prime example), and brash young conglomerate kings were pulling off breathtaking feats of *chutzpah* like that of twenty-nine-year-old Saul P. Steinberg, of Leasco Corporation, who took over Reliance Insurance Company in 1968 and then nearly succeeded in taking over Chemical Bank New York Trust Company in 1969.

NSMC's nominal business was distributing samples and employment guides, doing market research, and selling fad items like posters on college campuses through a string of part-time student representatives. It did indeed do these things. But basically it appears to have been a stock promotion whose goal was to exploit profit-hungry institutional investors.

Randell, it seems clear in retrospect, was never so interested in selling goods and services to youth on campuses as he was in selling shares of his company to Wall Street, and especially to the dignified but nonetheless gullible managers of the great financial institutions: Bankers Trust, Morgan Guaranty Trust, the State Street Fund of Boston, the Harvard and Cornell endowment funds. His real product was the "concept" that the youth market was a gold mine; his persuader was his own charming and forceful personality. By repeatedly predicting tripled earnings for the following year, he kept his stock selling at 100 times current earnings; then to fulfill his promises he had to juggle the books through the process that was whimsically called "creative accounting." Of course—besides being on the borderline of plain dishonesty, as the following passages show—this was a process of deferring disaster, of mortgaging the future, and inevitably disaster had to come. It came, sure enough, with the general market collapse of 1969–70.

In his heyday, Randell lived in a $600,000 castle on the Potomac, relaxed on a fifty-five-foot yacht, and impressed security analysts and institutional portfolio managers by talking to them on the radiophone from his $700,000 Lear Jet. Andrew Tobias, a Harvard graduate (1968) who had been a campus entrepreneur as an undergraduate and then worked briefly for a Princeton subsidiary of Gulf & Western, came to work for NSMC late in 1968, when he was only twenty-one, at a salary of $15,000 and stock options. During his twenty months in the job, and a few following months, he saw the company's sales go from $3 million to nearly $100 million and its stock, which had originally been offered for $6.00, go up the roller coaster to $143 and then down to below the original price. In these passages we watch a young man of his times undergoing a commercial education of a most disillusioning kind while he wrestles, none too successfully, with his conscience. Of course, a man writing about the experience of gradually discovering that his employer is engaged in something like a confidence operation has the problem of whether to present himself as a fool or as a knave. I must say that I feel Tobias confronts the problem forthrightly and, meanwhile, he gives us a privileged glimpse of the inside of one of all too many operations of that era that succeeded for a short time in making suckers of the investing public and of the big financial institutions too. Here is the "youth revolution" in Faustian perspective.

[CORTES] RANDELL'S EARNINGS PROPHECIES were self-fulfilling. By announcing phenomenal earnings projections he got a phenomenal valuation of NSMC [National Student Marketing Corporation] stock, which then allowed him to buy enough earnings to meet his projections. Then, to keep the momentum high, as all glamour stocks must, he would make another round of phenomenal projections. As long as he bought companies for a lower multiple of their earnings than the multiple at which NSMC stock was valued, earnings would increase more than equity would be diluted—so earnings per share would increase. As with a chain letter, investors and acquired companies don't get hurt as long as the snowball keeps growing exponentially forever: Impossible, but enticing if you're one of the first to sign up. Chain letters are illegal.

Also like a chain letter, NSMC's growth depended on confidence in the chain. If people fear the chain may be broken or that there is something shady going on, they will not participate and it will collapse. Randell managed to build an unparalleled mutual-admiration society that could allay almost any fears. The auditors probably figured that if something disreputable were going on, then White and Case, one of the largest law firms in the world, would not sit quietly as NSMC's counsel. White and Case was probably reassured by the fact that Peat, Marwick, Mitchell apparently had no qualms about the financial statements. Morgan Guaranty and Donaldson, Lufkin, & Jenrette, when they took their substantial positions in the stock, were

---

From *The Funny Money Game,* by Andrew Tobias (Playboy Press, 1971), pp. 84–88, 112–16, 154–74.

probably pleased that the Harvard Endowment Fund had already taken a position, while Harvard probably was pleased about the growing ranks of Harvard MBAs in the company, including two who assisted Cort full time. The MBAs may have heard about NSMC through favorable articles in *Business Week* and *Ad Age*. And everyone wanted a ride in Cort Randell's Lear Jet. (I flew with him from Las Vegas to New York; but that was before he installed the telephone. . . .) When you are in such good company, you don't try too hard to find holes in the story. You take a lot for granted.

I remember a psychology experiment we studied in college. Five students were hired as subjects for a "perception test." The first 4 to arrive were told how to behave and seated in a row in front of a movie screen. The last student to arrive was given no instructions and was seated at the end of the row. Two squares were projected onto the screen and the students were asked which was bigger. They were told to answer in order, from left to right, which meant the unsuspecting fifth student would always be the last to answer. Each student in turn said that, obviously, the left square was bigger. Then 6 shades of red were projected—which was darkest? The third, each said in turn. Some hand-drawn circles—which most nearly round? Although it was fairly close, each of the 5 decided the first circle was most nearly perfect. Then 4 lines—which was longest? The fourth line was longest; however, the first four students, by instruction, chose the second line. What do you think the fifth student said?

Perhaps after reading how Cort bought nearly $100 million worth of other companies' sales with funny money, you are tempted, as I was, to write a letter to the editor like one that appeared in *Business Week* in a 1970 issue. The letter said that if a price-earnings ceiling were placed on stocks, "stocks would not be overinflated, the financial community would not be in a mess" and funny money would be taken out of circulation. If all stocks were sold at ten times their earnings, the letter said, "price swings would not be severe, and people would not lose much of their savings and their jobs," and if "earnings increased, the price of the stock would increase by the same proportion."

Upon reflection, though, there are at least two flaws in this neat solution. First, everyone would want to buy the stock of a company that expected to show healthy earnings growth each year—and almost no one would want to sell it. There would not be enough to go around. How would you ration IBM stock, for example, which sells at around 50 times earnings because it grows about 20% a year? Second, the stock market is a key mechanism by which the nation, consciously or unconsciously, allocates its capital resources.[1] People invested tremendous sums in a company called Recognition Equipment for years before it made a profit at all, because they thought machines that could read numbers and characters (on checks, for example) would be tremendously important to data processing in future decades. The stock was selling at an infinite multiple, since there were no earnings; but finally the bugs were ironed out of the machines and investors' hopes were largely realized. How would you finance speculative ventures if not through speculative stock issues?

True, many new ideas will fail and the capital invested will be lost. However, the S.E.C. attempts to force companies to make it very clear to investors just how much risk is involved in their investment. In order to satisfy the S.E.C., many prospectuses for new issues have to make comments like this:

> Because what we are trying to do has never been done before and we are not very well qualified to do it or positive that people will care even if we can, there is absolutely no assurance that we will ever make a profit.

Until recently, this kind of statement only served to whet the excitement of speculators, like me, who saw what Omega Equities had done (25¢ to $25) and weren't going to let the S.E.C. or other conservative Depression-raised types keep them from cashing in.

I reasoned this way: Although similar to horse races or roulette, the market does have three slight redeeming qualities. First, in a casino you have less than a 50% chance of winning, while in the market as a whole the average investment should grow with the American economy, which some people feel will grow, despite minor setbacks, forever. Second, when you invest in Wall Street, your capital is gen-

---

[1] There is evidence that Wall Street is less "key" in this respect than they might have you believe. "Equity issues supply less than 5% of the new capital needed to finance business." (*Business Week*, Oct. 31, 1970.)

erally allocated to projects you might consider more worthwhile than the pockets of other gamblers and casino owners. Third, people who play the market are probably better able to sustain losses than some of the people hooked on the horses.

The first annual report NSMC issued in 1968, five months after the stock went public, showed sales of $5.5 million and pre-tax profits of $700,000. I was very proud of it and took it home to my roommate Humphrey. He read the footnotes (how dull, I thought) and asked some rather nitpicking questions (obviously prompted by envy). In retrospect, his most important question may have been, "What is this $1.8 million of 'unbilled receivables'? I've never heard of 'unbilled receivables.'" I hadn't either, and the footnotes didn't really clear it up. As best we could tell, this represented money clients had committed for programs that were nearing completion and would be billed soon. Anyway, Peat, Marwick, Mitchell's standard letter was on the last page saying they thought the report fairly represented our financial situation, and that was that, as far as I and my then $190,000 stock option were concerned.

I learned much later that $400,000 of the $1.8 million unbilled receivables Humphrey noticed were eventually received and that the rest would never be billed nor received. The figures may have been off; but I believe that was the gist of the true situation. Clearly, the announced earnings of $700,000 in 1968 would have suffered somewhat if NSMC hadn't reported $1.4 million of sales that never materialized. As far as I know, NSMC never reported costs that didn't materialize, only sales.

But in stretching things a little, NSMC management may have been reasoning: "We've promised Wall Street a dramatic increase in profits. If we don't show it, our stock collapses, we can't make acquisitions, we are stuck trying to make a profit internally (ha!). So we owe it to ourselves and our shareholders to be as liberal as our auditors will allow. And maybe even fudge a little. If it turns out that some of these hoped-for sales don't come through, the write-offs won't make a very big dent in *next* year's statement, because by then we'll have millions of dollars of acquired companies' earnings with which to absorb any of this year's rough edges. After all, our basic concept is sound and what big company didn't have to scramble a little when it was small?"

Speaking of unbilled receivables, I should recount an incident that seemed harmless enough at the time. We were still located in the Time-Life Building and all indicators were pointing up. Over the last few weeks we had heard progress reports of negotiations with Pontiac for what promised to be our first million-dollar contract. The deal seemed to be in that strange limbo stage where it was certain but not definite. (We had a lot of deals like that.) I was stretching my legs around 10 o'clock in the evening and found that the only 2 people left in the office were Cort and a secretary. Cort was seated at a typewriter rattling off about 3½ words a minute. Always on the lookout for brownie points, and incensed by the idea of our leader wasting his valuable time, I let it be known that I was the fastest 2-finger typist in the world. They were relieved to hear this, because the tricky spacing on the IBM Executive typewriter was giving them trouble.

Cort gave me a brief letter addressed to NSMC on Pontiac letterhead and explained the silly mix-up that had occurred. You see, this was a letter confirming Pontiac's intent to spend something over a million dollars with us in the coming year. It had been received just in time to meet the accounting deadline for one of the financial statements (it wasn't clear how the accountants would use this document, just that it was important). A ridiculous typographical error had been made by the Pontiac executive's secretary. She had hit a *t* where she should have hit a *w*. Instead of a sentence reading, "We are no*w* planning to spend umpty-ump dollars with your programs" (or words to that effect), we had a sentence reading, "We are no*t* planning to spend . . ."

Cort explained that the Pontiac executive had been reached by phone, had apologized for the error, had agreed to send a corrected letter, but upon hearing that the letter would come too late, had asked us to retype it for him. I cannot recall whether I asked or was told how the executive's signature was going to arrive at the bottom of the retyped letter. I do recall that I was supposed to match the format of the letter I was retyping exactly, with the exception of that silly typographical error. I did so, collected my brownie points and statements of wonderment at my dual digital agility, and went back to what I

was doing. I imagine that the corrected text was pasted over the in-
correct text on the Pontiac letterhead and that a Xerox was made
and shown to the accountants—but this is no more than a guess based
solely on the information I have related. Your guess is as good as
mine. I have absolutely no evidence that the retyped letter wasn't
entirely authorized by Pontiac. I also have absolutely no evidence
that any of the Pontiac plans were included as unbilled receivables.

We wound up doing little or no business with Pontiac. They
changed their plans.

In addition to the unbilled receivables, Humphrey was a little worried about the $486,000 shown as the "unamortized cost of prepared
sales programs." A footnote explained:

> The company's business is seasonal and coincides with the
> school year. Expenditures are incurred for printing, lay-out, and
> mailing preparatory to the commencement of various sales
> programs, most of which commence in the fall of the year and
> carry over into the spring.
>
> The company follows the practice of deferring these costs and
> amortizing them over the periods in which applicable income is
> derived. The amortization periods commence with the various
> sales campaigns and costs are written off over the lives of the
> programs or a maximum of twelve months, whichever period
> is less.

In other words, this annual statement covered the fiscal year ending
August 31, 1968. In August a lot of money was spent printing hand-
outs and mailings that would not produce revenue until after August
31—too late to be included in that year's income. So it was reasonable
to defer the $486,000 of expenses to the 1969 fiscal year, since that
was when the revenues from these expenses would come in. You can
see, though, that reasonable or not, this would be a good way to postpone a loss if the $486,000 of expenses only produced, say, $150,000
of revenue.

With my limited knowledge of accounting and the stock market, I
was fascinated by one other interesting numbers game—the relationship of Cort's personal finances to his company's. For a while Cort
owned 50% of the company stock, which was selling at 100 times

after-tax earnings. His salary was $24,000. If he had raised it by $10,000 he would have had $10,000 more income, less perhaps $4,000 in taxes, or $6,000. But NSMC's pre-tax earnings would be $10,000 less, and after-tax earnings would be $5,000 less. Valued at 100 times earnings, this $5,000 reduction would mean a $500,000 decrease in the value of the entire company, of which Cort owned half. So, theoretically anyway, Cort's own equity in the company would decrease by $250,000. If instead he lowered his salary by $10,000, or $6,000 after tax, his stock would be worth $250,000 more. And when S.E.C. regulations allowed him to sell it, the Internal Revenue Service would consider that $250,000 a long-term capital gain, not ordinary income, leaving him $175,000 after taxes.

Thus, roughly and hypothetically, Cort might decrease his after-tax income by about $175,000 if he raised his after-tax salary by $6,000. And vice versa. Which may explain why Cort generously paid many travel and entertainment expenses out of his own pocket; paid low salaries and gave large options; and even gave away bits of his personal stock to avoid paying executives large salaries.

I NATURALLY developed a number of different subrationalizations to my Great Rationalization that accounted for my playing along with NSMC, for remaining in the overheated steamroom. Perhaps they are most easily described with reference to a particular situation . . .

August 31 was the last day of NSMC's 1969 fiscal year. The second annual report could easily have been mistaken for a copy of *Venture* magazine. Inside the embossed cover were 64 pages of mostly full-color photographs describing a $67-million company going on $1 billion. The report was not saddlestitched with staples, like a magazine or pamphlet; rather, it was perfect bound, like a book. It was every bit as slick as reports of companies 10 or even 100 times NSMC's size, and really put NSMC's best foot forward. But isn't a company free to spend what it wants on its annual report, to highlight good news and bury bad news in footnotes, to radiate optimism and confidence in the midst of difficulties?

The content of the report was much like the press release quoted earlier. For example, the $20 million of mainly nonyouth-market insurance sales were described this way: "The newest division, Financial Services, at this time provides health, accident, and affiliated insurance coverage to students, young travelers and campers." The truth. Was the company required to describe the greenhouse and race-track specialties as well? The whole truth? I don't know. As usual, there was much that is misleading; hopes stated as plans, unprofitable projects about to be dropped described as ongoing, presumably successful. Nothing but the truth?

It didn't seem my place to tell our professional public-relations people just how far they could ethically go in applying make-up to the corporate physiognomy. Anyway, sophisticated investors usually consider financial statements the most important part of an annual report and disregard the trimmings just as naturally as a smart housewife notes the bones when she buys meat by the pound.

When NSMC's 1969 fiscal year ended (August 31), it was clear that the earnings projections Cort had made would again be impossible to meet without a little "creative accounting." He needed to show about $3.5 million in net earnings. Two problems were CompuJob, which . . . lost a lot of money despite the good publicity it produced for NSMC, and the Canadian arm of NSMC. So on November 30,[2] 90 days after the fiscal year had ended, an agreement was made to sell CompuJob back to Tan [Miller] and Ed [Swan] [from whom NSMC had bought it several years earlier] and the Canadian operation [back] to its managers. According to the footnote, "In the opinion of counsel in both transactions negotiations and agreements of sale were in effect consummated prior to August 31, 1969 . . ." These transactions allowed NSMC to add $369,000 in after-tax earnings, or about 10%, to its 1969 results. The $369,000 represented the "aggregate gain . . . as a result of the sale of the subsidiaries." Where did Tan and Ed and the Canadians come up with the cash to buy back these subsidiaries? No cash. The footnote explains that payment was made with 1-year and 5-year personal notes. Even though NSMC didn't get any money in fiscal 1969, it was able to show in earnings the money that would come in over 5 years. Don't worry about the

[2] This is the date I noted next to the footnote in my copy of the annual report; I can't remember whether this was the exact date, or an approximation. If an approximation, it was fairly close.

loans, by the way. The footnote says they are secured by 3,850 (original) shares of NSMC stock then valued at about $400,000, now valued at about $40,000.

How could something I saw everybody sweating over the night of November 29th have in effect been consummated prior to August 31? But I am not a lawyer or an accountant, and our lawyers and accountants were evidently on record saying this was okay. Moreover, the footnote was apparently sufficient notice to the public of what had happened.

I never learned what inducements persuaded Tan and Ed to take CompuJob off NSMC's hands. Whatever they were, the sale was made with so little fanfare that, while notice was being given in the footnotes of the report, CompuJob was mentioned in the big type up front as though nothing had happened. I whistled, all right, but at the system, not for the cops. I was beginning to see why a business-school (or law-school?) education might be helpful, after all.

Meanwhile, another footnote explains a new item on the balance sheet called "deferred new product development and start-up costs." Here was $533,000 that was spent in fiscal 1969 but that would be charged against the future, on the theory that at least $533,000 of revenue was likely to be derived in the future from those invested expenditures. Had such a sum been charged against 1969, earnings per share would have decreased by 10¢ per share (unadjusted for splits), and the stock might have sold for $10 per share less (100 times 10¢ per share), which would have made it more difficult for NSMC to acquire other companies. The same kind of calculation could be run for similar footnotes to show the relationship between an accounting decision and stock price. I am not saying NSMC should not have deferred this $533,000. That is a matter of judgment. Take my salary, for example, which may be included in the $533,000. A conservative management would probably have considered my salary an administrative expense and charged it against the period in which it was paid out. A go-go management would probably have considered my salary a research-and-development expense and tried to persuade the auditors to allow them to spread it out over the next 3 to 5 years. In the long-run, my salary would be charged against earnings either way. But to a glamour company, earnings now are worth far more than future earnings. I don't know how my salary was treated; but I think it illustrates some of the latitude a creative accountant enjoys.

The "unbilled receivables" are back, up to $2,800,000 from the $1,763,000 shown in 1968—only there is a twist. In the "1968" column of the 1969 annual report, which is shown for purposes of comparison, you would expect to see $1,763,000, as was reported in 1968. Instead, you see $945,000. This discrepancy is not explained in a footnote. Perhaps the missing $818,000 of 1968 assets had to be written off when it turned out they would not materialize.

You may recall also the $486,000 of "unamortized cost of pre-pared sales programs," which had been deferred in 1968 because these were expenses for printing up fliers and the like that would not produce revenue until 1969. Now that figure is up to $1,048,000. In other words, 1969 was charged with $486,000 that was actually spent in 1968; but 1969 was *not* charged with $1,048,000 that was actually spent in 1969. There are two ways of looking at these de-ferrals. If the $486,000 eventually brought in revenues of more than $486,000, and if the $1,048,000 eventually brought in more than $1,048,000—then this is an accounting method of "waiting for prof-its." Not counting your chickens, and all that. On the other hand, if the $486,000 eventually brought in less than $486,000 and the $1,-048,000 less than $1,048,000—then this is an accounting method of "postponing losses." Borrowing from the future with no hope of re-payment, and all that. Of course, it is hard to predict future revenues, so it is hard to accuse anyone of purposely trying to postpone losses (which violates the Generally Accepted Accounting Principles). You can only accuse him of being groundlessly optimistic. It is the man who feigns optimism in order to postpone losses he expects who is cheating the system. While we can't tell for sure whether NSMC's optimism was feigned or genuine, it appears to have been unjustified.

And now we come to what I would like to call the Killer Footnote. This note points out that if you don't include in fiscal 1969 figures the earnings of companies whose acquisitions were "negotiated and agreed to in principle before August 31, 1969, but closed subsequent thereto . . ." or the earnings of companies whose acquisitions were "agreed to in principle and closed subsequent to August 31, 1969 . . ."—then you have to exclude $3,754,103 in net earnings, leaving a profit of $110,977, or about 4¢ a share (unadjusted). Dig beal, as they say. In other words, if you don't count companies that were not legally part of NSMC in fiscal 1969, then fiscal 1969 barely broke even. *(If* you accept the rest of the creative accounting.)

So why was the stock selling at $140 a share? The company earnings were valued at a multiple about 10 times that of other conglomerates, and those earnings were apparently far from solid. A good time to sell, even though prestigious brokerage houses were still issuing "buy" recommendations.

Brave Alan Abelson dared to point this out in his column in *Barron's,* and the stock fell 20 points the next day. Not so much because of what Abelson pointed out, but because people knew that when Abelson roasted a company, its stock fell about 15%, so they figured they had better sell NSMC until it had fallen about 15%. This is an oversimplification, I admit; but widely read Wall Street columnists surely start as many trends as they discover. Their prophecies are self-fulfilling, too. It was rumored, incidentally, that the NSMC annual report was brought to Abelson's attention by someone who had shorted[3] 3,000 shares of NSMC stock. If so, that someone made $60,000 the next day, and considerably more thereafter. Abelson had called the cops and the snowball began to melt.

NSMC's reply to the charge that earnings came from companies acquired after the close of the fiscal year was that considerable expenses were incurred in expanding the core company's capabilities in preparation for the acquisition of these companies. If their earnings hadn't been added, neither would the extra capabilities have been necessary. (I thought that might be a euphemistic way of describing the massive costs of running unprofitable programs in plush surroundings in order to have the kind of story that would command a 100-times multiple.) Moreover, the Chairman of Peat, Marwick, Mitchell's Ethics Committee was present at the NSMC annual meeting to read the portions of the accounting principles code that re-

---

[3] Shorting a stock is the opposite of buying it. You sell it first, by "borrowing" it from your broker, and buy it later at a lower price, if you are lucky, to "pay your broker back." While shorts are supposed to be restricted to stocks listed on the exchanges, in practice stocks traded over-the-counter are sometimes shorted also.

quired acquisitions made shortly after the close of a fiscal year to be included in that year's statements.

People had begun to doubt, but Cort kept promising another tripling of earnings and, [in a] speech to the New York Society of Security Analysts, predicted that 78% of the higher 1970 earnings would come from internal operations, and only 10% from acquisitions that had not yet been made.

In any case, my first subrationalization for not publishing some kind of dissenting annual report was my not being sure, especially at the time, whether NSMC was exceeding acceptable limits of public relations, creative accounting, and corporate law, though I imagined those limits were being severely strained at the very least. Although I assumed the accountants and lawyers were given unfalsified records to work with, I really had no way of knowing. All that was handled at the very top where hands are presumably always spotless. I also assumed that major accounting and law firms would not risk bending their standards for the sake of a client, albeit lucrative. While it was obvious that the public image was a rather fanciful description of the company, I presumed that dollars were dollars and documents, documents when it came down to the assets and liabilities of a financial statement.

A second reason for remaining loyal was that it seemed more reasonable and practical for a company to correct an unfortunate situation rather than commit suicide. Should GM encourage class-action suits against its failure to work sincerely toward curbing pollution, or should it simply begin working toward that end? We all complained frequently to Cort's inner circle about the way the story was being told. The inner circle in turn complained to Cort. We kept getting signs that things would improve, such as the appointment of a Chief Operating Officer, Roger Walther, who was a straight talker and who was willing to stand up to Cort. The third annual report would be different.

A third reason was that if I turned out to be *wrong* in my youthful idealism and/or NSMC and its mutual-admiration society withstood my attack, I would have had a rather difficult time being hired anywhere else. Patrick Henry for President, and all that. Fourth, I had already decided how to split most of my imminent fortune over various . . . projects. I was almost ready to believe that my then $400,-000 stock options, with 18 months down and 6 to go, would indeed be worth something. It might be stretching things to say I was beginning to see Ecuadorian towns renamed in my honor—but you get the idea. I wouldn't have minded the 20% I was going to keep for myself, either. My ego was raving over its new clothes—Vice-President of the darling of Wall Street. I, too, wanted to believe.

Fifth, I figured that even if Peat, Marwick and White and Case were being fooled, there were a lot of insiders with more information and more experience than I to whom I could pass the buck. We had lured from Time Inc., a seasoned executive who was billed as being in line for the Publisher's job; we had lured from J. Walter Thompson a Vice-President with a tremendous track record; we had in-house attorneys and financial people; we had computer people from IBM; we had two Harvard MBA's assisting Cort full time. Did I have the nerve to call a press conference and expose the American Business Establishment? Not *this* kid. I would wait and cast the *second* stone. And I do believe I would have been attacking much more than NSMC with such a press conference. I would have been attacking all those wild glamour stocks of recent years, all those highly paid shingle-hanging professionals, and all those aggressive young entrepreneurs who expected to make a fortune in 3 to 5 years, while 60% of the people on earth struggled to get enough to eat. I would surely have been branded as one of the radical left who wear blue jeans.

Finally, I was very proud of and involved with my own projects, which I felt were exciting. In presenting the NSMC story, as I often did, I was enthusiastic about NSMC's legitimate good points—there were and are many—but I don't think I knowingly passed on much of the fiction. Of course, by remaining an employee I tacitly endorsed the company. And I obviously did not stress the seamy side of the story as I have here. In the case of the one tiny acquisition it was my responsibility to complete, I spent hours with the company's President (Yale '68) to expose all the myths—self-fulfilling prophecies, ineffective media, the works. Yale or no, I wanted to be sure he knew everything I knew before betting his little company.

But it turned out there was a lot I, and virtually everyone else with the possible exception of Cort and a few top generals, did not know.

Just when serious, secret negotiations were going on to acquire 3 huge companies—National Tape with $60 million in sales, Champion Products with $50 million, and Josten's, listed on the New York Stock Exchange with $70 million—acquisitions that would have assured NSMC's earnings projections and kept the ball rolling, the accountants finally found that something was very wrong and the lawyers advised NSMC to announce preliminary information to the public. On February 24, 1970, it was announced that there had been a loss of $1.2 million on sales of $18 million for the first quarter of fiscal 1970—September 1 through November 30, 1969—the year for which Randell had been promising tripled profits. Whatever confidence or credibility may have remained was obliterated 2 days later when it was announced that the company had made a "mechanical error in transferring figures from one set of books to another," such that the loss would actually be $1.5 million on sales of $14 million. Where was the sophisticated, computerized management-control system now?

Evidently, the net profit for all the subsidiaries in this quarter had been a respectable, if not synergistic, $2.2 million; but corporate overhead, the campus rep program and others whose losses could be deferred no further, and write-offs of some of the previous year's creative accounting had racked up a deficit of nearly $4 million.

I was in Cambridge on a rare three-day weekend when I first heard the news from my Yale '68 Subsidiary President. It came as a complete surprise. I had assumed from Cort's profit projections that subsidiary earnings would continue to be large enough to absorb the costs of keeping up the corporate image. Then I saw the silver lining: No doubt this was the great housecleaning! NSMC was paying its debts to the future, getting its accounting back in line, starting afresh with a clean slate. I figured the stock would suffer for a while, but that a profitable second quarter might restore confidence. In any case, it was pretty clear that 1969 earnings had been boosted to Cort's projections only by dumping problems on 1970. Soviet factory managers do the same thing, borrowing a couple of days' production from April to meet March quotas, then borrowing 3 or 4 from May to hit April, and then a week from June to hit May. Since the managers purportedly meet their quotas, they cannot ask for lowered ones. If anything, quotas are raised. When the reckoning comes, as it almost always does, the Manager is sent off to you-know-where.

If 1969 earnings had not been thus boosted, the stock would have fallen that much sooner, before acquisitions like Cliftex could have been made. Cliftex is a sports-jacket manufacturer in New Bedford, Massachusetts, that NSMC managed to buy for about 17 times its $1.2 million earnings, with 100-times-dubious-earnings stock. This one, and a couple of others, brought NSMC sales close to the $100-million level.

If 1968 earnings had not been thus boosted, perhaps NSMC would now have sales of about $8—not $80—million.

If 1967 earnings had not been similarly increased, NSMC might never have gone public in the first place. (In fact, on the suspicion that Cort's *own* business ventures never made a dollar of profit from the day he started, it was suggested we call this book *How To Succeed in Business Without Really Having One.*)

So the slate had finally been cleared, to the considerable embarrassment of the company. But had it? There was the possibility that this huge deficit was the minimum that creative accounting would allow, that the debt to the future had actually been increased to keep the deficit from being even larger.

The announcement explained at last why NSMC stock had been slipping so badly—from a high of $143 in December 1969 before the *Barron's* article appeared, to $72 the day before the February 24th announcement. The following day the stock dropped only another dollar.

The *Wall Street Journal*, which by now was running articles almost daily about the Street's favorite stock of 1968, asked Jimmy Joy, our appropriately named Financial Vice-President, just when company officers had first known there would be a loss shown in the first quarter. "About January 20th." And had anyone leaked the news to the investment community? "Absolutely not." Joy attributed the market's foresight to widespread speculation and rumor that things were awry.

Nothing affects the price of a stock more than its earnings. The first one to know about the loss NSMC would announce held valuable information. Because the first one to sell a stock trading at $143 a

share probably will get about $143. But as more and more people
start selling, the market price goes down. By the time the loss was
announced to the public, you could only get $72 for your shares. The
first kids in the lunch line pick out the best apples. The Securities and
Exchange Commission is the lunch-line monitor. They get most upset
when company "insiders" act on information before it has been publicly announced. Someone will always be first to buy or sell his stock;
but the S.E.C. wants to be sure that Irving Investor has some chance
of a good place in line. Otherwise the officers of a company could buy
their own stock, announce some good news so it would go up, and sell
the stock before they announce bad news. The NSMC officers were
probably not guilty of such manipulation when they sold more than
$1-million worth of their personal stock as it passed its peak of $143
—but it's hard to decide what is insider-trading and what is not. (Insiders are supposed to file monthly reports with the S.E.C. noting any
transactions they may have made in their stock.)

If a company officer gets the feeling that long-term prospects are
not too good, and so wishes to sell his stock, must he call a press
conference to announce his private doubts about the company's future? He might not get much of a Christmas bonus if he did. Must he
hold the stock indefinitely and only sell when it has hit rock bottom?
If the answer to both questions is "no," then what is the answer to
this one: If he is right and the company begins to announce bad
news from time to time, will he look bad for having sold out before
the fall? Yes.

So it's a sticky area for the S.E.C. to regulate, and a difficult one
for insiders to deal with. This insider knew of the Interstate acquisition
an hour before it was announced and (wrongly) could not resist the
temptation of running down to a phonebooth and calling a good
friend to recommend purchase of 100 shares. What better gift to a
friend than an inside tip likely to be worth a few thousand dollars?
What a great way to feel like a Big Shot. What a shame to let such a
valuable opportunity go to waste! Who would find out about a
measly 100 shares? You just found out. (As it happened, the market
had already pretty much "discounted" this news, and had pushed up
the stock price in anticipation. It didn't do my friend any good at all.
I guess I wasn't first in line, after all.)

At $72, I was only worth $100,000, but I would have gladly taken that paltry sum and retired to the business school or Bermuda if I could have. The Harvard Alumni Bulletin, to whom I had sent proud news of my Vice-Presidency about 8 months earlier, managed to record it in the March number. Randell was having problems of his own. His net worth was down from $48 million to $24 million, but he must have figured the jig was far from up. Even after he knew of the loss, he continued to predict big profits for 1970. He did not know that the people had renounced their faith.

In fact, the day before he was forced to resign, Cort talked optimistically with one of my colleagues and recommended purchase of the stock. If you play hearts, you know it takes *all* the hearts and the queen of spades to "shoot the moon" and score 26 positive points. Otherwise, the more hearts you have the more negative points you suffer. Once you let even a single heart slip, you've lost the moon and should pick up no more hearts. Yet how often have I, having developed the perfect strategy to the moon, let one heart slip but continued to collect the hearts, refusing to relinquish the fantasy and return to earth?

On February 10, Randell was reportedly asked whether he was worried that subsidiary presidents and his own key executives now held a majority of the stock and could force him out. He was quoted in *Fortune* as replying: "Who do they respect? Their confidence in me to succeed is what brought them here. Why do people like Morgan Guaranty buy the stock? Because they have talked to Cort Randell and they have confidence in what we are trying to accomplish. As long as I do a good job, I'll continue. If I don't do a job, I don't deserve to be President."

How about this earlier passage from *American Way* magazine:

We have a late dinner one night in New York at a midtown restaurant. Randell eats very lightly, as usual. He is introspective. "I'm lucky," he says, "but there has to be some reason in life for this whole thing happening other than making money." He comes close to feeling, he says, that providence has some different work for him to undertake someday. "I feel certain I'll know what great project I'm to begin," he says. "I don't know what it is, but I'm sure that someday—within a year, or five years, or even twenty years, I'll be told." As he talks this way it is not difficult to imagine him the founder of a philanthropic foundation, or sponsor of medical research, or college bene-factor.

Can you blame a man who is told several times a day he is a mar-keting genius, a visionary able to turn his vision into reality, and an awfully nice guy—for believing some of it? There is no question that Cort was a self-promoter. Perhaps he was more eager to think great things about himself than most of us. The fact that Cort was "deeply religious" (a church deacon) was probably also mixed into the mes-sianic equation someplace. But the media, the investment houses, the suppliers, the employees, and the hopefuls all did their share to distort Cort's self-estimation.

A week after his confident statement about continuing to run the company as long as he did a good job, Cort was forced by his chiefs of staff to resign. Five of his Board members, with the support of the subsidiary presidents, told him he would have to leave the company if NSMC were to stand any chance of regaining credibility in the in-vestment community. Their meeting was the culmination of several days of tense power maneuvers necessary to execute the coup suc-cessfully. Next morning the New York staff was assembled in the conference room to hear Cort, trembling and voice cracking, an-nounce his resignation.[4]

The announcement was brief, the reaction varied. Some of those present, particularly the secretaries, were taken entirely by surprise. Some may even have believed Cort's statement to *The New York Times* about resigning for personal reasons of health and much-needed relaxation. Everyone seemed to think they should carry themselves as at a funeral. In preparation for the euphemisms and false sentiment I expected to hear at this meeting, I wore my most cynical, detached frown. I heard Walther say something nice about Cort's having given so much to the company and wish him all the best; while I knew Walther must really have been thinking thoughts far less kind. Eloy and I couldn't feel sorry for Cort and his now-

[4] In its generally excellent article, *Fortune* said Cort was "remarkably com-posed" at this meeting. I was there; he was on the verge of tears.

$15-million net worth; it seemed to me his comeuppance was deserved and overdue. Yet, of course, I did feel sorry. He *had* become used to luxuries he would likely never enjoy again, he *had* been "an awfully nice guy" to me, he *had* been under tremendous pressure from everyone to produce, he *had* worked harder than anyone else, he *had* come to believe his own messianic creed.

Investors lost further confidence when Cort left and the stock continued its slide. Roger Walther was elected President and immediately began reducing NSMC's outrageous overhead—closing offices, firing recently wooed executives, discontinuing unprofitable programs —but trying all the while to keep up a healthy front. Having lost our original glamour, we would now bill ourselves as a terrific turn-around situation, another glamorous image of sorts to investors anxious to "discover" winners among losers. The media that had run glowing articles in the past felt foolish and wrote extra-glaring articles now. The last subsidiaries to be acquired struggled successfully for recision of their agreements, including Cliftex and my friend Yale '68, on the grounds that they had not been informed of the material change in NSMC's condition prior to their joining up. The rest of the subs tumbled around trying to decide who should run the company, now a string of subsidiaries stripped bare of 90% of the corporate umbrella and public-relations mirage.

After two months of Walther's leadership the subsidiaries decided on Cameron Brown, head of the large Interstate Insurance subsidiary, to carry the ball. At 55, Brown had the conservative image Walther, 33, may have lacked. Walther had not particularly wanted the job of cleaning up Cort's mess, either. He had made his fortune selling New England Travel Company, with his 2 partners, to NSMC (converting much of his stock to cash); why not enjoy it? Investors saw the third Chief Executive in 2 months, read of S.E.C. investigations, class-action suits, and suits against the parent by NSMC's own subsidiaries! The *Wall Street Journal* even uncovered a 1964 Post Office mail-fraud investigation of a Randell enterprise. The stock eventually reached a low of $3.50 in August 1970, down almost 98% from its high less than a year earlier.

While *you* had to go pay $3.50 for a share of NSMC stock, *I* had the option to buy it for $37 a share. Actually, by the time the stock was that low I no longer had my options. I was no longer with the company and you have to be an employee for options to be valid. In March, in the midst of wild confusion, the banks withdrew their lines of credit and, of course, no one would buy the company's letter stock. Nor would healthy subsidiaries lend the parent any money, at least for a while, since they were not sure of their own legal positions. This placed NSMC on the verge of bankruptcy. I sat in Jimmy Joy's office more than once waiting to ask for money to operate our refrigerator project and heard him talk on the phone to irate creditors. They sounded remarkably like the kind of conversations we used to have freshman year in my dorm about paying the telephone bill. Only NSMC's phone bill was about 1,000 times larger and there was no one to write home to as a last resort. The strategy had to be to make payments only when the final threat of suit was made (3 creditors owed $1,000 or more each, I learned, must file petitions in order for a company to be thrown into involuntary bankruptcy).

We could not meet the commitments we had made to schools to deliver refrigerators. In the case of Indiana State, I had been assured we would have the funds to deliver the 700 units that had been ordered; the campus paper announced their impending arrival. Then I was told by my boss to tell them we simply could not deliver. Then, he somehow got approval of the expenditure and told me to tell them it was on again. But I had to visit the student-government President and University Legal Counsel personally in Terre Haute to renegotiate the price of the lease now that our cost of capital had to be figured realistically. They were more than understanding and, having already collected $2 deposits from their impatient students, simply requested that we waste no time in making delivery. The refrigerators were actually loaded onto 2 trucks in Sydney before my boss told me that, unfortunately, we would not be able to deliver after all.

I was mortified by what we had done to the student government and the students of Indiana State. Especially when we had been billing University Products Corp., as the reliable, service-oriented company that was big enough to meet its commitments 100%. I decided to resign.

But what of the people who had invested in NSMC partly as a result of my enthusiasm? Didn't I have a responsibility to stick with the company to try to salvage something? A friend at one company that had put $10,000,000 (!!) into NSMC called me to remind me of my responsibility. I decided to stay.

One of the Directors of Harvard Student Agencies called me from Boston, told me he had heard some nasty stories about NSMC from his friends in the investment community, and told me I would be crazy, perhaps irresponsible, to stay. I decided to resign.

The concept of the company was still sound, I had a great job, in a few years my options might really be worth $400,000, things are rarely as bad as they seem, I must learn to have more patience, and so forth. I decided to stay.

I was very, very tired and so forth and so forth, and there were so many more "so forths" on the side of resigning that resign is what I did.

I left in April 1970, just in time for my 23rd birthday.

18. Saving Wall Street

THE DEPREDATIONS of Cornfeld, Randell, and their ilk—aided and abetted by the willing complicity of the great financial institutions and too-lax surveillance by the SEC under the business-oriented early Nixon Administration—certainly had an important role in bringing about the 1970 market collapse, in which far more money was lost by far more people than in 1929. It is fitting that the next voice to be heard should be the sober and responsible one of Donald T. Regan, chairman of Merrill Lynch, Pierce, Fenner & Smith, by far the largest of all brokerage firms. Regan was one of the small group of New York Stock Exchange leaders who in 1970 devoted themselves to picking up the pieces and putting them together again—arranging mergers to rescue failing firms from liquidation and raising appropriations from the NYSE membership to rescue the invested savings of customers of failed firms. Indeed, if the Merrill Lynch board of directors, led by Regan, had not agreed to rescue Goodbody & Company, there would have been—in the words of Robert Haack, then president of the NYSE —"a panic the likes of which we have never seen." True enough, the terms Merrill Lynch succeeded in exacting in the Goodbody merger were favorable ones (the Exchange agreed, as part of the transaction, to indemnify Merrill Lynch against losses resulting from it, to the extent of $30 million). True enough, too, Regan's progressive views on crucial Wall Street issues—NYSE democratization, negotiated commission rates—tended to coincide with the interests of the vast numbers of small investors who constitute Merrill Lynch's constituency. Still, Regan, on performance, deserves to be rated as one of the Wall Street leaders of the 1969–70 period whose self-interest was most enlightened.

In this entertaining passage from his book, Regan describes the White House dinner of May 27, 1970, at which President Nixon and members of his Administration met with Wall Street and industry leaders, at these leaders' suggestion, for the stated purpose of restoring public confidence in the stock market and the national economy. It was a triumph of government-business co-operation on the level of symbolism rather than substance. Although no significant business was transacted, although the taxpayers had to foot the bill for an elaborate meal, and although (as Regan recounts) the dinner was marked by a certain amount of rather macabre comedy, it worked —the dinner had the desired effect; the Dow-Jones industrial average, which had fallen from a previous high of around 1,000 to 630 and seemed to be hell-bent for much lower ground, made a record one-day gain merely on the *announcement* of the dinner; by the end of that week, the average was above 700 and the danger of panic was past.

The moral, Regan persuasively argues, is that close communication between Wall Street and Washington works to everyone's benefit and that (a point harder for some in Wall Street to accept) vigorous government regulation of the stock market is better for everyone, even the stock market, than the lax regulation that characterized the Nixon SEC in 1969. However, a comment on the context is necessary: in May 1970, despite the unpopular Vietnam war and the recent Cambodia invasion, the government still generally enjoyed the confidence of the business community, if not of the nation as a whole, and such confidence is essential to the effectiveness of co-operation. If such a dinner had been planned to stem a market collapse in, say, the autumn of 1973, after the revelations about Watergate, White House-directed "plumbers" operations, and the President's questionable personal financial dealings, the prospects for success would have been slim.

WASHINGTON AND WALL STREET, 1970

WHILE THE REVERBERATIONS from Investors Overseas Services' turmoil were being heard, other offshore funds were tottering. The best known of these was Gramco, which, like IOS, had a good number of celebrated American personalities associated with it. And, as the shakiness of offshore funds slowed down markets and spirits at home, domestic events were taking shape that would lead to the sensational three days in May.

In regular communication with the Nixon Administration, Bernard Lasker [Chairman of the New York Stock Exchange] pressed Wall Street's case during the crisis that was shaping up. Lasker drove home the significance of the failures on the Street to the President's official family. He told various members of that family that only a few people in Wall Street believed that the President's economic advisers were on the right track, or that the "game plan," described earlier, would work. Lasker was urging recognition of the fact that between Washington and Wall Street lay a special kind of credibility gap, and, indeed, the gap probably had sprung up between Washington and the rest of the business community as well. Out of Lasker's conversations was born the idea, which I touched on in an earlier chapter, that the President might host a dinner at the White House to talk intimately with some Wall Street leaders. Later the idea was expanded to include not just the Street but other parts of the business world also.

Initially, the news of the dinner was tightly held. The first public inkling appeared in the *New York Times* on May 23, when Terry Robards, who covered Wall Street for the *Times* (and covered it very well), reported that Henry Kissinger and Budget Director Robert Mayo

From *A View from the Street,* by Donald T. Regan (New American Library, 1972), pp. 142–59.

were soon to meet with a group of top businessmen, including members of the financial community, to discuss the stock markets and the apparently depressing effect that any and every Government action seemed to have on them.

Robards' report was accurate in every detail. He related that Lasker had had conversations with the President, and then had reported them to the Board of Governors of the New York Stock Exchange. As Robards said, Lasker told the Board that he had passed on to the President an analysis of what was wrong with the market—stressing to the President that the uncertainty about the Vietnam war and the disclosure of a growing Federal budgetary deficit were especially upsetting.

These two topics accounted for the selection of Kissinger and Mayo as spokesmen. Vietnam and the Cambodian invasion clearly fell within Kissinger's area of competence, while the budgetary deficit belonged to Mayo. Robards reported, again correctly, that Lasker had told the President that, besides declining stock prices, businessmen were disturbed by the spreading talk about the possibility of wage and price controls. And Lasker informed President Nixon that his analysis of the various alarming factors at work was based on conversations he had had the previous day with four leaders from the financial community. The conversations were held with Louis Lundborg, then Chairman of the Bank of America; George Champion, retired Chairman of Chase Manhattan; Henry Kaufman, a partner and the chief economist at Salomon Brothers, the largest bond firm and a leading institutional brokerage house; and with me—then the President of Merrill Lynch.

Gradually the plans for the meeting that would bridge the credibility gap began to unfold. Finally, announcement of the dinner was made officially on Tuesday, May 26, and the date was set for the following day—Wednesday, May 27. It seems to me an indication of just how hungry everybody was for good news that the market reacted so favorably to a coming event which, after all, was of itself hardly earth-shaking in importance. Yet the announcement was enough to spark the largest one-day rise in the market's history . . .

There is always a special aura about dinner at the White House.

On this occasion, 63 guests assembled at 8:00 P.M. Of them, 35 came from the Wall Street community: 14 were industrialists; seven were bankers, from various parts of the country; five were heads of big mutual or pension funds; and two came from insurance companies. On hand to greet the guests were some of the leading lights of the Administration.

From the Cabinet came Secretary of the Treasury David Kennedy, Attorney General John Mitchell, and Secretary of Commerce Maurice Stans. Paul McCracken, then Chairman of the President's Council of Economic Advisers, was there, along with Arthur Burns, in his new capacity as Chairman of the Board of Governors of the Federal Reserve. From the President's personal staff came Peter Flanigan, who was charged with liaison between the White House and businessmen and the various Federal agencies that are concerned with business. Among other people present who were close to the President were Charles Colson, special counsel to the President, and William L. Safire, the speech writer who specialized on economic matters. Despite the earlier reports, neither Kissinger nor Mayo was present. Dinner was in the State dining room, at a large square table. Dessert was served promptly on schedule at 9:30 P.M.

After dinner the President rose to talk to his guests. I took careful notes. He started off by saying that he thought the economy would turn up in the third and fourth quarters of the year. He said that the money stock had been increasing just before Dr. Burns took over at the Fed at an annual rate of 5%; but recently, under Burns, the increase had been doubled to 10%. He expressed regret over rising unemployment, warned that it might worsen for a while, and indicated his hope that it would not rise much more.

Then he turned to Cambodia. A huge map of Southeast Asia had been set up behind him, and the President referred to it as he explained the military strategy lying behind the thrust then under way. The President indicated that in his judgment the Cambodian operation should have a bullish effect on the stock market. He explained that the Cambodian move would not run up military expenditures, but in fact might constitute a long-run economy, since it would shorten the war and speed up the return of our troops from Vietnam. He expressed understanding of the fact that the invasion had brought to a boil a good deal of dissension, particularly among young people on the campuses. But he renewed his pledge that he would pull the troops out on time, and stated that this, in turn, would demonstrate to college students that he was keeping his promises, and that the Vietnam war was gradually winding down.

As for the Paris negotiations, the President expressed the view that they might move more quickly as the result of this Cambodian action. He regretted that the invasion had not been widely accepted publicly for what in fact it was: a well thought-out, fast-moving, well-executed and successful coup. He characterized it as the best strike by American forces since General MacArthur landed American forces at Inchon, but admitted that there was no public recognition of the fact. He finished his informal talk by repeating assurances that our troops would be out of Cambodia on schedule, if not ahead of it, and that the withdrawal of American troops from Vietnam would continue as planned.

After the President finished speaking, Lasker rose to explain the Street's perspective. (That, by the way, is often quite different from the perspective of the man in the street.) Lasker said that Wall Street was convinced that certain actions outside of the Street's normal sphere of interest were required before we could expect substantial recovery of the market. One of those actions was close adherence to the schedule of withdrawal announced when the Cambodian strike began. Another, closer to the Street's proper business, was a clear assurance that the Fed would take all the proper steps to support the price of Government bonds. At that time, Government bonds were selling at very heavy discounts—the lowest prices in recent history— with a deterioration of confidence in the bond market in general as a consequence. Finally, Lasker stressed that the Fed should continue to make money more plentiful.

At that point, the President called on Burns to speak to the matter of the money supply. Responding, Burns told the guests that he very well understood and sympathized with their nervousness about the shortage of liquidity. Indeed, he said that the Fed had taken extraordinary steps, following an unusual all-day meeting on the subject, to allay that nervousness. He stressed that the Fed was aware of its responsibilities as a lender of last resort and indicated that it had every intention of properly meeting those responsibilities. Burns declared that the Fed would not be handicapped by any rigid adherence to any theoretical formula affecting the money supply—demonstrating his considerable sensitivity to current practical needs. He also emphasized that, while the Fed would not finance inflation, it had the ability and every intention to meet the country's monetary requirements. I recall vividly my impression that once the current near crisis of liquidity was past, and once the obvious need for some easing in the money supply was behind us, Burns would be very inflation-conscious. His public positions assumed and expressed before the freeze of August 15, 1971, were to bear out this impression.

Following Burns' talk, the President, acting as the leader of a seminar on the economy, asked whether anyone present had any questions. The first came from John Bogle, the head of the Wellington Management Company in Philadelphia. Bogle asked about the young people in the country and how the President was going to deal with their attitudes. The President briefly characterized the mood of young people and followed that characterization with the interesting comment that "more guts" should be shown by junior faculty members on the campuses. He said they had an obligation to support their college presidents, and that they should insist that colleges be halls of reason, not halls of violence. If the heads of universities had such support from the junior faculty, they would be able to exercise much better control over the campus scene. But the alliance between the junior faculty and the student rebel movement had turned out to be incendiary, the President said.

Turning back to the war, the President told his guests that he knew very well that he could easily win lots of popularity by ending the war by Christmas—and bear in mind that this means Christmas 1970. He recognized the obvious: this kind of peace, one might say peace at any price, was what the country seemed to want, and it seemed to offer to him an easy way out. But he believed that if he were to take that easy way, the United States could never go to the help of any ally—Israel, Germany or any other—because we could not let down one ally without letting them all down. We could not pick and choose between allies. He added that he had not become President of the United States to witness the liquidation of all of our alliances and to see us lose our place of primacy in the hierarchy of nations.

All of this very serious talk was then interrupted by an odd incident, to which, as it happened, I was a close witness. In the seating arrangements, I was placed just down the table from the President, with Arthur Burns on my left and an otherwise unidentified Isidore N. Cohen on my right. I later learned that, along with his brother, Mr. Cohen was one of the principals of Joseph H. Cohen & Sons, a men's clothing manufacturer. They have offices in New York, and their primary plant in Philadelphia. The two brothers had recently sold their company to a big conglomerate, Rapid American, and so had become large stockholders in a large concern.

Reacting to the President's request for questions, Mr. Cohen got to his feet, as he put it, in an attempt to find out "what's going on in this country." Mr. Cohen's question, if that is what it was, turned out to be a 10- to 12-minute speech on the subject of his own opinions. They included an indictment of the Administration for its failure to act more vigorously; the bad advice given to the President by Dr. Burns and others about what was really going on in the economy; and a large helping of recommendations in a wide range of fields.

The moment was at first entertaining. Then it started to become quite uncomfortable. But the President took it good-naturedly, and, even though the other guests were squirming, and clapping to drown out Mr. Cohen, he refused to silence the man. He let Mr. Cohen speak his piece through to its end. A couple of times I surreptitiously reached out and tugged on Mr. Cohen's coat to get him to sit down—without much result.

When this incident had run its course—to everyone's great relief—the President picked up where he had left off. He told us that it would be very easy for him to clamp on price and wage controls and, more or less at the same time, to abandon Vietnam. But he believed that controls then would do more harm than good, and in a somewhat similar vein he believed that a sudden withdrawal from Vietnam would hurt too—particularly, it would hurt our ability to contain other aggressors. In that context, he seemed to be referring specifically to the USSR and to China; and he added that he would never see our ability thus limited while he was President. (Not until almost a year later was the President's intention to visit China announced.) At 11:05 P.M. the meeting broke up, to considerable applause. The President marked the occasion's end with a wry remark to those New Yorkers present that since they had missed their plane they might as well relax—a reference to the fact that the last plane leaves Washington for New York at 10:00 P.M.

At this distance from the event, I judge it to have been an important success. The *Wall Street Journal* the next day carried an article indicating that the guests were not at all enthused by what the President said, continued to be disturbed about the domestic impact of the Cambodian action, and were not really satisfied or gratified in any important way. My own judgment is different. I believe that the reaction was not so clear or simple as that, and on the whole considerably more favorable. I would say the consensus came closer to being this: that the President had diagnosed both the foreign and the domestic situations accurately; that with some time and a modicum of luck, his policies would succeed. I came away most impressed with his insistence on the fixed character of the Cambodian withdrawal date. He gave similar emphasis, with similar impression, on his determination to get the troops back from Vietnam on schedule.

On the way back on a charter flight—I was given a lift by John Loeb of Loeb, Rhoades & Company—I mused over this remarkable evening. One firm conclusion I came to was the sincerity of the President and his seven advisers. I could not and do not believe that the whole affair was just an elaborate show. The President did not shade the truth or try to force upon us any falsely optimistic prognostications. He was, after all, not only addressing a group that would be instrumental in spreading the information disseminated at the meeting throughout the country, but also he was talking to people with whom he would surely have to have future frank exchanges.

Of all the events of the evening, the most direct balm applied to the worst wounds of those present was administered by Dr. Burns. I did not know at the time, although I suspected it, that the Fed was in the process of increasing the money supply. Later publicly expressed confirmation of this impression was welcome news because it persuaded me as well as others that, in time, the bond market would turn around. I judged from Burns' comments that the mistakes of

1966 and 1967, when the Fed suddenly pumped so much more money into the economy, would not be repeated. Thus a compounding of inflation would be avoided, I thought, and a more orderly economic development could be expected. By mid-June, some evidence that this general interpretation was correct came to hand. The specific substantiation, as we have seen, was the rise in bond prices. And by the fourth quarter of 1970, there were glimmers of an upturn in the economy.

The White House dinner got its due share of publicity in the following couple of days. Once again Robards of the *New York Times* did a good reporting job in his account of the dinner in the Sunday edition, an account which included the menu—lobster cocktail, a white table wine, beef Wellington, a Chateau Lafitte Rothschild 1962, and coffee.

Of course, the verdict that the affair had been well worth its sponsorship was not unanimous. Philip Greer, writing in the *Washington Post,* complained that more heads of mutual funds should have been present, and he criticized the guests for telling the President not how things really were, but what he wanted to hear. Greer went on to say that "five will get you 10 in Wall Street that first, the dinner had nothing to do with the stock market rally and second, that the rally is a speculative bubble that will soon be just a memory."

Greer seemed to me, and still seems to me, to have been wide of the mark in this analysis. I respect him as a hard-hitting reporter, but in this instance I thought he was wrong. Indeed, I discussed the point with him and indicated my dissent at a luncheon some time later. My own judgment, as I've indicated, is that the dinner did mark a turning point in the stock market decline—that the idea was a good one, that the results were good, and that a line of communication was opened up which could have general value to the investing public and indeed to the economy as a whole. Of course the President can always go on television and speak to the nation, or call a press conference and be widely quoted. But the reception given such public signals by businessmen is quite different from the way they react when the signals are delivered, in the classic phrase, "live and in color."

While the President obviously cannot speak with great frequency to groups of business leaders, the fact that he did so in a moment of crisis strikes me as terribly important. Misunderstandings and garbles were pretty much ruled out by the means he chose. The general purpose of good communication was well served. Wall Street was in a crisis at the time, and a good deal of it had to do with Government monetary and fiscal policy, as well as with the war. The discussions dispelled some fear and clarified some thinking.

As I mulled over the importance of an understanding, or, if you like, even a tentative working partnership between Washington and the business community, the importance of good communication struck me more forcefully than ever. Naturally, my interest centers around individual shareholders, that being the strength and the primary concern of Merrill Lynch. Beyond the fact that 31-million individual Americans own stock lies the more significant fact, as a perceptive *New York Times* reporter wrote, "investors have become a potentially more powerful political force than ever before." It does not seem too farfetched to assume that these shareholders, who as yet have not clearly staked out a political identity, may someday do so.

They may, in the words of Donald Schwartz, a law professor at Georgetown University, become "surrogate for all citizens." Schwartz goes on to say that "this is the great potential in shareholder democracy. It will require a big shift in attitudes, but shifts in attitude are the products of education and communication." Americans affected directly and indirectly by the stock markets—through share ownership, pension and retirement plans, insurance policies, mutual funds, and other investments—form the largest single constituency in these United States. But until recently they have also formed one of the most completely forgotten. Within the past two years Wall Street and Washington have suddenly awakened to the political reality that investors are voters—and that they can be very angry voters when they believe their interests are neglected.

The arrival of the era of popular capitalism coincides with the coming of a new era of public skepticism and militancy. As fast as the number of investors grows, equally fast grows the number of consumers who complain. It is no longer sufficient to proclaim devotion to the public interest. The public now demands, quite rightly, performance in the public interest. Of all industries, the securities industry is perhaps uniquely vulnerable to the consequences of leaving the customer unsatisfied. For the basic capital of the industry is public confidence in the markets and the market makers.

Over the past two years, as we've seen, that confidence has been severely shaken. The effect of the shock waves passing through Wall Street and registering on the political seismographs in Washington has been to push market makers and lawmakers to recognize the importance of forming a new partnership to protect the interests of the investing public. Some form of collaboration, obviously, has existed since 1933 and 1934, when the landmark securities acts were passed. At that time the Congress wisely resisted the clamor for the government to regulate the securities industry in detail as retribution for the speculative excesses and dishonesty of the 1920s. Instead, the lawmakers adopted the principle of self-regulation, entrusting the exchanges and industry organizations with the responsibility for writing their own operating and financial rules and policing compliance by their members. The Securities and Exchange Commission was assigned the responsibility, among others, for supervising and ultimately enforcing *effective* self-regulation.

Under the stress of radically changing conditions and the inadequate response to change within the securities industry, the terms of the collaboration are shifting—precisely how much and toward what new balance of power and responsibility, it is now impossible to say. On his first day in office, the first SEC Chairman, Joseph P. Kennedy, spoke a blunt warning to his former Wall Street colleagues that still applies: "Times have changed and things that seemed all right four or five years ago are now out of the picture."

The new partnership, if one can so characterize it, will be what both sides work to make it. If the parties display wisdom, maturity, and farsighted responsibility (not their foremost characteristics in the past), free and competitive capitalism will be strengthened through reform, and public confidence fully restored. If, however, cooperation breaks down, ill-advised "reforms" may weaken the market mechanism, and we may wind up with what the late economist Joseph Schumpeter described as "capitalism in an oxygen tent."

Like so much else in American life, the relationship between Wall Street and Washington is a complex, many-faceted mixture of change and continuity. At one level, where headlines tell of woe and recrimination, the relationship appears troubled—and it is. At the working level of the marketplace, where most of the activity is reported in agate type, the relationship appears harmonious—and it is. (Merrill Lynch alone buys and sells more than $100-billion worth of Government and Federal agency securities each year.)

As the vast expansion of the Government securities market illustrates, the inhabitants of Wall Street and Washington, like Americans generally, have a talent for adjusting to unimagined situations in a practical and pragmatic way, inventing new means as new needs arise. But the talent for coping, for absorbing novel demands into the mainstream of continuity, is merely the bright side of another, thoroughly American trait. This is our tendency to remain preoccupied with immediate concerns almost until the moment the need for drastic change ("crisis") overwhelms us. It is not good enough to continue entrusting the future to luck and ingenuity. Too much is at stake. Moreover, crisis-driven reactions permit choice only among available alternatives, not necessarily the best ones.

The central question in our society, Peter Drucker reminds us in *The Age of Discontinuity,* is, "What do we have to tackle today to make tomorrow?" Applied to the partnership emerging between Wall Street and Washington, the question is, what must we—market makers and lawmakers alike—tackle now in order to insure strong and healthy popular capitalism tomorrow? The first thing we must do, it seems to me, is begin closing a communication/information gap that yawns like Grand Canyon. Hence I approve most heartily of the White House initiatives I have just described.

The brand-new institution, the Securities Investor Protection Corporation (SIPC) . . . has as its purpose to insure customers against the failure of their brokers, up to a limit of $50,000 ($20,000 in cash) for each account. Considering the cliff-hanging circumstances in which it was created, SIPC so far has proved a useful and workable institution—a better one in fact, than the creators had any right to expect. For throughout the months of dashing back and forth between Wall Street and Washington, it was obvious that everyone concerned was operating in the dark, uncertain of the most basic facts of the situation, except that they were grim and urgent. It was a subject of speculation, for example, just how many brokerage houses were in danger of failing, and therefore the size of the risk SIPC would face.

Actuarial data were nonexistent, and the schedule of premiums merely guesswork. Senator Harrison A. Williams of New Jersey, chairman of the Securities Subcommittee of the Senate Banking Committee and like Senator Muskie a key figure in the creation of SIPC, came away from the experience with some definite opinions. These were expressed in a candid, thoughtful address to the Investment Company Institute in April 1971, and are worth quoting at length:

> We in the Congress know far too little about how your industry works. Despite past studies there is a devastating lack of precise information concerning the exact condition of the securities industry and the causes of the problems which it is experiencing. To make changes . . . without knowing their effect could well bring about the very event we have so arduously worked to avoid: a major financial disaster on Wall Street.
>
> Each time the Congress has considered a specific reform . . . we were told by both the SEC and industry representatives that the immediate institution of such a reform, needed as it might be in the long run, could cause the failure of large numbers of broker/dealers. This in turn would accelerate the deterioration of the securities industry and cause a further loss in investor confidence.
>
> Neither the SEC nor the industry has been able to provide the Congress with the necessary specific information for the enactment of sound reform legislation. This is true simply because the information is not available. To obtain facts necessary to make sound legislative judgments is the sole objective of the study which I am about to undertake . . .

Studies of Wall Street by the Congress and the SEC and others will soon help provide the accurate information indispensable to successful partnership and sound reform. But there is more involved in closing the information/communication gap than assembling and analyzing data. After the studies are completed and reports published, the same gap could eventually reopen, inviting another crisis. The exchanges and other self-regulatory bodies, the Securities and Exchange Commission, and the Congress should be continuously linked in an expanded and modernized information system, so that the Federal overseers of the financial community are brought closer to significant developments there.

Some improved means of communicating current data will have to be devised because the fact of geographical separation (and its psychological consequences) hampers the oldest and best human information system—face-to-face talk. Unlike their counterparts in such world centers as London, Paris, and Tokyo, American leaders of finance and politics go about their professions in separate capitals. They are denied the daily opportunity to rub elbows—and ideas. They live within quite different climates of opinion. They read about each other's activities in the newspapers, which, by their very nature, filter out much of what's happening because it is "routine." Yet awareness of the other fellow's workaday routine is the first step to understanding him, his accomplishments, and his problems. Information seems to flow only when the system *stops* working well.

Now, it cannot be claimed that men with different interests and perspectives, merely by talking and listening to each other, will automatically agree. Very likely they won't. But the chances of one's taking the other by unpleasant surprise are greatly reduced and so are the misunderstandings that arise from rude awakenings. Through the late 1960s, the Wall Street–Washington relationship was essentially one of benign neglect—not to say blissful ignorance—on both sides. We have seen how prosperity concealed the shakiness of poorly capitalized and badly managed firms from men in Washington who weren't paying close attention anyway. When the winds of adversity brought these structures down, the lawmakers were surprised—and they, in turn, surprised inattentive market makers by proposing stringent measures to shield the investing public from the storm.

Of course, there may have been no way to avoid the crisis of 1970, regardless of how often and how candidly financial and political leaders communicated. Too much had been allowed to go fundamentally wrong. But the lack of communication inevitably generated an atmosphere of suspicion, and belated cooperation began in a setting that had overtones of confrontation. As the Securities Investor Protection Act was moving to final passage, the Governors of the New

York Stock Exchange sent a telegram to New York's Senator Jacob Javits: "We assure you and your colleagues of our cooperation in a spirit of constructive reform." Nothing less than that assurance would satisfy the industry's critics, who had seen too little evidence of such a spirit earlier.

Wall Street will have to make the psychological adjustment required to cooperate with Washington in good season and bad alike. This means shelving old prejudices and abandoning the wish that government would go away—except, of course, when it is needed. The government is in the securities industry to stay, on terms still to be decided. Acceptance of that reality is the premium the industry paid for its $1-billion insurance policy from the U.S. Treasury.

Perhaps the key to the adjustment required on the part of Wall Street is to expand its definition of professionalism. Men who are preoccupied with the short-term, often the minute-to-minute, fluctuations of the markets may perform well *as* capitalists, yet poorly *for* capitalism. Longer-term trends, particularly political trends, may have critical impact on the nature, strength and freedom of the markets, and time spent analyzing these trends is time well spent professionally. Any insight gained into future investment opportunities is an incidental bonus, as those who anticipated and profited from the rising concern for the quality of the environment can attest.

Wall Street can go a long way toward closing the information/ communication gap, but Washington has its part of the bridge to build, too. Even if data were flowing as the Congress desires, there is reason to doubt that the lawmakers and the SEC as now staffed could handle it. Outmoded ideas and narrow preoccupations flourish also in Washington.

One day in the early summer of 1970, Representative John Moss of California, a member of Congress deeply involved in the creation of SIPC, performing with seriousness and solid competence, spoke to a visitor off the record about "the whole business of legislating and its frustrations." With the authority of long experience in the Congress, he singled out the chronic shortage of staff personnel as "perhaps the greatest burden of the legislator and the biggest obstacle to good legislation." He had only one full-time assistant and three part-time assistants, he said. "Yet I must deal with agencies every day that come into the hearing room with four or five times the staff I've got. So we all have to look to industry for some of the expertise. Yet, they have their own special point of view and you know that, and you watch that. Nevertheless the industry can be very helpful because they can give you the facts."

The Congressman closed his reflections with a pair of conclusions beyond argument: "It is long past time that Congress recognized the need for competent, comprehensive staffing. It's time the press and public stopped laughing about our complaints and started helping their representatives do the kind of job people expect them to do."

Since 1934 the Securities and Exchange Commission has been responsible for overseeing the performance of the industry's self-regulatory bodies and for keeping the rules of the marketplace up to date. In recent years the SEC has fallen woefully short of its capacity to meet these responsibilities. "We seem to have lost confidence in the SEC," Congressman Emanuel Celler of New York declared during House debate on the SIPC bill. ". . . When we say the SEC will do this and that, I wonder what indeed the SEC has been doing all this while. If the SEC had been doing its duty, we would not have this sorry state of affairs." Similar misgivings and complaints were expressed on the Senate floor.

True enough, the SEC too often moves very slowly or not at all. Delays in important studies and rule-making decisions are measured in years. In part, however, this reflects the stepchild treatment the SEC receives from the negligent Congress. Although the SEC is grossly underfunded and understaffed, each year it remits to the Treasury revenues from various fees and charges that amount to almost as much as its budget. In fiscal 1969 the SEC actually turned in to the Treasury amounts larger than its total budget—in business terms, it made a *profit*. But Wall Street and the investing public pay dearly for this survival of old-style economizing into the age of the computerized marketplace. Perhaps if the very modest fees were increased, Congress would be more inclined to give the SEC the funds it urgently needs to expand its staff and modernize its operations. Merrill Lynch, for its part, would be pleased to support an increase in SEC fees.

So there are obvious shortcomings in Washington's end of the partnership, which the Congress alone can repair. And there are obvious temptations to take shortcuts, which should be resisted. One of these is to bestow more power and authority on institutions unable effectively to use what they already possess. The SEC needs a thorough overhaul, yet one of the commissioners recommends simply installing a much bigger power plant in the same Model T. "If there is any lesson that has been learned from our experiences over the past few years," he declares, "it is that the Commission must have plenary power to take whatever action is required in the public interest and should not have to wait and see what action a self-regulatory body will or will not take before it acts."

In spite of the sorry evidence in support of that view and the undoubted concern for the public interest inspiring it, I would question whether the "lesson" is that clear-cut. Or whether putting more responsibility on Washington would make Wall Street a more responsive and constructive partner. On the contrary, it might so enfeeble the principle and practice of self-regulation that the markets would pass into the oxygen tent owned and operated by the government. Then the dynamic force of popular capitalism might flicker out. The whole burden of self-regulation and government regulation needs to be examined, weighed, and parceled out differently. The assignments of the National Association of Securities Dealers, the Stock Exchange, the SEC and SIPC must all be redefined.

Senator Williams, in his speech quoted above, acknowledged that Congress, over the past 37 years, "has never really undertaken a careful review of the self-regulatory procedures embodied in the Securities Exchange Act." His study and others are correcting that oversight and will recommend reforms to strengthen the foundation of the Wall Street–Washington relationship. It is the crucial assumption, always subject to being proved anew, that the market makers will make and faithfully obey rules serving the public interest. In 1969–1970 faith in that assumption came dangerously close to collapsing among investors and lawmakers.

Self-regulation fell into deserved disrepute because of Wall Street's self-made problems in two areas . . . : operations and finance. Excuses, some rather plausible, can be made for the operational lapses of the securities industry, which, after all, experiences extraordinary fluctuations in its level of business. It isn't the easiest business to manage or plan on a long-term basis. But the financial irresponsibility revealed by the bear market was inexcusable. Too many of those engaged in the business of handling other people's money clearly didn't regard themselves as businessmen at all. Capital supposedly "invested" in the business was here today and gone tomorrow.

To enforce its rules, the New York Stock Exchange would have had to push distressed firms to the wall, compel liquidations, and expose customers to the hazards the Exchange sought to avoid. So as we've seen, the Exchange relaxed the interpretation and enforcement of its net capital rule. The hope, as the Exchange said in a special bulletin to members, was that if it allowed such firms to continue to operate, under closer surveillance "pending a scaling down of business and reduction of paper work backlogs," their liquidation would be "manageable." It was an awkward position, to say the least, and it proved to be an untenable one. The financial problems of the industry were too deep and fundamental, and the deficiencies in detection and monitoring safeguards too glaring, for such rescue operations to be adequate. By asking for emergency assistance from Washington in the form of SIPC, the industry tacitly admitted that the existing system of self-regulation, temporarily at least, had broken down.

The principle of self-regulation was sound and viable, but it had not been rigorously applied. Only under the spur of crisis did the SEC bestir itself. In 1970, for the first time in six years, its inspectors visited the New York Stock Exchange and checked on the enforcement of minimum net capital requirements for member firms. Some firms were required to file regular—even weekly—statements of financial condition. Firms were told to stop hiring salesmen and start hiring more clerical help to get paperwork unclogged. Highly individualized bookkeeping methods, which blurred the overall picture of the industry's condition, were ordered scrapped and replaced with a uniform system of accounting. (The system is not yet installed. The legal fight may go on for years.) These and other intrusions on management prerogatives were widely resented, but such pressure was necessary, and the self-regulators took the cue. "A few months ago, no governor [of the New York Stock Exchange] would have thought it proper to pry into the operations of a competitor," an SEC official told a *Wall Street Journal* reporter. "Now they're right down in the bowels."

So the Big Board tightened up its "early warning" rules on the debt-capital ratio of member firms, set up its special monitoring committee which directed emergency measures to prevent major failures, and launched the reforms I've explained aimed at strengthening the capital structure of Wall Street. Among the most important were the new rules governing the terms and duration of investment in brokerage houses, and the aggregate indebtedness permissible in relationship to capital. The main thrust behind such reform may be summed up just as concisely: capitalism is striving to regain its vitality, competition is being practiced and professionalism is being accepted. Wall Street may actually be becoming what Wall Street formerly claimed it was.

Truly competitive and professional market makers have less to fear from consumerists and Government officials than they do from colleagues who, contemplating reform, would rather sink comfortably into the oxygen tent. The decisive tests in the evolving partnership between Wall Street and Washington are likely to occur *within* the securities industry itself, between those who see what must be done *now*, today, to prepare tomorrow's free central marketplace, and those who see only today's trades and let tomorrow take care of itself. The outcome will determine whether the industry deals with Washington as a full partner, accepting responsibility, or a supplicant, accepting its fate.

Meanwhile, the SEC and the Congress, as overseers of change, ought to be undergoing simultaneous modernization that will permit them at least to stay abreast of the restructured securities industry. It is not clear that they will. Other regulators, such as the ICC and the FTC, have not found it easy or done conspicuously well. The pressures of competition and technology fall lightly, if at all, on the Government, and political pressures will not automatically bring a response attuned to novelty and change. On the contrary, competitive and modernizing forces in the securities industry could encounter stiff resistance from entrenched bureaucrats allied with the industry's stand-patters.

I am confident that this will not be the case, for Congress, in approving SIPC and placing the Treasury in a new role vis-à-vis the industry, clearly committed all concerned, including itself, to reform. All the musty corners should be swept clean—in Wall Street, the SEC, and the Congress—and the regulators as well as the regulated should cross the threshold of change. Whether the SEC would be more efficient under a single administrator, rather than its present five-man board; whether committee staffs should be expanded and professionalized; whether committee and SEC budgets should be increased, and by what amount—these are questions for the Congress to answer. What is important is that the lawmakers, when querying the market makers, see that these questions are also on the table. The new partnership between Wall Street and Washington should be an alliance of equals: men equally bound by the interests of the public they separately serve; and equally determined to apply their specialized talents to the common objective of expanding the prosperity of free men through free markets.

19. Madame

HELENA RUBINSTEIN (1870–1965), founder and lifetime proprietor of one of the world's most famous cosmetic enterprises, stood less than five feet tall, had a manner generally described as "imperious," spoke a half dozen or so languages in a thick accent (a friend said, "Madame never spoke any language very well"), and built a business empire that at her death had assets of many millions including factories, salons, and laboratories in fourteen countries.

Born in Cracow, Poland, in middle-class circumstances, she went at eighteen to Australia, where she had an uncle, and opened a beauty shop in Melbourne where she dispensed jars of her mother's favorite facial cream. Achieving immediate success, she returned to Europe to study dermatology with various celebrated authorities, then opened salons in London and Paris and, in 1915, in New York. In London in 1908 she married Edward J. Titus, an American journalist of Polish extraction; they had two sons, one of whom was to become board chairman of Helena Rubinstein, Inc. Following the breakup of that marriage (described in the first of the following excerpts), in 1938 she married a Russian prince with the resounding name of Artchil Gourielli-Tchkonia. They lived together happily until his death in 1956, after which she lived out her last decade presiding over her far-flung interests, restlessly traveling between a worldwide network of homes that were sometimes called the "Rubinstein Hiltons"—and putting together an autobiography. At her death her personal fortune was estimated at more than $100 million.

My Life for Beauty—purportedly written without assistance in the last year of her life, when she was ninety-four, but rumored at the time of publication to have been ghosted by one of her close business associates—is half autobiography and half beauty advice. It is interesting to note that in the autobiographical part Helena Rubinstein constantly and forthrightly interrelates her business life with her private emotional life, just as women in business have traditionally been supposed to do. (Men, of course, have long been required by a rigid social code to seem to keep business and private life separate, but as almost every businessman knows, this is usually the frailest of pretenses.) In the first selection, we see Madame quite openly seeking to save her marriage through a business trip from Paris to New York, which fails of its purpose but results in the greatest business coup of her career. (The price Lehman Brothers and associates paid for her business was $7.3 million, and the "fraction" at which she bought it back was $1.5 million.) How many a man, heartbroken about a failed marriage, has immersed himself in an anesthetic bath of work and thus mustered the energy and concentration to do the best work of his life! By telling this story in the round, Helena Rubinstein gives male business autobiographers a lesson in honesty and self-acceptance.

In the second selection we get a memorable, touching, and slightly intimidating glimpse of Madame as an ancient matriarch, casually issuing orders to subordinates "with one of our good moisturizing creams on my face" and making the astonishing revelation that she had never learned to use a telephone successfully.

On September 5, 1973, Colgate Palmolive Company, the household-products giant, acquired Helena Rubinstein, Inc. for 4,430,375 shares of Colgate common stock. Immediately after the acquisition Colgate stock had a small temporary sinking spell, which some analysts attributed to the hard bargain the Rubinstein firm had driven. Madame, it would seem, could not have managed the matter better herself.

THE YEARS IN PARIS after World War I were successful ones for me. I was able to make frequent visits to all the countries in which I had salons, including America. My business was flourishing everywhere. But Edward was expressing more and more openly his disapproval of my constant rushing around and of my frequent absences from our home in Paris.

I did my best to allay his anxiety, but I failed to take his objections seriously. I thought he was merely being possessive. The growth and development of my business meant so much to me that I did not understand the extent of his unhappiness. Often his words would be tinged with real anger, which should have warned me. "You work too hard," he would say. "It's not necessary. I want you here at home, where you belong." But I was so completely caught up in the web of my work and planning that I considered the business my first duty. I realize what a failure I must have been at that time as a wife, even as a mother.

And then one day Edward told me that he had fallen in love with a younger woman. I was hurt and bewildered, but I could not absolve myself from all responsibility. Yet I desperately hoped that I could do something to win back Edward's affection.

Just at the time of this terrible crisis in my marriage, I was faced with another crisis in my business life. The New York firm of Wall Street bankers, Lehman Brothers, offered me several million dollars for the American business. They promised, too, that every one of my staff would be kept on. I had received offers before, but none so tempting or so well timed. If I could free myself of the American business, I thought, my life could be lived happily in Paris, by Edward's side. Our marriage might yet be saved.

My decision was a quick one. I accepted Lehman Brothers' offer and hastily set sail for America, in order to sign the papers.

From *My Life for Beauty,* by Helena Rubinstein (Simon and Schuster, 1966), pp. 72–74, 106–8.

Many stories of this "take-over" have been circulated and many explanations given. It has been described as a brilliant financial deal, an example of "genius timing." But there was nothing especially clever about it. I sold the American corporation for one reason only—to save my marriage. It was a sacrifice, for my business had always meant more to me than money. Besides, every instinct told me that bankers would have neither the training nor the intuition necessary to operate a cosmetic company. I felt there was no alternative, however.

My stay in America was brief, only long enough to complete the transaction. The return trip to Paris seemed endlessly long. One day I felt elated; the next day I would be filled with doubts. When finally I arrived home, Edward told me that he had made up his mind. He was determined that we must separate.

It was a case of the two saddest words in any marital breakup—"too late." And I had no one to blame but myself.

I was numb. There was no fight left in me as I heard Edward say, "Nothing will ever change you, Helena. Your business is your life."

As it turned out, the same circumstances that had helped to wreck my marriage had their salutary effect in another direction. During my instructional tours of the department stores in the States, I had made many friends among the store owners and they kept in frequent touch with me. As time went on they complained bitterly of the way in which the American business was being run by the new owners. Some wrote regretfully that it would no longer be possible for them to sell the Rubinstein preparations. Distribution had been expanded and the new sales methods had vulgarized my products.

These distress signals helped to take my mind off my personal troubles, at least to some degree. Without publicizing the fact, I began to buy back some of the stock on the open market, until eventually I held one-third of it. Then as a substantial shareholder I wrote to Lehman Brothers, registering a strong complaint. For a while they ignored me, while the business diminished and the stock continued to fall in price. Unable to restrain myself, I circulated a letter to all of the stockholders, informing them that I felt the Rubinstein business was being jeopardized and urging them to add their complaints to mine.

Then came the Wall Street crash. Millions of dollars were lost overnight, and people were frantic. The value of the Rubinstein stock fell from sixty to three dollars per share. By that time Lehman Brothers were anxious to get it off their hands at any cost, and I bought back the controlling interest in the business for a fraction of what they had paid me. I desperately needed an interest which would keep me occupied so that I would have no time to think of anything else; besides, I knew in my heart that no one else could run the business as I could. Both the cosmetic and fashion businesses, I have learned over the years, are best run as personal enterprises.

Ahead of me once more was the lonely treadmill of work . . . never had I felt so utterly alone.

Today I still manage to get to the office daily whether I am in London, Paris, New York, or any of our other centers. Once a week I drive out to our regional factory to work with our chemists in the laboratory. It is still my greatest passion to see a new product at its birth, to sample a new scent, to cover my hands or face with a possible new cream or lotion, to share in the work of my staff. It thrills me to watch products develop, to perfect and push them into the realm of actuality, so that from a formula they join the hundreds of certified Helena Rubinstein preparations bringing to women the world over a promise—and a fact.

I travel less, but I still enjoy having my family and friends about me for a game of bridge and a pleasant meal. True, I spend more time in bed and often wonder how I managed, years ago, to sleep so few hours without feeling a moment's fatigue. Yet my age in years bothers me very little. Even today my life is filled with what many people would consider "a full quota of activities." I wake up early, and my day begins. While still in bed, I have a breakfast tray, a newspaper, and the morning's mail which I read with interest—even the circulars!

By eight-thirty my secretary arrives, and together we examine the day's mail. Letters mean a great deal to me, not only as a means of communication but as a close link between two human beings. I read them with care and, unless they require further attention or discussion, I endeavor to answer them by return mail. While my secretary

is with me, I often have a visit from my son Roy, my nephew Oscar
Kolin, my principal American lawyer, Harold Weill. Here in my bedroom we can informally discuss important company policy. Since they
all live nearby, it is a great convenience to hold these conferences at
home, first thing in the morning, before we go off to our offices. Perhaps because of the informality of these meetings we sometimes accomplish more than we would have at an official office meeting
involving divisional managers, sales managers, brand managers . . .
our whole hierarchy.

Over the years I have always preferred to deal with a small staff.
Large meetings irritate me because of the waste of time involved in
several people wanting to speak at once. I remember the pleasure of
working with one chemist on a new formula, with one art director
and one copywriter on an advertising campaign, with one accountant
balancing our books or preparing a financial statement. But as our
business has grown, more and more people have inevitably become a
part of the necessary equipment. I take pride in this expansion. I am,
after all, a "matriarch"—but I know from past experience that with a
small staff we often managed to do our work more quickly.

In the morning from my bed (unless I have an early appointment
which requires my getting up and dressed) I will also talk on the
phone to friends and business associates, until I rise around ten, for
my bath and personal beauty routine. I do not like the telephone and
to this day cannot manage to dial a number correctly by myself. But
I use it, since I must, to remind those around me that I am still interested in what they are doing and what they are thinking.

While still in the bath (I love a few drops of perfumed oil in the
water) and with one of our good moisturizing creams on my face, I
do simple stretching exercises to limber up. The steam from the warm
water increases the moisturizing effect of the cream, softening my
skin so that make-up foundation, rouge, and powder can be applied
with an evenness that produces a truly natural look. While I make up,
a maid brushes my hair and helps me to set it in my perennial
chignon. There are times when I would have liked a more frilly
hairdo, but I have always been a bit short on patience where my appearance was concerned, and besides, the day awaits me—decisions,
people, and time slipping by.

P